THE BURNING EARTH

THE
BURNING
EARTH

A History

SUNIL AMRITH

W. W. NORTON & COMPANY
Independent and Employee-Owned

For information about permission to reproduce selections from this book, write to
Permissions, W. W. Norton & Company, Inc., 500 Fifth Avenue, New York, NY 10110

For information about special discounts for bulk purchases, please contact
W. W. Norton Special Sales at specialsales@wwnorton.com or 800-233-4830

Manufacturing by Lakeside Book Company
Book design by Lovedog Studio
Production manager: Julia Druskin

ISBN 978-1-324-00718-0

W. W. Norton & Company, Inc., 500 Fifth Avenue, New York, N.Y. 10110
www.wwnorton.com

W. W. Norton & Company Ltd., 15 Carlisle Street, London W1D 3BS

10 9 8 7 6 5 4 3 2 1

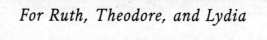

For Ruth, Theodore, and Lydia

CONTENTS

PART III

THE HUMAN EXCEPTION
(1945–2025)

THE BURNING EARTH

DREAMS OF ESCAPE

I HAD THE MOST THOROUGHLY URBAN OF CHILDHOODS in an Asian metropolis that grew vertically. My memories are of harbor lights and darkened movie theaters and air-conditioned shopping malls. I paid little attention to the natural world, though nature seeped into my life unnoticed. To this day the rain I love is the rain that thrilled me then: rain that arrives abruptly and falls in sheets from stacks of inky afternoon clouds.

"I believe that whatever time you are born into shapes your perception of humankind vis-à-vis the natural world," writes novelist Annie Proulx.[1] And so my perception rested on separation. I grew up in Singapore, an island-city that imported almost all its food and even its water, a city as committed as anywhere on the planet to remaking nature for human ends. From the 1960s to the present day, Singapore's land area has grown by 25 percent. The country's engineers have conjured land from water—land made from sand dredged from river beds, held up with pillars drilled into the sea floor, and then sculpted into highways and parks and public housing and the world's best airport. Even the climate was molded to the nation's needs. In a 2009 interview, Lee Kuan Yew, first and longest-serving prime minister of Singapore, reflected that "air conditioning was a most important invention for us, perhaps one of the signal inventions of history." Lee believed that climate was destiny. Air conditioning had "changed the nature of civilization," Lee said, "by making development possible in the tropics."[2]

As a young person I was conscious of the idea of "sustainability," which entered common use in the 1980s. But I was drawn to study history by what seemed to be the more urgent struggles for political and social freedom that I saw unfolding all around me in the last two decades of the twentieth century.

When nature first touched my writing, it entered unbidden through the archives. Amid the bloody accounting of Malaysia's coroner's court records, I stumbled on detailed descriptions of the neat rows of trees that provided cover for the buried bodies of Indian migrant workers on the rubber plantations in the late nineteenth century. As I traveled through rural Malaysia to interview retired rubber tappers, I was surprised by how many of the stories they told me were about trees. Once I met a man who had spent his whole life on the plantations. His memories of the terrain were vivid as we walked together, his purposeful strides leading the way, his tall frame forcefully upright at the age of 80—"there used to be a tree there," he said, "it just refused to be cut down. We all believed a powerful spirit lived in it, so we left it alone." A line from the French historian of the Mediterranean Fernand Braudel came to my mind—"the land, like our skin, is bound to conserve the traces of past wounds."[3]

A few years later, in 2012, I spent time in Yangon, Bangkok, and Mumbai within the space of a few months. I have always been drawn to the port cities of the Indian Ocean. Their architecture and their many tongues still bear traces of an ancient commercial world, even as their youthful cultures embrace an optimistic future. The romance of sail and spices brought me to study the sea. On this visit, I became aware of new risks.

Within recent memory all three cities had faced extreme floods. A monsoon deluge in July 2005 submerged a substantial part of Mumbai. Cyclone Nargis leveled Yangon in 2008, with a toll beyond counting in lives and homes lost. The Bangkok floods of late 2011 broke the fortress of levees that surrounded Thailand's capital, which was no longer able to contain a Chao Phraya River swollen by a summer of unusually heavy rains. In all three cities, extreme

The busy life of the Chao Phraya River, vulnerable to increased flooding as a result of climate change.

weather cascaded into political disaster because of misrule. In Mumbai, decades of unregulated construction had paved over the city's natural drainage. In Yangon, a military government clung to power at any cost, denying the scale of the tragedy and shutting out international assistance. In Bangkok, rapid growth had wrecked the mangroves that once held back the waters. In all three cities the poorest people suffered most, those who lived in makeshift housing in precarious and low-lying settlements.

Walking by the banks of the Chao Phraya on a breezy evening after a day of intense heat, I struggled to connect the scene before me with fears that half the city could be underwater by the end of this century. The river was crowded with noisy pleasure boats festooned with lights. Silent barges pulled their loads upstream. Some of those barges carried sand, mined in Cambodia and Myanmar, to supply raw materials for new skyscrapers in cities that had doubled in size in a generation. Cranes stood watch like sentries over the half-built shells of luxury riverside apartments. The scars of the recent floods were confined to private grief. The life of this great city went on.

Was it resilience I was seeing—or blindness? I began to wonder what these appearances of nature in every part of my research meant for the sort of history I wanted to write. It took me two books to begin to figure that out.[4] Now I understand, most of all, that I can no longer separate the crisis of life on Earth from our concerns with justice and human freedom that inspired me to become a historian in the first place.

The most compelling writing on nature often comes from deep feeling for the texture of a particular landscape and a sense of kinship with the other species that share it. This book rests on different foundations. It builds from a patchwork of attachments to many different places, distant from one another, most of them cities far from any wilderness. It is history for an urban, globalized, and divided planet, written from a position of empathy for the all-too-human dreams of fossil-fueled escape that now lie in ruins.

NATURE AND FREEDOM

ONCE UPON A TIME ALL HISTORY WAS ENVIRONMEN-
tal history. Life was governed by the seasons. When the weather
gods were fickle, misery followed. Human societies used their ingenuity to wield fire, dam rivers, cut down forests: all to mitigate the
risks of living. They harnessed the power of the animals they shared
shelter with. Every culture had its gods of beneficence; every culture
had dreams of plenty. A thousand years ago, those dreams grew
more insistent. The scale of human impact on Earth expanded with
the growth in human numbers. The range of possible futures inched
wider. But the twinned foes of famine and epidemic never receded
for long.

And then things changed. The most privileged people in the world
began to think that the human battle against nature could be won.
They believed that natural limits no longer hindered their quest for
wealth and power. They believed that instant access to the prehis-
toric solar energy embedded in fossil fuels made them invulnerable.
Their steam engines and lethal weapons conquered the world. In
pursuit of freedom, they poisoned rivers, razed hills, made forests
disappear, terrorized surviving animals and drove them to the brink
of extinction. In pursuit of freedom, they took away the freedom of
others. The most powerful people in the world believed, and some
still believe, that human beings and other forms of life on Earth are
but resources to be exploited, to be moved around at will.

ALMOST EIGHT HUNDRED YEARS separate the Charter of the
Forest—issued by England's King Henry III in 1217—and the Earth
Charter, published in fifty languages in the year 2001 by an international group of political leaders, scientists, and activists chaired by
Mikhail Gorbachev, the final leader of the Soviet Union. The two
charters are waypoints in a history of human freedom in relation
to nature.

The medieval Charter of the Forest was a companion piece to
the more famous 1215 charter of liberties (Magna Carta) decreed
at Runnymede by King John of England to placate rebel barons
resentful of overweening royal power. The forest charter "disaffor-
ested," or removed from the realm of Royal Forest, all the ecologically varied lands that the previous king, Henry II, had added to
it. It affirmed the customary rights of commoners—rights to collect
bracken and wood, turf for fuel, bark for tanning; rights to collect
herbs and berries; the right to allow pigs to roam. As it gave, so
it took: the charter recognized the property rights (the assarts) of
lords whose domains encroached on the Royal Forest, easing fines
for erecting structures or creating arable land. As forests became
lucrative sources of timber, lords restricted public access to their
woods—that is, they enclosed them as private property. Landscapes
on the margins of settled cultivation, woods and uplands and wetlands, were at the leading edge of this enclosure movement. Soon,
manor courts charged the provision of firewood or game from the
enclosed lands as theft. Local people fought back, invoking royal
promises of equal justice. To address these social conflicts, traveling
forest courts, Eyres, became a feature of English law.[1]

In the year 1227 a group of peasants from Bilston, a manor south
of Wolverhampton in the English Midlands, brought a case to the
royal courts at Lichfield. They charged that Juliana, widow of Roger
de Bentley, had put up unauthorized buildings and cut down trees
in the Royal Forest, where the plaintiffs claimed rights of common.

The men of Bilston alleged Juliana and her son were blocking entry to the woods that remained. The court's verdict in this case is unknown, but there were many other judgments like it. People took action. They uprooted or burned fence posts. They filled ditches. They occupied land. Sometimes the courts brokered compromise by specifying limits to common rights: only alder and willow, thorn and holly could be used for fuel and fencing, for these were trees that lent themselves to coppicing—cutting low on the trunk so that the trees can grow back. The forests were not inexhaustible; demand for them was. People knew from hard experience that the health and survival of their small communities was consonant with the health of the forest.[2]

The Charter of the Forest arose from social conflicts that drove rapid changes in how human societies inhabited the planet around a thousand years ago—conflicts between rulers and ruled, elites and commoners, settled agriculture and nomadic life. Twinned with the charter of liberties, the Charter of the Forest acknowledged that human freedom and flourishing lay in the richness of human and more-than-human life that the soils and forests and waters sustained. The capture of those resources by people with power narrowed and impoverished the ways others could live, eroding what an archaeologist and an anthropologist together have called the "basic forms of social liberty": the "freedom to move away," the freedom to "ignore or disobey commands," and the freedom "to shape entirely new social realities."[3]

What relation does this capacious notion of human freedom—freedom within the affordances of nature—have to the narrower history of freedom as the foundational political concept that defines modernity? Modern ideas of freedom arose together with a step change in the scale and scope of the human imprint on the rest of the living planet, and together with the growing power of western European societies over the lives of others far away. Thomas Hobbes put it this way in his 1651 political treatise, *Leviathan*: "The NUTRITION of a Common-wealth consisteth, in the *Plenty*, and

Distribution of Materials conducing to Life." Over the centuries to
come, the pursuit of "materials conducing to Life" would transform
the planet; their "distribution" would create vast inequalities in different peoples' access to that plenty.[4]

Into the pursuit of freedom there crept, over time, a notion previously unthinkable: that true human autonomy entailed a liberation from the binding constraints of nature. The unshackling of
fossil energy bolstered a way of seeing the world in which freedom
defied any limits on what it was possible for human beings to do and
to make—and for owners of capital to accumulate. "Freedom has
been the most important motif of written accounts of human history
of these [last] two hundred and fifty years," Dipesh Chakrabarty
observes. The liberal freedom from arbitrary government, the capitalist freedom of markets, workers' freedom, anticolonial freedom,
freedom from patriarchy, freedom from caste oppression, sexual
freedom—hidden within these histories, until a belated twenty-
first century reckoning, was their basic material underpinning: "the
mansion of modern freedoms stands on an ever-expanding base of
fossil-fuel use." That condition of possibility now exerts a new limit
on the choices of future generations.[5]

In the human struggle to expand the possibilities of life on Earth,
there is a surprising twist in the tale. From long before the Charter
of the Forest, a fundamental human aspiration has been the dream
of continuance: the dream that one's kin, one's name, one's works,
one's community would outlast the vicissitudes of drought and flood,
plague and famine, accident and disorder. In the second half of the
twentieth century, that dream met with astonishing, unforeseen success, as early death and debilitating illness lost some of their power
over a significant part of humanity. Economist Angus Deaton calls
this the "great escape" of modern history. It is a signal and surprising achievement in a century otherwise characterized by its terrible
innovations in mass killing.[6]

A child born in India in the 1940s could expect to live on average
thirty-five years; had they been born in Indonesia or Nigeria, the

prospects would have been just as bleak, and if in Brazil only modestly brighter. Life expectancy at birth in each of those countries, and for most of the Global South, has doubled in less than a century. The survival gap between the wealthiest countries and the rest of the world has narrowed. Infant mortality has fallen rapidly, though unevenly along the gradient of wealth and social status. Nowhere in the world today are rates of infant mortality as high as they were in Britain in 1900, at the time when it was the wealthiest and most powerful country in the world.[7]

This vast expansion in human possibility could be credited to an increase in environmental control. Sanitary engineers disrupted the conditions in which water-borne and vector-borne diseases thrived. Oil refineries churned out the fractionated petroleum products that made fertilizers to boost crop yields and antibiotics to fight bacterial infections. Coal-fired power plants or diesel-powered generators kept the lights on in rural obstetrics wards that made childbirth safer, at least some of the time.

And then, in the year 2001, a further threshold was crossed in the human ability to understand, and potentially to manipulate, every form of life on Earth. That was the year when an international team of scientists announced that they had completed the initial sequencing of the human genome—the complete genetic information in an organism contained in sequences of DNA, consisting of twenty-three pairs of chromosomes in the cell's nucleus, and a small chromosome in the mitochondria. It came as a "capstone for efforts of the past century" to understand the building blocks of life. At the time, scientists had already deciphered the genome sequences of 599 viruses and viroids, 31 eubacteria, a fungus, and 2 animals. This was different. The team's first claim for the significance of the human genome was its complexity—it was twenty-five times as large as any genome previously sequenced. Only then did they add: "And, uniquely, it is the genome of our own species."[8]

There was no triumphalism in the genome team's announcement, which conveyed a sense of wonder that "the more we learn about

the human genome, the more there is to explore." They acknowledged obstacles in the way of their scientific advances being deployed
"broadly and equitably." But still there was an exhilarating sense
of a barrier broken. Working together across borders, scientists had
finally found the key to "long-sought secrets" of life, with "profound
long-term consequences for medicine."[9]

The initial sequencing of the human genome was published the
same year as the Earth Charter. In 2001, at a "critical moment in
Earth's history"—amid "environmental devastation, the depletion
of resources, and a massive extinction of species"—the Earth Charter insisted that human well-being, and ultimately human freedom,
depended on "preserving a healthy biosphere with all of its ecological systems, a rich variety of plants and animals, fertile soils, pure
waters, and clean air." The relationship between human liberty and
ecological vitality had become toxic. But unlike the medieval Charter of the Forest, the 2001 declaration contained no enforceable pro-
visions. There would be no world court for the Earth, no global Eyre.
The statement articulated principles that could only be enacted, if at
all, by an interlocking architecture of administrative states, national
courts, international organizations, and multilateral agreements.[10]

Scientists' breakthrough in assembling the genome coincided with
awareness that all forms of life, including human life, were threatened by the destabilization of the core conditions that had made
Earth a hospitable home. An expanding horizon of possibility collided with a closing-in of constraints. The publication of the charter
marks a moment when people around the world began to ask: At
what cost has this basic freedom, the freedom to live, been won? In
the "great escape," were there also seeds of future imprisonment?

THE DREAM OF HUMAN freedom from nature's constraints is
under assault by viruses, burned by wildfires, drowned by floods,
scorched by extremes of heat. Many still cling to it, but an awakening has come to people around the world: "we cannot and will

not escape the constraints that constitute the parameters of our mortal existence," writes essayist and critic Maggie Nelson in *On Freedom*—"nor do I see why we would want to." In the wealthy part of the world, and in the context of the past seventy years, the last part of Nelson's statement is bracing and radical. In the broader sweep of human history, it was the norm. Egyptologist J. G. Manning puts it this way: "We have, some say, achieved an existence outside of nature, . . . and in control of our own destiny. But that of course, is an illusion, and one limited to those living in a handful of lucky nations." The real question, then, is how it ever became possible for a small minority, a minority-within-a-minority, to believe in the illusion of mastery.[11]

How have we reached this point of planetary crisis? It is the outcome of our creaturely quest for survival—the long and continuing struggle for food and shelter that still drives a large part of the human impact on the rest of nature. It is, conversely, the outcome of the elite pursuit of luxuries—animal, vegetal, and mineral—that has spanned ever more of the world, ever more relentlessly, over the last five hundred years. It is the outcome of energy-hungry economic systems, capitalist and socialist alike, that turned living nature into lifeless commodities, sometimes with the liberatory intention of expanding human freedoms. It is the outcome of our inability to imagine kinship with other humans, let alone with other species. It is the outcome of the mutating hydra of militarism, armed with the power to destroy every form of life on Earth. Over time, those roads to ruin have twisted together: "The planet is shaped by the sheer amazing force of human want, which has changed everything," observes novelist Samantha Harvey. To have any hope of undoing the densely woven braid between inequality, violence, and environmental harm, we need to understand its origins.[12]

PART I

SEEDS
OF
CHANGE

1200–1800

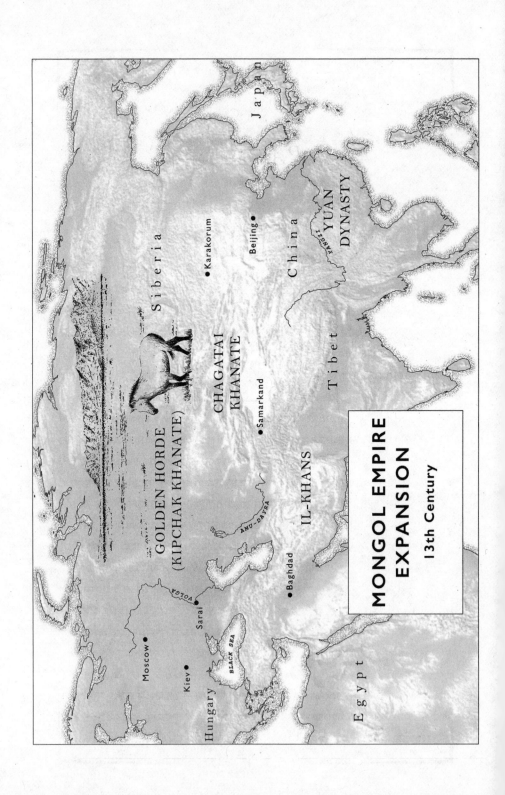

MONGOL EMPIRE
EXPANSION

13th Century

Japan

Siberia

•Karakorum

Beijing•

China

YUAN
DYNASTY

Tibet

CHAGATAI
KHANATE

•Samarkand

GOLDEN HORDE
(KIPCHAK KHANATE)

IL-KHANS

AMU-DARYA

•Baghdad

VOLGA

Sarai•

Moscow•

Kiev•

BLACK SEA

Hungary

Egypt

CHAPTER ONE

HORIZONS OF DESIRE

I N THE YEAR 1218, YELÜ CHUCAI (1189–1243), SCHOLAR and administrator from the nomadic Khitan people of inner Asia, made a political pilgrimage to the West. He delighted in the varied landscape of steppe and mountain. He expressed grudging admiration for Mongol military prowess under the leadership of Chinggis (Genghis) Khan. Yelü's description made Mongol armies seem like they, too, were a force of nature:

> Mountains and rivers crisscrossed; how lush was the verdant land! The covered wagons were like clouds; the army, like rain drops. Horses and oxen covered the plains; foot soldiers and troops in armor emblazoned the sky. Fire and smoke viewed each other from afar; fortified camps stretched for thousands of miles. Never has there been such magnificence throughout all history!

With a gardener's eye, Yelü observed new plants ("The flowers of the *pa-lan* are like those of the common apricot tree, but somewhat lighter in shade"), and he relished new tastes: the pomegranates of Khojend were "sweet with a tinge of sourness" and "excellent for quenching thirst"; the watermelons were "sweet, cool, and delicious." Yelü delighted in every sign of cultivation. He praised the gardens of Samarkand watered with "fountains, square ponds, and

Przewalski's horses, which played a vital role in the Mongol
Empire's military strength.

round pools," and marveled that "every third acre of land is irrigated
with over two hundred gallons of water."

In his audience with the Khan, who had summoned the sage from
his Buddhist hermitage to share his reputed wisdom, these "impressive scenes," were what Yelü told Chinggis to encourage. The ruler
should turn his back on the nomadic life, Yelü advised. He urged
Chinggis to stop harassing settled villages and to let their agriculture flourish. The Mongol treasury would bulge with the taxes that
flowed in.[1]

By contrast, Mongol soldiers and advisors saw nothing of value
in the cultivated agricultural landscape that they moved through at
such speed. They urged their ruler to demolish fields and let grass
take over, to make new pasture for the roving camp's horses and
sheep. The Mongols' power was rooted, quite literally, in steppe
grass. Each of the estimated 102,000 men in the Mongol army had
at least five horses. Perhaps half of all of the horses on Earth in the
thirteenth century were in the Mongol Empire. Horses' milk and
meat, at times their blood, furnished mobile soldiers with calories,
even in winter, when the horses foraged for grass under snow. In
the words of archaeologist Barry Cunliffe, the "partnership" that

humans established with horses on the steppe—a relationship of domination, to be sure, but also one of intimacy, care, and mutual dependence—"empowered humans, increasing out of all proportion their creative, and destructive, power."[2] The years from 1211 to 1230, immediately following Chinggis's fratricidal accession, were unusually wet. Rain made the grass grow faster: the Mongols' horsepower became their superpower.[3]

The Mongols' supreme god, Tengri, was the sky personified: the limitless sky sheltering the high, flat steppe. Under the umbrella of Tengri lived a range of natural and animal spirits: the wolf, the bear, and the eagle harbored special spiritual force. Chinggis's own mythology of origin held that he was descended from a union between the Blue Wolf and a wild doe. Before such wild and awesome power, what use could there be for agriculture?[4]

Few empires in history have faced as sudden and stark an ecological dilemma as the Mongols faced on their lightning sweep through the heart of the Eurasian continent. As the Mongols broke out of the niche that had sustained their way of life and their military power, the world of pasture and grass, they had to choose among fundamentally different ways to use land, find food, raise animals, manage forests, and rule people. They had to choose between competing visions of human life on Earth.

IN THE DECADES FOLLOWING Yelü's pilgrimage, Mongol forces pushed south through China, leaving a trail of death behind them. The debate that Yelü had tried to adjudicate remained unsettled. When Chinggis's grandson, Kublai, began the final advance against the southern Song Dynasty of China in the 1260s, he confronted the largest, most populous, and wealthiest agrarian state the world had ever known. He had to learn to rule over a landscape, and a society, that was the antithesis of the Mongols' own. By the end of the eleventh century, more than twice as many people lived in southern as in northern China—a reversal of a long historical pattern. China's

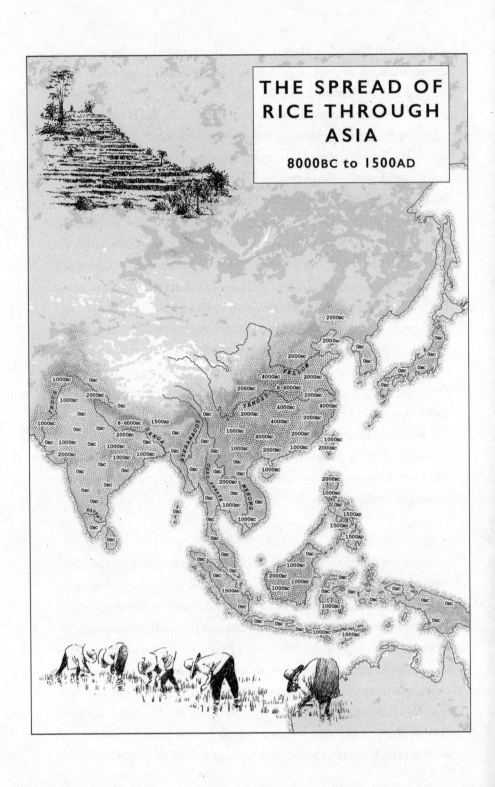

THE SPREAD OF RICE THROUGH ASIA

8000BC to 1500AD

population reached around 115 million people by the start of the thirteenth century: a third of all the people alive in the world. Such stunning growth was possible because of the spread of rice.[5]

Rice sustained more human lives than any other crop until the advent of industrial agriculture. Compared with most grains, its properties are miraculous. Rice draws nutrients directly from water. Soil planted with rice improves rather than deteriorates over time. Only around 5 percent of the harvest needs to be kept for seed, whereas wheat demands a much larger proportion. Wet rice cultivation was the most productive and the most labor-intensive agriculture in the world. In China under the southern Song, the productivity of rice reached new levels.[6]

China's rice revolution began along the old trading route between southern China and Champa, a coastal kingdom on the Indochinese peninsula bordering Cambodia—it was the prodigal return of a Chinese crop that, through the uncoordinated efforts of Asian farmers over millennia, spawned more than one hundred thousand varieties. Almost all the rice grown in the world belongs to a single species, *Oryza sativa*, first cultivated in the middle stretches of the Yangzi valley as early as ten thousand years ago. From there it began a winding, prolonged, journey south and west: a journey we can trace through genetic, linguistic, and archaeobotanical fragments. Wet rice cultivation reached Taiwan, Korea, and Japan by 2500 BCE; rice arrived in Southeast Asia shortly afterward, likely taken by migrants from southern China. In India, rice cultivation may have developed independently, adapting strains of Gangetic wild rice; over time, rice grown in India appears to have hybridized with shorter-grained *japonica* varieties from East Asia, hinting how early the continual movement of knowledge and seeds had begun. By the second millennium, BCE, rice cultivation supported large sedentary populations along the Ganges Valley and eastern India, as well as in southern India and Sri Lanka.[7]

Sometime in the tenth century, one of those artisanal varieties of *Oryza sativa* returned to Chinese shores. "Champa rice"—an early-ripening variety that was more tolerant of drought—arrived on merchant ships in Fujian. It passed between family farms by word of mouth and power of example. Its revolutionary possibilities grabbed official attention. In the year 1012, the Song emperor, Zhenzong, sent to Fujian for thirty thousand bushels of Champa seed to be distributed to other southern provinces. Government agricultural officers demonstrated the new technology and offered villagers incentives to adopt it. Within decades, the area planted with rice in southern China doubled. A second annual crop was added. Rice cultivation moved up hills and seized brackish swamps. By the 1300s, Guangdong was exporting rice back to Champa.[8]

. The jeweled green surface of lowland paddy fields, bunded and cut with sluices; the chiseled, stepped terraces that ascended steep mountains—they were so ordered and so expansive as to seem an eternal feature of the landscape. But paddy fields, too, were the result of human conflict over different ways of inhabiting the Earth.

Kublai Khan had reasons to turn China's agrarian world upside down. The most pressing of them was a simmering conflict with his brother Arigh Boke about how far to adapt to settled society. Arigh Boke spoke for traditional Mongolian ways; he feared that his brother had caved to the temptations of sedentary luxury. But Kublai chose a different path, and provoked his brother into open rebellion. The wisdom of two women in Kublai's life—his mother, Sorghaghtani Beki, and his wife, Chabi—appears to have convinced him to make peace with Chinese agrarian society. When Kublai was a child, Sorghaghtani had held a personal realm in northern China. She was at pains not to interfere with its agriculture and had encouraged toleration of Chinese cultural norms. Her son took that lesson to heart. Chabi, too, urged Kublai not to allow his camp followers to turn agrarian land into pasture. Kublai prevailed over his brother, in the end, by denying Arigh Boke's forces the agrarian resources they disdained but could not do without.[9]

In 1261, Kublai's government opened the Office for the Stimulation of Agriculture: this was a fundamental change of approach. The bureaucrats who worked at the office produced detailed reports on growing rice and on the cultivation of silkworms. It is because of the Yuan Dynasty's efforts to create a permanent archive of agricultural innovation that a record still exists of two twelfth-century scrolls by Lou Shu—scholar, administrator, painter, and poet—that bear witness to every step in the making of China's "carpet of green." The original works have been lost, but not before Kublai's Office for Agriculture had copied and transcribed them.

Lou Shu came from a long line of scholar-officials in Ningbo, in coastal eastern China. Disappointed but undeterred after he failed the imperial civil service examination, which would have been a ticket to secure employment for life, he served instead as a local magistrate in Lin'an, near the southern Song capital at Hang-zhou. In his spare time he turned to art to express his vision of a harmonious agrarian society. Lou Shu "diligently attended to people's affairs" and "consulted with farmers and sericulturalists," his grandson recorded. Lou Shu's work is ethnographic in spirit, humble and observant. He depicts lives of toil with empathy; he pays as much attention to women as to men. Lou Shu insists that the wealth of China is built on the hard work of its farmers, and he admonishes the wealthy to remember this: "The couple in damask silk gauze, / Should think of the one who wears coarse hemp." Lou Shu celebrates the productive beauty of the landscape vivified by the farmers' labor. A sense of hope suffuses the sixth tilling poem, "Planting Seeds," with its vision of nature and human hands working in concert.

> The old grains send out new shoots,
>   Plums ripen, and rains make plentiful.
> Down in the fields, begin to plant the seeds,
>   When walking slowly, the arms swing continuously
>   back and forth.
>
> Next morning, look at the level fields,
>   Green, needle-like spikes ripple in the wind.

Carefully watch these one inch roots,
So the rows will have the space needed for ripening.

The poet observes and instructs, he praises and advises: "carefully watch these one inch roots." The skill of planting lives in muscle memory: in the swing of the arms, in measured movement through the fields. The man in the scroll looks concentrated but also loose, fluid. The seeds tumble from his hand like spray. "This is how we obtain every grain of food," Lou Shu writes, and, moving from the single farm to the known realm, he concludes thereby that, "The whole world is properly fed." Lou Shu hoped that, over time, improvements in irrigation would provide farmers a measure of freedom and leisure—even a chance to find love. "The setting sun shines on young willows, / The farmers, with laughter and songs, relax / with young maidens."[10]

In choosing to preserve the scroll, Kublai's officials endorsed this late-Song idyll of a harmonious society. A decision had been made about the future shape of China. By 1262, just a year after opening the state Office for Agriculture, Kublai passed an edict prohibiting nomads from allowing their animals to roam on farmland.[11] Upon

Yuan dynasty copy from Lou Shu's twelfth-century *Pictures of Tilling and Weaving*, showing the planting of a rice field.

Terraced rice fields in Guizhou, China.

becoming the emperor of a unified China, Kublai styled himself as a successor to previous holders of the Mandate of Heaven and not as a conquering cultural outsider. His reign achieved a new fusion of nomadic power and settled resources.

THE TRANSFORMATION OF THE world began with desire, even as most human lives scrabbled for subsistence: the desire of powerful rulers for symbols of rank and distinction—for pearls and pepper; for gold and silver and sugar. Already by 1300, the products of distant places were arrayed in hoards within Eurasia's royal treasuries. The harder they were to find, the more they were worth. The Mongols built an empire on ecological contrast: traders along the overland routes across Eurasia "had access to the produce of utterly different climatic zones, from desert to tundra." In centuries to come, the pursuit of spices and precious metals would compel millions of people to move across oceans and continents.[12]

In 1300, in the midst of a pan-Eurasian exchange of knowledge and plants, Rashid al-Din—Jewish convert to Islam; cook, physician, and vizier of the Il-khan branch of the Mongol Empire in

Persia—set up his House of Healing on the outskirts of Tabriz. It was a hospital, a medical college, a publishing house, and a botanical garden all in one. Rashid and his polyglot group of students of surgery translated Chinese medical texts into Persian. They investigated the properties of medicinal plants. They hoarded the dried root of Chinese rhubarb, native to Gansu and northern Tibet, for its cathartic and astringent properties; they procured cinnamon, exclusive to the island of Sri Lanka, as a painkiller and a tonic. Caravan and seaborne routes converged. The transmission of knowledge through written and printed texts enhanced the search for what was new and exotic. Paper was among the most revolutionary of all China's technologies, and the Mongol Empire spread it to many parts of the world where it was previously little or never used.[13]

The immediate region around the House of Healing was heir to the legacy of a tricontinental Islamic Empire, which had created pockets of irrigated agriculture from a profusion of plants from across Eurasia and the Indian Ocean. To the east of Tabriz was the Mongol highway to China, which the Moroccan intercontinental wanderer, Ibn Battuta, described as "the safest and best country for the traveller," where "a man travels for nine months alone with great wealth and has nothing to fear."[14] To the west lay Europe, where an agricultural efflorescence unfolded in parallel with China's embrace of rice. Between 800 and 1300, farmers and their lords had wrested large parts of western and central Europe from forest and marsh into arable land and planted endless fields of wheat. The most palpable effect of these changes was to sustain more people and more domesticated animals on Earth. Between 900 and 1200, the population of China more than doubled, from around 60 million to 140 million people; over a longer period, from 800 to 1300, Europe's population grew from 25 to 70 million. It took the Mongol empire's fusion of steppe, field, and ocean to force these agrarian worlds into a newfound proximity, which, for all its uniqueness, the House of Healing embodied. The pulse of human life on Earth quickened.

"Few other events in the history of European civilization," French

historian Marc Bloch wrote, "have had such weighty consequences"
as the growth in human numbers that peaked in the twelfth century.
The same was true for China, and across rice-cultivating regions
of Asia. Social density allowed the "greater ease and frequency
of exchange," Bloch observed. The Franciscan Bartholomew the
Englishman published his *De proprietatibus rerum* ("On the Properties of Things") around 1240, part encyclopedia and part travel-
ogue. In his writing, the adjective "populous" was used as the highest
praise, along with "fertile." Italy, he observed, had "the most populous cities" (*civitates populosissime*); Paris "receives people coming
from all parts of the world"; Picardy was "abounding in peoples."
The horizons of his world expanded; Bartholomew wrote of places
few Europeans had seen, but which now entered the consciousness
of the literate elite. India, he said, was "amongst all the regions of the
earth . . . the most populous." Human density brought a new sense
of possibility. It also brought new kinds of desire, and among them
the desire for spices loomed large.[15]

In the imagination of European consumers, spices came from distant and mythical lands to the east, all known vaguely as "India."
The spices that arrived in Venice from Alexandria, dried and packed
in bales or boxes, grew on plants unknown. They called forth fevered
fantasies. Isidore of Seville, seventh-century philosopher, had imagined India's pepper forests "guarded by serpents." He speculated
that "the natives burn the trees when the pepper is ripe and the fire
drives away the snakes. It is the flame that blackens the pepper. . . ."
Isidore's image of snake-vines coiled around pepper trees inspired
manuscript illustrations well into the sixteenth century. The myth
held that these substances were hard to procure because they had to
be wrested from the menace of wild and faraway forests by the hands
of unfamiliar people. Stories like these gave western Europeans the
notion that to find the source of spices would be a heroic quest, pit-
ting men against a hostile nature—and Christians against infidels.[16]

After 1250, European travelers began to fill out their knowledge
of the spice route as they traveled through the vast Mongol Empire.

Europeans adjusted their perception of where India was in relation to China; for the first time, they understood that a major source of spices lay beyond "India," in archipelagos to the south and east. Marco Polo brought "Java" into European literature, though he never traveled there and his account fused Java with other islands of Indonesia. South-south-east from the kingdom of Champa, he said ("according to the testimony of good seamen who know it well") lay "the biggest island in the world . . . ruled by a powerful monarch and paying no tribute to anyone on earth." "It is a very rich island," Polo wrote, "producing pepper, nutmegs, spikenard, galingale, cubebs, and cloves, and all the precious spices that can be found in the world." He was sure that "it is from this island that the merchants of Zaitoun and Manzi in general have derived and continued to derive a great part of their wealth." His revelation was a siren: "this is the source of most of the spice that comes into the world's markets," he speculated. A young Christopher Columbus pored over the travel accounts of Marco Polo and Pierre d'Ailly, tantalized by the treasures that awaited the intrepid traveler. In margin notes, he scrawled: "great treasures," "much incense," "pepper, cinnamon, nuts"—and in Japan, "gold in the greatest abundance."[17]

The quest to monopolize the traffic in luxuries—luxuries chased by a small minority at first, and slowly widening their social reach— would affect soils and mountains and forests, airs and waters, mammals and birds and fish. But not yet. For within the whirlwind of the Mongol exchange of goods, plants, and knowledge, lay hidden the catastrophes that would bring it to a sudden end.

WITH THE DAWN OF THE fourteenth century came a change in the weather. With a change in the weather came acute pressure on the margins of viability of human and animal life. China experienced not only a marked shift toward cooler conditions, but also a slew of superstorms and an unrelated upsurge in seismic activity. Two earthquakes, in 1303 and 1305, caused an estimated 270,000 deaths. The snowstorms that struck the Mongolian heartland led thousands of people to seek shelter in the vicinity of the Great Wall. The official Yuan chronicle noted that, by 1308, "the refugees from the north totaled 868,000 households, and everyone lived on disaster relief from the court." As part of the Yuan Dynasty's adaptation to traditional ways of rule in China, the state had conceded relief to its subjects in times of hardship. Now China's rulers faced desperate claims from their own Mongol kin. Between 1307 and 1310, Helin province alone distributed 36 million kilograms of grain, and 40,000 *ding* of paper money, to people fleeing the freezing Mongolian steppe.[18]

The following decade, Europe faced a similar string of catastrophes. Between 1315 and 1317, torrential rains flooded the fields, ruining the harvests. To a German observer, the rain was a portent of biblical catastrophe: "there was such an inundation of waters that it seemed as though it was *the* Flood." When an English poet described the weather as "so cold and unkynde," he used "unkynde" in the sense of uncharacteristic: weather behaving at odds with its own nature.[19] The English clergy walked barefoot in penitence after the failed harvest of 1315. The following season, grain yields were 43 percent below the annual average. The crisis continued into 1317, when "a thusent winter / ther bifore com nevere / non so strong" (never before had there been a winter so harsh as this). Across Europe, millions died. The poor suffered most as the price of grain rose sharply amid the crisis. A memorial in the German town of Schmidtstedt is devastating in its simplicity: "In the year of the Lord 1316 here were buried 100 × 60, 33 × 60, and 5 humans, who have died in the year of dearness. God have mercy on them." After the rains came a cattle plague. Half of the cows in England died.[20]

Things in China were about to get even worse. Between 1314 and 1320, after a "super snowstorm of the vast steppe," further disasters followed: "sheep, horses, camels, and all other animals died, people scattered and sold their children into slavery." While inland areas suffered from cold, the coasts drowned. Between 1319 and 1332, repeated typhoons and storm surges caused devastation. The

Yuan Shi, the official chronicle, observed: "typhoon and tsunami, houses in the Run, Chang, and Jiangyin prefectures washed away and people are hungry"; "The sea overflowed and broke the dikes and drowned over 17,000 people."[21]

The repeated onslaught of disasters eroded the authority of a Yuan state that was already overstretched, already riven with conflict between the Mongol ruling elite and Han Chinese, already printing too much money. Historian Li Tana argues, "climate [was] a major factor in the downfall of the Yuan dynasty," which "had had the misfortune to found their dynasty in an age of great climatic instability."[22]

The biological entity that did more than anything else to halt the expansion in human numbers and prosperity in the fourteenth century was *Yersina pestis*, the bacteria that infects human beings with the plague. The emergence of the plague pandemic that would come to be known as the Black Death—a name it acquired in Europe in retrospect, centuries later—owed everything to the environmental reshaping of the medieval world. *Yersina pestis* is endemic to wild rodents on the Central Asian steppe. Once before, almost a millennium earlier, it had caused a pandemic in Mediterranean Europe: the Plague of Justinian (541–49 CE). The development of a new strain through genetic mutation, sometime in the middle of the thirteenth century, made the germ more virulent and easier to spread. The ecological disruption unleashed by Mongol expansion—the rapid movement of people, animals, plants, and pathogens across ecological zones—created prime conditions for the mutation to develop. A fateful transition took place when *Yersina pestis* found a home among rodent populations that lived close to densely settled human populations; fleas transmitted infection from rodents to people. The trade in grains and furs carried the plague far and wide.[23]

Intermittent outbreaks of plague in China are recorded in the 1330s. It reached the cities of the Golden Horde, in southern Russia, by 1345–46. From there, the epidemic followed overland trading routes to the Crimean coast; it traveled in the holds of Genoese merchant ships to the Black Sea and to Italy. The plague arrived in Constantinople in 1347, and from there it burned through Europe and the Middle East. The catastrophe was sudden and all-consuming. "In the face of its onrush, all the wisdom and ingenuity of man were unavailing," wrote Giovanni Boccaccio, Italian man of letters, who lived through it. Neither earthly nor divine power were of any use: "all sick persons were forbidden entry, and numerous instructions were issued for safeguarding the people's health, but all to no avail"; the "countless petitions humbly directed to God by the pious" proved just as futile.[24]

The Arab writer, Abu Hafs Umar Ibn Al-Wardi, observed the plague's devastation of Palestine and Syria—until he, too, succumbed to the illness in 1349. In Damascus, "the plague sat like a king on a throne and swayed with power, killing daily one thousand or more and decimating the population."[25]

For al-Wardi, the plague takes on human characteristics of a conquering army. In other accounts, by contrast, the plague represents nature alive and awry. An account from a monastery in southern Austria found portents of the plague in a mythic succession of disasters: "in the country where ginger comes from, a deadly rain fell, mixed with serpents and all sorts of pestilential worms . . . Not far from that country dreadful fire descended from heaven and consumed everything in its path; in that fire even stones blazed like dry wood." Widespread was the sense that the plague was a form of divine punishment: "this is surely caused by the sins of men who, while enjoying good times, forget that such things are the gifts of the most high giver." Everywhere, preachers called for repentance. In many parts of Europe, beginning in Germany, Jews became a scapegoat: they were accused of poisoning wells and rivers; they faced expulsion and murder.[26]

As the plague moved through western Eurasia, it squeezed the thin margin of security hard won by those who had cleared land and planted new crops. "Our former hopes have been buried with our friends," the Italian poet Petrarch wrote. He skewered the presumptions of his generation, which had grown complacent in prosperity. "How transient and arrogant an animal is man! How shallow the foundations on which he rears his towers!" The great monuments to human power that adorned the cities of Eurasia looked different, now. There is sarcastic fury in his conclusion: "Go, mortals, sweat, pant, toil, range the lands and seas to pile up riches you cannot keep; glory that will not last."[27]

For what was Eurasia's agrarian transformation, if not a bet on the future? Now that future lay in ruins. A chronicle from Rochester, in England, observed in 1348: "The shortage of labourers and of workers . . . was then so acute that more than a third of the land throughout the whole kingdom remained uncultivated." Before his death from the illness, John Clynn, one of the Friars Minor of Kilkenny, left some pages blank in his notebook as a gesture of hope: "I leave parchment for continuing the work, in case anyone should still be alive in the future. . . ."[28]

The Black Death was the most lethal pandemic ever to affect human society. The numbers only hint at the scale of suffering, pieced together from local archives, and available only where births and deaths were recorded. Somewhere between seventy-five and two hundred million people died across Eurasia during the Black Death. The plague took the lives of between 30 and 60 percent of the population of Europe and the Middle East, following the forward march of conquest, connection, and expansion that had allowed for a leap in the scale and density of human habitation. French historian Emmanuel Le Roy Ladurie, pioneer of climate and demographic history, observed that the Black Death marked the beginning of an alteration in the conditions of life—"the unification of the world by disease."[29]

IN RECENT DECADES, THE computer-driven statistical power of the natural and social sciences has newly made visible patterns of long-term change. Today, analyzing these patterns drives the field of climate history, as we urgently want to know how anomalous our current trajectory of anthropogenic climate change might be compared to previous eras of climatic variability. (The short answer is: highly anomalous.) The data that climate historians use comes from written traces of human experience—travel accounts, administrative records, manorial account books, sermons—but it also comes from a natural archive of tree rings and ice cores. These are called "proxy" data. The testimony of wood and ice stands in for the silence of human voices.

Beginning in the 1960s, the research of historical geographers suggested that medieval Europe had experienced a run of four centuries of warmer, wetter weather: a "medieval warm period." With an expanding natural archive, historians of different European regions added detail and nuance to this picture. Developments in economic and social history seemed to be driven by causes previously obscure: "It was the benign climatic and biomedical environment that was most responsible for the rise of European power and wealth, the clearing of land, the revival of cities, and above all the expansion of the population base fourfold from 900 to 1300."[30] Warmer weather extended the growing season; plentiful rains boosted the harvest. At first the evidence for warming was primarily European; and then new data from other continents hinted it was widespread, and nothing less than a global Medieval Climate Anomaly that affected Mesoamerica, India, and China as well as Europe. The timing, intensity, and synchronicity of this pattern admits many regional variations, and uncertainty remains: Iran, for instance, does appear to have experienced warming, but it began and ended earlier than in neighboring regions.[31]

If there *was* a worldwide climatic shift, this would explain why so many societies, so far apart and so different from one another, simultaneously expanded cultivation, built cities, and erected monuments. It would explain why so many states and empires came to the point of collapse in the fourteenth century, again more or less synchronously. The circulation and borrowing of new ideas and

The Hindu epic *The Churning of the Ocean of Milk*, carved
into the walls of the south gallery of Angkor Wat, Siem Reap,
Cambodia. Once among the largest cities on Earth, with a
sophisticated infrastructure of water control, Angkor's decline
in the fifteenth century is sometimes attributed to climate
shocks, though recent evidence suggests a gradual retreat
rather than a sudden collapse.

technology; the binding as well as destructive effects of conquering
empires—these go some way to accounting for the highs and lows
of prosperity and disaster, but they also leave much unexplained.[32]

Abrupt changes in climate, volcanic eruptions, and earthquakes
acted upon a world on the move; they acted on a world being molded,
imperfectly, to serve human needs. Unseasonal rains defeated dikes
made to control them. Floods washed through soils unimpeded
after whole forests had been burned or pulled up by their roots. Prolonged frosts slowed the growth of grass that fed horses that carried warriors over vast distances. Plague-carrying fleas stowed away
amid animal furs in the holds of merchant ships. Cycles of unaccus-
tomed cold and rain affected a profusion of life forms, stimulating
new kinds of inquiry by botanists and physicians, travelers, and pil-
grims. Curious observers of nature wrote in new genres, inscribed
on a medium that spread across Eurasia: paper, wrought from cel-
lulose fibers taken from wood, beaten in water, pressed on screens

and dried. When the eleventh-century Jewish trader Madmun bin Hasan-Japheth, chief merchant of Aden, sent a gift to his business associate in India, Abraham bin Yiju, he sent what was most precious: "two sets of fine, large paper—government paper, the like of which no one has."[33] This ingenious product of plant fibers allowed human beings to see, name, categorize—and, just maybe, control— nature in a new way.

The human attempt to script and harness nature would grow more elaborate in centuries to come. Around the world, states and societies consciously widened their margins of safety. The scale and complexity of human societies grew and so did the range of possible futures before them.

CHAPTER TWO

WINDS
OF DEATH

THE SPECTATORS ARRAYED ALONG THE BANKS OF Suzhou harbor were unlikely ever to forget what they saw that day in November, 1405. An armada of 317 ships crowded the port, ready to set sail for the southern seas (Nanyang). The expedition was under the command of the eunuch admiral, Zheng He, confidant of China's Yongle emperor.

The admiral presided over a total of seven Indian Ocean voyages between 1405 and 1433; he died on the last and was buried at sea. The first voyage alone carried some twenty-eight thousand men—more than the population of the average large European town at the time. Its biggest vessels were hulking, nine-masted, two-hundred-foot "treasure ships." On multiple voyages, the Chinese fleets twisted through the Indonesian archipelago, stopping in Java and Sumatra. They traversed the Bay of Bengal to Sri Lanka. Crossing the western Indian Ocean, they voyaged from the Arabian Peninsula down the littoral of eastern Africa, traveling as far as Malindi on the Kenyan coast. A smaller offshoot venture possibly made it down to Mozambique. The world had never seen such a spectacular naval display, and nor would it again for centuries.[1]

Treasure ships sailed from China carrying gifts of gold brocade and fine silk, gauze and porcelain. The fleet was a floating bank, stocked with a panoply of currencies to cater to different ways of measuring value. The vessels returned to China packed with tribute from foreign rulers as a sign that they acknowledged the Emperor's

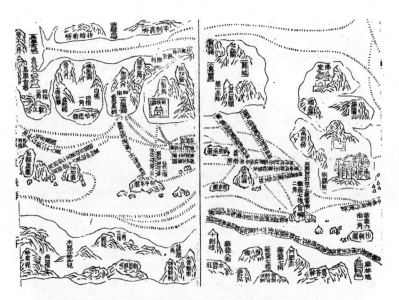

Zheng He's sailing charts, as published in 1628 in *Wubei Zhi*
("Treatise on Armament Technology").

supreme authority. There was little choice in the matter. On one of
the early voyages, a Sri Lankan king dared to refuse tribute—he
was seized, brought to China, and executed. Zheng He's armada
was an awesome display of China's power. The treasure voyages
were backed by a threat of punishment, but never of conquest. For
the Ming Empire at the height of its power, always concerned with
nomadic threats at its northern borders, there was simply no need to
colonize territory overseas.

Indian Ocean rulers quickly learned to be forthcoming with gifts.
Malindi sent the Emperor a pair of giraffes, which resembled, to
astonished Chinese eyes, the auspicious *qilin* of their mythology:
dragon-like creatures with flesh-covered horns, deer-like bodies
covered in scales, cloven hooves, and ox tails. The Chinese court
painter and poet Xendu composed an ode to the giraffe, describing
it as strange but intimate, a communicative, sensitive being coming
from "a corner of the western seas, in the stagnant waters of a great
morass," with the familiar features of the qilin.[2]

The giraffe was soon followed by other animals. Zheng He's fifth

Giraffe with Attendant by court painter and poet Xendu.

voyage, which reached Aden, brought back "an arkful of African animals, including antelopes, leopards, lions, oryxes, ostriches, rhinos, zebras—and more giraffes." At the beginning of the fifteenth century, none could match the Chinese emperor's power to summon all the plants and gems and creatures of the world, offering a glimpse of the scale and diversity of the living planet. Not everyone in the Ming court admired the search for exotica. "A prince should not . . . value strange things," the Confucian classic *Shujing* had decreed, "fine birds and strange animals he will not nourish in his kingdom." A powerful faction in the Chinese court felt that exploration had reached its limits. True wealth resided at home, they thought, in local soil cared for and cultivated. Above all, Confucian administrators thought, the voyages were unnecessary. China's manufacturing prowess was so great that the world's merchants would bring their treasures unprompted to its shores.[3]

For Europeans, more was at stake in voyaging beyond their shores. Their societies were only beginning to recover from the demographic catastrophe of the Black Death. With the collapse of the Mongol Empire, the overland route from Europe to Asia had closed. The rise of the Mamluks in Egypt had defeated the last Crusader kingdom in Acre. And then, in 1453, Ottoman forces encircled Constantinople, capital of Byzantium. The last vestiges of the Roman Empire, which had lasted more than a thousand years, collapsed in sixty days. Only at the western corner of Eurasia, with the fall of the Muslim kingdom of Granada in 1492, did the advance of Muslim power meet defeat by the Christian "reconquest." That lone military triumph was fire for the crusading spirit that would drive Iberian mariners across the Atlantic.

Caravels began as simple fishing boats with triangular sails. Nothing in their humble origins hints at the ecological impact they would come to exert on the world. Bolstered by Portuguese royal patronage under the rule of Prince Henry ("The Navigator"), shipwrights turned caravels into wind-harnessing machines: three- or four-masted ships outfitted for trade and war, square rigged on their front masts

and lateen rigged at the rear. Caravels sailed close to the wind, built
to capture its energy more efficiently. Iberian navigation improved
through experiment, but in 1400 European techniques were hardly
more sophisticated than the methods used by the Polynesian way-
farers of the vast Pacific, who made their way by the positions of
hundreds of stars, alive to signs of land-swell and the luminescence
of marine life, able to read the pink tinge of clouds that hovered over
reefs and the convective billows that rose higher and thicker over
land. Denied the generally predictable winds of Asia's monsoonal
oceans, European sailors' windborne struggles in the Atlantic would
eventually equip them to sail under almost any conditions.

By the 1410s, Portuguese ships had broken from the shoreline to
venture into the deep Atlantic. The Portuguese claimed Ceuta on the
coast of Morocco in 1415. Sailors learned that if they sailed north
on their return from the mid-Atlantic islands, then they could ride
the westerly Gulf Stream back to Europe without battling head-
winds. In 1426, they conquered the island of Madeira, which would
emerge—and just as quickly fade—as the world's most important
producer of sugar.

The colonists' first act on Madeira was to set the island alight. By
the time the Venetian traveler and slave-trader Alvise Cadamosto
visited the island two decades later, the settlement's birth in fire had
passed into legend: "So great was the first conflagration," he wrote,
that the settlers had to "flee its fury and take refuge in the sea." The
flames "razed the great part of the forest, and cleared the ground
for cultivation." Portuguese fleets forced their way south. They first
rounded the bulge of Cape Bojador in 1434: mariners called it "the
cape that juts out," at the westernmost point of the African continent, but its Arabic name captured more fully the promontory's menacing aspect—Abu Khatar, "father of danger." Caravels reached the
coast of Ghana in the 1470s. Defeating spirited local resistance, they
built a fortress at Elmina in 1484. High walls of dark brown stone
guarded the castle, ensconced in the cove of a natural bay. Elmina
began as a market for gold from the forested mines of Akan (el mina:

"the mine"). Soon, it would launch the bloody Atlantic commerce in enslaved human beings.[4]

Starting out with no more chance of success than so many failed attempts of earlier years, Christopher Columbus crossed the Atlantic for the first time in 1492. Giovanni Caboto (or John Cabot) sailed from Bristol to Newfoundland five years later, furnished with a patent letter from King Henry VII of England, instructing him to "conquer and possess" those lands for the Crown. Vasco da Gama followed the southwesterly monsoon winds of April to reach Calicut the same year, 1497, guided across the Indian Ocean by a skilled local pilot. Pedro Álvares Cabral made landfall in Brazil in 1500, also in search of India. In just eight years, armed Iberian sailors had found a seaborne passage to India—a long-held European dream—while stumbling upon two continents of which they had no inkling at all, soon to be named for the Italian mariner Amerigo Vespucci.[5]

THE EARLY LETTERS OF the Iberian mariners who accompanied Christopher Columbus to the Americas abound with descriptions of island landscapes, always compared with the terrain and the seasons they knew. Columbus himself saw trees "as green and lovely as trees are in Spain in the month of May"; but on the island he called Hispaniola, it was November. The physician Diego Álvarez Chanca, who penned the only surviving account of Columbus's second voyage, described Dominica as "green even up to the water, which was delightful to see, for at that season, there is scarcely any thing green in our own country." They wrote of trees and flowers and birds they did not have names for.[6]

Amid his bewilderment at where in the world he was, Columbus imagined an agricultural landscape in the image of Europe: Hispaniola's "hills and mountains, fine plains and open country, are rich and fertile for planting and pasturage," he reported. On his second transatlantic voyage, Columbus came prepared with the whole ecology of agrarian Europe to "transplant," including a menagerie of animals. "We brought pigs, chickens, dogs, and cats," wrote Michele de Cunco, and "they reproduce here in a superlative manner, especially the pigs." The Iberians imported the botanical heritage of the Mediterranean: barley and wheat, leeks and onions, cucumbers and broad beans, citrus fruits, olives, parsley, and vines. They planted cuttings of sugar cane, which had come to Madeira from the eastern Mediterranean—and traveled to the Antilles with Columbus, who had married Filipa Moniz Perestrelo, daughter of a Madeira sugar baron.[7]

Within two months of his crew's arrival on Hispaniola, Columbus reported, "the greater part of the people we employed fell suddenly ill." The people of Hispaniola and its neighboring islands lost everything. They lost their homes; they lost their mounds of fertile black soil; they lost the forests and streams that gave them spiritual sustenance; they lost their understanding of how the world was ordered. They lost their language. They lost their kin. Columbus and his men raped, murdered, and enslaved people without compunction. There is no reason to think the Iberian invaders were inherently any more violent than, for instance, the Mongol raiders who sacked Baghdad in 1258; but the imbalance of destructive power between the Taino and the firearms-bearing Iberians and the lack of previous contact combined to devastating effect. Medieval Eurasia had suffered cascades of plague and war and famine. Never did any society see its path to social and cultural continuance extinguished so fully as the Indigenous peoples of the Caribbean did.[8]

The Europeans brought a lethal mixture of conscious intention and invisible force. Their intentions were the residue of religious warfare. The messianic commitment of Columbus and his companions to reoccupying the Holy Land underpinned everything they did: it shaped how they understood the world. That mission gave them two sets of ideas that would do incalculable harm. The first was an overweening lust for gold—previously remote, inaccessible, and firmly in Muslim hands. Religious rivalry fed the gold-addled fantasies of medieval Europe. Iberian colonizers saw their own quest in the biblical story of King Solomon, about a ruler who surpassed "all the kings of the earth in riches and wisdom" (1 Kings 10:23), blessed with wealth from the gold mines of Ophir. Closer to them in time, medieval accounts of Chinggis Khan's wealth also spurred Iberian greed. Gold was never far from the minds of the Spanish conquerors: Columbus mentions it no fewer than sixty-five times in his account of the first voyage alone. In its pursuit, the conquerors abandoned any limits to their violence.[9]

The promise of gold meant the promise of funding for endless holy war. Another idea possessed the voyagers, also with roots in the religious conflict of Iberia. The Christian *Reconquista*—the seizure of the Iberian Peninsula from Muslim power—had led to the forcible conversion of many Jews and Muslims: sometimes it was their only alternative to capture, expulsion, or death. A class of converts accommodated to the new order, and some of them even prospered. Old Christian families grew envious. They insisted that only those with Christian ancestors were of "pure" lineage. *Limpieza de sangre*, "purity of blood," emerged as a new vocabulary for ordering human beings. The violence of Iberian conquest fed on a set of ideas about human descent that saw local people as "like beasts," "naked as the day they were born." To see the Taino in this way removed any shred of moral doubt about their destruction, at just the moment when the conquerors envisaged a new level of human domination over the rest of nature.[10] An elite among European Christians seized the freedom of other peoples on the grounds that they lived too close to nature to be fully human. Ideas of race underpinned a new sense of human exceptionalism that applied only to one part of humanity.[11]

Ecology combined with intention: the destruction of the Taino was a direct result of the violence, enslavement, and starvation inflicted on them by Iberian invaders. It was the outcome, too, of germs that traveled in the bodies of human beings and animals from Europe. Caribbean societies were accustomed to the illnesses distinctive to their own hemisphere, but they had been insulated from

Eurasia's disease pool by the Atlantic Ocean. That barrier broke with the arrival of ship after ship from Spain.

We will never know just how many people died on Hispaniola in the three decades after 1492, nor how many had lived there before. A likely figure for the precolonial population is between two and three hundred thousand people, an estimate that relies on the prolific work of the friar Bartolomé de las Casas, who became an advocate for the Indios, as the Spanish called them, as well as censuses by Spanish administrators seeking to divide the spoils and boost their coffers, traces of archaeological evidence, and insights from demographic models. Wherever they begin, demographers agree that by 1508, only around sixty thousand Indigenous people remained alive on Hispaniola. And then, in 1518–19, an epidemic of smallpox decimated the surviving population. "It has pleased our Lord to bestow a pestilence, of small pox among the said Indians, and it does not cease," reported the Jeronymite friars who governed the island, sent to restrain the worst excesses of the conquistadors. Gold production dwindled—because everyone was dead.[12]

Amid the ruins of Hispaniola, a few species found a path to survival while many others disappeared. The small mammals native to the island—*hutia*, likened to rabbits, and a small species of dog—were hunted to extinction by colonists. But the creatures that accompanied Columbus now thrived on an island without natural predators. With the collapse in native cultivation, the animals made more of the island their own. They sculpted its ecology to create new habitats. Cattle and "innumerable" wild horses roamed free, domesticated cats turned wild, the dogs became "worse than wolves," and the pigs were happiest of all. "We should remember," Las Casas admonished, "that we found the island full of people, whom we erased from the face of the earth, filling it with dogs and beasts."[13]

THE POPULATION OF THE Americas stood somewhere between fifty and eighty million people in 1500. The largest states, those of the

Aztecs and the Incas, had experienced a growth in population and cultivation comparable to medieval Eurasia. Within a century, the population of the Americas had collapsed by 90 percent, the people of a continent slaughtered by men from the other side of the Atlantic, and by the Eurasian infectious diseases the invaders carried within their bodies and in the holds of their ships: smallpox and measles, diphtheria and influenza, malaria and whooping cough. A century into the catastrophe, the French essayist Michel de Montaigne lamented the multiplying devastation of the early Iberian voyages: "So many goodly cities ransacked and razed; so many nations destroyed and made desolate; so infinite millions of harmless people of all sexes, states, and ages, massacred, ravaged, and put to the sword; and the richest, the fairest, and the best part of the world topsy-turvied, ruined, and defaced for the traffic of pearls and pepper."[14]

Twenty years ago, paleoclimatologist William Ruddiman suggested that the mass killing that accompanied the Iberian conquest of the Americas was so colossal that it triggered the planetary cooling that would be known as the Little Ice Age. Ruddiman's hypothesis was that the depopulation of so much cultivated land allowed for the regrowth of carbon-devouring tropical forests.[15] The idea that the Iberian invasion not only destroyed a continent but impacted the global climate was initially astonishing (though perhaps it wouldn't have been to observers in the sixteenth century). Mounting evidence from ice cores bolstered Ruddiman's case. Mass spectrometers and gas chromatographs allowed wisps of premodern air, embedded as bubbles in Antarctic ice, to tell a new story. They testify to a noticeable dip in atmospheric concentrations of carbon dioxide in the sixteenth century, reaching a low around 1610. The abrupt and total end to cultivation over such a large swath of the Americas "probably overwhelmed the usual forces controlling Earth's global climate," one recent study concludes. There remain too many wrinkles for this finding to be seen as settled. The ice core data is inconsistent. Some samples suggest that the fall in carbon dioxide levels happened later than would be explained by the Iberian conquests. And it is difficult to disaggregate the climatic effects of ruin and destruction in the Americas from the countervailing impact of the continued growth of cultivation, and loss of forests, across many parts of Eurasia and Africa.[16]

There can be no question about the devastation of indigenous cultivation in the Americas, even if its climatic impact remains open to debate. Inca agriculture, as sophisticated as any on Earth, raised potatoes, quinoa, and corn, all carefully adapted to the stark, water-scarce mountain landscape of the Andean highlands. Llamas played a vital sustaining role as both food and transport. The kingdom's religious culture venerated the living planet. The power of plants and animals animated its divinities, including Apu, the mountain deity, and Hurkaway, the serpentine goddess guarding the treasures beneath the Earth's surface. The Inca realm sprawled from Ecuador to the Chilean desert and reached as far west as the Amazon basin. Through the *mit'a* system of coerced labor, the empire raised an army to build an infrastructure of roads, cisterns, granaries, irrigation channels, and terraces carved into steep hillsides. In his chronicle of the Inca kingdom that had fallen many decades before his birth, Garcilaso de la Vega, born to a Spanish father and an Inca mother from a noble family, described the intensively sculpted landscape that had decayed: "In this way the whole hill was gradually brought under cultivation, the platforms being flattened out like stairs in a staircase." Deposits of precious metals in the Andean plateau were no secret to the Incas. They had mined small quantities of silver for centuries, to create beautiful objects of adornment and ritual importance.[17]

It was hardly a kingdom at peace. In the years leading up to the Spanish conquest, a war of succession between two sons of Huayna Capac, Huáscar Capac and Atahualpa, had brought suffering and destruction. The chronicle of the Quechua nobleman and writer, Felipe Guaman Poma de Ayala, describes a cascade of suffering: "And in this life we have seen the eruption of volcanoes and the rain of fire from the inferno and solar sand over a city and its district";

after those signs of a world awry came "the pestilence that God sent of measles, smallpox, croup and mumps, of which many people died." And "another pestilence that God sends," a plague as sorrowful as any in nature, "is the bad Christians to rob the possessions of the poor and take their wives and daughters and use them."[18]

The "bad Christians" arrived in the Inca capital in 1532, a ragtag band of a few European and many Indio soldiers under the command of Francisco Pizarro. They took Atahualpa hostage and forced the kingdom's implosion. A decade earlier, the Spanish had conquered the mighty Aztec Empire. From there they moved north into New Mexico, and south into Venezuela and Colombia. The list of their conquests was an epitaph for the societies, and ecologies, they destroyed. The Iberians found that the riches that lay in the Andean ground surpassed their most avaricious dreams. The story goes that Indigenous Peruvian Diego Gualpa stumbled (quite literally) upon a rich outcrop in 1545, a decade after the Spanish conquest. With every retelling, his discovery grew more fated. Over the following century, the mines of Potosí would produce half of all the silver in the world.

The conquistadors' fevered search for gold in the Caribbean had brought short-lived profit and lasting ruin. The discovery of the world's largest deposits of silver, on the high plains of the Andes, went many steps further: it catalyzed a chain reaction that would reshape the demography and ecology of the whole world.

Silver miners worked in open pits and down shafts cut at steep angles into the hillside—they were Quechua and Aymara speakers from the arid *puna*, and enslaved Africans, brought by the Spanish through Brazil and Argentina. Miners labored with hammers and pickaxes wrought of imported Basque iron. Mine shafts collapsed all too regularly, crushing workers or maiming them. At first many mines were in native hands. They smelted ore with *guairas*—furnaces driven by wind, powered by what was easily to hand: llama dung, the *yareta* plant, or charcoal. Indigenous owners participated in the boom at first, but they were edged out by European claim-owners

Theodoor de Bry's *Mining in Potosi*, depicting the toil of
workers in the silver mines, an illustration from the *Historia
Americae sive Novi Orbis* (1596).

and absentee landlords. Guairas gave way to bellows furnaces, share
work to wage labor. However many workers arrived in Potosí, the
mine owners wanted more. In 1572, Francisco Álvarez de Toledo,
Viceroy of Peru, sent to restore order amid warring factions of Span-
iards, revived the old Inca institution of the mit'a: the labor draft.
Luis Capoche, a mine owner himself, admitted that of what emerged
from the mines, "we could say it was rather blood than ore." The
mines reached so deep underground that, in 1600, the Hieronymite
friar Diego de Ocaña wrote: "It is a portrait of hell to enter inside,
because seeing so many caves, and so deep, and so many lights in
diverse parts, and to hear so many blows of those striking with the
iron bar, it is a din that causes a man to lose his judgement and even
his senses."[19]

Mining the ore was only the beginning. In the 1550s, a Seville
merchant named Bartolomé de Medina devised a way to extract
pure silver from ore using mercury as a reagent. Medina's technique
showed promise but supplies of mercury were hard to find; at first
it had to be shipped from Spain, as the most volatile and toxic of
cargoes. A decade later, enormous deposits of the vermillion sulfide

ore known as cinnabar—from which liquid mercury is extracted, burned off, and condensed—were found in Huancavelica, in Peru's southern highlands, eight hundred miles across forbidding mountains from Potosí.

Workers called Huancavelica *la mina de la muerte*—the mine of death. The labor draft brought thousands of men to the mercury mines: groups of "fifty or one hundred, chained up like criminals, with branches and shackles of iron." The roads were "so covered" with people, one Spaniard observed, that it seemed to him that "the kingdom was moving." Metallic mercury is the most toxic of substances. As the wind carried mercury vapor from the refineries, it seeped into water bodies, into the bodies of fish and animals, into the clothes people wore. Mercury poisoning causes tremors and headaches; it robs people of sleep, makes their muscles twitch, disorients them and confuses their senses. In larger concentrations, mercury damages the kidneys and ravages the lungs. The workers of Huancavelica, and those at the ore-crushing mills of Potosí, ingested the poison through their skin, in their breath and food and water.[20]

The quest for silver harmed every form of life, human and more-than-human. It brought some people so much wealth that Potosí, which had grown to become the largest city in the Americas (with a population of around 160,000 people in 1610), was "the richest, most opulent, and most renowned of any [city] known on the entire planet." The refinery furnaces sucked up so much energy that they ate the forests around Potosí. Mules and llamas carried a dirty burden to the point of exhaustion. The hillsides lay denuded and despoiled, as an anonymous chronicler reported in 1603:

There also used to be in this mountain . . . deer with antlers, and now not even grass is found on the mountain, not even where you find the roots of trees, which is what is most alarming, since all of it is a rocky mass with very little or no earth on it, spread over with the tailings from the veins, which are of live rock.

These would not be the last lands ruined by the human search for wealth in rock.[21]

A CENTURY AFTER THE first Iberian conquests in the Americas, the most truly lucrative market, for Europeans, remained China. The Pacific route from America to Asia was already known to Europeans by the time of the Potosí discoveries. In 1519, an expedition commanded by Ferdinand Magellan sailed from Spain to circumnavigate the globe. The mission returned home in 1522, its success having come at a terrible cost. Only one of the five ships in the fleet made it back. Most of the fleet's crew was dead: drowned, starved, or felled by scurvy. The storm-battered Pacific crossing had proved too risky to be worth the investment—until silver changed the equation. In China, the value of silver relative to gold was twice what it was in Europe. The Ming paper currency did not command widespread confidence and it struggled to hold value. Bronze coins worked for everyday transactions, but they were insufficient for large purchases. The Chinese government demanded taxes in silver. China's demand for silver seemed without limit at a time when trade was expanding and population was growing. European traders made a fortune. Silver reals from the Potosí mint traveled both east and west from America to China: shipped on from London and Amsterdam, around the African continent and across the Indian Ocean, and taken directly on ships that crossed the Pacific from Acapulco every year between 1565 and 1815. The ships that undertook these annual trans-Pacific voyages were known as the Manila Galleons. Europeans had little else to offer that was of value in the Chinese market, but the silver was enough. The Dutch East India Company alone exported almost five hundred tons of silver to Asia between 1610 and 1666.[22]

Manila was the hinge that swung open trans-Pacific trade between the Americas and China. The Spanish inveigled their way into this trading port at the mouth of the Pasig River in 1570, and they followed their script from the Americas: they captured the king,

Soliman, and massacred the town's Moro inhabitants. The Spanish built a fortress at the heart of the city, enclosed by pentagonal stone walls twenty feet thick. Within the walls—the area of Manila still known today as *Intramuros*—they built neat town squares and imposing churches in the image of home. Beyond the walls lay the Parián, a settlement of Chinese traders who had been in Manila long before the Europeans. Manila's trade could not have functioned without the Chinese, but the Spanish regarded them with racial contempt and religious suspicion. Manila's urban ecology was born of hierarchy. Chinese merchants were forbidden from building in stone, a privilege reserved for the Spanish ruling class. So the Parián was a city of wood. Time and again, it burned to the ground. In 1603, Spanish settlers carried out a pogrom against the Chinese, fueled by the local bishop's fevered accusations of witchcraft and sodomy. Tens of thousands of Chinese were killed. And still the traders returned because the opportunities were too lucrative to turn away from. Zhou Qiyuan, a Chinese coastal official, said of the Manila traders in 1617: "they are at ease on the ocean's waves and treat their boats as though they were fields." Thirty or forty Chinese ships arrived in Manila every year. They carried "silks, cottons, China-ware, gunpowder, sulphur, iron, steel, quicksilver, copper, flour, walnuts, chestnuts, biscuits, dates, and all sorts of stufs [textiles], writing-desks, and other curiosities." They took back enormous quantities of silver—and seeds that would change what the poorest Chinese ate in the century to come.[23]

Another Spanish pogrom against Manila's Chinese, even more brutal, followed in 1640. That year's Manila Galleon failed to arrive, wrecked in a Pacific storm. The prospect of financial ruin sparked rumors and fueled anxieties that spilled, again, into collective violence. Such were the bonds that stretched across the world's oceans, binding profit and loss, silver and sustenance, mercury and murder.

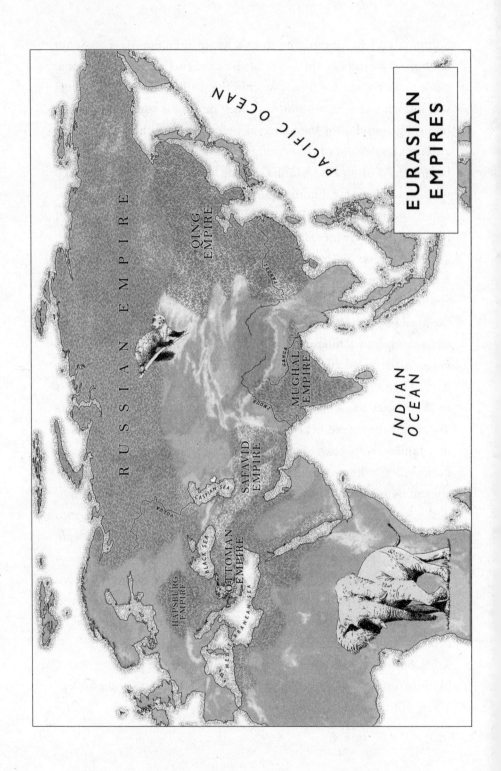

EURASIAN EMPIRES

RUSSIAN EMPIRE

QING EMPIRE

MUGHAL EMPIRE

SAFAVID EMPIRE

OTTOMAN EMPIRE

HAPSBURG EMPIRE

PACIFIC OCEAN

INDIAN OCEAN

CASPIAN SEA

BLACK SEA

MEDITERRANEAN SEA

VOLGA

INDUS

GANGA

MEKONG

CHAPTER THREE

LAND AND
FREEDOM

A SINGLE FAMILY PLAYED AN OUTSIZED ROLE IN drawing the Russian Empire beyond the Urals in the sixteenth century. Of obscure origins, the Stroganovs began as salt traders. They proved canny in their investments and as they grew prosperous, they assumed the trappings of nobility. The Stroganovs' sprawling estate at Perm marked the eastern edge of the Russian Empire. Beyond lay Siberia. In 1574, the tsar made the family a large grant of land there. In return, they supplied the ruling family with sable fur, its rarity a mark of royal distinction. The Stroganovs—private merchants acting in the name of an empire, akin to armed, chartered European merchants in the Indian Ocean—used their own militia to seize more and more land from Indigenous people. Siberia was home to dozens of dispersed communities—the Yukaghirs and Koryaks, who had inhabited the region since ancient times, as well as Turkic and Tungus tribes who had migrated later. They herded reindeer and subsisted on a profusion of wild berries, on protein-rich mushrooms and freshwater fish. When the khan of Siberia, a descendant of the Mongols, failed to comply with the Stroganovs' demands for trading concessions and territory, the fur-traders received the tsar's permission to advance.

The constant movement of people propelled Russia's expansion during the sixteenth century. Servicemen, gunners, musketeers, and cavalrymen moved at the command of imperial authorities. Many others packed their meager belongings and set out in search of more

land and plentiful food or in flight from the most oppressive landlords. Amid the wooded wetlands of the Dnieper and Don rivers,
armed bands of peasant settlers took the initiative. They came to be
known as Cossacks—from the Turkish word *kazak*, or "free man."
To wrest cultivable land from forest was a mark of liberty. Within
self-governing Cossack societies, known as hosts, men (and men
alone) held regular assemblies to elect their own leaders. Cossacks
proved formidable warriors for the Russian Empire. In return, imperial rulers did not intrude too much upon the settlers' quest for freedom. Now, with funding from the Stroganovs, the Cossack army of
Vasili Timofeevich pushed the empire's frontiers outward.[1]

Timofeevich, known as Yermak, rose to power after years of
working on the Stroganov trading fleet up and down the Volga. His
exploits passed into legend. In a collection of eastern Russian folk
songs dating from the sixteenth century, compiled in the early twentieth, Yermak's journey appears as a quest for freedom:

> In Astrakhan we cannot live; to live on the Volga is to count as
> thieves; to go to the Yaik is a great journey; to go to Kazan—
> there is the Terrible Tsar, the Terrible Tsar our Lord Ivan
> Vasilyevich;—to go to Moscow is to be arrested, scattered
> throughout different cities and placed in dark prisons. Let us
> go to Usolya, to the Strogonovy, to Grigory Grigoryevich, to
> the Voronovy; let us take a supply of lead, powder, and grain.

In a three-day battle on the River Irtysh in October 1582, Yermak's
army (supplied amply with "lead, powder, and grain") overcame the
forces of Kuchum Khan of Siberia. Traders, trappers, and merchants
followed the trail of fortified settlements east of the Urals. Imperial Russia arrived at the shores of the Pacific Ocean in 1639, when
explorer Ivan Moskvitin reached the Sea of Okhotsk.[2]

No landed empire expanded its territory as much as Russia did in
the centuries between 1500 and 1800. Successors to the Rus princes
of Kiev, the rulers of Moscow established their own empire in the

fourteenth and fifteenth centuries. Their sense of mission was burnished by an adapted form of Byzantine eastern Christianity. Their techniques of rule owed much to their Mongol overlords, from whom they had broken away.[3]

Theirs was an empire of ice and wood. Settlement proceeded "wherever the *sokha* [plow], scythe and axe have gone," as the saying went. Settlers seized the animal life of the coniferous northern taiga and the mixed forests further south—foxes, hares, minks, and beavers, their furs commanding high prices in the markets of the Black Sea. The empire expanded in every direction. In 1550, Russia covered an area of 1.1 million square miles with a population of around 6.5 million people; by the 1720s, this had grown more than five-fold to 5.9 million miles: a realm stretching across northern Eurasia to the Pacific Ocean.[4]

At the edge between forest and steppe, migrants found an abundance of fish and game. They found buttery black earth (*chernozem*) more fertile than poor northern soils. Centuries later, the dissident poet Osip Mandelstam would write an ode to these lands where "circumference is not all circumscribed," where the black soil had a life, and perhaps a will, of its own. Forests vanished as human settlement advanced. Over three centuries, the southern and western regions of Russia lost between half and two-thirds of their forest cover. As settlers moved east into the grasslands, they adapted to an ecology less familiar. The traditional horse-drawn Russian wooden plow, the sokha, was no use here, tripped up by soils that were tangled with the matted roots of steppe grasses. Ukranian settlers did better with the heavier, wheeled "plug" plow, pulled by oxen, that they brought with them. Migrants built houses with clay and bricks rather than wood, just as local people had always done. They set fire to the grasslands so that they could plant unending fields of rye.[5]

The Russian peasantry's quest for freedom clashed with the liberty of nomadic people to herd, hunt, and raid farming villages. Across Eurasia, the advantage was now on the side of sedentary societies, empowered by agrarian wealth and furnished with new ways of fighting wars. As the Russian Empire grew, conflict ignited at its boundaries. Heavily armed Russian fortifications at the empire's borders proved effective: the 1571 Tatar raid upon Moscow turned out to be the last. The imperial regime's success against its nomadic opponents marked the triumph of one way of using land and animals over another. By the 1630s, Moscow's forces had built a line of fortifications along the southern frontier with the still-powerful khanate of Crimea. The Belgorod Line strung together city fortresses, punctuated by small wooden forts. With newfound security from Tatar raids, Russia's nobility demanded more control over their labor force. Agricultural workers on newly opened lands could leave too easily, the nobility complained, and when workers were unhappy, they simply moved on. The imperial authorities first restricted and then, through a 1649 law, eliminated the freedom of peasants to leave landed estates. Upon a landscape that had changed so much in two centuries, mobility turned to immobility. A new era of serfdom began, and it would last for another two centuries.[6]

RUSSIA WAS AN EMPIRE of rivers with the great Volga at its heart—running from northwest of Moscow to the Caspian Sea, slicing through the border between forest and steppe. And across Siberia, waterways were crucial. To unearth the secrets of Siberia's terrain was a task that fell to a remarkable and unheralded cartographer, Semyon Remezov. Remezov was the second generation of his family to be born and raised in Siberia. He lived in Tobolsk, administrative heart of the Russian Empire east of the Urals. Making a living as a draftsman and surveyor, Remezov's reputation for skill landed him in charge of drawing a comprehensive map of Siberia. He traveled, he consulted the holdings of libraries, he compiled many maps that surveyors had been sending back to Moscow since the start of the seventeenth century.

Remezov's *Book of Siberian Maps* (1699–1700) is a singular work of art and mapmaking. He worked within a long tradition of

Russian cartography in which rivers were paramount. In Siberia, as in much of Russia, rivers were the only viable means of long-distance transportation; their condition at any moment, flowing or frozen, set the limits of what could be done. Remezov painted a river's eye view of the world. He brought the ecology of the region to life with sketches of animals and trees. He juxtaposed different scales from page to page in his notebook—here, a whole river basin; there, a single silver mine.[7]

In each village we see a pattern of change also replicated at larger scales: regional, interregional, and continental. In bare outline, it looks something like this: pioneer migrants set out from their homes with danger and uncertainty as their companions. They clear forests, tempted by free land and a remission of taxes. They settle land secured by arms and fortifications.

There are two possible endings. In one, the settlers flourish, enjoying the bounty of fertile fields. In the other, the imperial state takes away what it once gave freely, sweeping in to lock peasants in place. The story ends differently, always badly, for those who barely feature in the plot—nomadic peoples, dispossessed of an entire way of life: a hard and often violent way of life that would only be romanticized long after its passing. It ends badly, too, for countless living creatures. Their habitats vanish. They have nowhere to shelter from human pursuit, as parts of their bodies turn into commodities or curiosities to be enjoyed in places far away. By the end of the seventeenth century, sables had been hunted to the brink of extinction in Siberia—and since sables were connected in the food chain to dozens of mammals, more than two hundred birds, and many plants, other species felt their loss.[8]

SETTLEMENT AND CULTIVATION ACROSS the Russian Empire took place over a greater expanse than any other. But Russia was not alone. Throughout early modern Eurasia, landed empires devoured land and resettled people. First established by a small

group of Turkic warriors in Anatolia in the fourteenth century, the
Ottoman Empire reached its furthest extension in the second half of
the seventeenth, stretching west to east from Hungary to the Caucasus, and north to south from the Ukrainian steppes to the Arabian
Peninsula. Ottoman power came from the empire's ability to extract
value from the diverse ecologies within its realm, procuring and dis-
tributing grain, salt, and mineral riches.[9]

For the scale and density of human life that expanding empires
could sustain, China and South Asia, followed by western Europe,
always loomed largest. Fewer than 10 million people lived across the
whole of the Russian Empire in 1500, and just over 10 million by
1700. Compare that with China, where the best estimates put the
population around 91 million in 1500, and close to 100 million by
1700. The figures for India are even higher, though on a less secure
statistical footing: 131 million people in 1500, and 168 million by
1700. France, a fraction the size of Russia, was home to 14 million
people in 1500, and 21 million by 1700.[10] The settlement of Russia
resembles Remezov's art: it unfolded like a light wash of paint across
page after page. In Eurasia's agrarian heartlands, the art of human
settlement was more like a thickening, or what Italian painters called
impasto: textured layers of paint on a canvas that had been painted
over for centuries. The question, everywhere, was how many more
layers the canvas could sustain.

China, like Russia, was a society on the move in the seventeenth
century—across a more modest, if still huge, expanse but involving
a vastly larger population. People sought safety through a century of
upheavals—tenants revolted against landlords; farmers faced a spi-
raling succession of freezing, harvest-ruining winters; the dynastic
transition from the Ming to the Qing sparked forty years of intensive
warfare. China's experience of the colder temperatures and diminished rainfall of the Little Ice Age tore at its social fabric. In the lower
Yangzi valley in the 1640s, floods turned to drought, accompanied
by locusts and yet more floods. By the winter of 1641, a local administrator noted, "there was no rice for sale on the market." Local

people ate "chaff, leaves, bark, roots of grass"—and a great many of
them died.[11] Millions left their homes in search of sustenance, and
on the road they starved. The Chinese scholar-official, Chen Zilong,
wrote a moving poem about the plight of refugees:

> The little cart jolting and banging through the yellow
>   haze of dusk;
> The man pushing behind: the woman pulling in front.
> They have left the city and do not know where to go.[12]

Through these hellish decades, agrarian settlement did not just
continue—it intensified in the regions of southern China that had,
since the Song era, been home to most of the country's population.
Written in the late 1600s, an administrative guide, *New Descriptions
of Guangdong Province*, marveled at south China, "so warm that
the land produces three crops in a single year." The author extolled
the region's agrarian richness:

> They grow two crops of rice in the early field and then plant
> brassicas to make oil or indigo for dyeing, or grow turmeric or
> barley, rape or sweet potatoes. Once the main-field crops have
> been harvested they soak the straw in sea-water and burn it
> for the salt. On flat hills and ridges reeds, sugar cane, cotton,
> hemp, beans, aromatic herbs, fruits and melons are grown in
> profusion. The people are all extremely industrious and devote
> themselves so diligently to their farming that truly no patch of
> land is wasted and no hands are ever idle.

In troubled times, the bedrock of security was land—land that was
nourished and cultivated, planted and weeded and harvested without a wasted inch.[13]

It needs no leap of imagination to see how vulnerable China was
to the sustained but erratic cooling that climatologists now agree was
happening in the seventeenth century. As the ecological basis of China's

power and wealth came under strain—from the length of the growing season to the soundness of flood defenses—it is no surprise that the Mandate of Heaven, the Ming Dynasty's right to rule, teetered. What is more puzzling is how millions of Chinese farmers, many of them migrants to new lands, found ways to survive and even to flourish: in the *Description of Guangdong* lies a clue as to how.

It is a dark irony of early modern environmental history that from the Iberian ruination of the Americas came the seeds of China's survival. The Manila Galleons that carried the silver of Potosí and the Portuguese vessels that took the treasures of Brazil to the Indian Ocean—they also bore humbler cargo. They packed American plants previously unknown in Eurasia—potatoes and sweet potatoes, maize, peppers, chiles, peanuts, squash, tomatoes, pineapples, and papayas. These food crops brought about a "second agricultural revolution" in China, successor to the Song-era bonanza of Champa rice.[14]

Sweet potatoes arrived in Fujian as early as the 1590s, brought by the Manila merchant Jin Chenlung. Jin offered the crop to the provincial governor to fight hunger—which is just what it did. Around the same time, sweet potatoes arrived in Guangdong by way of Vietnam, and from the Portuguese outpost on Macau Island. The tuber spread quietly and steadily, mostly in the hands of small farmers. "It is treated like grain in Fujian and Guangdong," an imperial administrator observed in the middle of the seventeenth century. The sweet potato took its place amid an intensively engineered ecology. As the Guangdong gazetteer had noted, it grew alongside the staples of rice, sugarcane, and cotton, and with yellow ginger, cabbage, and many fruits. The crop spread to island frontiers of Chinese settlement, Hainan and Taiwan, where it thrived. A 1717 district manual from Chu-lo county, Taiwan, describes how sweet potatoes had become integral to local cuisine: boiled and eaten plain, ground into flour for noodles or steamed cakes, and brewed into a heady liquor. As people's palates became used to them, the properties of the sweet potato must have seemed miraculous to Chinese farmers. Adapted to arid regions of the Americas, the crop needs little water and thrives in stingy soils. It takes a tenth as much labor as rice and provides more calories in each serving. Measured by modern nutritional standards, sweet potatoes are unusually rich in minerals and vitamins as well as in starch, protein, and fiber.[15]

Sweet potatoes made human communities viable in unforgiving environments. Migrant farmers could now occupy lands that had been too hilly, too dry, or too eroded for paddy. The most energetic sculptors of upland environments were the Hakka—a southern Chinese community with its own distinctive dialect, infused with the cultural traditions of the Indigenous She people whom they incorporated or displaced as they moved uphill. The Hakka followed the rivers, like so many migrants in the early modern world. As they arrived in each hilly place, Hakka would employ local people to burn forests. They carved terraces of paddy into slopes made fertile by the ashes. They planted small plots of sweet potatoes, peanuts, and tea. They mined rock, made paper, logged timber, burned charcoal. Easy river transport gave Hakka settlers a ready market for their produce.[16]

Elsewhere in China other American crops played a similar role, even if they never grew as widely as sweet potatoes. Millions of people from Sichuan and Hubei moved in the 1600s to Shanxi. They could not have thrived without peanuts and maize. With every act of settlement by Han migrant families, the Indigenous inhabitants of forested and mountainous lands in China found their own margins of survival had become narrow.

By the end of the eighteenth century, the Qing Empire occupied double the land area it had inherited from the Ming, putting China not far behind Russia in size and with ten times its population. The Qing Dynasty was both the last nomadic empire as well as the last imperial dynasty to rule China. An interethnic coalition of Jurchens, Mongols, and other mobile peoples had united as Manchus, their base in the sprawling lands of Manchuria, northeast of the Great Wall and reaching up to Siberia. Once in power, the Qing played a double game: they insisted on, even reinforced, their Manchu ethnic distinction while they also incorporated and shared power with the Han Chinese majority. A hybrid imperial culture fused classical Chinese precepts with values honed by generations of nomadic life. The Manchu always retained a distinctive view of the relationship between human beings and animals, and hunting remained, for the Qing court, a mark of valor, masculinity, and martial acumen. Every young Manchu boy was trained to ride and to hunt; Chinese boys were not. "The hunt is also training for war," the Kangxi emperor wrote. Court scribes kept a proud count of the Kangxi emperor's personal kill, among his victims were 135 tigers and 96 wolves.[17]

To the northeast, the Qing Empire arrived at the frontiers of Russian expansion. Just as Siberia provided the Russian imperial elite with the furs they craved, so too did Manchuria beckon to the Qing with its exotic life. Manchu and Chinese alike adorned their robes with fur trim, a practice that would have been considered vulgar in Ming times. Steppe mushrooms lent their distinctive flavor to imperial banquets, perfectly matched with the taste of wild game. More valuable still was wild ginseng, treasured for its medicinal properties. Before Qing expansion, Manchuria was already part of a constellation of trade in wildlife and wild plants that included southern China, Japan, Korea, and Russia. Now trappers, hunters, and traders moved north in force. So lucrative was Manchuria's animal and botanical life that up to a quarter of all the American and Japanese silver imported into China ended up in Manchuria, used as currency to pay for furs and skins and rare foods. China's Manchu rulers restricted Han migration north of the Great Wall, but they could not prevent it entirely. Luxury demand from China's courtly elite wounded the ecology of Manchuria. In the eighteenth century, the fur trade collapsed—because there were few animals left to hunt.[18]

Imperial China expanded south and west. In 1683, Qing forces moved to incorporate the island of Taiwan, which had been the refuge of a renegade Ming loyalist. They advanced into Tibet and Mongolia. The sternest challenge to Qing ambitions in central Eurasia came from Zungharia, a nomadic empire created by a new alliance of Mongol tribal groups, now under pressure from both Russia and

China. The Kangxi emperor's provisional victory against Zungharia
in 1698 did not last as Zunghar forces regrouped. The showdown
came in 1755 when the Zunghar leader, Amursana, rallied disaf-
fected Mongols into rebellion.[19]

The Qianlong emperor fought a war of extermination. His
aim went beyond conquest: it was the destruction of the Zunghar
as a group. In twentieth-century language, his war could only be
described as genocidal. "Show no mercy at all to these rebels," the
emperor commanded his generals: "Only the old and weak should
be saved." There is no counting how many died in battle, and still
more died of hunger, thirst, and disease. Here, as in the Americas,
conquest meant the erasure of all that was there before—including
names. Zunghar, thick with meaning and memory, became the ano-
dyne Xinjiang (literally "New Frontier"), as if the land were empty.
Wherever the steppe's ecology allowed cultivation—in the Ili River
basin, in desert oases—farms followed. A mixed band of settlers
moved in to reshape the landscape, their migration sponsored by
the Qing state: Han Chinese cultivators, Manchu bannermen, Hui
Muslims, and many others. The relentless imperial quest for land
to settle and for resources to extract—in Central Asia, as in Russia
and China—put pressure on Indigenous peoples whose way of life
depended on constant mobility, and on ready access to pasture and
forest that were fast disappearing.[20]

When Tsebek-Dorji tayishi, a leading Kalmyk noble, appealed to
his followers in the 1770s to embark on an exodus, he presented it as
a heroic bid for ecological freedom. The nomadic Kalmyks inhabited
the Russian Empire and had their origins in Zunghar. Under enormous pressure from Russian and German settlers, the leaders of the
Kalmyk khanate dreamed of a return to their original homeland—
the very lands that had been crushed by Qing forces fifteen years
earlier. The Russian state "wants to make peasants out of you,"
Tsebek-Dorji told his followers. His view of the future was bleak:
the Kalmyk lands would be taken and made unrecognizable, he
thought. "In a little while, the Don, Terek, and Kuma will also be

colonized, and you will be pushed to the waterless steppes," Tsebek-Dorji warned, "and the only source of your existence, your herds, will perish." With a pastoral ecology, the very "source of existence," under mortal threat, Tsebek-Dorji presented his people with a stark choice: "either to carry the burden of slavery, or to leave Russia and thus to end all your misfortunes."[21]

Their misfortunes were far from over. At the chosen moment of departure, blessed as auspicious by the Dalai Lama who was revered by the Buddhist Kalmyk, the waters of the great Volga refused to cooperate. Weakening ice left the Kalmyk on the river's west bank stranded and unprotected against Russian reprisals. Those on the eastern bank who began the exodus found themselves pursued by Russian troops. When imperial soldiers had to turn back, unequal to the terrain, the Kalmyk then faced attacks by Kazakh fighters determined to revive old enmities. The refugees froze and starved across steppe and desert. They lost their herds of sheep and their horses died. Only a third of those who embarked on the journey survived. They arrived in a region now called Xinjiang, no longer Zunghar, held securely by the Qing state.

The Kalmyk flight for ecological freedom ended with just what Tsebek-Dorji had feared—in the end the Chinese, not the Russians, "made peasants" of the Kalmyk. The outcome was the same.[22]

CHINA'S CARPET OF CULTIVATION unfurled toward the borderlands. Diversity retreated to the edges of the empire. In India, that never happened. India sustained as much human life as China did, held together in a different balance. Throughout the early modern era India remained more ecologically diverse than China, its animal life more varied and profuse. India's society was more militarized, more polyglot, and even more mobile than China's. India's rulers never achieved the level of social control that their Chinese counterparts did. India's landscape resembled a mosaic: tiles of intensive cultivation pressed against scrub and forest, pasture and desert.

Unlike in China, the boundary between settled and nomadic life followed no neat geography of heartland and borderland in India. It cut an invisible and jagged line through every part of South Asia. The growth of settled cultivation under the Mughal Empire depended on the endurance of a pastoral world. Landscapes of green abutted swaths of brown and ochre. Beyond the bounds of the Mughal Empire, in Tamil-speaking South India, armed chieftains in the plains offered protection to rice-cultivating villages in the river valleys. The promise of security spurred fresh migration and turned some warrior groups into farmers. The frontier between pastoral and agrarian life was everywhere, and everywhere it was in motion. Human and animal life in India were interdependent, even symbiotic—far more so than in China.[23]

Contemporary with the Qing Dynasty in China, the Ottoman Empire, and the Safavid Empire of Iran, the Mughal Empire was the last horse-borne, Central Asian empire to rule in South Asia. The Mughals rose to power a century before the Manchus, and at their peak they held most of the Indian subcontinent. Like the Manchus, like the Ottomans, the Mughals' success came from their ability to adapt to and harness the wealth of a vast agrarian society.

When Zahir-ud-Din Muhammad (1483–1530)—the first Mughal emperor, known as Babur—arrived in India, he confronted an ecology both alluring and threatening. Descended from Timur on his father's side and Chinggis Khan on his mother's, Babur established his power in Kabul, Afghanistan, and from there launched a shock raid upon India. Babur reflected on his encounter with an agrarian society so different from his own. "The greater part of the Hindustani country is flat," Babur observed of the Yamuna River valley. He noticed that "autumn crops grow by the downpour of rain themselves," while other plants took intensive work; they had to be "watered constantly" by rivers, irrigated from wells using waterwheels or leather buckets lifted by yoked oxen. Even as he planned to tax the agrarian wealth of the Ganges valley, Babur noted that its ecology offered "forests of thorny trees in which the people of those

districts hole up and obstinately refuse to pay tribute." Accustomed
though Babur was to nomadic Central Asian societies, the scale of
mobility he observed in India astonished him—"Large cities in which
people have lived for years, if they are going to be abandoned, can
be left in a day, even half a day, so that no sign or trace remains."[24]

Babur grasped the dilemmas of rule that his Mughal successors,
and later the British too, would have to contend with: how to extract
as much land tax as possible from a society that was densely popu-
lated but far from sedentary. Across India a substantial portion of
the population—perhaps one in five men—was armed, and actively
participating in a competitive marketplace for military and artisanal
labor. They poured into the Mughal army and also bolstered the
forces of defiant local kingdoms. The Mughal Empire amassed territory under the reign of Emperor Akbar (r. 1556–1605), and again
between 1630 and 1690: by the end of the seventeenth century, the
Mughal realm ran from Gujarat in the west to Bengal in the east,
with outposts far into southern India.[25]

The motor for the empire's expansion was the land tax. As in
China, India's cultivators had to pay their taxes in imperial coin to
satisfy the government's wish to control the money supply. Such was
the demand for bullion that India initially received even more American silver than China, most of it by way of Europe. The Mughals collected their taxes through layer upon layer of intermediaries. Large
landowners (zamindars) submitted to the imperial treasury a third
of the value of staple crops like rice and wheat, and a fifth of the
value of commercial crops—tobacco, poppy, sugar, and indigo—and
then kept for themselves a substantial cut of what their tenants grew.
Often zamindars delegated their responsibilities to subsidiary holders
of rights to the land. Those rights could be traded, sold, or granted
as favors by imperial administrators. The question of who owned a
given plot of land became fiendishly complicated. To reckon with the
scope of his domain, Akbar ordered an exhaustive survey of India to
establish a basis for taxing the land. His surveyors documented the
productivity of the soil, the area under irrigation, the market price

for each crop. It was a tabular inscription of India's landscape: field by field, orchard by orchard. With knowledge came power—in a society as complex as India's was, that power had limits.[26]

The Mughal appetite for revenue drove an assault on the wilderness. "It was customary that wood-cutters and ploughmen used to accompany [Akbar's] troops," a Mughal document recorded, "so that forest may be cleared and land cultivated." The incentive was the same one that had drawn so many Russian farmers to the steppe forest and so many Chinese to Sichuan: "There was a general order that whosoever cleared a forest and brought land under cultivation such land would be his zamindari."[27]

When Akbar's forces followed the course of the Ganga to reach Bengal in the 1570s, it was still heavily forested. Mughal horses could go no further than the regional capital at Rajmahal. They wilted in the humid heat; the terrain of rivered jungle did not let them pass. To advance, Akbar's chronicler Abul Fazl wrote, Mughal forces "chose the river route, in this season full of turbulence, and with constant rain and tempest."[28]

Following the armies, and sometimes ahead of them, moved a gathering band of holy men, cultivators, artisans, and woodcutters. The settlers' quest unfolded through a braided landscape of earth and water as turbulent and animate as any on the planet. The Bengal delta is made and unmade by rivers that descend from the Himalayas bearing a freight of silt, swollen from June to September by the monsoon rains. The rivers scour new channels whenever obstacles block their path.

Human choices and ecological happenstance collided: the Mughals moved into Bengal at just the moment that the great rivers began an eastward migration, jolted into a new course by tectonic shocks. The Ganga deserted its existing channel to the Indian Ocean through the Hooghly River, forced its way further east through the Padma and the Meghna, and merged with the waters of the Brahmaputra. The gifts of silt now fell to the eastern part of the delta. The west became, in the melancholy language of hydrology, moribund.

Muslim holy men, *pirs* in the Sufi tradition, led the migration. They assembled groups of followers bound to their leaders' charisma. Stories of the pioneers' prowess spread: stories told anew in every successive generation. The power of the pir flowed from his mastery of the dark forces of the forest, his bravery in the face of predators, his ability to channel the life force of other species. In the Sundarban region of the eastern delta, the legend of Zindah Ghazi, protector of woodcutters and boatmen, tells of how he subdued the ferocity of a local tiger so completely that he rode upon its back, padding benevolently through the tamed forest.[29]

India's Mughal rulers induced self-organized groups of settlers to cut down trees and plant rice. Within a short span of years, Bengal became a land of paddy. As early as 1607, the French traveler François Pyrard observed:

> There is such a quantity of rice, that, besides supplying the whole country, it is exported to all parts of India, as well to Goa and Malabar, as to Sumatra, the Moluccas, and all the islands of Sunda, to all of which lands Bengal is a very nursing mother, who supplies them and their entire subsistence and food. Thus, one sees arrive [at the port of Chittagong] every day an infinite number of vessels from all parts of India for these provisions.[30]

English merchant William Methwold wrote, a decade later, of Bengal's "abundance of such things as that countrey produceth, that is the most plentifull in the East." Bengal's textile industry was already famous before the Mughal conquest. In the 1510s, the Portuguese apothecary Tome Pires had observed that, in Southeast Asia's great entrepôt, "Bengali cloth fetches a high price in Melaka, because it is a merchandise all over the east." Now the rapid growth of rice production after 1660, spurred by land grants and tax remissions from the Mughal state, yielded so much that it freed more Bengalis from the fields. A significant portion of the population—perhaps up to 5 percent, and many of them women—turned to weaving, spinning, and dyeing in the household workshops that made Bengal the leading producer and exporter of cotton textiles in the world.[31]

Bengal's textiles, desired "all over the east," beckoned to merchants from much further west. They paid in silver. An early English trader in India saw that "India is rich in silver, for all nations bring coyne and carry away commodities for the same; and this coyne is buried in India and goeth not out." The Portuguese were the first to arrive, establishing a settlement in Chittagong in 1528. A century later, the Dutch and then the English set up trading posts along the Hooghly River. The English East India Company built Fort William in 1697, along the Hooghly's banks. Around it grew the town of Calcutta. European merchants shipped textiles home to cater to changing fashions among the wealthy. And then they saw there was even more money to be made by muscling in on the longstanding trade between Bengal and ports across Southeast Asia.[32]

WITHIN SIXTY YEARS OF building Fort William, the English East India Company had not only maneuvered and battled its way to power in Bengal—it had also seized the *diwani*, or the right to revenues from India's richest agricultural lands. What followed was an earthquake in the global distribution of power as Indian farmers' taxes paid for the company to raise an enormous army. For the first time, traders from the western fringes of Eurasia had breached their coastal strongholds to exert real power over the agrarian heartland of South Asia. Neither regional Asian powers nor Britain's European rivals would concede without a fight. The Seven Years' War between Britain and France was fought in the Atlantic and Indian Oceans as well as on land, deciding the political futures of both Canada and India in the process. Only by the early nineteenth century, at the end of the Napoleonic Wars, did the British position in Asia become unassailable. They had been brought there by a desire to monopolize the animal, vegetal, and mineral products of the Indian soil—and then the spiral of conquest took on a life of its own.

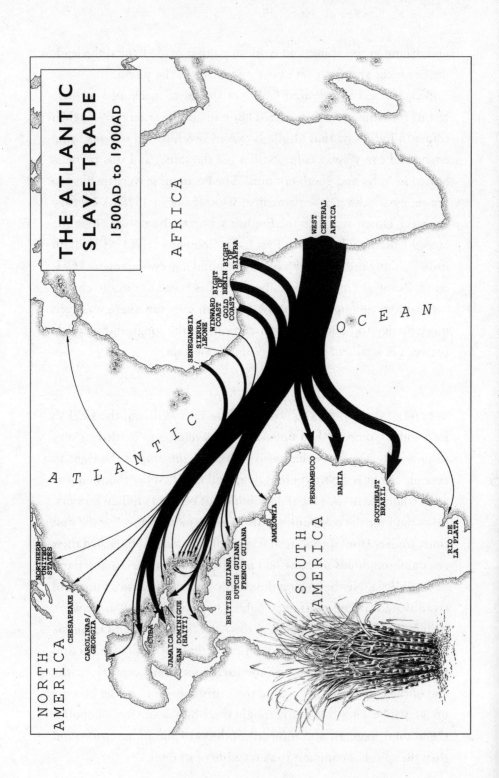

THE ATLANTIC
SLAVE TRADE
1500AD to 1900AD

AFRICA

OCEAN

SENEGAMBIA
SIERRA
LEONE
WINDWARD
COAST
GOLD COAST
BIGHT OF
BENIN
BIGHT OF
BIAFRA
WEST
CENTRAL
AFRICA

ATLANTIC

NORTHERN
UNITED
STATES
CHESAPEAKE
CAROLINAS/
GEORGIA
CUBA
JAMAICA
SAN DOMINIGUE
(HAITI)
BRITISH GUIANA
DUTCH GUIANA
FRENCH GUIANA
AMAZONIA
PERNAMBUCO
BAHIA
SOUTHEAST
BRAZIL
RIO DE
LA PLATA

NORTH
AMERICA

SOUTH
AMERICA

CHAPTER FOUR

SUBURBS
OF HELL

O BSERVING THE CAPE COAST CASTLE IN 1682, built on Ghana's Atlantic shoreline by the English Royal Africa Company, the French trader Jean Barbot wrote, "the keeping of the slaves thus under ground is a good security to the garrison against any insurrection." Denied light and space, only their ears gave captive people a sense of where they were. At every moment they could feel the breath, and hear the cries, of their fellow human beings. Extreme sensory deprivation began at the coastal fortresses where hundreds of enslaved people were imprisoned together.[1]

Millions of Africans suffered a violent removal from all the richness of life that sustained their human communities. They were taken from soils and plants and animals, revered hills, and precious water bodies—and from those they loved. Slavery took millions of Africans "out of the dark beauty of their mother continent into the new-found Eldorado of the West," W. E. B. Du Bois wrote in *Black Reconstruction*; and there, dispersed across the Americas, "They descended into hell."[2]

The ecology of West Africa had long afforded spaces of refuge and ample possibilities of escape. Hubs of intensive cultivation West Africa had in abundance, but they were spread across a patchwork of forest and scrub. Rulers knew not to press too hard upon their adherents, for they could easily move away. Land for cultivation was increasingly scarce in many parts of Eurasia, most especially in China and western Europe. By contrast, in the regions of Africa where people were most mobile and land most plentiful, to amass population was to amass power. Ambitious leaders accumulated strength in numbers by enslaving defeated enemies. Slavery was not always a permanent condition in West African societies: unfreedom was on a continuum with unequal kinship.[3]

Warfare propelled African systems of slavery. Enslaved people were sold into caravans that made the punishing journey across the Sahara—the trans-Saharan trade in human beings involved an estimated six million people between the seventh and nineteenth centuries; another four million people were taken from eastern Africa to points around the Red Sea and Indian Ocean. Many more enslaved Africans were moved shorter distances, to the kingdoms of their captors. Torn from their homes and their kin, captives were forced into households as servants and subordinates. But enslaved people were also valued as future mothers, as healers or artisans, in ways that might bring them acceptance, even power, over time. The hell of Atlantic slavery was something altogether different.

Following the Portuguese in the fifteenth century, English, Dutch, and French merchants arrived on the coast of West Africa. At first their aim was gold, but soon they saw even greater profits to be made in trafficking enslaved human beings. Europeans brought desirable products, none more desired than Indian cloth, sought-after in West Africa for adornment and ritual use. Textiles made up two-thirds of British exports to West Africa during the peak decades of the slave trade, and up to half of the woven cargo was of Indian origin. Indian textiles fueled the acquisitive desires that captured, tortured, and enslaved millions of people. One British trader described West African purchasers smelling the textiles to check for the distinctive scent of Indian indigo dye, which alone was a guarantee of the quality and color-fastness of the product. They were sniffing for the traces of Indian earth. Along with cloth, Europeans brought guns into a competitive world of emerging African states—Dahomey, Asante, Oyo, Koyo, and Niger—each seeking an edge over its rivals. Firearms gave Europeans an immediate, lethal advantage in their dealings with local powers: and as guns spread throughout West Africa, they swelled the number of enslaved captives arriving at the coast.[4]

In captivity, enslaved people were deprived of the most vital link that any human being can have to the land: growing food. Over the course of the seventeenth century, enslaved people arrived at coastal prisons from ever further inland. They had known many landscapes. They had grown cocoyam and plantains, black-eyed peas and pineapples; they had raised fowl and goats; they had caught fresh fish. Now, crowded in coastal fortresses, they were forced to subsist on corn, malagueta pepper, and palm oil, ground into a stodgy porridge called cankey. To profit from the trade in human beings, captors spent the bare minimum to keep their captives alive—and they often got it wrong. Dalby Thomas, chief factor of Cape Coast Castle, spelled out the brutal calculation in 1704, when he noted to his bosses in London that trading in human lives was not like trading in other commodities: human beings, he found, almost as if surprised, "eat and dye[die] as too many have done of late."[5]

In the holds of cargo ships, enslaved people were deprived not only of light but even of breathable air. Roiling waves intensified their suffering. Olaudah Equiano described firsthand the slave ship's assault on every sense: "The closeness of the place, and the heat of the climate, added to the number in the ship, which was so crowded that each had scarcely room to turn himself, almost suffocated us." So violent were the floating prisons that their impact reverberated across species. Sharks learned to crowd behind slave ships, following them all the way across the Atlantic, hungry for the broken bodies that would be thrown overboard. Sailor Samuel Robinson described a typical encounter, feeling shaken by "the very sight of him slowly moving round the ship, with his black fin two feet above the water, his broad snout and small eyes, and the altogether villainous look of the fellow." Even in the face of that terror, still the prospect of freedom from the slave ship beckoned. Equiano imagined the many souls that inhabited an enveloping ecology underwater: "Often did I think of the inhabitants of the deep much more happy than myself," he wrote; "I envied them the freedom they enjoyed, and as often wished I would change my condition for theirs."[6]

BETWEEN 1492 AND 1866, 12.5 million enslaved human beings crossed the Atlantic Ocean. At least half, and perhaps two-thirds, of those who survived the Middle Passage were chained to a single substance.[7]

Sugar first entered the European palate by way of Egypt along with Sicily and other Mediterranean islands. It arrived as a fine spice akin to cinnamon or nutmeg or cloves—coveted, exotic, and very expensive. And then something changed to set sugar apart, something unleashed by the addictive effect of sweetness on human desire. Sugar became more than a rare luxury: around its cultivation there gathered a storm of human and ecological harm. Portuguese colonists transplanted a Sicilian prototype of the sugar plantation to the Atlantic island of Madeira, where, with capital from Genoese and Flemish investors, they prospered from the labor of enslaved Guanches and enslaved Africans. Madeira became the largest producer of sugar in the world. Those who financed the trade grew enormously wealthy. Sugar laid waste to the island so that within a few decades the boom collapsed. A thoroughly deforested Madeira was left to cultivate wheat and wine.

Madeira's ruin marked a new phase in the history of human exploitation: a tightening of the knot that ties human suffering to the destruction of other forms of life. Madeira wrote the script—rise and fall, boom and bust, intensive exploitation followed by sprawling waste. Many other places would follow. There was nothing unique about turning expanses of land over to growing a single crop. There was nothing unprecedented in the speed with which the forests of Madeira were razed by new settlers. "To exhaust the land" was the imperative of Chinese provincial governors in Ming and Qing times. But their aim was always to secure food for a growing population. Investors in Portuguese sugar ventures wanted something else—they wanted to extract maximum profit in the shortest time. Planters hastened their reward with the terror of the whip and the peril of the boiling house that extracted sugar syrup from the cane. Madeira inaugurated a new form of cultivation for the rapid gain of distant investors. Only in the nineteenth century would this system acquire the name we now use for it—capitalism.[8]

Once Madeira had been sacrificed, investors simply moved on. Just under half of all the enslaved Africans who crossed the Atlantic were taken to Caribbean islands, which jostled for first rank in sugar production. Each dominated for less than a century before being surpassed by newer plantations with fresher soils: first Spanish Hispaniola, and then British Barbados, and then Saint-Domingue, until the French were overthrown by the Haitian revolution—and, finally, British Jamaica. Looming above them all was the colossal territory on the South American mainland that the Portuguese called Brazil: destination of no fewer than 40 percent of all the enslaved people who ever crossed the Atlantic. Sugarcane thrived in the wet heat of Brazil's Atlantic forest: the profits from sugar soon outweighed the profits from the brazilwood that had given the land its name.[9]

Martim Afonso de Souza—the swaggering admiral who led the first Portuguese assault on the Brazilian interior in 1530, burning and pillaging as he went—ordered the construction of a mill in São Vicente to crush cane brought from the Portuguese settlement on the Atlantic island of São Tomé. Traveling through Brazil, naturalist and chronicler Gabriel Soares de Sousa was impressed by the "famous mill of Mem de Sai," which he described as "well constructed with a solid building and a curing house, a crushing machine worked by slaves and other facilities": so easily did human lives appear in Portuguese eyes as but a *facility*—an "amenity or piece of equipment for a particular purpose." Many ventures collapsed. Already by the 1580s ruined plantations dotted the landscape. Along the banks of the Sergipe River, Soares de Sousa saw that "there was formerly a mill on the stream built by Antonio Dias Adorno." The mill, he learned, was "abandoned when a dam broke, which had cost much to build, so it is like a graveyard." Soares de Sousa was optimistic: "it will not be so for long for the land is good enough to repay the investment of much capital." Failed investors fought to recover their losses. "Of those who came none had love for this land," a Brazilian planter admitted, "all want to act on their own behalf, even if it is at the cost of the land, because they expect to depart it." Here lies a profound insight into why the plantation economy was so destructive of every form of life.[10]

Plantations simplified nature. Planters cut or burned through delicate forest ecosystems so that a single crop could thrive. Sugar's war on the land demanded a colossal amount of work. Using only hoes, enslaved workers dug four- or six-foot squares up to nine inches deep; each bunded cane hole made a home for two young plants, nourished by manure carried in buckets on workers' heads. Children and older people were made to wage an everyday battle against the jungle. They did the unending work of weeding. They hunted rats, which had first crossed the Atlantic on European ships, and now flourished unchecked. At harvest time the cane fields hummed with the rush of wind moving through stalks taller than the tallest men. Backs bent, workers cut stalks six inches from the ground using sharp, curved bills. Mills churned through the night to crush cane through rollers; and, all too often, to maim the limbs of tired workers. The cane juice traveled through pipes to the horrific modernity of the boiling house. In a large copper vat the juice was stirred, skimmed, and stirred again. The Boiler, an enslaved person with practiced skill, declared when the juice was ready to move to the next stage in the process, where it went to be burned again and again, the liquid darker and denser with each reduction. Debilitated by heat, workers suffocated on sick-sweet fumes. Jesuit priest and writer Padre Vieira recoiled at the sight of a Brazilian boiling house in the seventeenth century: "who sees all the confused and tumultuous machinery and apparatus of that Babylon can not doubt though they may have seen Vesuvius or Mount Etna, that this is the same as hell." At the point of crystallization, specialist workers tempered the thick liquid sugar with lime juice and left it to cool. The molasses that remained was distilled into rum that found an eager market in colonial North America.[11]

Violence was the engine of the plantation. Violence underpinned every act and order. Planter João Fernandes Vieira published in 1663 an advice manual for sugar planters. He gave stepwise instructions on seeds and soils, on maintaining the machinery of the mill; he gave some of his most detailed instructions under the heading, "Punishing the Slaves." Enslaved people "deserving of punishment," he declared in a bloody string of imperatives, "should be tied to an oxcart and punished with a whip, and after being well-lashed they should be cut with a razor or knife and then treated with salt, lemon juice, and urine and then placed for some days in chains." If the enslaved person was a woman, Vieira noted, "she will be whipped in a shirt of baize and it should be done inside a house with the same whip." Across the Americas, from the seventeenth to the late-nineteenth centuries, enslaved human beings faced these horrors. C. L. R. James—Trinidadian historian, poet of cricket, Marxist theorist, and giant among Caribbean intellectuals—put it starkly in the opening pages of *The Black Jacobins*, his monumental history of the Haitian revolution, published in 1938:

> The slaves received the whip with more certainty and regularity than they received their food. It was the incentive to work and the guardian of discipline. But there was no ingenuity that fear or a depraved imagination could devise which was not employed to break their spirit and satisfy the lusts and resentment of their owners and guardians—irons on the hands and feet, blocks of wood that the slaves had to drag behind them wherever they went, the tin-plate mask designed to prevent the slaves eating the sugar-cane, the iron collar.

The truly pious were to be entrusted with this savagery. Vieira's manual insisted that only Christians, "fearful of God, mindful of the estate . . . respected by the neighbors, courteous, seeing to the necessity of others, affable and reasonable . . ." could inflict such terror.[12]

Violence on human beings accompanied a violent assault on the rest of nature. Sugar plantations had a limitless appetite for timber to fire the vats. Furnaces swallowed forests. Woods fell for pasture to feed the domestic animals that were a vital source of muscle power. Denuded hillsides threatened human settlements with mudslides after every rainfall. Sugar ruined the soil: "The fertility of this island is much abated from what it was in the Time of its first Plantation," John Ovington wrote from Madeira, the first of the sugar lands to lie wrecked, "and the continual breaking up of the Ground has, in many Places, impoverished its Productions." To hold up a collapsing ecology, British planters in Barbados imported wood from New England and coal from Britain; they built windmills to drive the rollers, they burned cane waste (bagasse) to keep the boom going for as long as they could.[13]

Enslaved people were alienated permanently from their homelands. Amid the brutality of life on the plantations, they came to know new soils. They harnessed hereditary knowledge to sustain the communities they forged in the face of suffering. In small kitchen gardens and on meager plots of land, enslaved people cultivated plants that had crossed the Atlantic in folds of clothing or had been hidden in smuggled packages, and they cultivated plants that they found locally: yams and sorghum, legumes and peanuts. Home cultivation brought another burden at the end of each day of toil. Frenchman Pierre Moreau, who traveled in Brazil between 1646 and 1648, described the "little pieces of land on which, during the limited time [enslaved people] have for rest (after a twelve-hour day) they sow peas, beans, millet, and maize."[14]

Nobody knew the land more intimately than those who found refuge in rivered thickets beyond the plantations. In every society across the Caribbean and the Americas where enslaved Africans were taken, significant numbers rebelled. They formed maroon communities. The most resilient persisted for decades, or even centuries, against the worst of odds: Saramaka and Ndjuka in Suriname; San Basilio, Colombia; Esmeralda in Ecuador; Le Maniel in Haiti; and the Leewards and Windwards in Jamaica. "Maroon" comes from the Spanish *cimarrón*, a word used to describe confined livestock that had escaped. In its shifting meaning and translation lie two countervailing histories: a history of dehumanization, wherein human beings who escaped slavery were likened to feral animals; and a history of what historian Alvin Thompson calls "elemental freedom"—the freedom "that all living creatures seek."[15]

Throughout the Americas, a landscape of forest and scrub and hills menaced those who came to destroy maroon communities. John Stedman, a Dutch mercenary who spent five years fighting the maroon communities of Suriname, described a long march that tested his band of men at every turn:

> We continued our march till 8 o-clock when we arrived at the Society Post in *Soribo* in Pitica, in a most shocking condition, having waddled through water and mire above our hipps, climb'd over heaps of fallen trees, creep'd underneath them on our bellies—scratched and tore by the thorns or macas that are here of many kinds, stung all over by Patat or Scrapat lice, ants, and *wassy-wassy* or wild bees. . . .[16]

Brazil was home to more maroon settlements than anywhere else. Quilombos and mocambos, as they were known, lay scattered across the coastal wetlands, the forests, and hills of Bahia. Quilombos receive nervous notice in official records as early as 1575; by the seventeenth century, they had become an obsession for Portuguese and then Dutch authorities. The largest quilombo was in Palmares, in a forbidding landscape around fifty miles inland from the coast— its name means "place of wild palms." Palmares grew large enough to constitute a self-governing polity. Most of its residents had roots in Congo and Angola (from which they gained the name Ngola Janga) but also among the renegades were Indigenous Brazilians,

Jews, and Muslims. Slaveowners and colonists waged endless war against maroon communities. Military expeditions tried and failed to defeat the free settlement. Only in 1694 was Palmares conquered and destroyed. The spectacular violence used against maroon communities served as a warning and an example: "That which is proper is only to extinguish them," the city council of São Paulo declared, "and conquer them so that those who are still domesticated will not join them and those who are in rebellion will not aspire to greater misdeeds." The quilombos persisted on what Angolan writer Allan da Rosa calls the "precarious stability and joy of minuscule, marginal resistance, with personal relationships simmered in the waters of exhausted dreams."[17]

The soil was the quilombos' means of sustenance, the terrain their tool of defense. Their settlements were configured for rapid flight—when the early Dutch expeditions first arrived to attack Palmares, they found the settlement had emptied out. Maroon communities forged underground networks of trade to supply themselves with food and weapons from towns, and when those networks failed, they raided settled villages. Palmares was guarded to the north by impassable swamps, its southern approach was fortified by spikes hidden in long grass that had grown on cleared forest land. The residents of Palmares relied on the landscape and on their knowledge of its many rivers: the Ipojuca and Sirinhaém, the Camaragibe and Jacuípe. Their freedom was always fragile. For a few quilombos, it lasted for generations. When the Brazilian authorities arrested her in Belém in the 1870s, along with 135 fellow quilombolas in the lower Amazon region, they asked Maria Candida who her owner was. "I've never had an owner," she replied, "I was born in the forest."[18]

IN THE SEVENTEENTH CENTURY, Europeans began to acquire a taste for tea, coffee, and chocolate. In the societies those narcotic foods came from, they were appreciated for their bitterness; in Europe, sugar became their essential companion.

Jean-Étienne Liotard's 1744 painting, *A Lady Pouring Chocolate*, shows a young woman preparing drinking chocolate; on the tray in front of her sits a bowl of sugar.

Sugar sweetened the coffee served in the cafes of London and Amsterdam. "You have all Manner of News there," a French visitor observed of a London coffeehouse at the end of the seventeenth century—"You have a good fire, which you may sit by as long as you please; You have a Dish of Coffee; you meet your friends for the Transaction of Business, and all for a Penny, if you don't care to spend more." That "transaction of business" now involved investing in plantations across the Atlantic in the hope of quick profit. The falling cost of a "dish of coffee" brought it within reach of customers with fewer means. The true cost was out of sight. Only in the eighteenth century did abolitionist pamphlets start to draw European consumers' attention to the way their sugar was stained with "the blood of their fellow creatures." It took even longer to see how sugar also harmed creatures that were other than human.[19]

Laid out before investors, amid whispered rumors and jubilant yells along the corridors of Exchange Alley and the Amsterdam Bourse, was a botanical and mineral menu that they could order from and bet on: pieces of Earth they could rearrange and redistribute. Daniel Defoe—novelist, journalist, merchant, and spy— enumerated London's exchanges: "Fish Markets, Herb Markets,

Corn Market, Meal Markets, Hay Market, Leather Market, Hinds & Skins, Coal Markets, Bay Market, Broad Cloath Market": each assembled plants and animals from nearby farms and from distant continents. With the commercial energy of London came "new squares, and new Streets rising up every Day to such a Prodigy of Buildings." The city's population quadrupled in the sixteenth century, doubled in the seventeenth, doubled again in the eighteenth. One in every six Britons found themselves in London at some point in their lives. Men came to work in the port; they staffed the warehouses and outfitters and sailmakers' workshops that kept it running; a fifth of the girls and women who arrived in the city went into domestic service, and another fifth into London's largest industry: the manufacture of clothing. By the middle of the eighteenth century, London had the second largest population of any city in the world after Beijing—a leap from the medieval era, when London was tiny compared with the major cities of Asia and not even among the biggest in Europe.[20]

Cities cut lives short. Defoe lamented "the terrible Appearance of Death in so many dismal Shapes." London assailed its residents with a new ecology of crowding, and a new chaos of smells: the stench of rotting animal carcasses, the fug of unwashed linen, the reek of open sewers; the pervading smell of sickness and fear. Amid the "saucy stink" of London a slew of "olfactory offenses" came before the courts and brought neighbors to blows. Mixed with it all, permeating everything, was the smell of smoke. Diarist and pamphleteer John Evelyn, a founding fellow of the Royal Society, described London's "clouds of smoake and sulphur, so full of stink and Darknesse" in his 1661 pamphlet *Fumifugium: or The Inconvenience of the Aer and Smoak of London Dissipated.* Evelyn likened London to "Mount Aetna, the Court of Vulcan, Stromboli, or the Suburbs of Hell." Padre Vieira had used just the same analogies to describe the boiling houses of Brazil's plantations. The smoke of London came from a substance that the city's residents burned to heat their homes through harsh, damp winters: stuff brought by barge from

Newcastle to substitute for the timber that was now scarce. They called it sea-coal. Unlike any other world city, London already drew much of its energy from mineral sources by 1600.[21]

The prodigious urban growth of England and the Netherlands would have been impossible if farmers had not produced more food, more efficiently. England's farms doubled, perhaps trebled, their output in the five hundred years between 1300 and 1800, and especially after 1600—new crop rotations diminished the need to leave fields fallow, while new seed drills and threshing machines hastened planting and harvesting. As grain flowed, the culinary culture of England's elite became ever more carnivorous. Cooks were enjoined in popular songs to "Break that deer; . . . rear that goose; lift that swan; sauce that chicken." Margaret Cavendish, poet and philosopher, was a rare voice of dissent when she observed, in her 1653 *Dialogue Betwixt Birds,* that man behaved as if "all creatures for his sake alone / were made for him to tyrannize upon."[22]

Urban demand burrowed into rural soils. Soon the pull of the city began to change the land and the water and the lives of animals. Amsterdam financiers devised new ways to accumulate funds to pay for the restless remolding of nature that their continued wealth now depended on. What remains the world's oldest active bond was issued by the Lekdijk Bovendams water board to finance the reconstruction of the 33-kilometer-long dike between Amerongen and Vreeswijk that had collapsed in 1624. One of a handful of copies of the water bond, dating from 1648, resides in my university's Beinecke Rare Books and Manuscripts Library—and to this day it pays Yale interest amounting to 25 guilders a year. The quest to tame water spurred financial innovation.[23]

Few societies on Earth engineered water as fast or as intensively as did the Dutch in the seventeenth century. The first half of the 1600s saw Dutch engineers embrace the serial drainage of lakes in North Holland. Amsterdam merchants clubbed together to invest 10 million guilders in the effort—more than they had invested in the spice-seeking, textile-gathering journeys of the Dutch East India

In Yale's Beinecke library, a 1648 copy of the world's oldest
active bond, issued by the Lekdijk Bovendams water board.

Company. The land area of the Netherlands swelled by a third.
Grand projects spurred hundreds of smaller ones: Dutch farmers
expanded their holdings one coastal polder at a time. It was a power
as precious as alchemy: to turn water into land.[24]

Just as Dutch reclaimers had taken their skills east of the Elbe in
the medieval era, so too did Dutch hydrological knowledge travel in
the seventeenth century. In the person of Cornelius Vermuyden—
descended from several generations of water engineers, his craft
honed draining Brabant and Beveland and Flanders—Dutch expertise traveled to England. In the flat marshlands of eastern England,
the Fens, new riches beckoned. King Charles I commissioned Vermuyden to lead the Hatfield Level drainage project in the late 1620s:
a scheme in the Isle of Axholme, Lincolnshire, which set out to dry
70,000 acres of land by using drains, dams, and sluices to channel
the Don, Idle, and Torne rivers. Vermuyden stood to profit hand-
somely, promised possession of a third of all the drained lands. Travelers through the Fens in the 1630s observed the scale of the work
with some bemusement: "a little Army of Artificers, venting, con-
triving, and acting outlandish devises."[25]

One overriding idea drove the Hatfield project, an idea that would have a global career with incalculable effects on the ecology of the planet—the idea that some lands were "waste." The meanings of "wasteland" accumulated from the fourteenth century, in step with the expansion of settled cultivation. It slipped back and forth across European languages: "waste" evoked lands that were "desolate and uncultivated," from the Anglo-French with roots in the Latin *vastus* ("empty, desolate"). By the seventeenth century, it had acquired in English a more specific, more intentional meaning—land "unfit for use," at a moment when it seemed that human ingenuity might finally override that unfitness. Vermuyden described the marshy Fens as a landscape of "diverse wastes, waste grounds and commons . . . subject to be surrounded and drowned with water in such a manner that little or no benefit is or can be made." One of his strongest supporters insisted that "the most civilized Nations have by so much art and industry endeavoured to make the best improvement of their Wastes, Commons, and all sorts of barren land." The "benefit" from draining wetlands that had been held in common would now accrue to landowners—and to a profligate English state in need of revenue.[26]

The Fen villagers put up a vigorous fight. Residents of neighboring counties protested the inundation of their own lands that followed from the diversion of rivers to drain the Fens. "Thus have strangers prevailed to destroy our inheritance," wrote Richard Bridges from Sykehouse, Yorkshire, in 1630. The drainage scheme, he observed, would undermine land "which our ancestors left for a sink and receptacle of inundant waters for our future safety." Bridges decried the absence of precaution in the pursuit of immediate profit at the expense of "future safety." Other critics of the scheme deployed religious arguments against its hubris: they cautioned the engineers "not to intermeddle at all with that which God hath ordained"; they believed that "fens were made fens and must ever continue such."[27]

Critics disagreed with the engineers' characterization of the Fen landscape as waste. Flooding need not be feared, the commissioners of Suffolk noted: it was a transient and not a permanent state, and it brought life to the soil. Water, overflowing, "much enricheth those grounds." The wetlands sustained a richness of human and more-than-human life that was now in danger: "many thousand cottagers," a pamphleteer noted, lived from collecting "reeds, fodder, thacks, turves, flaggs, hassocks, segg, fleggweed for fleggeren collars, mattweeded for churches, chambers, beddes, and many other fenn commodytyes of greate use both in towne and countreye." The wetlands sustained a "variety of fish and fowl, which here have their seminaries and nurseries; which will be destroyed on draining. . . ."[28]

Villagers took direct action. Protests sparked across the Fens. The Dutch migrant workers that Vermuyden brought in to build the Hatfield Level were attacked by locals. In Edgehill, in 1642, a group of protesters occupied land that was newly drained and enclosed. They "broke the sluices, laid waste to their lands, threw down their fences, spoiled their corn, demolished their houses, and forcibly retained possession of the land."[29]

Supporters of the scheme pressed their case. They imagined a world where Fen villagers would no longer be icebound in winter with "no help of food, nor comfort of body or soul." They promised liberty from air that was "cloudy, gross, and full of rotten harrs," freedom from waters that were "putrid and muggy," and escape from "spungy and boggy" ground. They promoted the deepest human dream: a better future. The drainers argued that their opponents wanted to hold the region back and deny it the means of flourishing. If still the promises failed to persuade, then the improvers wielded the force of arms and the power of the courts, which combined to ensure that protesters would not impede the completion of the King's scheme.

Even before the drainage of the Fens, England's political and commercial elite had foreseen victory over the power of nature. Francis Bacon—philosopher, early member of the Royal Society and, at the same time, Attorney General and Lord Chancellor under King James I—looked forward to the time when nature would be "bound into service" and made a "slave." His language carried more than a hint of masculine violence against a "nature" that had long been depicted as feminine: "hound nature in her wanderings," Bacon urged his followers, until nature was "put in constraint, molded, and made . . . new by art and the hand of man." The reality was messier than the dream. Improvers faced resistance at every turn. The drama would play itself out around the world for centuries to come: the defense of local ecologies confronted the march of Progress. Progress often prevailed—but not always.[30]

AS CULTIVATION IN EARLY modern Europe crept over marshlands and inched up hillsides, agrarian expansion reached new lands and new intensity: these were fresh pages added to an existing medieval script. At first glance, western Europe's environmental transformation was not so different in kind from southern China's or Bengal's.

And then environmental change in Europe metastasized. What set western Europe's trajectory apart was the way its impact spilled across the Atlantic. Agrarian Europe annexed another hemisphere by decimating Indigenous agriculture so thoroughly that it is plausible that the destruction even registered upon the Earth's climate— and then filled the archipelagoes of Atlantic islands with a captive labor force. The blood and toil of enslaved people from West Africa generated wealth for European investors, who used it to reshape nature on both sides of the Atlantic.

Among the world-shaping, parallel movements of people across Eurasia between 1600 and 1800—the movement of Russian peasants to the steppes, Chinese cultivators to Sichuan, Muslim settlers to Bengal—it was not immediately clear that the movement of Europeans to North America would be as consequential as ultimately it was. Many early European voyagers came to North America in search of fish and furs, not land. Their journeys resembled the fitful encroachment of Russian hunters, trappers, and fishers into Siberia. Only gradually were seasonal encampments occupied continuously.

Even before the settler conquest of North America's lands, the life of the ocean recoiled before the force of European "fishing plantations." Between 1530 and 1620, Basque whalers in the Strait of Belle Isle hunted the right whale and the bowhead to the verge of extinction. Later in the seventeenth century, Dutch and Basque whalers slaughtered a further thirty-five or forty thousand whales: the Western Arctic flowed with cetacean blood. French and English fishers discovered in Newfoundland the "largest single fishery on the planet." The average European ate between four and five times as much cod in 1650 as in 1500; cod brightened the tables of poorer families, an affordable and accessible source of protein. The profits of the Newfoundland fishery were as vast if never as visible as those from Potosí silver. It was easy to believe that the bounty would last forever; only a few prescient observers worried about the future. Pierre-François-Xavier de Charlevoix—Jesuit priest, traveler, and historian of New France—wrote in 1720:

> The number of [codfish] seems to equal that of the grains of sand which cover this bank. For more than two centuries since, there have been loaded with them from two to three hundred ships annually, notwithstanding [which] the diminution is not perceivable. It might not, however, be amiss to discontinue this fishery from time to time.

By the time Charlevoix penned his warning, European perceptions of North America had begun to imagine endless land for the taking.[31]

The earliest dreams of permanent European settlement in North America conjured a land of plenty. Richard Hakluyt—English clergyman, pamphleteer, and promoter of colonization—wrote in the 1580s that the lands of North America may absorb "thousands of idle persons" from the British Isles, putting them to work in "sawing and felling of timber for masts of ships and deal boards, in burning of the fires and pine trees to make pitch, tar, rosin, and soap ashes, in beating and working of hemp for cordage: and in the more southern parts in setting them to work in mines of gold, silver, copper, lead, and iron. . . ."[32]

For the first settlers, amid a landscape so unlike the ordered, regular fields of Europe, the dream of plenty was a mockery. They froze through a string of winters that are etched in tree rings as the imprint of America's Little Ice Age. They endured hunger and fell to "cruell diseases as Swelling, Flixes, Burning Fevers." "Though there be fish in the sea, foules in the ayre, and Beasts in the woods," wrote John Smith, the plucky and self-regarding leader of the collapsing Jamestown colony, "their bounds are so large, they so wilde, and we so weake and ignorant, we cannot much trouble them." The scale of the landscape was forbidding. An early description of Plymouth colony, Massachusetts, complained of a "hideous and desolate wilderness, full of wild beasts and wild men. . . ." Puritan clergyman Cotton Mather described New England as an expanse of "dismal thickets."[33]

And then America began to mesmerize the settlers. Puritans saw an Eden in its vastness. The settlers' ideas of what it meant to possess land denigrated the practices of Native communities. Their clash of perceptions is at the heart of William Cronon's environmental history of New England, *Changes in the Land*, which retains its power forty years after it was published. For Indigenous communities in New England, Cronon argues, property rights "shifted with ecological use." They made claims "not [on] the land but [upon] the things that were on the land during the various seasons of the year." The affordances of place lay embedded in their names, strung together on a necklace of seasonal movement. Wabaquasset was the place to find "flags or rusks for making mats"; Narragansett was the "small island where we get pitch," Seconchqut, the "the late spring or summer place." In the act of renaming the land after places in Britain—always with the prefix "new"—settlers asserted an absolute and exclusive claim to the land. Puritan minister Francis Higginson argued that "the Indians are not able to make use of one fourth part of the Land" because they "change their habitation from place to place"—and so, he thought, they forfeited their claims to it. "In a vacant soyle," wrote clergyman John Cotton, "hee that taketh possession of it, and bestoweth culture and husbandry upon it, his Right it is."[34]

The Narragansett leader, Miantonomo, countered the settlers' claim to property with an account of their ecological recklessness, their violence toward the land and everything on it. "Our fathers had plenty of deer and skins, our plains were full of deer, as also our woods," Miantonomo said, "but these English having gotten our land, they with scythes cut down the grass, and with axes fell the trees; their cows and horses eat the grass, and their hogs spoil our clam banks, and we shall all be starved."[35]

As settlement intensified, fear gave way to ambition, ambition to megalomania. The royal charter for the Massachusetts Bay Company gave it rights to everything, and "for ever":

> TO HAVE and to houlde, possesse, and enjoy all and singuler the aforesaid continent, landes, territories, islands, hereditaments, and precincts, seas, waters, fishings, with all and all manner their commodities, royalties, liberties, prehemynences, and profitts. . . . and every parte and parcell thereof, unto the saide Councell and their successors and assignes for ever.

The subsequent history of English settlement in North America was an exercise in wish-fulfillment: fictive claims to sovereignty came first, and then settlers fought to make them real. Settlement followed the rivers south and west toward the Appalachians. News of America spread among the artisans of British towns, and even the remote farming communities of the Shetlands. Emigrants set out in growing numbers beginning in the 1630s. They went "to plant" and "to settle": those are the words that recur most in the maritime customs registers that recorded in shorthand the muddled hopes and compulsions that led migrants across the Atlantic. They went for "bread," which signified more than food alone: "bread" meant freedom from scarcity. Those who moved were rarely the poorest; many had a little capital that they could use to start their new lives. Like Hakka pioneers and Russian peasants, they went in search of land and liberty.[36]

English philosopher John Locke—who wrote the constitution of the Carolina colony of his patron, Lord Shaftesbury—declared that America had shown that "the *chief matter of Property*" was no longer "the Fruits of the Earth, and the Beasts that subsist on it, but the *Earth it self*; as that which takes in and carries with it all the rest. . . ." Benjamin Franklin—writer, inventor, and diplomat—imagined how North America would look "to the Eyes of Inhabitants in Mars and Venus." Franklin thought settlers were "*Scouring* our Planet, by clearing America of woods." His sense that a deforested landscape reflected a "brighter light" fed his sense of racial supremacy ("perhaps I am partial to the complexion of my Country," as Franklin put it): "we have so far an Opportunity, by excluding all Blacks and Tawneys," he wrote, "of increasing the lovely White and Red." The "Red" referred to Native communities that Franklin could romanticize now that he believed they had been politically defeated, though in many parts of America that was far from the case.[37]

All the while, settlers quite determinedly took the corn, the lands, and the lives of Indigenous people. In *A Mercy*, a novel set in early-colonial Virginia, Toni Morrison imagines the story from the perspective of the dispossessed. Lina, a Native woman who has lost her family and her community, walks with Florens, an enslaved girl with whom she lives in the extended household of planter Jacob Vaark. "Imagine," Lina says to Florens:

One day a traveler climbs a mountain nearby. He stands at its summit admiring all he sees below him. The turquoise lake, the eternal hemlocks, the starling sailing into clouds cut by rainbow. The traveler laughs at the beauty, saying, "This is perfect. This is mine." And the word swells, booming like thunder into valleys, over acres of primrose and mallow . . . "Mine. Mine. Mine."[38]

Much later, geographers and historians would describe the lands of North America as "ghost acres" that provided an outlet and an escape for millions of people from the crowded lands of northwestern Europe. They were ghost acres not only because they were out of sight of the European mainland, but also because they were haunted by loss and death.

The violent competition among European states crossed the Atlantic. The line of English settlement stopped where the French staked out New France over a territory larger than they had any real prospect of ruling. To the south, both bordered the lands of New Spain. Native polities fought longer and harder for their autonomy than settlers' history books would ever acknowledge. At the edges between polities was the "middle ground" of the Great Lakes and their fur trade, where hierarchies were more fluid and racial boundaries were looser. In these unstable societies, ecological knowledge—of animal habitats and patterns of migration, of river currents and the advance or retreat of ice—was both a condition of survival and a pathway to gain.[39]

The ocean-spanning conflicts of European powers converged. In North America, the Seven Years' War unleashed limitless violence between French and English soldiers—and by both groups upon Native communities. English forces approached an Abenaki village by the Saint Lawrence River, suspected allies of the French, with one aim: to "kill everyone without mercy." They burned the village to the ground. That was not enough to satisfy their bloodlust: "Those who the flames did not devour," wrote a participant in the attack, "were either shot or tomohawk'ed." Victory in war allowed the British to grab a swath of French territory at the heart of the continent, from the Great Lakes in the north, through the Ohio Valley, and down to the Mississippi. The British Crown then sought to reconcile two contradictory goals: to appease restive settlers set on expansion while making concessions to Indigenous allies. The compromise was the Royal Proclamation of 1763, which prohibited white settlement west of the Alleghenies, carrying an implicit acknowledgment of Native sovereignty. Settlers defied the decree. "Neither royal nor provincial proclamation," Benjamin Franklin wrote, "nor the dread and horrors of a savage war, were sufficient to prevent the settlements of the lands over the mountains."[40]

It was as if the westward movement of settlers were itself a force of nature. Thomas Jefferson—Virginia tobacco planter, slaveowner, and Founding Father—stated, "the spontaneous energies of the earth are a gift of nature." In American national mythology, the animate earth conspired with settlers in their expansion, so that "the plow is to the farmer what the wand is to the sorcerer." Alexis de Tocqueville observed that American settlers soon became "insensible" to the dimensions and splendor of their landscape—for they were too busy changing it. "Their eyes are fixed on another sight," Tocqueville wrote, preoccupied with "draining swamps, turning the course of rivers, peopling solitudes, and subduing nature."[41]

PART II

BREAKING THE CHAINS

1800–1945

CHAPTER FIVE

REVOLUTIONS
IN LIFE AND DEATH

O N THE SIBERIAN HIGHWAY, TOWARD THE END OF the nineteenth century, Anton Chekhov's carriage overtakes two ramshackle carts weighed down with men, women, and children, and filled with their modest possessions. Chekhov describes the carts' occupants simply, as if it is all his readers need to know— "They are migrants."

Chekhov is on an arduous quest to visit Sakhalin Island, the frigid encampment where Russia's prisoners—political exiles and convicts alike—are sent to endure hard labor. A social activist and physician as well as a renowned writer of fiction, Chekhov would return from his journey to pen a searing exposé of abuse at Sakhalin. He looks at the carts again. This time, Chekhov's empathy, the profound empathy that infuses his fiction, comes to life: "I gaze at them and think: 'To cut loose from a life which seems to be going unusually badly, and to sacrifice for this one's own locality, one's own beloved domestic nest, can only be done by an exceptional human being, a hero. . . .'" Chekhov sees heroism where others write of "waves" and "flows" and even "hordes" of migrants, effacing the individuality and the hopes of people on the move. He can only imagine the migrants' inner lives; his reportage quotes only a few words from the migrants themselves. But he allows for the possibility of fear and courage and yearning—in a way that state officials, and the archives they have left to historians, do not.[1]

The great migration to Siberia, which Chekhov witnessed on the

road, involved around six million people between 1851 and 1914.
They were part of a worldwide unmooring. Around two hundred
million human beings left their places of birth in the nineteenth century to undertake journeys near or far. Somewhere in the region
of fifty-three million people left Europe's shores, most of them for
America. The same number again, probably far more, moved around
different regions of Asia: from China and India to Southeast Asia,
and from China's river valleys to the far northeast of the country.
The numbers—an amalgam from official censuses, shipping registers, local records, and retrospective statistical models—are so fuzzy
that any claim to exactitude would be absurd. The moth-eaten fabric of state surveillance left many people out, and left room for others to hide. Allowing for every caveat, statistics still give us an order
of magnitude. The nineteenth century saw people move further,
faster, and in larger numbers than ever before. The world's population would grow many times larger in the twentieth century, but its
distribution across the land surface of the Earth would not change as
fundamentally as it did in the nineteenth.[2]

The scale of human migration altered, to use a nineteenth-century
image, the "face of the Earth." Chekhov sees just how this has happened. He describes the remaking of the Alexandrovsk Valley, on the
western coast of Sakhalin Island, by the shores of the Tatar Strait. It
has taken "heavy, truly 'hard' labour" to change the land, he writes:
"Nowadays, in place of taiga, quagmires and ruts, there stands a
whole town, roads have been laid out, one sees the greenery of meadows, rye fields and vegetable gardens." All of it took "toil and struggle" that was both material and emotional. Chekhov writes of "the
frosts, the cold rains" that workers have endured. He also writes of
the migrants' "yearning for their homeland," as well as "the insults,
the birch rod" and other cruelties they suffered at the hands of their
employers. Chekhov wants to evoke, in his readers' minds, "appalling pictures." This is the true cost of the rush to modernity, Chekhov
says, this is the hidden labor behind the transformation of nature.[3]

The necessary condition for the nineteenth century's amplification of human impact upon the Earth was the steam engine: its conversion of long-buried fossil energy into the power not only to make things but also to move people on a scale previously undreamt. Command of that productive power let its wielders reorder the human and more-than-human world. For the first half of the century, that power was confined to the states and capitalists of northwestern Europe and the eastern United States, and then it spread more widely.

Even in the high age of the railroad, Chekhov's testimony reminds us, millions of migrants simply walked or relied on animals to carry them. Large stretches of Earth lay beyond the reach of infrastructure—and beyond the reach of extractive profit. And so began a war, or rather a hundred small wars, to bring ever more of it into the fold.

THE ENERGY OF THE nineteenth century came from burning what had once been alive. Industrial flames devoured the crushed remains of ancient forests and all the life they had once contained—amphibians and early reptiles and enormous insects. They consumed life that had been buried in freshwater swamps and starved of oxygen, compacted by tectonic movements. Old life, shaped into a form of rock that we call coal.

In the second half of the eighteenth century, British tinkerers and inventors were the first to animate machinery with the energy from burning coal, which until then had been used primarily for heating. Scottish engineer and chemist James Watt invented his steam engine in 1769, improving on the first fuel-burning engine devised early in the century by ironmonger and Baptist preacher Thomas Newcomen. That their devices would bring such far-reaching change was not a foregone conclusion. The industrial revolution came to Britain first because the island's landscape had already been so thoroughly altered in the centuries prior. British agriculture had grown highly commercialized and unusually productive in the eighteenth century. The enclosure movement made private fields of common lands, creating a class of landless laborers in search of work. Britain was already the most urbanized society in the world, and home to what was by 1800 the largest city on Earth, year after year absorbing newcomers from the countryside. Britain had plentiful deposits of coal, socially familiar through long use in London's domestic hearths and close enough to a heavily engineered system of waterways to be mobile. Capital for investment was abundant: it came from the innovation of joint stock corporations that allowed people to pool their funds with minimal risk; it came from the profits wrung from the labor of enslaved people on the sugar plantations of the Caribbean. Britain exported people to, and imported grain from, lands seized from Indigenous Americans in the seventeenth and eighteenth centuries. Raw cotton from India, under the heel of the East India Company, fed the mills of Lancashire, while the imports of finished textiles from Indian artisans were shut out. Tested and emboldened by a century of intercontinental warfare, the British state was uniquely good at raising money—and its navy at forcing markets open at gunpoint.[4]

Steam generated by coal prevailed over water power in the English textile industry because its use wasn't tied to hilly, often remote, riverine locations. Investors embraced steam engines because the new technology allowed them to concentrate their labor force in the factories that clustered in growing cities. The factories' armies of workers were swollen by new migrants looking for work, many of them driven out of the rural economy by the enclosure of common lands, their wages in the city now depressed by competition, their daily lives under intrusive surveillance.[5]

E. A. Wrigley, Cambridge historical demographer and economic historian, describes the use of fossil fuels as nothing less than a break with the entirety of human history. Fossil energy represented a "breaking free from dependence on photosynthesis." It was a kind of freedom that would previously have been beyond the reach of human imagination: a freedom that people could hardly have known *how* to want. In what Wrigley describes as an "organic" economy—that is, every economy ever until the advent of fossil fuels—plant photosynthesis was the source of, and limit to, all that it was possible for human beings to make. With sudden access to a vast stock of fossil energy, human productive power was decoupled from the growth cycles of timber, from the seasonality of rainfall and river flow. It was suddenly possible to imagine the unimaginable: freedom from wind, water, and earth.[6]

In the eyes of contemporaries, only the language of magic could adequately capture how Watt's engine bestowed mastery over the elements. Mechanical engineer and patent agent John Farey, Jr., wrote that steam power reminded him of "oriental fables of those beneficent and laborious genii" who could "raise populous cities in the midst of deserts, excavate subterraneaous palaces, create fountains and cascades of water; and transport their favourites from place to place." Here was a force, Glaswegian physician and scientist Andrew Ure wrote, that could be "made to animate millions of complex organs, infusing into forms of wood, iron, and brass, an intelligent agency." Here was a power "at the command of man," which transcended the majesty of animal muscle: "the trunk of an elephant, that can pick up a pin, or rend an oak, is nothing to it." Here was a power, above all, "to which no limits can be assigned."[7]

The steam engine expanded human beings' ability to feed and adorn and clothe, to educate and entertain themselves. Farey's account of steam's epochal power listed its many uses:

Steam power is also applied for twisting silk, for spinning flax and worsted into thread, and winding sewing thread into balls; coining money, cutting diamonds, grinding glass plates, grinding spectacle glasses, making lace, printing books and newspapers, making pins, bending card wires and button shanks, dressing hats, making weavers' reeds, grinding snuff, grinding drugs of all kinds, making mustard, grinding chocolate, making lozenges, making soda-water, and even for chopping sausage-meat.[8]

Tens of thousands of migrants arrived in Britain's industrial cities every year: they came to work in factories; they apprenticed themselves to trades; they worked as tailors and ironmongers; they worked in quarries and mines to furnish the factories with the fuel and ore they needed. They came because rural life had become precarious and oppressive for those without land. "I took it upon myself at once to become my own master," one anonymous worker wrote to the journal *Working Man's Friend*. On first encounter, Britain's industrial cities must have felt like another planet: the water ran a rainbow of pungent textile-factory dyes; enveloped by smog, it felt different just to breathe. "You stand in Manchester," journalist Angus Bethune told readers of the *Morning Chronicle* in 1850, and this is what they would see: "There is smoky brown sky over head—smoky brown streets all round piles of warehouses." "The tinge of darkness in the atmosphere may be seen making a line of at least forty miles in length," observed Scottish chemist Robert Angus Smith, who would go on to study the phenomenon called acid rain. The Reverend John Molesworth, who organized the Manchester Association for the Prevention of Smoke, declared at a public meeting in May 1842 that Manchester's smoke was all that people "saw, tasted, and felt." Molesworth's might well have been the world's first pressure group against air pollution. Manchester appears, barely disguised, as "Coketown" in Charles Dickens's *Hard Times*. Looking at the sky, "interminable serpents of smoke trailed themselves for ever and ever, and never got uncoiled." It was amply clear to those who lived through the first blast of industrial growth that burning fossil fuels changed everything: the air, the water, the soil—even people's bodies.[9]

Other species suffered the assault of the new industrial world. Robert Holland, a botanist who worked with the North Lancashire Agricultural Society, described the effects of smoke on Manchester's

The brittle bark of a London plane tree, well adapted to protecting the tree from air pollution.

parks: "trees stunted, dying, flowers struggling to bloom and some-times their species scarcely recognisable." The smoke was like a dis-torting coating that turned nature mutant. Lancashire ornithologist F. S. Mitchell described how the "vitiated atmosphere" of Manches-ter affected birds, destroying their sources of food, and stripping them of the shelter of "protective foliage."[10]

Through any ecological disruption, some species find a niche to flour-ish. One Mrs. Haweis, horticulturalist, published a farsighted guide to a new nature: she called it *Rus in Urbe, or Flowers that Thrive in London Gardens and Smoky Towns.* Smoke paved the way for the triumph of the London Plane, a cross between the American sycamore and the eastern plane tree. Its brittle bark, which flakes and renews itself, acts like an outer shield, protecting the tree against attack from the tiny toxic particulates of pollution. Once an adornment to the city's most exclusive neighborhoods, half of all the trees in London today are planes.[11]

As people struggled for breath, they saw in smoke the hope of a better future. Anti-smoke activists in Manchester had a diffi-cult time mobilizing support so long as smoking chimneys were a symbol of progress. "Thank God, smoke is rising from the lofty chimneys," the Irish writer, William Cooke Taylor, wrote from Bolton in 1842, because its absence "indicates the quenching of the fire on many a domestic hearth, want of employment to many a willing labourer, and want of bread to many an honest family." There could be "permanently smokeless cities," thought William Nicholson, smoke inspector of Sheffield—but who would want them, he mused, when "a smokeless country, with its purer air, clear skies and more sunshine would be a country of universal poverty." Witness, here, the birth of an idea so powerful that it has reverberated around the world for almost two centuries: the idea that the degradation and sacrifice of nature is the necessary price of a human freedom from want.[12]

It was not long before people wondered how long the boon would last. By 1865, English economist William Stanley Jevons observed, in *The Coal Question*, that "coal in truth stands not beside but entirely above all other commodities. It is the material energy of the country—the universal aid—the factor in everything we do." In Jevons's mind, coal represented a break in human history: like a portal to the future, it had created a temporal gulf between those who used it and those who did not. Without coal, Jevons wrote, "we are thrown back into the laborious poverty of early times."[13]

Jevons knew that buried stocks of coal were not infinite. Once coal had burned, Jevons warned, it was gone: "we are drawing more and more upon a capital which yields no annual interest, but once turned to light and heat and force, is gone for ever into space." British meteorologist Rollo Russell believed that any quantity of emissions would vanish into the atmosphere, which "freely spreads high above all mountains and flows ever in mighty currents at levels beyond the most elevated regions of the solid earth." It would be another decade, at least, before scientists began to realize that these traces of fossil fuel combustion were far from "gone for ever."[14]

By the time Jevons penned his warning, Britain's industrial production was no longer unmatched, its economic leadership no longer assured. Britain's advantage lasted no more than a few decades.

The British government's ban on the export of industrial secrets could not be enforced, for British inventors had few incentives not to sell their wares to others. Visitors smuggled out plans, samples, and prototypes. In the opening decades of the nineteenth century, Belgium was the first country in Europe to experience industrial growth. Steam engines imported from Britain powered a textile boom around Ghent. Belgium's power looms were fed by the mines of Wallonia, part of an arcing line of coal-seam that wound through the Nord-Pas-de-Calais region of France and up into western Germany: a seam buried under the lowlands that traversed a stretch of valleys through the Haine and the Meuse, the Canche and the Sambre, the Rhine and the Ruhr—soil that would be soaked in the blood of twentieth-century wars. By the 1830s, France witnessed such a spurt of industry that economist Jérôme-Adolphe Blanqui observed, "industrial conditions were more profoundly transformed than at any time since the beginnings of social life." Germany followed in the 1850s, and within two decades the Ruhr Valley ascended to the top rank of industrial powers. Its only rival, by then, lay across the Atlantic Ocean.[15]

The Centennial Exposition of 1876, held on the banks of the Schuylkill River in Philadelphia, was America's "birthday party." A century after the American Revolution and a decade after the Civil War, the Exposition thrilled an audience of ten million people. Brazil and Mexico, Britain and Japan were among the thirty-six countries represented. London's Crystal Palace Exhibition of 1851 had been the first to celebrate a new industrial age; Philadelphia's showed that the future belonged to America. The Exposition displayed a vision of nature reshaped by technology. It sat at the gateway city to a hub of metalwork and glasswork and dyeing: an industrial region that sat above three-quarters of the world's store of the anthracite coal that was almost pure carbon, knitted together by the Pennsylvania Railroad, the largest industrial corporation in the world. The Exposition embraced agriculture and horticulture. A women's pavilion, the first of its kind, celebrated the economic achievements of women. Proud exhibits from Britain and America showed off the power of industrial weaponry in this era of global empire: breech-loading rifles, made from strengthened steel, which shot standard-ized, manufactured bullets.[16]

Most memorable and most intimidating was the fifteen-acre Machinery Hall. Its centerpiece was the largest steam engine ever built, designed by George Corliss of Rhode Island, who, in 1849, had invented a stationary steam engine more efficient than Watt's. On the Exposition's opening day, US president Ulysses Grant stood alongside Emperor Dom Pedro of Brazil to pull the engine's start-ing levers. William Dean Howells, writer and critic, declared in *The Atlantic Monthly* that the Corliss engine was like "an athlete of steel and iron with not a superfluous ounce of metal on it." He described the flywheel, the engine's heart, as bearing "a hoarded power that makes all tremble." Unperturbed next to the giant engine, "the engi-neer sits reading his newspaper, as in a peaceful bower." The din of the boilers was safely out of hearing range, in a different building. The Corliss engine aroused Howells's patriotism. The world "would be a barren place without the American machinery," he thought; "America is voluble in the strong metals and their infinite uses." Howells was not alone in his sense of awe. An aging Walt Whitman sat for half an hour in silent contemplation of the Corliss engine at the Exposition. An anonymous correspondent wondered if Whit-man alone might have the "magician's touch . . . to evoke the melody and beauty now surely latent alike in the water-driven saw-mill and the big Corliss engine." If he did, it was because Whitman had a rare "eye for nature that is not limited in its range to nature untouched by man."[17]

There were moments in the nineteenth century when the past life embedded within the fossil-fuel economy became suddenly and shockingly visible. Just two years after the Centennial Exposition, miners down deep shafts in Bernissart, Belgium, hit something that looked unlike coal—it looked suspiciously like a bone, but they weren't sure. That evening, the mine supervisor took fragments of

The Corliss Engine in Machinery Hall, at Philadelphia's Centennial Exposition of 1876.

it along to the Café Dubruille; a local doctor examined them, and confirmed their suspicion. It *was* a bone. Upon further investigation by zoologist and paleontologist, Pierre-Joseph van Beneden, it emerged that the miners had stumbled upon a pit that contained the first complete skeletons ever found of dinosaurs that would be identified as iguanodons: thirty-one of them, alongside a profusion of fish, crocodiles, turtles, and a lone salamander. Before the remains were excavated, piece by piece, artist Gustave Lavalette arrived to draw them in their original resting place. He depicted the dinosaurs at the moment of their demise, arranged in "death poses."[18]

To the miners faced with a mass grave of a herd—a family?—of iguanodons, perhaps it would not have seemed bold to suggest, as humanities scholars have recently done, that we should think of fossil fuels as our "kin." What had happened to cause such sudden death, they might have wondered. By what chance had these stubborn traces survived, intact, the crushing force that had turned the vanished life of primeval forests into the fuel of the nineteenth century?[19]

By 1885, fossil fuels had overtaken all other energy sources in the

A wood engraving from 1880 showing the discovery of
iguanodon fossils in a coal mine at Bernissart, Belgium, in 1878.

United States. The same decade, Japan became the first Asian country to undergo sustained industrialization, orchestrated by an ambitious Meiji state that used the language of "restoration" to justify
a revolutionary response to the fear that Japan would fall victim,
like so many of its neighbors, to European or American imperialism.
Between 1874 and 1894, Japan's production of coal increased twenty-
fold. Industrial muscle gave Japan victory over the Chinese Empire
in the Sino-Japanese War in 1894–95, and an even more stunning
victory against Russia in 1905. In India, too, a corridor of extractive
industries had emerged by the 1880s along the rail line between the
Raniganj coalfields and Calcutta, though Indian nationalists argued
that the country was less industrialized than it ought to be, inhib-
ited by British policies that locked India into exporting raw materials. In 1880s' Calcutta, commissions of enquiry took up the question
of the city's "smoke nuisance"; smoke inspectors adopted a practice
from Britain's northern cities, producing daily color-graded sketches
of the smoke's intensity, sketching an archive of a changing sky. In
1898–99, Calcutta's inspectors recorded "black smoke" emanating
from a sample of eighteen factory chimneys for between ten and seventeen minutes in every hour on average.[20]

The 1890s also saw the earliest recognition of how the century of coal might affect the planet in the distant future. In Stockholm, the Swedish chemist, Svante Arrhenius, carried out a series of painstaking manual calculations of how much heat the Earth received from a full moon. Arrhenius was an electrochemist by training, and his radical doctoral thesis on electrolytes had so perturbed the examiners that it only barely passed. He was concerned with the history of previous ice ages and what might have caused them. Arrhenius narrowed in on the role of carbon dioxide in the atmosphere. He estimated that halving the amount of atmospheric CO_2 would lead the planet's temperature to fall by between four and five degrees Celsius—and that doubling it would raise temperatures by five to six degrees. Arrhenius recognized that burning coal released significant amounts of carbon dioxide into the atmosphere; he speculated that a warming Earth would be no bad thing for Sweden over the long term. His far descendants, he thought, would live "under a milder sky and in less barren surroundings." Arrhenius had glimpsed, however uncertainly, the greenhouse effect. He thought it would take about three thousand years for CO_2 to double; he could never have imagined that it would jump by 30 percent over the single century to come.[21]

BY THE END OF the nineteenth century, still only a small proportion of the world's population labored in factories. Hubs of industry, linked to one another by intercontinental trade, were like brightly lit outposts that hugged the coasts of oceans, the fringes of forests, the edges of prairie and planted expanses of grain. It was the use of steam in transportation, more than in production, that truly changed the world. Railroads took a large, migrant labor force to build, and then, once built, they hastened and multiplied the migration of people across continents. Railroads devoured wood and ore in their construction, and then hastened and multiplied the movement of wheat and cotton and cattle across half the world. Railroads consumed coal, seemingly without limit. And they reordered the landscapes they cut through simply by changing what it cost to turn whole forests into timber to be sold far away.

By 1850, twenty years after the first rail link between Liverpool and Manchester, Britain had 3,000 miles of railroad, and the United States in the region of 4,000. By 1871, Britain possessed 13,000 miles of rail track, and the United States around 41,000. Over the next three decades, spurred by the construction of the Transcontinentals, the US rail network grew to 175,000 miles of track. Germany's rail network more than quadrupled between 1860 and 1900 to reach 32,000 miles. American railroad companies, and the steel manufacturers that supplied their carriages and tracks, became the largest corporations in the world; they generated fortunes for America's new capitalist elite. The mania reached Asia when the Marquess of Dalhousie, governor general of India, inaugurated the construction of India's railways in 1853. In British India, as in the United States, the state took on the risks of railway construction while the profits went to private investors: in India, they were guaranteed a handsome return of 5 percent. Over the second half of the nineteenth century, the Indian railways expanded to encompass 24,000 miles of track, by far the largest rail network in Asia.[22]

To build the railroads, hundreds of thousands of men left their homes. Some of them were accompanied by wives and sisters and daughters, but many traveled alone. In Britain they were called "navvies," derived from the "navigators" who had built the canals of the eighteenth century. They numbered a quarter of a million by 1850. They came from every corner of Britain and from an Ireland reeling from the aftermath of terrible famine; they came from continental Europe as refugees from war and failed revolutions; they came as plucky seekers of opportunity and higher wages. Across the British Isles, navvies blasted and hammered the land into something new.

Broadside ballads—printed on cheap paper and sold on street corners, set to commonly known folk tunes—told of the hardships and triumphs of life on the tracks. One beloved ballad, "Paddy Works on the Railway"—"Paddy" was a generic and often demeaning term for an Irishman in nineteenth-century Britain—narrates the history of the mid-century through the life of an itinerant Irish navvy: "In eighteen hundred and forty-two / From Hartlepool I moved to Crewe / And found myself a job to do / a-working on the railway." The chorus, interspersed with verses of adventure and mishap, is plaintive: "I'm weary of the railway / Poor Paddy works on the railway." Another song called "Paddy" conveys the circular journeys many migrant workers made, back and forth across the water. Its final verse sings of the bittersweet return:

> Now to the harvest I will go,
>   And tell them there of all I know,
> I'll tell them of each friend and foe,
>   That I met on the Railway
> Then off to Ireland I'll repair,
>   And tell them all the wonders there,
> For never a one in County Clare,
>   Ever saw or heard of a Railway.

As he toils on the railway, the navvy looks forward to the stories he would tell back home. The colonial relationship between Britain and Ireland is plain in the final lines. Ireland sees none of the prosperity of this new age of steel and steam; life back home still follows the rhythms of the harvest, not the clock-time of the railroad.[23]

Rail labor could be the work of a lifetime. To build the Transcontinentals across North America, more than one hundred thousand Chinese workers crossed the Pacific. Their suffering and their labor were erased in triumphal accounts of how the railroads knitted the American nation back together after the Civil War. Chinese workers dug and exploded railway tunnels through the Sierra Nevada and the Rocky Mountains. It was crushing work; or, as one observer described it, "bone-labor." Most came from Guangdong province in southern China and set sail from the British-controlled port of Hong

Kong for the "gold mountain," as they called the United States—in
that name lay many dreams. They left a country consumed by civil
war over the millenarian Taiping Rebellion, led by Hong Xiuquan
who claimed to be the younger brother of Jesus Christ, an upris-
ing in which people died in numbers that defy reckoning; perhaps
twenty million people were killed in fifteen years. Refugees from the
fighting were assailed by "at least eight different kinds of troops who
march and counter-march around their former homes." Those who
could muster enough to pay labor recruiters to take them to North
America were among the more fortunate. Theirs were journeys
in search of freedom from terror. New trials awaited them across
the sea.[24]

The Chinese workers who formed 90 percent of the workforce of
the Central Pacific Railroad company carried what traces of home
they could. A traveler through the region noticed that railroad stores
"sold pipes, bowls, chop-sticks, large shallow cast-iron bowls for
cooking rice, lamps, joss paper, Chinese writing-paper, pencils and
India ink, Chinese shoes, and clothing imported ready-made from
China." Further north, through the harsh winters of Montana, Chinese laborers worked on the North Pacific Railroad. They reshaped
the rugged landscape around them. "For more than 20 miles," a visitor to the worksite reported, "workmen are seen digging, chopping,
lifting, blasting, cursing, and shouting. Trees are crashing down,
earth is flying from countless shovels and huge rocks are being riven
and scattered from all sides." All we know about the lives of many
Chinese workers is what they left behind. Since the 1970s, archaeol-
ogists have excavated their residential camps, discovering fragments
of small objects that hint at the workers' struggles to forge community and to keep up a respectable appearance to their fellows: metal
razors, toothbrushes with bone handles, and clothing fasteners.[25]

In India the 1860s saw the construction of a railway line between
the coastal metropolis of Bombay and the inland city of Poona. Like
the Sierra Nevada, the Western Ghats posed a formidable obsta-
cle: engineers had to turn "the stupendous natural inequalities of

the precipitous hills into a series of uniform inclined surfaces," until the "whole rugged and inhospitable region has been smoothed down." Within three decades, the railway had reduced India to "one-twentieth of its former dimensions." The railway consolidated the state's control over Indian territory and precipitated a renewed assault on nature. India's railways demanded a "prodigious consumption of mineral or vegetable food, in the shape of coal, coke, or wood," vast quantities of iron and steel, and water to supply the engines. India's ecology menaced every scheme. Storm surges threatened the stability of railway bridges and the lives of thousands who built and used them. In 1897, a bridge collapsed amid late-monsoon rains in Mysore—the packed train that was crossing at the time tumbled into a river in flood, and 150 passengers died. As infrastructure diverted watercourses and altered drainage channels a surge of malaria followed.[26]

Railroads deepened the chasm of freedom in the nineteenth century—the chasm between those who had it, and those who lost it. For white settlers in North America, Australia, and New Zealand, freedom meant the freedom to move, and freedom to acquire land without the least regard for the many Native communities who had prior claims to it. "There was nothing but land . . ." the narrator Jim Burden says in Willa Cather's 1918 epic of migration to the Midwest, *My Ántonia*: "not a country at all, but the material out of which countries are made." The US Congress passed the Homestead Act in 1862, granting to every settler family 160 acres of land after five years of continuous residence and "improvement," for nothing more than a token registration fee.[27]

Homesteaders needed homes. Chicago firms distributed by rail millions of house construction kits, issued in standard sizes to a balloon-framed pattern; they were made of light, milled wood and held together by nails. Chicago firms also shipped out vast quantities of wood for fences to mark the edges of each family's property and to protect crops from livestock. On an 1871 estimate, the value of the fences alone was around $1.7 billion. "Who can impress the forest, bid the tree / Unfix his earth-bound root?" the usurping king Macbeth had asked in the play that Shakespeare wrote almost three centuries earlier at the threshold of Europe's aggressive turn to empire and conquest. Now the Chicago timber merchants were doing just that. The mixed hardwood forests of northern Michigan, Wisconsin, and Minnesota had their earth-bound roots unfixed; they were taken apart to be transported, as timber, to farmsteads across the Great Plains. In place of forests grew cultivated fields, which demanded more wood for fencing from even further away. A visitor to northern Michigan in 1868 lamented that "the Pioneer is insensible to arguments touching the forest supply; to him, the forest is only fit to be exterminated, as it hinders plough and obstructs his sunlight."[28]

The twinned thrust of the railroad and settler colonization renewed the long war of dispossession against Native American communities. German traveler Ernst von Hesse-Wartegg wrote, approvingly, in 1877: "Civilization sweeps like a storm across the plains and smashes what will not bow down or give way before it." Native communities did not bow down, neither did they give way without a fight. As Cheyenne trading networks were ruptured by the Transcontinentals, they fought to preserve their treaty-defined rights; they sabotaged rail tracks and raided settlements. The Lakota, whose expansive mobility across the Plains clashed with new settlement, waged war to resist the Northern Pacific Railroad's incursions into their lands. Settlement was war. By deceit and legal sophistry, by sheer force of numbers backed by the force of the railroad and industrial weaponry, the US empire thrust across the continent. Indigenous Americans lost their expansive landscapes; their spatial horizons were squeezed into the confinement of reservations.[29]

Settler conquest also brought devastation to the Indigenous peoples of the Argentine *Pampas*. In Argentina, too, the railroad and the quest for land—to grow wheat and graze cattle—emboldened racial violence. Histories of empire, north and south, came together: Argentina's settlers dreamed of nothing less than re-creating the

United States in the southern hemisphere. The "conquest of the desert," led by the forces of Julio Argentino Roca, unfolded across the grasslands from 1878 to 1885. Roca's army waged a ruthless war against the nomadic people of the Pampas, who had either resisted or found ways to coexist with the ranching and grazing economy of early settlers. Now they were in the way. "Peopling the desert means to suppress the *indios* and to occupy the frontier," President Nicolás Avellaneda declared. Argentinian forces executed more than ten thousand *indios*; faced with starvation, exhausted from flight, cut off from their ecologies of survival, a further one hundred thousand or more Indigenous people died during the war. The ways that rulers described the land conveyed their vision of what it should be. To see the grasslands of Argentina as a barren "desert," to "occupy" it, was to imagine a different ecology in its place: an ecology of cultivated fields and an endless horizon of wheat, which would free small farmers from hunger, and turn large ones into major exporters.[30]

IN THE CENTURY OF the industrial revolution, the deepest impact of human activity and ambition on the Earth remained the oldest—growing food. "All ends in the same," wrote Richard Jefferies, chronicler of English rural life: "iron mines, coal mines, factories, furnaces, the counter, the desk—no one can live on iron, or coal, or cotton—the object is really sacks of wheat." The railway, the steamship, and the telegraph combined to extend the lands planted with the staple crops of human existence: wheat, corn, and rice. At the same time, demand for the "drug foods" surged among European and American industrial workers who craved small comforts to take the edge off the drudgery of factory labor: coffee, tea, and chocolate sweetened with sugar.[31]

The use of enslaved labor on agricultural plantations gave way, gradually, to other forms of unfreedom. Resistance by enslaved people combined with the moral and political pressure of humanitarians—a coalition of forcefully eloquent, free

African-Americans, white middle-class women and men, and radical philosophers—to bring about the end of the British Empire's
slave trade in 1807. It took until 1834 for slavery itself to be abolished
in the Empire, and slaveowners received ample financial compensation. Elsewhere, it took the industrial-scale bloodletting of the US
Civil War, repeated revolts, and national movements for independence in Latin America to defeat the laws that protected slavery—
which persisted in Cuba until 1886, and in Brazil until 1888.

But the economy of the plantation, which had shattered the lives
of millions of enslaved Africans since the sixteenth century, did
not just survive the nineteenth century, it grew to dominate the
lands surrounding the Indian Ocean as well. In the 1830s, the same
decade that slavery was abolished in the British Empire, the first
ships departed Indian ports for Trinidad and Mauritius. The ships
carried Indian men, women, and children who had signed punitive
and binding contracts of indenture under pressures of debt, and
not infrequently deceit. They went to work on sugar plantations.
The age of abolition inaugurated a new history of confinement—
and a redoubled transformation of the Earth in service of an
industrial hunger.[32]

The most extensive environmental changes of the nineteenth
century involved wheat. Over centuries, farmers had fought for
improved yields: gains built up from trial and error in manuring
and draining and watering and breeding. Wheat was grown much
as it had always been in the 1800s, and its spectacular growth came
from devoting more and more of the surface of the Earth to the crop.
Rice colonized fewer new soils than wheat, but paddy expanded too,
as thousands of small farmers moved into the silt-rich river deltas
of Southeast Asia—the Irrawaddy, in Burma; the Chao Phraya, in
Thailand; the Mekong, in Vietnam.[33]

In North America, the tallgrass prairie of wild rye, switchgrass,
and bluestems and the shorter grasses of the drier west and the
Rocky Mountain foothills—all turned to acres of wheat and grass.
Multifarious human and more-than-human ecologies made way for

a single crop. Following the rail lines, settlers clustered in Minnesota, Ohio, and Kansas; in the 1880s, migration was so intensive, the spread of cultivation so rapid, that the Dakotas alone produced more wheat than all of India exported in a year. In the last decade of the nineteenth century, the heart of the wheat boom moved north to the Canadian prairie, first to Manitoba and then to Alberta and Saskatchewan. Across the Atlantic, Europe's granary lay in the *chernozem*, the fertile black soils, of Ukraine, which were planted with wheat almost as fast as the Great Plains. By the end of the century, the wheatlands unfurled like a roll of ochre paper across Argentina and Australia. Wheat took over the arid lands of Punjab, in India's northwest, made possible by the British construction of the most extensive network of irrigation canals anywhere in the world.[34]

In Punjab, one British official observed, "irrigation was not designed to assist agriculture and diminish the losses from seasonal vagaries, but to create it where it did not exist."[35] Between the 1890s and the 1910s, more than a million Punjabis moved west to the region bordered by the Beas and Sutlej rivers on one side, and the Jhelum on the other. Theirs was an eager, state-sponsored migration to newly built "canal colonies" that covered 13 million acres. Migrants went, as ever, in search of security, leaving an eastern Punjab where land was scarce and life was hard. Migrants took courage from the colonial government's lavish promises of plenty. Village communities broke up as some families seized the opportunity to migrate and others chose not to go, or were turned down by recruiters for being too poor or too unhealthy. A Punjabi folk song warns aspiring migrants against needless ambition: "Allah will give us food and water; / Why have you gone to the canals?"[36]

The allure of land proved irresistible. The colonial state did not just decree that each parcel of land take a regular, repeating shape "in complete squares"; the state also chose the canal colonies' population to conform to Victorian notions of race, fitness, and heredity. Asked how he chose future colonists from among the large number of applicants in any given village, British rural administrator James

Douie was straightforward: "I looked at their chests," he said, and he proceeded to make voyeurs of his audience in London by showing them slides of unclothed Punjabi bodies. One of his fellow officers had focused on the applicants' hands, as if they held the key to future success. British administrators in India had a global view of how the movement of people was changing the Earth. Douie knew that when he mentioned "colonization," his audience would think immediately of "the prairies of the United States, or the pampas of Argentina"— but in India, too, he told them, a similar movement was underway.[37]

Not all migration to the new lands of wheat was permanent. As steamships made ocean voyages cheaper, faster, and less treacherous, they also at last opened the prospect of return. Beginning in the 1870s, Argentina's wheat boom depended on the oscillating migration of laborers from the Po Plains of Italy, where livelihoods had suffered because cheap American wheat was being imported to feed urban Italians. In Argentina they came to be known as *golondrinas*, or swallows—suggesting that their trans-Atlantic journeys were as seasonal, and as natural, as the migration of birds. "We Italians are the worker bees of the Argentinian hive," boasted journalist Luigi Barzini in 1902, "In fact, Argentina exists because of Italian labour." Along the rail lines from Buenos Aires, new settlements came up with familiar names—Nueva Torino, named for the city of Turin, and Colonia Cavour, named for the hero of Italian reunification. The characteristic village gates of Piedmont and Lombardy now adorned the Pampas, complete with village squares and churches in an Italian style. Most of all, Italian migrant workers would have recognized the furrowed, watered fields they went to farm: just like at home— but so much bigger. They transplanted, across the South Atlantic, the alfalfa that they knew so well, for use as hay and forage.[38]

Throughout the world, rail and steam elongated the journey of grain from farm to table, twisted and stretched it across continents. In the process, wheat turned from an item of commerce into a form of capital to be invested in land, machinery, and speculative ventures to generate further wealth. The grain elevators of Chicago—giant warehouses for storing, sorting, and grading wheat—allowed the produce of hundreds of individual farms to be piled together and sold as an abstract commodity in markets around the world. For farmers, grain elevator receipts functioned as a form of money: they could be exchanged for cash or used as checks. Traders bought wheat as a physical product—they also bought promises of future wheat, betting on its price rising or falling in the meantime.[39]

Futures markets were not new. Medieval merchants in Mediterranean Europe, and traders at the Dōjima Rice Exchange of Tokugawa Japan, had devised contracts agreeing prices for future deliveries: they did this to hedge against a ruined harvest, or a superabundant one that would drive down the market; they priced in the ever-present risk of loss in transit. Chicago's trade in futures was on an altogether larger scale; it remade landscapes around the world in the expectation of future profit.[40]

Between the 1850s and the 1900s, the world grain trade grew almost ten times larger, from 3.8 metric tons to 37.7 million. In 1850, Britain was self-sufficient in wheat; by the end of the century, it was the world's largest importer by far. A single, global market in wheat drew in North America, Australia, Argentina, Russia, and India. China alone, among the major producers, remained outside it—Chinese wheat and rice were grown only for domestic consumption through a century when China's trade was devastated by the debilitating conjunction of civil war and European aggression. The telegraph brought about a convergence in prices. In 1903, a tsarist official witnessed an astonishing scene: "On the market place in Nikolaiev (one of the most important southern ports) I had an opportunity to observe a fact which a short time ago would have been altogether incredible"—when farmers arrived at the market, their first question was: "what is the price in America, according to the latest telegram?" By that year, Russia surpassed the United States as the world's largest exporter of wheat, barley, rye, and oats.[41]

Steamships did even more than rail to enlarge the global market in rice, a crop that grows best in river deltas. Rice expanded simultaneously with wheat and always provided a larger proportion of the daily calories of people for whom it was the main staple. The completion of the Suez Canal in 1869 cut the journey time between Asia and Europe—the journey between London and Singapore was between ten and twelve days shorter than before—and so catapulted Burma into the position of the world's largest exporter of rice. Until the 1850s, Burma's ruling Konbaung Dynasty had banned the export of rice. Its kings held to a fundamentally different conception of the value of rice as a food. Rice, Burma's rulers thought, should provide sustenance for the local people; it was not a commodity to be sold abroad. The East India Company had other ideas. Following the defeat of the Konbaung Dynasty by British forces in 1852, Burmese rice began to reach European markets, where it was used not primarily as food but rather as starch, as animal feed, and as an ingredient in liqueurs and brandies. By 1905, Burma's rice exports had grown almost twenty times larger than they had been in 1855, and over the same decades, the expanse of Burma given over to paddy expanded from 700,000 acres to more than 6 million, much of it at the expense of forest. By the turn of the twentieth century, Burma's rice exports to its close neighbors—to Bengal and Madras in India, to Singapore and Malaysia—surpassed the traffic of rice to Europe.[42]

Burmese farmers grasped similar opportunities in the Irrawaddy delta that their counterparts in Punjab sought in the wheat lands of the canal colonies. But where the colonial state encouraged cultivation of Punjab with grants of land and start-up costs to farmers, Burmese rice farmers were on their own. They had little money to invest. To get started in rice farming, to tide them over until the harvest, to generate cash for the small things that with a little security they came to desire—canned milk, tinned biscuits, soap, glassware, calendars, illustrated magazines—Burmese farmers depended on loans. Local shopkeepers and moneylenders in the bazaar not only charged ruinously high interest, they could not keep up with demand, so a group of people from across the sea moved in and took over. Originally a caste of salt traders, the Chettiars, from the arid deep south of India, flourished as merchant bankers by following the British expansion into Southeast Asia. By the turn of the twentieth century, around 350 Chettiar firms operated in Burma, with a working capital of 150 million rupees. With networks of agents dispersed through rural Burma, Chettiar banks were willing to risk lending to small farmers, where British banks would not.[43]

In Burma, just as in North America, an injection of new investment in agriculture changed the landscape and spurred the movement of people. For Burmese families, the independence of small-scale rice farming made wage labor unattractive; so, millions of Indian migrants from the coastal regions of southern and eastern India, men without land or with plots too small to be viable, found work milling and processing rice. They hauled jute sacks on the docks of Rangoon; they built and staffed the Burmese railway and the fleet of steamboats up and down the Irrawaddy. Burmese rice became a lifeline for the growing cities of South and Southeast Asia, just as Ukrainian wheat had for urban Europe. Food security came at a price—it created a knot of dependence that would leave large numbers of people vulnerable if anything were to happen to cut these ties.[44]

THE INDUSTRIAL REVOLUTION AND the agrarian revolution collided in an explosion of animal flesh. The nineteenth century brought a profound change in the conditions of human life on Earth—part of that change was a newfound capacity to slaughter animals on a scale out of all proportion to anything that had been known before. In killing, as in wheat, the United States led the way. At the beginning of the nineteenth century, anywhere between twenty and forty million wild bison roamed the Great Plains of North America; their presence was so marked that they shaped the ecology of the grasslands, favoring the development of "buffalo grass" that could stand heavy grazing. George Catlin, adventurer

and painter, described in the 1840s the awesome sight of a bison
herd: "several thousands in a mass, eddying and wheeling about
under a cloud of dust"; they sounded, he said, like "distant thunder." By 1900, the thunder was silent. Bison had been exterminated
from the land.[45]

The railroad was, in William Cronon's words, "a knife into the
heart of buffalo country." The beasts were helpless before the most
lethal products of the foundries of New Haven, Connecticut, and
Springfield, Massachusetts. Hunters wielded Springfield .50-caliber
rifles from the backs of rail carriages. Hunters shot for sport. Hunters shot for meat. They shot for status and for profit. In the 1870s,
tanners in Philadelphia found a way to make bison hinds into supple
leather to be used as flexible belts in factory machinery. Carnage followed. The plains were littered with animal carcasses: "a dead, soli-
tary, putrid desert." Political intent as well as financial gain drove the
slaughter. Send settlers "power and lead, if you will," wrote Philip
Sheridan, architect of the conquest of the US West, "but for the sake
of a lasting peace, let them kill, skin, and sell until the buffaloes are
exterminated." So grievous would be the harm this inflicted upon
the Indigenous peoples of the plains, Sheridan knew, that it would
pave the way for conquest: "then your prairies can be covered with
speckled cattle."[46]

Buffalo country became cattle country; what followed was a
bonanza of beef. At the beginning of the nineteenth century, the
average European ate 15 kilograms of meat each year; a little over
a century later, they ate 50 kilograms of meat, and Americans
even more. The dinner table of the Turner family, millworkers in
the northern English town of Huddersfield in the 1870s—working
people who could hardly be described as wealthy—exemplifies the
change. Meat had become a daily necessity, where for earlier generations it would have been a luxury. In a typical week, the Turners
ate: "on Monday a bit of cold meat, on Tuesday a hash . . . on Satur-
day a bit of sausage, and on Sunday the usual joint."[47] Refrigeration

brought meat into the same global marketplace as grain. Chicago meatpackers harvested ice from the lakes of Illinois and Indiana and shipped it in from as far away as Boston.

Humans had always struggled against decay, salting and drying meat to store it for future need. The ability to freeze animal flesh marked a new front in the battle. Refrigerated train cars, writes historian Reviel Netz, author of *Barbed Wire*, marked a "spatial separation between the killing of animals and the life of humans"—and a temporal separation, too.[48]

The techniques of factory production now turned to dismembering animal carcasses. Frederick Olmstead described a Cincinnati slaughterhouse as "a sort of human chopping-machine where the hogs were converted into commercial pork." The quest for efficiency that characterized the industrial revolution now made the most of every dead pig—turning it not only into pork to eat and fats to cook with, but also into household brushes and combs, and lubricants for factories. William Cronon hints at the broader moral shift that came from separation, as packing plants "distanced their customers from the act of killing." What set in, Cronon writes in *Nature's Metropolis*, is a sort of forgetfulness: dismembered and processed into so many commodities, every animal's "ties to the earth receded, and in forgetting the animal's life one also forgot the grasses and the prairie skies and the departed bison herds. . . ."[49]

At the dark heart of animal slaughter in the nineteenth-century world stood the Chicago stockyards, by far the largest in the world. By the 1880s, the stockyards possessed a hotel and a tavern for traveling traders and an imposing Exchange Building where deals were done away from the screams and the smell of blood and flesh. Few newcomers would ever forget what they saw or convey the experience of the stockyard as viscerally as Rudyard Kipling. He described the sight of "nearly all the pigs ever bred in Wisconsin" crammed together in a holding pen. Ejected a few at a time, lifted by their hind legs, "they rose in the air, suspended from the railway of death." The pigs feel sheer terror, first mute and then deafening:

Oh! it was then they shrieked and called on their mothers, and
made promises of amendment, till the tackle-man punted them
in their backs and they slid head down into a brick-floored passage, very like a big kitchen sink, that was blood-red. There
awaited them a red man with a knife, which he passed jaun-
tily through their throats, and the full-voiced shriek became
a splutter, and then a fall as of heavy tropical rain, and the
red man, who was backed against the passage-wall, you will
understand, stood clear of the wildly kicking hoofs and passed
his hand over his eyes, not from any feeling of compassion, but
because the spurted blood was in his eyes, and he had barely
time to stick the next arrival.

While he abhorred the death inflicted upon cattle and pigs in Chicago, Kipling reveled in the death inflicted by Britain's imperial
armies upon Asians and Africans. In "Brown Bess," Kipling writes
in loving praise of the muzzle-loading musket that supplied British forces for more than a century: "So she followed her red-coats,
whatever they did / From the heights of Quebec to the plains of
Assaye / From Gibraltar to Acre, Cape Town and Madrid, / And
nothing about her was changed on the way; / (But most of the
Empire which now we possess / Was won through those years by
old-fashioned Brown Bess.)" By the time Kipling composed his ode,
Brown Bess had given way to weapons far more lethal. Scottish-
American gunsmith Hiram Maxim's invention could fire six hundred rounds every minute.[50]

If Kipling failed to equate the mass animal death in Chicago with
imperial killing, some of the leading natural scientists of the nineteenth century deployed their power to kill for other purposes and
drew different conclusions about the human place in nature.

Alfred Russel Wallace—English naturalist, explorer, and co-
discoverer, with Charles Darwin, of the theory of evolution
through natural selection—had spent many years in the 1850s and
1860s traveling through the Indonesian archipelago. Wallace was

a cultured and intelligent man, more sensitive to cultural difference and to human suffering than many among his generation. But
emboldened by the zeal of scientific mission, aided by the racial
privilege that gave him easy access to Chinese and Dayak labor, and
protected by an armory of factory-made guns—Wallace went on a
killing spree.

Without shame, Wallace describes how he shot at an adult orang-
utan repeatedly until the wounded creature fell "with a crash and
thud like the fall of a giant." His legs and his hip bone were broken. The base of his spine was "completely shattered." Bullets were
lodged in his neck and in his jaw. Wallace had the corpses of the
many orangutans he shot skinned and their bones boiled to make
"perfect skeletons" to be shipped off to Europe for display in muse-
ums of natural history. It is hard not to believe that the ability to
inflict death gave Wallace an overwhelming sense of entitlement to
subdue any living being for the purposes of his research.[51]

Five years into his time in Southeast Asia, isolated and stricken
with malaria, Wallace came to a startling, fevered realization. "Why
do some die and some live?" Wallace asked, reflecting on the vast
variations in flora and fauna he had seen on his travels. His answer
was that "on the whole the best fitted live." Wallace had discovered
"the long-sought-for law of nature that solved the problem of the origins of species." In no fit state to publish his thoughts, Wallace shared
his insight with his hero, Charles Darwin, who had been thinking
along similar lines. They presented the work jointly, though Darwin
would receive the greater share of both acclaim and infamy.[52]

The ideas of Wallace and Darwin punctured the presumption of
human uniqueness in nature, much to the dismay of religious authorities. They built on the work of German naturalist and polymath
Alexander von Humboldt, and before him the Swedish biologist and
creator of the modern system of taxonomy, Carl Linnaeus, who, in
Systema Naturae of 1735, included human beings in his scheme of
animal classification.[53]

Published at a time when there seemed no limit to European

empires' ability to subdue nature, the logic of natural selection was deployed to justify, rather than to challenge, racial hierarchy and European domination. In the end, there was little to separate Wallace's worldview from Kipling's. Wallace wrote:

> If the tide of colonization should be turned to New Guinea, there can be little doubt of the early extinction of the Papuan race. A warlike and energetic people, who will not submit to national slavery or domestic servitude, must disappear before the white man as surely as do the wolf and the tiger.[54]

Of all the technologies that fostered a sense of invulnerability in the minds of people with power, few were as important as the portable firearm. The magnified scale of both animal and human killing was no coincidence: both were in service of a project of conquest—of lands, and soils, and minerals, and energy—and people.

A late-century surge of competitive imperial conquest now unfolded around the world. The "steady pounding fire" of Maxim guns "produced a profound moral, as well as a devastating physical, effect," wrote an agent of Cecil Rhodes's British South Africa Company, describing the brutal British war against the Ndebele kingdom of Zimbabwe. No corner of the Earth was safe. In Southeast Asia, the French invaded Vietnam and Cambodia in the 1860s. In the 1870s, the British took control over most of Malaya through treaties with local leaders, negotiated at gunpoint. The British conquest of Burma was complete by 1885. The final phase of the Dutch conquest of Indonesia, which had started in the seventeenth century, led to a genocidal war in Aceh, lasting until 1908. And at the Berlin Conference of 1884–85, the European powers cynically divided the African continent among themselves, creating fifty colonies under the doctrine of "effective occupation." The last European power to acquire colonies, Germany, now waged brutal wars of extermination to suppress the Maji Maji rising in Tanzania, and against the Herero people in Namibia. British expansion in southern Africa brought ruin to independent kingdoms. The United States, too, embarked on an empire of conquest in the 1890s, annexing Hawai'i, Puerto Rico, Guam, Cuba, and the Philippines—all in 1898. Not to be outdone, a rapidly industrializing Japan sought its own regional empire: first, through the takeover of the island of Hokkaido, in 1869—seizing the lands and ruining the livelihoods of the Indigenous Ainu—and then, in 1910, annexing Korea.[55]

AGHAST AT THE UNDIGNIFIED spectacle of Chicago street vendors shouting for the attention of passersby, Kipling reached for an unexpected analogy: the salesmen reminded him of starving people at famine relief camps in India, he said; and he added that "I had sooner watch famine relief than the white man engaged in what he calls legitimate competition. The one I understand. The other makes me ill." Why, in a century of unprecedented abundance of grain, was Kipling so familiar with the image of famine camps in India? And what about them did he "understand," such that they disgusted him less than the voluble commerce of migrants to an industrial American city?[56]

Between 1876 and 1879, amid the global agricultural boom, the Deccan Plateau and parts of northwestern India suffered from famine as severe as any ever recorded. Simultaneously, famine took the lives of between nine and thirteen million people in the five northern provinces of China—Shandong, Zhili, Shanxi, Henan, and Shaanxi. Over the same grim years, famine affected Java, Egypt, and the northeast of Brazil. In the 1890s, famine again ravaged Siberia (in 1891–92) and central India (1896–97 and 1899–1900). In southeastern Africa, between 1895 and 1900, prolonged drought combined with a locust plague and cattle disease caused havoc. The Rinderpest panzootic spread through sub-Saharan Africa starting in 1889, when Italian colonial settlers introduced the disease to Eritrea. It crossed the Zambezi river in 1896, at a time of harvest failure, decimating herds already weakened by the drought-induced scarcity

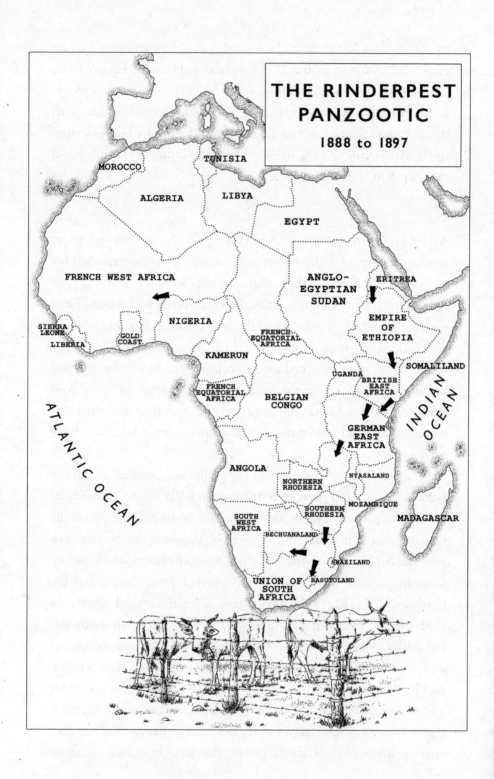

THE RINDERPEST
PANZOOTIC
1888 to 1897

MOROCCO
TUNISIA
ALGERIA
LIBYA
EGYPT
FRENCH WEST AFRICA
ANGLO-
EGYPTIAN
SUDAN
ERITREA
SIERRA
LEONE
GOLD
COAST
NIGERIA
EMPIRE
OF
ETHIOPIA
LIBERIA
FRENCH
EQUATORIAL
AFRICA
KAMERUN
SOMALILAND
UGANDA
BRITISH
EAST
AFRICA
FRENCH
EQUATORIAL
AFRICA
BELGIAN
CONGO
INDIAN
OCEAN
GERMAN
EAST
AFRICA
ATLANTIC OCEAN
ANGOLA
NYASALAND
NORTHERN
RHODESIA
SOUTHERN
RHODESIA
MOZAMBIQUE
SOUTH
WEST
AFRICA
MADAGASCAR
BECHUANALAND
SWAZILAND
UNION OF
SOUTH
AFRICA
BASUTOLAND

of pasture. Around the world, the death toll of the late-nineteenth-century famines was likely in the tens of millions but rarely in the official record do we learn the name of a single person who died.[57]

It would take almost another century for climate scientists to decipher the clues to discover that the intensive droughts, the trigger if not the root cause of the global famines of the 1870s and 1890s, were due to unusually powerful episodes of what came to be known as the El Niño Southern Oscillation. Signs of synchronicity were already clear at the time. The same telegraph lines that transmitted the price of wheat instantaneously around world furnished meteorologists with enough data to sense that the droughts of the 1870s and the 1890s were somehow connected: they just were not sure how. At the close of a century in which the wealthiest and most powerful nations in the world felt confident in their mastery over nature—including a newfound capacity both to preserve and to extinguish human and animal life—the famines brought a sign that the Earth and the atmosphere had many mysteries still in store.[58]

Every social fissure widened. The suffering was most acute for people without the security of land and family. Poor people without claims upon patrons or kin had nothing to fall back on—often they were elderly, or they lived with disabilities. Within families, women and children, and especially girls, fared worst in the desperate search for food. The destructive pattern of the 1870s' and 1890s' famines was comparable across continents. Drought provoked rapid rises in the price of grain just as agricultural laborers found themselves without work and without income. Their bodies weakened by hunger, most of the victims of famine died from infectious diseases—cholera, dysentery, and malaria thrived amid a maelstrom of ecological and social disruption. In India, famine coincided with an epidemic of bubonic plague that had arrived by ship in Bombay in 1896. The epidemic would persist for a decade, thriving on the large-scale migration sparked by famine, and spreading along the railway lines to rural areas. Plague claimed the lives of 12.5 million Indians, more than 80 percent of those who died worldwide in the epidemic.[59]

To anyone mesmerized by the march of progress, famines on such a scale ought no longer to have been possible by the 1870s. Steam had changed the world, after all. Midwestern farmers felt that the railroad had brought a miracle—"rail steadied the farmer's year like a hand laid upon the turbulent heel of heaven," Richard Powers writes in *Gain*, his epic novel of nineteenth-century American capitalism. The power of coal and new forms of preservation and storage promised to decouple food markets from seasonal fluctuations. In the 1860s, British engineer Edward Merrall predicted that the railway would consign India's famines to the past: episodes of scarcity in India were "not general, but partial and local," he observed, and so shortages in one area could "very easily be met by an increased supply of food from other and more fortunate districts." The railway promised to secure the driest parts of India by connecting them with places that "never want water."[60]

Boosters were blinkered by their own inflated ideas of how far the railways reached. However impressive the maps and statistics of railway expansion, large parts of the rural world were not near rail lines. This was deliberate and self-reinforcing: states and investors saw no reason to build railroads to regions of precarious rainfall or limited mineral wealth, or to places without obvious strategic value. On the road to Siberia, from Tyumen to Tomsk, Chekhov reported that one should not believe the official story that rail had tied Russia together: "this hideous, pock-marked strip of land, this foul smallpox of a road, is almost the sole artery linking Europe and Siberia!"[61]

A century after the famines, in the 1970s, India's National Sample Survey found that still 72 percent of all journeys in rural India were made on foot. In North China, the Taiping Rebellion and its aftermath wrecked the waterways and undermined the Qing state's capacity to buffer insecurity or to step in with relief. While the infrastructure of the nineteenth-century mitigated the vulnerability of well-endowed farmers to seasonal fluctuations, it deepened the environmental insecurity of those—a substantial majority of people in the world—who could not access that infrastructure, or didn't have the purchasing power to benefit from it. The interlocking of global grain markets only deepened the vulnerability of those locked out.[62]

Even if the railway had gone everywhere, the risk of famine would still have lurked in the inequalities of wealth and landholdings that deepened in the nineteenth century. Writing in 1851, C. H. Lushington, India's Railway Commissioner, had cautioned that the agrarian lands of the Ganges valley were "sublet in very small portions," and worked by farmers "without capital who live from hand to mouth." They lacked the surplus of grain that would make it "worth their while" to sell in distant markets connected by rail. Lushington worried that railway lines would cut through small holdings, dividing them further; he feared the "serious and tangible injuries" that would come from the way the railway built over natural floodplains. A quarter of a century later, his fears proved prescient. Even if markets "work like clockwork," one historian of famine observes, they can only "make the most of existing resources, given their initial distribution across a community." And grain markets never were like clockwork: the shape they took came from government decisions, which in turn responded to pressure from merchants and investors and also reflected deep-seated beliefs about whose lives were worth saving. For those without land or income, the only path to survival lay in being able to appeal to others' sense of obligation, charity, or mortal fear.[63]

The British government of India, wedded to the doctrine of free trade, pleaded helplessness before the brute forces of nature: life and death in India were governed by an unpredictable monsoon climate, they insisted. India was ineluctably a land of famine. This is what Kipling meant when he wrote that famine camps were a phenomenon he could "understand," though Chicago he could not. For a British elite that trumpeted its technological mastery over the world, backed by steam and liberalism, admitting that nature reigned supreme in India could have been discomfiting. But it proved convenient enough, for it displaced responsibility for starvation onto Indian society, which had apparently failed, unlike white Europeans, to transcend the dictates of nature.[64]

By the last quarter of the nineteenth century, the claim that famine was a "natural" disaster rung hollow. Even Florence Nightingale, so fêted by the British establishment as the nursing heroine of the Crimean war, admitted that "the land of India is not especially subject to famine." India's farmers were "industrious," she said, and they "compare favorably with other races in capacity to take care of themselves." Nightingale concluded that the famine showed that, as colonial rulers, "we do not care for the people of India." A *New York Times* correspondent went further, describing a "state of society in India whose only parallel in recent times was to be found in American slavery." Others turned to satire amid so much suffering. Villiyappa Pillai, court poet of the south Indian kingdom of Sivagangai, penned a narrative poem in which the lord Siva tells starving villagers that he, too, was powerless to act; instead, he advises them to seek redress from the local landowner. The famine was neither a divine punishment nor a natural disaster, the poem suggests: it was entirely man-made—even the gods were helpless before the political economy of the British Empire.[65]

The famines spurred a further migration of people—not pioneers or settlers, but refugees who took to the roads in search of bare subsistence. They were people whose rains and soils, whose landlords and governors, had betrayed them. In India, hungry people moved in the hundreds of thousands to British famine relief camps. They received a minimal cash wage and basic rations in exchange for the hard labor of extending India's infrastructure to benefit those already well off: they laid roads, built bridges, dug irrigation canals. For those in drought-affected parts of South India, the coffee and tea plantations of Ceylon (Sri Lanka), a short journey across the Palk Strait, provided jobs. Two decades later, in the regions of southern Africa worst affected by the fatal convergence of famine and cattle plague—rural Transvaal and Bechuanaland—whole villages were abandoned by people who moved in search of survival. South African mine owners would leap at the chance to exploit a new source of migrant labor.[66]

Migration was not an option open to all. Village officials in India, concerned with preserving order, tried to stop people from leaving. Recruiters at the emigration depots rejected as unfit for labor those whose bodies were weakened by what they had suffered. Writing of the desperate attempts of people to escape Sakhalin Island during the Russian famine of 1891–92, Chekhov observes how the landscape itself limits human choices:

> But among the obstacles which restrain people from escaping, the path to the sea is more formidable than the waves. It is not the crossing of, or even the fear of drowning in, this sea that is difficult and frightening, but the route to the sea itself. The impassable taiga, the mountains, the permanent damp, the mists, hunger, the lack of human beings, and in winter, the dreadful frosts and snow-storms—it is these things that are the true allies of surveillance.

When faced with climatic disaster, the impossibility of migration, for so many people, stands out as much as the scale of departure.[67]

Commenting on the Victorian famines, Alfred Russel Wallace, a committed socialist, began to question the power structures that had made his own work possible. Wallace argued that the oppressions of imperial rule were a blot on the amazing scientific advances of the nineteenth century. Two decades of recurrent famine in India, he wrote, were "a disgrace to our rule." "The final and absolute test of good government is the well-being and contentment of the people," Wallace insisted, "not the extent of empire or the abundance of the revenue and the trade. Tried by this test, how seldom have we succeeded. . . ."[68]

AT THE HEART OF imperial power, in the industrial cities of western Europe and North America, administrators and scholars and investors were sure, by the end of the nineteenth century, that they had mastered nothing less than life itself. Confident that natural processes were both predictable and controllable, wise administrators discerned statistical regularities across so many individual instances of birth, death, illness, and migration—from there, they could draw conclusions about the population as a whole. Over the course of the century, even at the level of individual and family experience, it became clear that something fundamental had changed. In 1800, in every part of the world, fewer than half of all people born survived to adulthood. By the end of the century, in western Europe, North America, and Japan, the average lifespan broke the barrier of forty years for the first time in human history; by 1900, life expectancy at birth in most parts of Europe was between forty-six and forty-eight years.[69]

This revolutionary change in the conditions of life was a cumulative result of the nineteenth century's environmental history. The span of Europeans' and Americans' lives expanded because swaths of prairie had been planted with wheat and hundreds of millions of cattle and pigs and poultry were killed for meat. Diets improved for all but the poorest people. So did the level of control that municipalities could exert over the ecology of infectious disease, particularly after English doctor, John Snow, discovered the waterborne transmission of cholera through an ingenious epidemiological study that pinpointed an outbreak to use of a single public tap on Broad Street in London's Soho district. Improvements in the conditions of life, such as the regulation and testing of municipal water supplies, were no benevolent gift from social elites—labor unions, socialist parties, and local associations fought hard for them, often in the face of neglect and indifference.[70]

But this is, at best, half of the story. The other half is that the nineteenth century birthed new weapons of mass destruction and witnessed an apogee of mass death in imperial wars and in the famines that swept Asia and Africa and Latin America. The environmental transformation of the nineteenth century world was built on the differential value of different human lives, depending on where they lived and on the color of their skin. The same changes in the land that brought undreamt-of security to those in the industrialized parts of the world brought suffering and vulnerability to those whose grip on the conditions of life, beginning with the use of the land they were born on, was torn from them. All the while, nestled in a history of exploitation—amid the abuse of people and animals and earth—lie the stories of Chekhovian heroes.

CHAPTER SIX

IMPOSSIBLE CITIES

When sixteen-year-old Abraham Kahn first arrived in Paris in 1876, his prospects were shaky. He came with the exodus of Alsatian Jews after their homeland's annexation by Prussia after the French defeat in the crushing war of 1870. The son of a cattle dealer, Kahn left for Paris with no more than a few family contacts and an appetite for self-improvement. By day Kahn, now known as Albert Kahn, found work as a clerk in the Goudchaux banking house. By night, he studied law and philosophy with a tutor just a year older, a man named Henri Bergson. Long after Bergson attained renown as a philosopher, he would remain a friend to Kahn.

Goudchaux was a small firm that specialized in mining ventures. Kahn proved a diligent worker at first, and then he grew bolder. After a visit to South Africa in the 1880s, Kahn ventured a risky investment in the diamond mines, just as they were being recast by industrial machinery. Kahn made a fortune from his privileged access to shares in Cecil Rhodes's De Beers company, which now controlled the diamond supply. When Kahn invested in the newly discovered gold mines of the Witwatersrand, the profits were even quicker to arrive, and he had the foresight to sell before mining shares crashed in the late 1890s. Kahn brokered French investment in Japanese railways, which began his lifelong love of Japan. He became a partner at the Goudchaux bank; before long he had turned it into Banque Albert Kahn.

Twenty years after leaving home, Albert Kahn was one of the

wealthiest men in Europe. In 1898, he bought a vast estate in wooded Boulogne, on the outskirts of Paris. Kahn preferred to avoid public attention, since he made his money in a France gripped by antisemitism following the false charges of spying leveled at army officer Louis Dreyfus, also an Alsatian Jew. For the rest of his life, the Boulogne estate would be Albert Kahn's salon and his solace.[1]

Kahn made his money from the global rush to turn nature into commodities. The centerpiece of his home in Boulogne was an exquisite garden. To create its illusion of natural beauty took immense labor: it was a "titanic project." Kahn's garden was a mosaic of seven ecological zones, a whole world in miniature: alpine, French, and English gardens; a rose orchard; a blue forest and marshes, a golden forest and meadow; and a Japanese garden, his true treasure. His gardeners dug ravines and streams, built walls, shifted mountains of soil: the rocks in Kahn's Vosges-style forest alone weighed six tons and arrived by rail from Gérardmer. From Japan came the "earth, rocks and various species"—and even an entire tea house, dismantled and carefully reassembled—to lend the garden a "character of sincerity."[2]

As a businessman, Kahn prospered from the ever-closer integration of the world by steam and telegraph. He clung to the liberal faith, already tattered in his day, that the global extension of commerce would bring an end to war. But Kahn saw trouble ahead. Alfred Nobel's invention of TNT—so vital to Kahn's ability to profit from the blasted rock of deep mines—found other uses. By the turn of the twentieth century, the French military had adapted Nobel's invention into cordite, and the British had developed melanite. These highly explosive compounds were loaded into the most lethal products of industrialization: semi-recoilless rapid-fire artillery that expended hundreds of shells every hour; machine guns that shot hundreds of rounds a minute. British and German shipyards competed to build bigger and deadlier naval vessels. Military commanders had gained unprecedented power to destroy life—all forms of life. These developments went hand in hand with more benign ones. An autodidact, and ultimately an optimist, Kahn believed in the power of education to break down barriers as jealous nationalisms swept Europe.[3]

Kahn's first foray into philanthropy began the year he bought the Boulogne estate. In 1898, Kahn launched his Les Bourses de Voyage Autour du Monde: a scheme of grants for travel, "to provide specially qualified teachers the opportunity to tune in with the life of the planet." The utopian aim of the scheme was described most eloquently by B. Ifor Evans, a grant recipient, as the "extension of vision, and with it of sympathy." Scholars were inducted into the Société Autour du Monde. They attended lavish Sunday lunches, where they met Kahn's literati friends: Auguste Rodin and Thomas Mann, Paul Valéry and H. G. Wells, Rudyard Kipling and Rabindranath Tagore. The cuisine was refined; the champagne flowed freely; Kahn himself, it is said, drank only milk.[4]

ALBERT KAHN'S PARIS FELT to many like the center of the world. To the forty million visitors to the Exposition Universelle in 1900, multitudes more than had ever visited any event anywhere, Paris was a city of the future, bathed in electric light. The Paris exhibition was like the world in microcosm, laid out in the shape of a flattened letter "A." One arm stretched from the Champs Elysées to Hôtel National des Invalides, the other from Champ de Mars to Trocadéro; a bend in the Seine marked the horizontal bar. Not everyone was impressed: "All the styles are confounded in a frightening merging of inimical periods," one visitor complained; he scorned the excess and the kitsch.[5]

In a new century, it seemed, anything was possible. Exhibitions of industrial machinery depicted innovation so restless the newest machines anticipated their own obsolescence: within years, they would lie "outmoded and, as if by magic, transformed into junk." The conquest of distance that had crowned the nineteenth century now attained a vertical dimension. Among the Exposition's most compelling attractions was the Cinéorama, which used a new technology—the motion picture—to depict a new angle of vision. Viewers were treated to a voyage by hot-air balloon, and they could look down upon the Earth from on high: the bird's-eye view, once accessible only to imaginative flights of fancy, unfolded before them frame by frame.[6]

The exhibition displayed a world at Europe's command, sanitized of the violence of conquest. The colonial exhibits depicted exotic and distant lands, their traditional glories faded. The centerpiece of the fair's colonial section was a plaster reproduction of a tower from the temple of Angkor—swallowed by the jungle, forgotten by time, rediscovered and lovingly restored by French explorers. Or so the story went. It hosted daily performances of Cambodian dance.[7]

The universal exhibition assembled diverse ecologies—just as Eurasian royal collections had done centuries earlier, but now for public consumption rather than private pleasure. This profusion of the things of the world delighted the audience: hardwoods from far-away forests fashioned model houses, petroleum from distant wells powered motor cars, Malayan and Brazilian rubber furnished bicycles with tires. The fruits of nature were hammered and remolded by technology; they could even be re-created, as "piles of artificial stone, artificial marble, imitation gold and iron, and simulated porcelain." On display in Paris were all the energies propelling the planet toward a new state of being. If there was a hint of the hidden cost of the twentieth century's cornucopia, it lay in the Trocadéro exhibition called Le Monde Souterrain: the World Underground. Dioramas depicted the latest mining technology piercing the Earth—drilling, drilling, drilling ever deeper.[8]

Underground scenes would not have been unfamiliar to a French audience. In the 1860s, Félix Nadar's photographs of Parisian sewers had depicted the subterranean city with startling clarity, embedding in viewers' minds a metropolis planned and ordered beneath as well as above ground. The same decade, Jules Verne's *Voyage au centre de la Terre* captured public attention with its world of volcanic tubes and buried oceans still home to creatures that had vanished from the

Earth's surface. The mining exhibition revealed the underground riches that now lay within reach.[9]

The highlight was an elaborate re-creation of the gold mines of the Transvaal, in South Africa. The poster advertising the Transvaal experience depicts the social order of the mines, without a hint of the brutality that really sustained it. In the top half of the picture, dressed in a suit and hat, the figure of a sole white man crouches down, his face lit by a lamp; beneath him, a mass of Black workers are bent low to their work, their faces barely visible. "The mine is deep, the rock is hard and sparkles under the tool," wrote Louis Rousselet in his exhibition guide, and "all the hard work is done by the Negro without complaining." Rousselet reached straight for the argument the mine owners used to pay Africans less—the African worker, he declared, thinks "only of returning as soon as possible to his tribe . . . [with] a hoard large enough to be considered a chief." The Black worker has a "smiling and placid air," Rousselet noted, in contrast with the white manager, brow furrowed, who alone worries whether the quality of the ore will suffice, whether there is enough of it, whether profits would meet expectations. "After this long journey," Rousselet promises, "we find ourselves dazzled near the Transvaal pavilion where we can witness the various manipulations of the gold ore that we have seen extracted"; here lay the true "wonders of the Underground World." Visitors emerged from the exhibition stunned.[10]

THE SOUTH AFRICAN POLITICAL activist R. V. Selope Thema saw the world-historical significance of the city on the veld: the establishment of Johannesburg, he wrote, was "a turning point in the history not only of southern Africa but of the whole continent." We could go further: it was a turning point, too, in the environmental history of the world. Everything changed with the discovery of a reef of rock only inches thick that ran from Randfontein to Modderfontein, bearing gold amid white quartz pebbles, silica, sand, and pyrite. The seam was first claimed by two men named Harrison and Walker in 1886.[11]

Within a decade of Harrison's and Walker's discovery, a quarter of the world's gold came from the Witwatersrand—a scarp above the high plains of South Africa, crossed by north-flowing rivers that give the region its Afrikaans name, "Ridge of High Waters." In the 140 years since then, the region has produced around 40 percent of all the gold ever mined on Earth. For a decade either side of 1900, Johannesburg was probably the fastest-growing city in the world: forty thousand people lived there in 1892, one hundred thousand by 1904 and more than double that by 1911. It was as if the city had emerged from nowhere—or from underground.[12]

If the hot-air balloon ride at the Paris exhibition's Cinéorama had floated over Johannesburg, viewers would have seen a city rise like an island amid the highveld's tall red grasses: a city growing out from a 40-mile ribbon of mines in a diagonal line following the gold seam. The Victorian explorer, Henry Stanley, saw it first from a train window: "a lengthy line of chimney stacks, engine houses, tall wooden frames supporting the headgear, stampmills with clusters of sheds, huts and offices." Approaching the mines, the floating camera may have lingered over the brittle red and ochre crust of the dry earth, broken and cratered, its flatness punctuated by paler yellow hills made of pulverized rock—shapeshifting hills, their fine dust carried on the wind, and also "redeemed" hills, now stabilized with grass and made to seem natural. Beneath the surface lay levels upon levels of interlocking shafts and passages and tunnels.[13]

To extract gold from the impure deposits of the Rand took more work, and cost more money, than it had in the gold rushes of Australia or California earlier in the nineteenth century. To extract profit from unyielding rock, mine owners suppressed wages. They had a ready model in the racially segregated mining compounds of Kimberley, in the northern Cape province of South Africa, where diamonds had been discovered in the 1860s. By the end of the nineteenth century, the goldmines employed close to 93,000 workers.

Just over 10,000 of them were white: they came from across South Africa, but also from Britain and the United States, Germany and Canada. They monopolized the best jobs. Many brought skills they had gained working in the factories of industrial cities: they worked as boilermakers, electricians, wire-splicers, steam drivers, machine rock-drillers, and engineers. The hardest work, the work most dangerous and least compensated, was done by Africans. They made up 90 percent of the workforce. The Chamber of Mines was explicit about how much depended on Black labor: "The continuance and expansion of the mines, and prosperity, contentment and existence of the white population depend, in a large measure, on an adequate supplementary supply of cheap labour through the coloured races."[14]

Most of the African workers on the goldmines were migrants. They came from across southern Africa. Many moved back and forth between the mines and their rural homes, bridging the always-on rhythm of industrial mining with the seasonality of the harvest. Before long, most workers on the Rand came from Mozambique— they were a mixture of Tsonga and Nguni speakers, known on the mines as Shangaan, from the name of their nineteenth-century ruler, Soshangana (c. 1780–1858). Of all the migrant communities on the mines, Shangaan workers were the most exploited, the most surveilled, the longest serving, and the least endowed with margins of choice. The Portuguese conquered southern Mozambique in 1895 and made life for local people even worse. The colonizers demanded a hut tax in cash and extorted forced labor. The Witwatersrand Native Labour Association contracted with the Portuguese colonial authorities for the exclusive right to recruit labor from south of the Save River. Migrant workers traveled under cover of darkness packed onto freight trains.[15]

Gold heightened the strategic value of South Africa to the British Empire. The struggle to control that mineral wealth provoked the South African War of 1899–1902, in which British imperial forces defeated the two independent Afrikaner republics, Transvaal and the Orange Free State, established by the descendants of early Dutch settlers as they moved inland and encroached further on African territory. It was a brutal conflict. Afrikaner civilians were placed in concentration camps, among the first instances of this new weapon of war. Their farms were destroyed.

The British victory was a triumph for mine owners and investors. Their long-held dream of ever-cheaper labor came to fruition. Pass laws tied African migrant workers more tightly to their employers, restrained their freedom of movement, and cut their wages. The South African war had pitted two groups of white settlers—British and Afrikaners—against one another, and many Black leaders supported the British in the hope that they would be rewarded for their loyalty in a postwar settlement. The opposite happened: Africans' rights were sacrificed to a race-based rapprochement between the English and the Afrikaners, culminating in the Union of South Africa in 1910.

When mines resumed production after the war, their demand for workers grew insatiable. Worried that they could not recruit enough Africans from the surrounding region—Africans who had heard stories of the wretched conditions on the mines, and who preferred to retain their autonomy—mine owners turned, quite unexpectedly, to China. Between 1904 and 1907, 63,296 Chinese workers traveled to South Africa to work on the mines, recruited directly by the miners' association. The Chinese workers were stricken by beriberi, a debilitating disease of vitamin deficiency, on the voyage out. When they arrived, they were corralled into trains headed to the mines that bound Chinese workers with contracts of indenture. The experiment was hardly a success: no fewer than nineteen thousand of the workers deserted their employers; more than three thousand died of exhaustion or injury or assault. Thousands more participated in riots, protests, and go-slows. Humanitarian campaigners in both Britain and China cried foul, called the indentures a form of disguised slavery. White miners, for their part, screamed about being undercut by the "Yellow Peril." The scheme was quickly abandoned. Mine owners had no trouble hiring workers from nearer by, however harsh the work on offer. The mines of the Witwatersrand employed 210,000 African workers by 1915, a number that had almost trebled in twelve years.[16]

How long could it all last? A newspaper published in faraway Warragul, Victoria—a region of Australia that had lived through the rise and fall of its own mines—struck a note of caution: once the Witwatersrand had "given up its treasures," the editors thought, Johannesburg would "vanish as rapidly as [it] sprang into existence and fame."[17]

JOHANNESBURG DID NOT VANISH. The rand's treasures seemed inexhaustible. With the gold mines South Africa experienced its "first" and "second" industrial revolutions simultaneously: the first, a process of steam-powered mechanization, had begun in Britain a century earlier; the second was a late-nineteenth-century spurt in chemical and electrical industries led by the United States and Germany, propelled by the expansion in world trade by steamship and railway. Now a panoply of both industrial and chemical technologies assaulted the grudging rock of the Witwatersrand. One observer noted the "immense power utilised on the fields and the large consumption of fuel" by winding engines and steam drills, water pumps and generators to illuminate the dark recesses underground. Engineering workshops made machine tools on site, filled with the cacophony of "ordinary lathes, screw-cutting lathes," and machines for "shaping, drilling, slotting, planing, shearing." Smiths' vast workshops sharpened thousands of drills a day, which passed to the hands of African workers.[18]

The mines of the Rand were at the forefront of developments in chemical engineering. They harnessed the invention of Glaswegian chemist John MacArthur and the pharmacist brothers William and Robert Forrest, who discovered in 1887 that gold could be leached from finely ground ore with a solution of potassium cyanide. The MacArthur-Forrest process was put to work on the Rand in 1893. It unleashed a torrent of gold, as output increased tenfold—and over the century to follow it would leave a trail of toxic pollution. Three years later, the Nobel Company of Sweden opened a factory at Modderfontein to produce dynamite, an explosive made of nitroglycerin, to blast down to new depths.[19]

Along with coal and explosives and steel, the mines devoured wood. Steamships brought Oregon pitch pine, cut from the Cascades, to make headgears, battery frames, and rock-houses. Mine engineers found "native timbers" wanting, but still cut acres of trees for mining poles, tramcar sleepers, and fences: they cut down camel thorn and sweet thorn and knob thorn; the very smell of the air changed as they felled sneeze-wood and stink-wood. Mine owners planted whole forests of blue gums, transplanted from southeastern Australia: finding the local ecology "inferior," settlers simply replaced it with an imported nature of their own design.[20]

African workers on the Rand labored deeper underground than anybody else on Earth. Their daily reality resembled the subterranean dystopia of early science fiction. Each shift began by clearing the previous day's debris, generated by the sheer force of blasting rock. The workers hammered steel into the rock face to drill holes for dynamite charges. Each miner had a minimum depth to drill; if he failed, he received a "loafing" ticket, and not a cent for the day's work. After 1910, the miners used machine drills, which created an enormous quantity of atmospheric dust in hot, airless conditions. The average depth of the mines was 800 feet in 1889, by 1916 they reached on average 1,600 feet below ground. The deeper the miners worked, the greater the risks they faced—deeper shafts were harder to ventilate. Water drills moistened the air to dissipate the dust but in turn made the shafts unbearably humid.[21]

At the end of their shifts, the miners waited. They waited sometimes for hours for the cage lift to bring them back to the open air. They waited until all the ore—more precious to the mine owners than the miners' lives—had been removed. In shallower mines, tired of waiting, workers sometimes clambered up to the surface. A

medical officer described the condition of the youngest minework-
ers after the ascent: "staggering, breathing rapidly and with obvious
difficulty, nostrils expanded, pupils dilated and pulse very rapid."[22]

The social and atmospheric circumstances of deep mining eviscer-
ated the bodies of workers. They collapsed from heat stroke. They
died of exhaustion. They died of malnutrition. Matebo Ramapiai,
a Basuto worker on the gold mines of Henry Nourse and Company, left Johannesburg in 1902 to return home to Lesotho. He felt
ill when he boarded the train and felt worse on the journey. When
the train pulled into Bloemfontein station, Matebo was too weak to
get off the train. His three traveling companions lifted him off: "we
laid him down at the corner of the wire fence near the goods shed,"
they said, where he died the same afternoon. Matebo had been ill-
fed and ill-treated, the coroner's inquiry found, and he was suffering
from scurvy.[23]

While they worked, tiny bits of silica lodged in the miners' lungs.
Fibrous tissue would form to repair the scars left by shards of blasted
rock, and it became difficult for the miners to breathe. Silicosis is a
disease created by the dusty environment of the mines. Elsewhere it
would be generated by factories and construction sites. And under
close, humid conditions underground, the tuberculosis bacteria—
introduced to South Africa by Europeans—found a place to thrive.
The incidence of tuberculosis on the mines jumped from 4.03 to 6.22
per 1,000 in just a few years. The environmental history of gold left
its imprint on the history of the human body: on individual human
bodies, and on the collective body of miners.[24]

The ruins of the miners' lungs mirrored the ruins of the veld.

AT THE END OF each day, workers returned to dormitories that
housed up to four thousand men each. The Swiss missionary Henri
Junod, who visited in the early twentieth century, described the
mine compounds as "the most complete triumph of modern indus-
trialism." He felt horror at "the dark dormitories with their dark

stalactites of dirty old clothes that hung everywhere, the treeless courtyard, the yards cluttered with old scrap-iron." Junod's fellow missionary, Charles Bourquin, wondered "how our blacks can leave their forests, their lakes, their lovely rivers, to live for perhaps one, two, three, four years under these horrible conditions." Missionaries condemned the deracination and anomie of life on the mines. Compounds were, in the eyes of white social reformers, a place of "environmentally determined demoralisation," where the ugliness and risk of the built environment undermined the possibility of an ethical life.[25]

On the mines and in the compounds, Black workers fought for the right to breathe. The mine owners of the Rand made the same calculations that shipowners had made two centuries earlier as they outfitted vessels to transport enslaved Africans: How much air did a person need? What was the minimum "air space" they could get away with providing a human being? The question arose in connection with the scheme to bring Chinese workers to the Rand. Given the plan's sensitivity in relation to humanitarian campaigners at home—and in relation to the racial politics of the white-settler colonies in the British Empire, which clamored to pass anti-Chinese immigration laws—the mine owners had to promise that Chinese migrant workers would be treated humanely, and that they were temporary. But they confronted a problem.

A spokesman for the vast Rand Mines complained: "if 300 cubic feet of air space has to be provided in the compound for the Chinese, the kaffirs will soon have to be treated in the same manner, with the result that every mine on the Rand will be put to enormous expenditure in providing additional compound accommodation." He estimated it would cost one and a quarter million pounds to do so—admitting, with this calculation, that African workers lived with far less than even the meager minima of "air space" that European industrial medicine had begun to codify. Once again, the mine owners fell back on spurious claims about innate racial habits. African workers wouldn't *want* more air space, they said, since "it is a well-known fact that the natives prefer a crowded room, and, however much air space is provided, insist upon huddling together."[26]

THE SUFFERING OF AFRICAN miners upheld the global economic system. The rock and soil of the highveld were the substance on which international commerce rested. Week after week, seventy-five-pound bars of gold from the Rand arrived in London. They passed straight into the hands of the famous refiners—Johnson, Matthey and Raphael, and the Rothschild Mint and Refinery—who fashioned them into standard ounce bars of 22-carat pure gold and 2-carat copper alloy: Cape Bars, they were called. Every Monday morning, commodity brokers sold them on the London bullion market, the most active in the world. London was also where the Rand mining houses arranged a host of financial services, including insurance. This steady flow of South African gold shored up London's position at heart of the global economy.[27]

Witwatersrand gold came to market just as the world economy embraced a single monetary system based on the gold standard. An expanding universe of domestic paper money—bank notes, checks, bills of exchange—was convertible to gold on demand in most countries. The Bank of England's gold reserves, in turn, backed the proliferation of international financial transactions. To this system the supply of South African gold was pivotal, even if much of it did not end up in London: the mere knowledge that the Rand's mines would always produce more gave people confidence in convertibility. "England has no need of a mountain of gold," wrote Sir Hartley Withers, editor of *The Economist*, in 1909: "Our banking system is happy in the possession of other reserves besides its metal"—the "psychological reserve," of confidence itself, was most vital. Over the decades from 1880 to 1914, supplies of South African gold sustained an expansion in the global money supply. The brutalization of South Africa's landscape, and South African society, made possible many other assaults on forests and rivers and animals around the world.²⁸

The growth of Johannesburg around the mines of the Rand tightened the knot binding social inequality (here in the form of white supremacy), technologies of destruction (Maxim guns to kill, dynamite to blast rock), and the capacity to exploit nature for profit (expanding human control into the deep Earth). Proconsuls and governors and investors turned mineral wealth into imperial power. The same lust for gold that had propelled Iberian adventurers to harness the Atlantic winds now brought prospectors to the highveld.

Environmental change had long been driven by human desire for precious objects; now the miners' capacity to move earth had multiplied using steam drills and blast furnaces and dynamite charges. Ready access to gold meant control of an economic system that was integrated by railroads and steamships, more restless than ever before in its search for new frontiers of profit.

IF JOHANNESBURG WAS THE "second greatest city after Paris"—the ironic title of an animated film about the brutality of mining capitalism by the South African artist William Kentridge— then Baku, on the edge of the Caspian Sea, was "commercially and ethnologically the Johannesburg of Russia." Baku's wealth was not embedded in ore: it oozed from the earth as a dark, viscous slime so valuable that it came to be known as "black gold." Like Johannesburg, Baku was a magnet for ambitious or desperate people from around the world: prospectors and engineers, diggers and cart-drivers, migrant workers and fugitives. The city's population was fifteen times larger in 1900 than it was in 1870. By 1901, half of all the world's petroleum came from Baku's oil wells, crammed into just a few square miles in the Bibi-Eilat and Balakhani-Saboonchi-Ramani fields.²⁹

Baku, like Johannesburg, grew in defiance of its environment. In the 1870s, British traveler and petroleum booster Charles Marvin wrote: "As the place develops its disadvantages—the heat, dust, absence of good water, rainlessness and want of vegetation—will largely be mitigated." Thirty years later another British oil journalist, J. D. Henry, editor of the industry publication *Petroleum News*, thought Marvin's prediction had come to pass: "Baku is greater than any other oil city in the world. If oil is king, Baku is its throne."[30]

For centuries, the area around Baku had been known to travelers as the place of "eternal flame." Spontaneous eruptions of oil from underground, "gushers," spouted from the soil when deposits of natural gas ignited periodically. From ancient times, their oil was valued as an illuminant, a heating fuel, and a lubricant. Marco Polo probably had Baku in mind when he wrote: "Near the Georgian border there is a spring from which gushes a stream of oil in such abundance that a hundred ships may load there at once." And long before it was oil's "throne," Baku was a site of worship. The Baku Ateshgah was built sometime in the seventeenth or eighteenth century, though it is possible that an earlier structure stood on the site centuries before that. The temple was devoted to the worship of fire, melding Zoroastrian, Hindu, and Sikh traditions. It sat atop a spring of natural gas that fed its flames day and night so that a German traveler described it as looking like a fairy castle. The British trader George Forster noticed that the temple had been built by "a society of Moultan Hindus, which has long been established in Baku [and] contributes largely to the circulation of its commerce."[31]

Fought over by the Russians and the Persians for more than a century, Baku came fully under Russian control under the Treaty of Gulistan in 1813. The Russian Empire made precocious use of Baku's oil. In 1823, they built the world's first paraffin factory in Baku. They dug the first oil well in 1846, more than a decade before the discovery of oil in Pennsylvania. But as American oil came onto the market, Baku was at a disadvantage: American oil was lighter and made better kerosene for lamps; it was easier to transport over long distances. Baku oil merchants struggled against climate: the

Volga and the Caspian Sea lay part frozen for half the year, and all the while American oil arrived on schedule at Saint Petersburg.

And then, in the 1870s, two things changed: the Tsarist state gave up its monopoly over Baku's oil fields, opening them up to private bidders. And the barons of Baku discovered a new use of oil, as fuel for transportation—a use so revolutionary that it would leave a mark on the atmospheric chemistry of Earth.

In the early years, Baku's oil fields were a free-for-all. Charles Marvin described the oil fields in 1883: "In place of highways are innumerable paths and tracks, and these seam the oil-soddened surface in every direction, and with a network of pipe-lines, petroleum channels, and ponds and lakes of oil, [they] utterly bewilder the stranger." By that time, prospectors had struck more than four hundred wells; by the early twentieth century, close to two thousand wells were in operation. Oil suffused the city's atmosphere: "over the town hangs a dense black cloud of smoke, and long before you reach it you perceive the all-pervading smell of oil, which you will breathe everywhere and taste in everything."[32]

ONE FAMILY PLAYED A pivotal role in Baku's rise: a famous family of arms manufacturers from Sweden. The Nobel family enterprise had started in the early nineteenth century. A born tinkerer with a taste for designing weapons, the patriarch, Immanuel Nobel, scented opportunity in Russia after being rebuffed by the Swedish military. He moved his business to Saint Petersburg in the 1830s, and set up a factory for the manufacture of artillery shells, mortars, and underwater mines. Immanuel's factory thrived for a time, and then failed under the weight of debts and unpaid orders. Immanuel's son Ludvig, possessed of a fierce work ethic, tried again: he established the Machine-Building Factory Ludvig Nobel in the 1860s, which manufactured gun carriages and ammunition shells made from an iron-carbon alloy known as chilled cast-iron. The strong axles and wheel rings of gun carriages led to a lucrative byproduct for civilian use, marketed and sold around the world as Nobel wheels. They were popular because they could withstand the harshest environments: "bogs, quagmires, spring thaws, rocks, potholes—these were the testing grounds of the Nobel wheel."[33]

A second brother, Alfred, remained in Sweden. Alfred Nobel invented dynamite, which expanded the destructive power people could wield over rock—including the gold-bearing rock of the Witwatersrand—and over enemy armies. It was the oldest brother, Robert, who struggled to establish himself. His ventures in brick-making and trade failed. Disappointed and embittered, he accepted Ludvig's offer of a job. In 1873, Robert first traveled to Baku in search of supplies of walnut hardwoods for the Machine-Building Factory. What he found there was more lucrative than timber.[34]

Robert inaugurated the Petroleum Production Company Nobel Brothers (Branobel) in Baku in 1877. To move their product, the Nobels built the world's first oil pipeline, completed at a cost of $50,000, and defended by armed Cossack guards against the protests of irate drivers of the *abras*—the mule-drawn carts traditionally used to haul barrels of oil. That same year, the Nobels brought into service the world's first oceangoing oil tanker, built by Lindholmen-Motala in Sweden to Ludvig's exacting specifications. It was called *Zoroaster*, in a gesture of respect to the awesome power of fire. The ship carried 21 watertight iron tanks and held 250 tons of cargo. Its successor tankers were named *Buddha* and *Nordenskjöld*, *Brahma* and *Socrates*. The quest for oil, it seemed, was a new path to enlightenment.[35]

The Nobels visited Pennsylvania to study Standard Oil's steam-powered drills. Over the next twenty-five years, Nobel Brothers opened five hundred wells in Baku, which produced 150 million barrels of oil. Many of the twelve thousand employees of the Nobel Company lived in a planned settlement that anticipated the company towns of the twentieth century. It was furnished with schools and libraries and a walled garden that grew on soil imported from 160 kilometers away. Its water came from the Volga, brought by

An engraving from the *Illustrated London News*, July 3, 1886,
showing the Nobel Brothers oil well at Baku.

Nobel tankers as ballast on their return journeys after they had
unloaded their precious cargo of oil. The workers' colony was called
Villa Petrolea.[36]

Engineers Henri Neuburger and Henri Noalhat wrote a rapturous
account of Baku in 1900. Viewing the world with a complacent sense
of European superiority, they described Baku as "an advanced post
of our old European civilisation" in "an almost barbarous country."
They reveled in its skyline of "innumerable factory chimneys [from]
which shoot up to heaven thick clouds of smoke" and its glorious
waterfront "lined with grandiose buildings [and] hotels of the first
rank." Every evening the city shone "with the glare of the electric
lamp." Neuburger and Noalhat saw a city that had been wrought
from emptiness—from the "solitudes of oriental Armenia." The triumph of technology and industry over nature, the emergence of this
impossible city, was nothing less than "a conquest over barbarism."[37]

Baku's "hotels of the first rank" were full of financiers and engineers. The global interests involved in Baku's oil industry by the start
of the twentieth century formed a jumble of subsidiaries and holding companies and cross-investments. The giants were Nobel and

the Russian General Oil Corporation, but Shell and the Oil Financial Corporation had a growing presence. They bought interlocking stakes in smaller firms: the Baku Oil Society, Mirzoev Brothers, the Caspian Black Sea Company. The French Rothschilds plowed money into the Transcaucasian Railway linking Baku to the Black Sea port of Batumi. Demand for Baku oil surged after the Russian Caspian Fleet and the Transcaucasian Railway converted their engines from coal to fuel oil. In the 1890s, the rest of the Russian Navy also switched its fleet to oil-burning engines, though as a precaution they used hybrid engines that could go back to coal. The city's waterfront was clogged with barges: "the night scene at Baku, the range of lights, as they rise on the hills, skirt the promenade, light up the wharves, landing piers, and passenger steamers, is one of exceptional beauty." But still, in an age of tankers and pipelines, older ways of moving oil proved durable—oil was "carried on camels into the inner-most parts of the Asian continent, and on yaks into the wild regions of the Himalayas."[38]

A significant portion of the oil industry of Baku always remained in local hands. Foremost among the local oil barons was Haji Zeynalabdin Taghiyev (c. 1823–1924). The son of a bootmaker, Taghiyev apprenticed himself to a bricklayer at the age of six. He trained as a mason and stonecutter. He made a modest living until he purchased a gusher on a plot of land in Bibi Eibat—and promptly he became a millionaire. Renowned as a civic leader, Taghiyev reshaped the city. His bounty funded the first Azerbaijani theater, the first school for Muslim girls, and Baku's first Russian-language newspaper, *Kaspii*, all of which Taghiyev founded. He was, appropriately, the first person in the city to own a motorcar. Oil was a ticket to the modern world.

By the early twentieth century, Baku's population of two hundred thousand came from "nearly all European nations, Central Asia, Asia Minor, Persia, Arabia, and even Abyssinia." The city was gripped by newspaper fever: sixty Russian and Azerbaijani-language newspapers emerged in the decade after 1905; many of them folded just as quickly. New political institutions navigated the untold opportunities and the social risks of the oil boom. The Muslim Social Democratic Party (Humma) and Muslim Union (Ittifaq al-Muslimin) debated religious reform in an age of plenty. In Baku's public sphere, a clamor of political ideologies debated one another—"a tapestry of French democracy, Russian and German federalism, Russian liberalism, Tatar Pan-Turkism, Young Turk radicalism, Iranian constitutionalism, and European socialism." They each held out contending visions of freedom—all premised on endless oil.[39]

Oil workers labored long hours for little gain. Baku became a hive for radical politics. From an unassuming basement cellar in the old Tatar quarter of the city, a small band of Communist party workers churned the printing presses of Russia's secret headquarters for the production and distribution of printed propaganda, hidden from the Tsarist secret police. The very infrastructure that exported Baku's oil by train and tanker now doubled as a route for subversive ideas moved by couriers carrying concealed packages. In the spring of 1903 Baku's oil workers came out on strike. That summer, in solidarity, the city's workers staged a general strike. State security forces crushed the protests. Again, the following year, oil workers laid down their tools in a coordinated work stoppage. One of their leaders was a Georgian named Iosif Dzhugashvili—a man soon to be known to the world as Stalin.[40]

BAKU LACKED THE UNBREAKABLE barriers of race that structured the South African goldmines. But in a febrile atmosphere of sudden wealth and visible inequality, distinctions of language, ethnicity, and religion grew sharper, and so too did competition over jobs, housing, and the use of public space. In 1905, the embers of social division were rekindled by the political ferment and mass public demonstrations against the Tsarist regime that came to be known as the First Russian Revolution. Baku's Armenian and Azerbaijani communities, longstanding neighbors, turned on each other;

both sides claimed provocation by the other, as street fights spiraled into communal violence. Bands of angry men torched the oil installations. Italian traveler Luigi Villari witnessed the scene. He saw "great sheets of iron torn to shreds as though they had been paper, broken machinery, blackened beams, fragments of cogged wheels, pistons, burst boilers, miles of steel wire ropes."[41]

Industrial machinery suddenly seemed fragile; whole infrastructures collapsed overnight. In every direction, Villari wrote, "streams of thick oozing naphtha flowed down to channels, or formed slimy pools of dull greenish liquid; the whole atmosphere was charged with the smell of oil." Twenty years earlier, the scent of oil had been a beacon of prosperity. Now it marked the stench of ruins. Henry described the oilfield fires of 1905 as "the most appalling the world has ever known, or probably ever will know."[42]

Baku's rise and catastrophic fall showed how fragile a boom founded on buried gifts could be: how quickly things could fall apart when the social pressure that accompanied rapid development caused an explosion. Machines turned to scrap; oil wells burned; all that remained were relics. Baku would boom again, in the 1960s and in the 1990s, but never again would it be the world's oil metropolis. In an era of extractive capitalism, frontiers closed fast. Investors packed up and left, leaving the ground hollowed out and poisoned.

ENSCONCED IN THE SPLENDOR of his Boulogne garden, Albert Kahn was worried. Though he had made a fortune from the extractive boom of the early twentieth century, he felt that the world was changing faster than he could fathom. As he prepared for a round-the-world business trip in 1908, to the United States and Japan, Kahn had an idea. He was drawn to the power of a creative innovation, the color photograph, to document how the world was being reshaped, for good and ill, by infrastructure and technology. Sensing a hidden gift for observation, Kahn encouraged his young chauffeur, Alfred Dutertre, to take up photography and bought him a Verascope camera. "Kiddo, I'll be taking you on a big journey soon," Kahn announced, to Dutertre's surprise, in October 1908. In his diary, Dutertre recalled that Kahn sent him out with an extravagant shopping list:

> *a second Verascope camera*
> *A 'Pathé' film camera*
> *a wax cylinder phonograph, as well as:*
> *4,000 Lumière glass plates for taking photographs*
>   *in black-and-white*
> *a few hundred autochrome plates for color photographs*
> *about 3,000 meters of film stock for cinematic recording*
> *a few hundred wax cylinders for sound recording*

Kahn had Dutertre trained by the very best: he took film recording lessons at the Pathé studios. A month later, Kahn said: "Kiddo, take two days off to go and say goodbye to your parents because we will be leaving for Japan, starting a world trip on Friday, November 13."[43]

Soon after he returned from Japan, Kahn dreamt up a photographic project far more encompassing, even outlandish—no less than a visual archive of the whole planet. Kahn's confidant, geologist Emmanuel Jaquin de Margerie, described the ambition behind it: "While there is still time, Mr Kahn was wanting to create what he called the Archives de la Planète, that is, to put into effect a sort of photographic inventory of the surface of the globe as inhabited and developed by Man at the beginning of the twentieth century."[44]

The Archives de la Planète would be a photographic record of the diversity of human cultures and ecologies. The archive fed on a sense of urgency ("while there is still time") to capture the world on the threshold of irreversible change. For all that we believe that ours is the first generation to live with the awareness that human actions are changing the fabric of the planet, the Kahn archive was an early effort to grapple with just that problem. As Kahn put it, his archive would "fix once and for all, the look, practice, and modes of human activity whose fatal disappearance is just a question of time." Kahn's archive was haunted by the imminence of loss.[45]

Kahn chose as director of the archive Jean Brunhes, professor at the University of Fribourg. Brunhes, protégé of the geographer Paul Vidal de la Blanche, had pioneered a new approach to understanding the reciprocal relationship between human societies and the environment. He rejected the idea that geography was destiny, an idea that had dominated nineteenth-century European and American thought. Brunhes and his students saw the dance of culture and nature as perpetual, and infinitely mutable. They emphasized the importance of locality, captured in the French term "milieu"—so difficult to translate that it moved directly into English.

Above all, Brunhes shared Kahn's enthusiasm for new technologies of vision. He saw special power in the aerial view. Introducing his sweeping *La Geographie Humaine* in 1910, Brunhes appealed to his readers' visual imagination—an imagination opened by exposure to entertainments like the Cinéorama of the Paris exhibition:

> Let us go up some hundreds of yards above the earth in a balloon or an aeroplane, somewhat after the fashion envisaged by the Swiss geologist Suess at the beginning of his great book, *The Face of the Earth*. Then, ridding our mind of all knowledge of man, let us try to see and note the essential facts of human geography with the same eyes and in the same way as we discover and disentangle the morphological, topographical, and hydrographic features of the earth's surface. From this imaginary vantage-point what shall we see? Or, better still, what are the human facts that a photographic plate would register just as well as the retina of the eye?

Brunhes invoked the power of "a general glance over the earth," to unveil "an entirely new and very abundant set of surface phenomena: there are towns and railways, cultivated fields and quarries, canals and irrigation tanks and salt-pans; and here and there, in particular,

there are masses of groups, of varying density, of human beings."
Brunhes conveys ambivalence about the scale of human impact upon
the Earth. Human settlements are found just "here and there," insig-
nificant in relation to the expanse of nature untouched by human
hands; but they form "masses of groups," and their presence, sculpt-
ing the planet, merits attention "in particular."[46]

Brunhes shared with Kahn a sense of living through momentous
change. His own vision for the archive was to "establish a dossier
of humanity seen in the midst of life," at a "unique moment" when
"we are witnessing a kind of 'moulting,' an economic, geographic,
and historic transformation of unprecedented proportions." Kahn
had a wistful sense of "fatal disappearance"; Brunhes, by likening
global change to "moulting," suggested it was a natural process—
the premodern world was sloughing off its skin so that the modern
could emerge.[47]

Brunhes's politics held their share of contradictions. He believed
that a "glance over the earth" could slice through cultural differences
and political boundaries; he believed that all cultures were changing
and so too were the ecologies sustaining them. He was also close to
the "colonial" faction in French politics: believers in the "civilizing
mission" in Asia and Africa, tethered to their faith in European cultural and racial supremacy and, in Brunhes's case, to the missionary
zeal of Social Catholicism.

From 1909 to 1931, Kahn's Archives de la Planète sent photographers to fifty countries—all of them men, except for Madeleine
Mignon and Marguerite Mespoulet, who had received travel grants
from Kahn's foundation. Together, they took the world's largest
collection of seventy-two thousand autochromes, using a technology invented by the brothers Louis and Auguste Lumière, and first
demonstrated at the Paris offices of the periodical *l'Illustration* in
1907. The Lumières' technique was to spread 140 million particles
of potato starch, each 0.01 millimeters in diameter, on glass plates
covered in sticky varnish. The granules were dyed red-orange,
green, and violet, interspersed with lampblack and rolled under high

pressure. Light from the camera lens passed through the dyed grains before reaching the photographic emulsion of gelatin silver-bromide or silver iodide.[48]

The Kahn archive assembled a kaleidoscopic portrait of the world—its effect came from aggregation. But the images were synchronous: the photographers visited each site once, and often stayed only for a short time before moving on. The archive tried to convey temporal change through spatial contrast; its photographs juxtaposed "pre-modern" and modern parts of the world as if they were on a continuum, with Mongolia on one end and New York City on the other—as if the parts of the world least affected by technological change were ghosts of what the industrial world once was, and as if their own future transformation was inevitable, ordained by Progress. Railways cut through prairie; dams tear through forests; deep shaft mines strip the Earth. The inventory captures a moment in the long human struggle to harness and control the rest of nature, a moment when the advantage seemed to lie decisively with technology.

In 1910, Kahn traveled to Norway: he went in pursuit of an investment as well as a photographic opportunity. Auguste Léon accompanied Kahn as the first photographer to be employed by the Archives de la Planète. Léon photographed pristine landscapes and rural communities. He also turned his lens on the object of Kahn's investment: the Norsk Hydro plant, completed five years earlier to harness the energy of the 300-foot Rjukan waterfall, purchased by the enterprising Sam Eyde in 1902. The size of the plant was impressive enough, but its real promise lay in an invention of Eyde's business partner, Kristian Birkeland: he had patented a way to conjure nitrogen from air using powerful electric arcs. The arcs simulated the effect of lightning, which was the only natural way to split inert diatomic nitrogen to make it usable by plants. Kahn's interest in the plant was a likely catalyst for further French investment, edging out competition from the German chemical conglomerate, BASF. There was another prospect on BASF's horizon—the discovery of a way to create artificial nitrogen by a chemist called Fritz Haber—but Birkeland's process

Albert Léon's photograph of the power station at Vemork,
taken in 1911 on Albert Kahn's visit to the Norsk Hydro plant.

still seemed, at the time, the more promising. It was no accident that
Norsk Hydro became embroiled in European geopolitics. In the first
decade of the twentieth century, synthetic nitrogen had two main
uses—making artificial fertilizer and making explosives.[49]

Léon's photograph of the Vemork power station stands out as an
exception among the photographs he took in Norway. Most of the
other images depict untamed wilderness, where human intervention
is nowhere in sight. Léon took many portraits of rural life. One auto-
chrome slide shows a group of children on a dairy farm, and it seems
somehow timeless. But Trond Erik Bjorli, curator of the Norwegian Museum of Cultural History, notes the unspoken relationship
between that image and the picture of the power station: "the dairy
farm will shortly be gone, drowned [by the dam] . . . and the siblings
look vulnerable standing there."[50]

SOME OF THE MOST haunting autochromes in the Archives de
la Planète were taken in 1913 by Marguerite Mespoulet. She traveled to Connemara, in western Ireland, and produced a vivid portrait of a rural community struggling to survive: she photographed
peat diggers and farmers, fishers and weavers; she depicted the lives
of women as few of Kahn's photographers managed to do. Mespoulet was entranced by the peat-digger's way of life ("he works alone,
under the sky, his feet in water, with just the birds and the clouds
for company"), but she did not romanticize poverty. What was visible here in Connemara, she noted in her diary, was connected to
what was out of sight, across the Atlantic. "The young men leave for
North America, the young women too," she wrote, "and when the
old people die, the houses are abandoned and fall into ruin." She saw
"hardly a village where one doesn't find sad skeletons of little grey
houses invaded by nettles."[51]

Kahn's project was utopian, outward-looking, idealistic, and cosmopolitan. Yet it also promoted the French colonial enterprise with
free publicity. Kahn upheld a turn-of-the-century vision of endless

Hibiya Koen, Tokyo:
Kahn's archive contained
many images from
Japan, a country to
which the banker felt
deeply attached.

and inevitable progress, but he viewed this outcome with ambivalence. His archive portrayed the dignity of older and less imposing
ways of inhabiting land and water, suggesting at the same time that
they were doomed. The archive was made possible by the triumph of
global capitalism, personified by Kahn the international banker—
despite which its most lasting achievement is the visual testimony of
capitalism's human and ecological cost. It was a "universal" archive,
cloistered away in a mansion on the outskirts of Paris and not seen
by the public until the early twenty-first century. From this knot of
contradictions, a new planetary consciousness emerged: an "extension of vision" open only to a few. To be able to see the whole planet
was, in a sense, to possess it.

CHAPTER SEVEN

NITROGEN NIGHTMARES

THE FIRST SHOT OF THE "FIRST GREAT CARBON-fuelled war" was fired at the back of a Gräf and Stift double phaeton—an automobile named for a two-horse-drawn carriage with outsized wheels. At a moment when motorcars were starting to replace horses on the streets of Europe, this model, the *Bois de Boulogne*, was the top of the line: graceful and open-topped. It was the pride of an Austrian firm that had started, back in 1893, as a bicycle service workshop in Vienna. It ran on petrol from the wells of Austrian Galicia. On June 28, 1914, it carried the heir to the Austro-Hungarian throne, Archduke Franz Ferdinand, and his wife, Sophie, through the streets of Sarajevo. The bullets fired by Gavrilo Princip, a Bosnian Serb nationalist, assassinated them both, thrusting Europe's rival military alliances into war.[1]

No historical event has been more debated, studied, or commemorated than the First World War. It was "not only a war of steel and gold, but a war of bread and potatoes." It was, in varying interpretations, the last gasp of a dying aristocratic order, the inevitable crisis of capitalist competition for markets, or the tragic outcome of statesmen's inability to anticipate the consequences of their actions. Long seen as a European conflict, the global dimensions of the war are becoming clear. The belligerents also spread their tentacles to every corner of the world in search of timbers and fibers, grains and minerals. It was not only an imperial but also an ecological catastrophe: it slaughtered animals, devoured forests, feasted on minerals, and left its poisonous trace in soils that remain toxic more than a century later.[2]

"IT IS THE DELUGE, it is a convulsion of Nature," British minister of munitions and future prime minister, David Lloyd George, told an audience of Glasgow ship workers in December 1915. The war seemed so sudden and so far beyond anyone's control that only the metaphor of a natural disaster could capture its force. The war's manufactured destruction was on such a scale that it still seemed, paradoxically, that only nature could achieve it. The war was a "cyclone which is tearing up by the roots the ornamental plants of modern society," Lloyd George said; it was an "earthquake which is upheaving the very rocks of European life."[3]

Though the destruction appeared to be a force of nature, few saw more clearly than Lloyd George how far the war required the exploitation of nature by machinery:

> The making of a gun or shell-case, for instance, involves the metal trades, blast-furnaces, steel works, iron and steel foundries, forges, stamps, drops and dies, rolling-mills, drawn rod and wire works—and behind them, the colliery and the iron-ore quarry. It requires factories, and these in turn require machinery, covered electrical plant, factory equipment and machine tools; engines, pumps, turbines, road and rail transport; boiler-making and constructional engineering work. The explosives for filling and propelling the shell from the gun involve the output of chemical works, dye works, gas works, and a great deal of very careful laboratory experiment, investigation and testing.[4]

War required a global ecology, one that drilled down to the very building blocks of matter. As an article in *The Scientific Monthly* noted, "Of the 80 known chemical elements, 30 were required in

modern warfare." Another observer wrote of the "absolute dependence of the modern fighting man upon chemistry." That "absolute dependence" became a vise. Germany confronted shortages
of tungsten—crucial to steelmaking—which had, until the war,
arrived in shipments from Russia and Burma; copper and nickel,
tin and mercury also became scarce. In August 1914, industrialist
Walther Rathenau established the Wartime Raw Materials Department (Kriegsrohstoffabteilung). Governments intervened to manage
nature; cycles of growth and harvesting were planned in a new way.
On both sides of the conflict, shortages forced people to recycle and
repurpose. Scrap metal was turned into cartridges, soldiers' helmets,
and buckles; cooking fat was turned into explosives.[5]

The war immediately became a struggle to monopolize elements
and compounds scattered around the world. No need was more desperate than the need for nitrogen. The calculation was stark: "Nitric
acid is essential for explosives, and nitrates for the fertilizer which
produces food." When the war began, German cruisers from the
East Asia Squadron, en route back to Germany, were positioned off
the coast of Chile, potentially blocking Allied access to the world's
main source of nitrates: the caliche substrate of the Atacama Desert. The Royal Navy gained the upper hand, as well as the nitrate
supplies, after the Battle of the Falkland Islands in December 1914.[6]

In a struggle for survival, Germany turned to an invention
achieved just before the war by the troubled genius of Fritz Haber.
The Habers were an assimilated Jewish family from Breslau, Prussia
(today Wrocław, Poland). Fritz lost his mother in infancy, and had
a difficult relationship with his father, Siegfried, who ran a successful business manufacturing dyes. He was driven to prove himself.
Haber's ambition and ability propelled his singular ascent to the pinnacle of German science—he was given a ready outlet in the febrile
atmosphere of imperial Germany's quest for international power. As
a student, Fritz Haber felt "a power that seemed only to bring unending bounty": it was the power of fossil fuels, as "coal awoke from the
deep, and its limitless riches rose to the light of the working day."

The next step, the *second* industrial revolution, lay in harnessing the power of chemistry and chemical industries. In that quest Germany became preeminent, and Haber led the charge.[7]

In the first decade of the twentieth century, surging global demand for nitrogen fertilizer had spurred a race to capture and make usable the plentiful nitrogen in the air. The success of Norsk Hydro in using electric arcs to fix atmospheric nitrogen held great promise—Albert Kahn was an early investor—but it proved so energy-intensive as to be prohibitively expensive. Haber, now holding a chair at the University of Karlsruhe, found another way. The practical urgency of the nitrogen question piqued his ambition. With his assistant, Englishman Robert le Rossignol, Haber made ammonia from hydrogen and atmospheric nitrogen using a new catalyst—no longer iron, but osmium and later uranium—subjected to searing heat and crushing pressure. Le Rossignol made a signal contribution: he designed a new valve that could tolerate the intense pressure in order to let the gases move through the equipment. Their next task was to convince the vast chemical conglomerate, BASF, to back them.[8]

The personal cost of Haber's triumph fell most heavily upon his wife, the brilliant chemist Clara Immerwahr. She was one of the first women to receive a PhD in Germany, only to find her career as a scientist blocked by prejudice while her husband became a celebrity. "Consider the other side!" she wrote to her doctoral advisor, Richard Abegg in 1909, "what Fritz has achieved in these eight years, I have lost. . . ." Fritz's success, she said, came from his "overwhelming assertion of his own place in the household and in the marriage," and from his "supreme contempt for everyone else and the most common routines of life. . . ."[9]

Even after its triumph in the laboratory, it was not certain that Haber's experiment would lend itself to mass production. Its success was down to the initiative of the thirty-five-year-old Carl Bosch, a charismatic chemist and engineer with BASF. Early experiments at using Haber's process on an industrial scale faltered. The reactors had an unfortunate tendency to explode under intense heat and pressure. The solution came to Bosch "after a Friday night of bowling and drinking." He designed a double-walled tube with soft iron on the inside, and a high-carbon steel on the outer layer. At the International Congress of Applied Chemistry, held in New York in the fall of 1912, BASF chemist August Bernthsen announced: "we have achieved a complete technical solution of the problem of producing ammonia from its elements, and the walls of our first factory for synthetic ammonia are already going up in Oppau. . . ." Haber's contract gave him royalties on BASF's output using his technique; he became a very rich man.[10]

The outbreak of war was a blow to BASF. Out of reach now were the mineral salts, quicklime, dextrin, and pyrites that its chemical factories swallowed. BASF employees in countries aligned with the Allied powers found themselves interned, their factories taken over, their patents voided. As the war dragged on, the company found a new lease of life in the German military's desperate need for explosives. Pushed by Haber, who advised the government, BASF developed a way to make nitric acid—the essential ingredient in the manufacture of explosives—by oxidizing synthetic ammonia. The BASF factory became a mainstay of the German war effort. Many years later, after another and even more catastrophic war, Bosch's deputy, Alwin Mittasch, would write to a colleague that he regretted his role in devising a way to make nitric acid from ammonia; if not for that invention, he thought, "the war would have ended in 1915 and world history would have been different—better, on the whole!"[11]

THE PROMISE OF SYNTHETIC nitrogen had been that it would feed a hungry world. During the war, the focus on churning out nitric acid for explosives meant that nitrogen fertilizer remained scarce. Germany kept its military supplied with arms but could not feed its people. At the start of 1915, to bolster the supply of meat, a great slaughter of pigs began—the *Schweinemord*. More than nine million pigs died in a state-sponsored killing. On and off the battle-fields, animals bore the burdens of war: pigs, dogs, sheep, mules, and camels died in the millions.

By the winter of 1915, bread and potatoes were rationed; after the brief glut of pork, meat became scarce. Lady Evelyn Blücher, an Englishwoman in Berlin, wrote that "long processions of women waiting for hours before the butchers', grocers', and bakers' shops were to be seen everywhere." Profiteering was rampant. Food riots spread through the cities. Women attacked shuttered shops. The British naval blockade of Germany, the "hunger blockade," cut off food imports almost entirely. A punishing winter in 1916 ruined the domestic harvest. The denial of food was a weapon of war, wielded in full knowledge of its lasting effects: "the physical and mental weak-lings produced by starvation are likely to beget their kind . . . to the detriment of the next generation," a British nutritionist declared.[12]

Germany's ally, the Austro-Hungarian Empire, fared no better in feeding its people. Before the war, Austria-Hungary was largely self-sufficient in food, though unevenly so: industrialized Austria depended on the uninterrupted supply of grain and meat from a hinterland of large estates in Hungary. The conscription of men and too many draft animals precipitated a 40-percent drop in farm output over the course of the war. The Russian occupation of Gali-cia early in the war, followed by battles to recapture it, wrecked Austria-Hungary's richest grain lands. Only half the usual amount of mineral fertilizer fed Austria's fields during the war; makeshift solutions—lime-nitrogen and crushed bones, large injections of potash—altered the chemistry and eroded the fertility of the soil.

Wartime price controls shook the incentive for farmers to sell their produce. Changes in the landscape soon followed. Deterred from marketing food by fixed grain prices, large farmers turned arable land into meadows and pastures for grazing; they converted food for human consumption into animal feed. Others sold their produce on the thriving black market. Peasantries everywhere in Europe fell back on the oldest of survival strategies. They adapted their production to the subsistence needs of their households now shrunken by conscription and uncountable loss. They cut their consumption to the barest of margins. Those without land suffered most. A survey of children in Vienna just after the war found more than half undernourished, and nearly a quarter severely so. Desperate need called for improvisation. Vienna's ornamental parks, its pockets of unbuilt land, its apartment balconies and roof terraces—all became vegetable gardens. Communal and cooperative solutions to provisioning displaced an unreliable market.[13]

In Ottoman-ruled Lebanon, Syria, and Palestine, too, hunger encroached as the infrastructure for the distribution of food seized up. The military commandeered trains. They seized camels and donkeys and took away horses and mules. Jaffa farmers who had thrived on the export of oranges from heavily irrigated lands now had no fuel for their generators and no means to get their produce to market. To compound the disruption of armies and governors, a swarm of locusts arrived in 1915, riding upon southerly winds from an unusually moist desert. That year came to be known as 'Am al-Jarad: "the year of the locust." The hungry creatures devoured no less than 80 percent of the summer crop: they ate olives and almonds, citrus fruits and plums and prickly pears. It was "as if the sea itself has gushed forth onto the earth," wrote Yusuf al-Haddad from Lebanon—a sea of locusts. In parts of Syria that year, the civilian death rate from starvation and the diseases of hunger approached 16 percent of the population.[14]

If food shortages exhausted the Central Powers' war effort, in Russia they provoked the social and political crisis that culminated in the revolutions of 1917. Food, a Russian historian writes, "superseded all other problems" during the war. The mobilization of more than fifteen million troops wrenched young men from the farms—millions of plough horses followed. Farming households lived in fear of having their land, their animals, and their sons taken away. Inflation ate through savings. The government, mired in corruption, failed to coordinate food supplies. Informal markets readily took their place. The later years of the war saw the rise of "bag men" (*meshochnichestvo*) from the cities who scoured the countryside for food, sacks in hand; when inflation became debilitating, they switched from cash to barter. Such was their ingenuity that in some regions the "bag men" imported twice as much food to urban areas as the government did. The state and the market had failed. To survive, people tacked between collective solidarity and subterfuge.[15]

THE MAELSTROM PRESSED HARD upon the fields of Europe, and on mines and forests and quarries much further away. But the ultimate outcome of the war owed most to an earlier, nineteenth-century environmental transformation. Writing more than thirty years ago, Israeli historian Avner Offer was the first to see this: "The distant causes of Germany's collapse in 1918," he wrote, "may be found on the new frontiers of farming which opened up during the last third of the nineteenth century." Without wheat, meat, and timber from Canada and the United States, Britons would have faced the same privations as Germans; instead, they adjusted to a strict but relatively equitable program of rationing. Assailed by German submarines, the North Atlantic shipping corridor became the Allied lifeline. Through the Panama Canal—described by James Bryce, British ambassador to the United States (1907–1913), as the "greatest liberty that man has ever taken with nature"—the grain of western Canada poured into Britain. So, too, did Canadian wood, after Britain's own productive forests halved in size in a few short years. Two-thirds of the Allies' wheat came from North America in the last two years of the war; 80 percent of Britain's meat and cooking fats came from the United States. Without Australian wool, Allied armies would have struggled in the wet northern winters. Canada provided up to a third of the ammunition expended by British forces in France. And with the money they earned from exporting produce, Canada, Australia, and New Zealand together

mobilized 1.2 million soldiers for the war. They suffered dispropor-
tionate losses.[16]

When the United States entered the war in 1917, its economic
power proved decisive. The US food administrator, Herbert
Hoover—a mining magnate who had coordinated US food relief to
Belgium at the start of the war—declared that "food will win this
war—starvation or sufficiency will in the end determine the victor."
The Food Administration guaranteed a high minimum price for
wheat, so American farmers planted more of it. Hoover pushed pork
exports to Europe harder than some Allied governments welcomed.
His wartime reign marked an unprecedented effort by the federal
government to support farmers; it brought the state into people's
homes, and to their tables, in a new way. For Hoover, son of a midwestern farming family, the war turned on the plenitude of America's vast agricultural lands. He told troops aboard the *Olympia*,
sailing to Europe in 1918, "My father and your own, side by side,
redeemed the West from the Wilderness. . . ."[17]

Appealing directly to women, Hoover's Food Administration
asked Americans to stint on wheat and meat voluntarily in solidarity
with their European allies—and to hold off the need for rationing.
War gardens, "Victory Gardens," encouraged urban Americans to
grow their own vegetables as a patriotic duty. If they lacked the desperation of the makeshift garden plots in European cities, American war gardens brought urbanites a new sense of connection with
the soil; a new knowledge of plants; a new, and short-lived, sense of
collective provisioning.

THERE WAS ONE OTHER product of nature that North America
had in such abundance as to secure the Allies' military victory. The
Great War began with the technologies of the nineteenth century:
with human, animal, and mechanical power. It was meant to be a
war won by coal, rail, and horses: one for every three soldiers. Germany's abundance of coal bolstered its military planners' confidence

in a quick victory. When Winston Churchill, First Lord of the Admiralty, had persuaded the British government to buy shares in the Anglo-Persian oil corporation just before the war, he believed the strategic value of oil would only grow. It grew faster and more thoroughly than Churchill, or anyone else, could have predicted. In 1914, few leaders gave much thought to oil. By 1917 Walter Long, British Secretary of State for the Colonies, called oil "the greatest motive power." French prime minister Georges Clemenceau told US president Woodrow Wilson that oil was "as vital as blood."[18]

To a war of attrition, the internal combustion engine delivered mobility. Taxis ferried French troops to the front; trucks carried men and material. Diesel-powered submarines gave the Germans their most powerful weapon at sea. Most pivotal in the land war was a new kind of armored vehicle, driven by a petroleum engine and mounted with machine guns. In secretive planning, a host of code names for this new war machine invoked ancient techniques to channel water and sculpt the land: it was called a cistern, a reservoir, and eventually it acquired the name that stuck—a tank. The British military began the war with 827 motor cars and 15 motorcycles; by 1918, its cars numbered 23,000 and motorcycles, 34,000. The US entry into the war brought an infusion of motor vehicles: 50,000 in 1917 and 1918 alone. The Allied countries manufactured close to 150,000 aircraft in four years, while Germany produced 48,000.[19]

War machines were thirsty for oil; most of it came from North America. The United States produced 65 percent of the world's oil in 1914, and 71 percent by 1918; Mexico rose to become the second largest producer in the world, displacing Russia after the revolution stopped the flow from Baku's oil fields. The wartime quest for petroleum tore through mangroves and rainforest in the Huasteca region of Mexico. Loggers set forests alight as the quickest way to clear them. In hurricane season, lightning strikes exploded jerry-rigged storage tanks. The city of Tampico rose on a crest of oil. The *Gulf Coast Oil News* observed in May 1917 that "Tampico's tugs,

launches and barges were working as they never worked before."
The Pánuco became an "oil highway"; the life of the river bore the
brunt of repeated spillages and accidents. Oil brought unprecedented
power—and unprecedented destruction.[20]

Petroleum-powered vehicles burst open a vertical dimension to
the conflict. Oil launched the war into the sky, submerged it undersea, dug it underground. For many combatants, only images recalled
from epics could make sense of the destruction from above and
below. A South Indian Muslim soldier, lying wounded on a hospital ship, wrote to his family that God must have given the Germans
their "fowls of the air, dragons of the earth and poisonous crocodiles
of the sea." A wounded Garhwali soldier turned to Hindu mythology when he described German aircraft as "like the great bird of
Vishnu in the sky." "This is not a war," a Punjabi Rajput soldier
wrote home, "this is the end of the whole world."[21]

The war inaugurated a level of technological control over the environment that would eventually become all-encompassing. As geographer Jean Brunhes had seen, the aerial view changed everything.
Even more powerful than their bombs, at least initially, was the new
angle of vision that aircraft made possible. Air power brought the
gift of sight. Stuck in the trenches and unable to advance, warring
armies could now assemble photo mosaics of aerial images to map
the enemy's position. Among the Allies, the French took the lead.
Aircraft, equipped with 26-centimeter handheld cameras, were met
as soon as they landed by mobile laboratories on trucks. German
photographic technology was further advanced; German aircraft
mapped Belgium from the air with a level of detail never seen before.
Every ridge was visible. It was hard not to believe that air power
granted men mastery over the Earth.[22]

In the second year of the war, the air itself turned murderous.
While urging BASF to convert its factories to make nitric acid, Fritz
Haber also advised German military technicians on a terrible new
way to maim and kill. At the second Battle of Ypres, in April 1915,
German forces unleashed clouds of chlorine gas.

After the war, Canadian military physician John George Adami pieced together the events of that shattering day from war diaries: "*Thursday, April 22nd* was like a warm day of the Indian summer in Canada. It had been absolutely cloudless, with a faint haze and light breeze, which veered round to the north-east." And then that breeze turned mutant. Around five that evening, "there appeared, rolling along the level ground, a dark-green cloud, yellow where the light caught it, broken here and there by the black of exploding shells." The first victims "staggered in, weak and semi-stuporose, with bloodshot eyes and hacking cough. Some had attacks of vomiting; all had intense dyspnoea, rapid heart-beat, and the severer cases a ghastly ashy colour of skin." The prosaic language of medical diagnosis only underscored the novelty of the terror.[23]

German philosopher Peter Sloterdijk argues that April 22, 1915, marked a turning point in life on Earth. It signified "the introduction of the environment into the battle between adversaries." He invokes the "prophetic" words spoken by Shylock in *The Merchant of Venice:* "You take my life / When you do take the means whereby I live. . . ." Sloterdijk overstates his case; Shakespeare was not prophetic so much as observant. As historian Emmanuel Kreike has argued in *Scorched Earth,* armies had for centuries targeted the "means whereby" enemy populations lived. Kreike uses the term "environcide" to describe an ancient practice that hastened with the early modern European wars and sped up further through innumerable colonial wars that followed in the Americas, Asia, and Africa. It involved the willful destruction of the ecological conditions for survival: torching fields and breaking dams and poisoning wells. But Sloterdijk is right to point to the escalation that took place during the Great War. Poison gas made possible "an attack on the enemy's primary, ecologically dependent vital functions" beginning with the basic act of breathing. As such, "human respiration was assuming a direct role in the events of war." Gas masks protected soldiers from their "immediate milieu, the breathable air" that had suddenly turned toxic.

There began a new quest: for insulation from the elements made lethal by human intervention.[24]

At his grand residence in Dahlem, Fritz Haber celebrated the innovation of Ypres on May 1, 1915. Decades later, his own son, Lutz Haber, would write: "In Haber, the OHL [German military command] found a brilliant mind and an extremely energetic organizer, determined, and possibly unscrupulous." The night of Fritz's celebration, his wife, Clara, took her life using her husband's military pistol. Many whispered that she was driven to suicide by dismay at her husband's complicity—more than complicity, his leading role—in the dawn of chemical warfare.[25]

In grim succession, chlorine gas was followed by yet more lethal phosgene; then by mustard gas that blinded its victims first before killing them slowly from internal bleeding. The Allies were fast to catch up in poisoning the air. When the United States entered the war, the Edgewood Arsenal, in Maryland, arose to become the largest chemical weapons facility in the world. What had been "a little wilderness, the home of wild ducks, geese, and game of all kinds" was remolded, just four years later, into "a maze of chemical plants . . . covered with a network of roads, railroads, pipelines and all that goes with a huge manufacturing plant and proving ground for chemical warfare agents." In the eyes of painter A.Y. Jackson, who served in the Canadian army on the Western Front, poison gas altered the elements, even light itself, into something eerie and almost beautiful. In rough notes for a painting he would call *Gas Attack, Lievin*, he scrawled impressions of an environment transformed: "Sudden bursts of flame . . . coloured glow . . . Bright green lights behind clouds, grey rolling along horizon . . . below star a shower of orange . . . gas clouds, cool greys."[26]

The 190,000 tons of chemical agents used during the First World War killed 90,000 people, and injured 1.3 million. In a book aptly titled *The Shock of the Old*, historian of science David Edgerton points out that many more men were killed and maimed by weapons much older—the weapons of the nineteenth century.

A. Y. Jackson, *Gas Attack, Lievin.*

"Of the 10 million who died in the Great War in Europe," Edgerton writes, "and they were overwhelmingly soldiers, 5 million died from artillery fire and 3 million from small arms in combat." Expanding "dum-dum" bullets—invented in Calcutta by an Englishman to strike terror into Asians and Africans—had been outlawed in "civilized" but not in "savage" wars. The years 1914 to 1918 showed that distinction to be meaningless. John George Adami described their horrific effect: "The soft metal of [the] body of bullet mushrooms against the bone, causes great shattering of bone, and as the metal spreads it brings about great laceration and destruction of the soft parts, with gaping wound of exit." An even simpler metal artifact from the American prairie—barbed wire—caused untold suffering in the trenches and scarred the landscape of Europe.[27]

The killing fields exposed the creatureliness of the human body in the face of steel death machines—"our hands are earth, our bodies clay and our eyes pools of rain," German officer Erich Maria Remarque would later write in his war novel *All Quiet on the*

Western Front. The technologies of war promised the conquest of nature—and laid bare the fragility of life.[28]

In the letters of Indian soldiers, the freezing rain of the northern winter is a sharper presence than poison gas. The harshness of climate contained all of the harshness of war. In many testimonies from the front, nature was itself a protagonist in the conflict. "The cold is so great it cannot be described," one soldier wrote to his family in South India. A Garhwali soldier recovering from his injuries on a hospital ship wrote home: "Here an extraordinary amount of rain falls and the men's feet become frost-bitten from the snow. Six months have passed since I saw the sun, because there is constant rain and clouds." Others turned to humor amid intolerable suffering. "The cold here is excessive," wrote signaler Nattha Singh, and then he told his friend a story: "One day, three or four of us signalers were working at the telegraph and telephone. When the message we were at was finished, a Jat added through the wire 'if this cold continues for another month or two we shall leave the earth with pleasure.'" Thinking of this, Nattha Singh said, "I laugh out loud."[29]

The scale of devastation in the war could be apprehended only through extended natural similes, for how else could it be conveyed? Sowar Sohan Singh wrote home, in July 1915: "There is conflagration all round, and you must imagine it to be like a dry forest in a high wind in the hot weather, with abundance of dry grass and straw. No one can extinguish it but God himself—man can do nothing." Amar Singh Rawat wrote, from the hospital for wounded Indian soldiers in Brighton Pavilion, that "the condition of affairs in the war is like leaves falling off a tree, and no empty space remains on the ground. So it is here: the earth is full of dead men and not a vacant spot is left."[30]

Even the most defiled ground could become sacred. Aliou Diakhatte, a *tirailleur* from Senegal on the Western Front, told an interviewer, almost seven decades after the war, that he had found himself unable to kneel to pray in the trenches—"so I took some earth in my hand and I put it to my forehead. And I prayed to God in that way."[31]

THE WAR WAS NO kinder to the animals that had been, for a thousand years, men's most trusted companions in battle. The advent of the tank in 1916 may have replaced horses with machinery in shock attacks, but right to the end, horses hauled men and material. Horses fought and horses died. American veterinarian Ernest Harold Baynes contrasted the "terrific, automatic, but unadaptable power of a motor car" with the "more moderate, intelligent, and highly adaptable strength of a horse." The internal combustion engine had failed to make horses redundant.[32]

In all, around sixteen million horses were deployed during the Great War. Half of them died. They died from bullet wounds, barbed wire tore their flesh, they fell from exhaustion. The average life expectancy of a horse on the front was but ten days. The horses' suffering caused distress to the soldiers they served. "The number of dead horses and mules shocked me," English poet Robert Graves wrote; "human corpses were all very well, but it seemed wrong for animals to be dragged into the war like this." Care and affection, as much as utility and command, bound men and horses together. Canadian general Arthur Currie wrote:

> Among the few bright things of the soldier's life none touched him more deeply than the mutual attachment of man and horse. . . . The very work of tending a horse was a distraction which relieved the trooper or the gunner from the otherwise unrelenting tension of warfare. The few minutes of pleasant companionship made him more ready for the battle of a new day.[33]

In death, as in life, men and animals were conjoined. Bengali medical officer Sisir Prasad Sarbadhikari's memoir of the war—recovered, translated, and movingly rendered by literary scholar Santanu Das—describes a scene from the battle of Ctesiphon: "The corpses of men and animals were strewn everywhere. Sometimes the bodies lay tangled up; sometimes wounded men lay trapped and groaning beneath the carcasses of animals." Horses appear frequently in the folk poetry of Russian soldiers in the Great War. They appear as companions, sources of comfort, reminders of home; the fates of men and the fates of horses are bound together in suffering.

> Horse, my faithful black horse,
> are you and I off to battle?
> The first bullet killed the horse,
> the second bullet struck me down.

Bullets did not distinguish between humans and other animals.[34]

Ernest Baynes, the veterinarian, wrote of a lasting debt that human beings now owed to another species: "we can pay it in part, and lasting shame to us if we don't, by greater kindness, greater decency, more thought and consideration for other horses all over the world. . . ."[35]

IT WAS THE DEAD trees that haunted Paul Nash. Nash had studied at London's Slade School of Fine Art. In the years before the war, he had made a name for himself as a painter. Though he suffered all his life from severe asthma, Nash enlisted as an infantry officer to serve in the Ypres Salient in March 1917. After being injured in a fall and invalided out several months later, Nash was appointed Britain's official war artist after a successful lobbying campaign by his supporters. In depicting the ruins of Europe, Nash fused sensitivity to suffering with a bold, expressionist style. In a letter to his wife, Margaret, he wrote: "Sunset and sunrise are blasphemous mockeries to men; only the black rain out of the bruised and swollen clouds or through the bitter black of night is fit atmosphere in such a land."

Paul Nash, *We Are Making a New World.*

Although Nash was employed as a propagandist, he was frank in private about the critical charge of his work. "I am a messenger who will bring back word from the men who are fighting to those who want the war to go on for ever," he wrote to Margaret. "Feeble, inarticulate will be my message, but it will have a bitter truth, and may it burn their lousy souls."[36]

Trees stand deformed and splintered as far as the eye can see. The cratered, puddled ground appears lunar. Each charred tree represents a human figure, every one a grave for fallen men. The sun pierces the landscape, breaking through a mountain wall the rusty color of dried blood. Human death and the death of nature lie entwined: "I have tried to paint trees as though they were human beings," Nash wrote to Margaret. The title of Nash's painting is *We Are Making a New World.* It is a bitter mockery of those who orchestrated the war; but it is also a simple truth.

CHAPTER EIGHT

WAR ON
EARTH

M*ODERN TIMES* (1936) WAS THE LAST GREAT MOVIE
of the silent era, and the final outing for Charlie Chaplin's
globally beloved everyman character, the Little Tramp. Amid the
deepest economic crisis of the modern era, Chaplin parodied how
the factory assembly line crushed the human soul. Rarely seen as a
film with an ecological subtext, *Modern Times* is an indelible artistic
statement on how human nature and the material world were mis-
shapen by machinery in the two decades after the First World War.[1]

The film's opening juxtaposes sheep with human beings, as if to
show that all forms of life were being turned into automata by the
doctrine of efficiency. A scene of sheep being herded through a narrow passage on an industrial farm blurs into a crowd of faceless, hat-
wearing men exiting a subway station. There is a lone black sheep
among the flock, portent of how Little Tramp will stand out, an
agent of glorious chaos, amid the mass of industrial workers.

The mechanized slaughter of the First World War awakened writers and artists in Europe and America, and across the colonized
world, to ask where the fevered pursuit of wealth and power would
ultimately lead. But their call for precaution was only ever the view of
a minority. The postwar years witnessed not a slowing down, but a
speeding up. The technological innovations of wartime—beginning
with the much-augmented use of the internal combustion engine and
extending to the new view of the Earth that came with aerial shots
in motion pictures—shattered limits to how far people could travel

Charlie Chaplin, *Modern Times* (1936).

and what machines could do. By 1929, there were more than twenty-seven million cars on America's roads, one for every household: no other country came close. On a visit to Ford's factory in Detroit, Chaplin heard stories of workers who had suffered nervous break-downs under relentless pressure to produce more.

Chaplin reflected on what mass production meant for human autonomy. In 1931, as the economic boom of 1920s gave way to mass unemployment, Chaplin met Mahatma Gandhi in London, in a "humble little house in the slum district off the East India Dock Road." Chaplin asked about Gandhi's "abhorrence of machinery." Gandhi replied: "Machinery in the past has made us dependent on England, and the only way we can rid ourselves of that dependency is to boycott all goods made by machinery." Gandhi's concern was for the living planet as well as for political freedom. "God forbid that India should ever take to industrialization in the manner of the West," he had written in 1928, for "if an entire nation of 300 million took to similar economic exploitation, it would strip the world bare like locusts." Few among Gandhi's fellow nationalists in India—including Jawaharlal Nehru, the Mahatma's protégé among the younger leaders—agreed with him. What India needed, many of them thought, was what British rule had blocked: an industrial revolution. Both his visit to Ford factory and his meeting with Gandhi left an impression on Chaplin as he plotted the Tramp's swansong.[2]

In *Modern Times*, the Little Tramp goes to work on an assembly line. A wrench in each hand, he tightens bolts. Chaplin revels in physical comedy as the conveyor belt moves faster and faster, leaving the Tramp flailing to keep up. And then the hapless Tramp is chosen by the factory manager to try out a new contraption—the Billows Feeding Machine, designed to feed workers automatically so that they could keep working through lunch. The machine goes awry, and assaults the Tramp with a corn cob. In its absurdity, the feeding machine embodies the industrial worker's final alienation from eating as a communal activity, and from food as a product of the soil. The Tramp is driven to the limits of his sanity, and starts assaulting his fellow workers. Thrown out of the factory, he finds work as a singing waiter.

In the final scene, Little Tramp and his love, the Gamin (played by Chaplin's wife, Paulette Goddard), are shown walking toward distant hills on a stretch of open road. It is not quite an escape from modern times—the road and the factory are bound together, after all—but the happy ending shows the couple's reengagement with the natural world, with the land and the open sky, after the unnatural hell of the factory.

All was not well on the open American road by the time of Chaplin's film. In 1936, the Great Plains suffered from severe drought for the second time in three years. Grasslands revolted, having been plowed up by generations of settlers for wheat, a crop ill-adapted to the arid conditions. Ferocious winds whipped up eroded topsoil, flinging dust storms toward the cities of the East Coast. Crops withered. Farm families embarked on another great migration west. A new generation of agricultural economists and soil scientists, brought into the Department of Agriculture under FDR's New Deal, diagnosed deeper ills. A 1936 report submitted to President Roosevelt, *The Future of the Great Plains*, presented the Dust Bowl as the inexorable result of settler expansion, and above all as the outcome

of the notion that nature could be conquered as if in a war. The
hope for the future was that, "The land may bloom again if man
once more makes his peace with Nature." Historian and sociologist
Lewis Mumford expressed optimism that the right lessons would be
learned, that "instead of exploitation by mere spread and plunder,
a stable and orderly culture of the earth and its resources will take
its place."[3]

The decade to follow would be neither stable nor peaceful.

BUILT UPON FRAGILE COMPROMISES after the First World
War, the global order collapsed in the 1930s. The great depression
shook the foundations of trans-Atlantic capitalism and emboldened
the Soviet alternative of forced industrialization. The accompanying rush to collective farming scattered a wreckage of famine across
Ukraine. "To slacken the pace would mean to lag behind, and those
who lag behind are beaten," Joseph Stalin declared in 1931: "We
have lagged behind the advanced countries by fifty to a hundred
years. We must cover that distance in ten years. Either we do it or we
will go under."[4]

Germany, Japan, and Italy tore up international agreements that
brought them little benefit. Surveying the possibilities before them,
German, Japanese, and Italian leaders understood only too well how
thoroughly the nineteenth-century British Empire had reshaped the
Earth: seizing, deploying, and exploiting the products of nature on
a planetary scale. "We have got most of the world already, or the
best parts of it," a British naval commander admitted amid the rising
tensions of the 1930s: "We only want to keep what we have got and
prevent others from taking it away from us." "The Era of Expansion . . . has come to an end," sociologist Lewis Mumford declared of
the US West. But as latecomers to the imperial game, what the Axis
powers sought was another great transformation—another redistribution of both people and nature. It would come at inhuman cost.[5]

The notion of *Lebensraum* ("living space") obsessed Nazi ideologues even before they seized power in 1933. Friedrich Ratzel, who coined the term in a 1901 essay, was a pioneer of "bio-geography." He understood modern states as akin to natural organisms in pursuit of living space, each haunted by Thomas Robert Malthus's early-nineteenth-century vision of a "perpetual struggle for room and food." Anxiety about land and sustenance became a self-fulfilling spur to imperial expansion. "Nature knows no political boundaries," Adolf Hitler had declared in *Mein Kampf*. "First she places living creatures on this globe and watches the free play of forces." Richard Walther Darré, Minister of Food and Agriculture in the Nazi government, insisted on Germany's need to break the binding limits of its territory: "The natural area for the settlement by the German people," he said, "is the territory to the east of the Reich's boundaries up to the Urals." In a 1936 speech, Darré boasted: "we will settle this space, according to the law that a superior people always has the right to conquer and own the land of an inferior people." This was a view that straightforwardly defined how every European empire had justified its expansion.[6]

A comparable fear of ecological limits motivated the Japanese search for new soils and new resources in mainland China: "The critical problem of population and foodstuffs seem all without solution," the Japanese Kwantung Army's commanders noted to justify their annexation of Manchuria in 1931. Philosopher Watsuji Tetsuro penned a treatise on climate and culture in the 1930s, insisting that the "submissive and resignatory" peoples of tropical lands were crying out for Japanese imperial domination in order to "set this teeming power," the power of earth and atmosphere, "in motion."[7]

The Nazi regime made repeated references to the environmental history of the nineteenth century—to the claiming of the world by Anglo-American settlement, which had left the Reich no choice, the Nazis believed, but to replicate that history of expansion in Eurasia. Darré's own early life had been spent in a land of settler opportunity underwritten by British investment and protected by British gunboats: he grew up in Buenos Aires, Argentina, the port through which the grasslands of the Pampas filled the empire with refrigerated beef.

Nazi proponents of "blood and soil" invoked the medieval colonization of the lands beyond the Elbe by German-speaking peoples; but America always loomed large in their imagination. Frederick Jackson Turner's theory of the American frontier, of westward expansion as national destiny, reverberated through German intellectual circles. Germany's version of the American "West" lay to the east. Heinrich Himmler imagined a future in which German settlers had at last subdued the "endless primeval forest" of eastern Europe, and made there "a paradise, a European California." Hitler himself insisted on the need to "set about the Germanization of the land by bringing in Germans and to regard the indigenous inhabitants as Indians." What that would mean for eastern Europe's inhabitants did not need spelling out; for decades German novels and popular histories celebrating the exterminatory violence of American settlers had found an enthusiastic audience.[8]

Without quite the open admiration the Nazis had for the total annihilation of native populations, Japanese planners saw Manchuria in comparable terms: "like the colonial days in American history, a new State is in the making, the vast virgin plains, unhampered by tradition, ready to welcome armies of fresh immigrants."[9]

Global war began not in Europe but in Asia. On July 7, 1937, a minor skirmish at the Marco Polo bridge, in Beijing, led to a full-scale Japanese invasion of China. The international order strained—and then snapped. On September 1, 1939, having secured a pact with the Soviet Union a month earlier, German forces invaded Poland. Within months, much of western Europe was under German control. In 1940, Japanese forces moved into Indochina after it came under the control of the Nazi-installed Vichy regime in France. Japan was now within striking reach of British- and Dutch-controlled regions of Southeast Asia. The decisive, worldwide escalation came in 1941: on June 22, Hitler invaded the Soviet Union in Operation Barbarossa; and then, on December 7 and 8, the Japanese army and navy simultaneously attacked Pearl Harbor and launched an invasion of Southeast Asia. Within three months, Japanese forces had conquered Malaya, Burma, the Dutch East Indies (Indonesia), and the Philippines. It took Allied forces six months to regroup and recover from the stunning Axis advance. The balance of military power was shifted, most of all, by the entry of the United States. By the end of 1942, the fortunes of war had changed. Though the war dragged on to wreak another two and a half years of murder and destruction, the German army's defeat at Stalingrad, and the Japanese navy's defeat by American forces at the Battle of Midway, gave the Allies a decisive advantage.[10]

Like the First, the Second World War was waged by workers rushing to make more guns, more aircraft, and more steel with the rock and metal, the coal and oil, grabbed from every corner of the Earth. It was a war against nature, described in the language of natural forces.

When the war began, it was as if the environmental history of the previous 150 years had been concentrated and ignited. The transformations of a century were reenacted, this time scattered and compressed into less than a decade. Millions of people and their animals moved to cultivate lands on the margins of habitability. Geologists scrabbled for minerals and put miners to work ever deeper underground. Armies of laborers hacked roads into mountainsides and felled woods for rail tracks. In the Soviet Union, workers and soldiers packed up and moved 2,600 factories, piece by piece, across the Urals.

Again, belligerent powers scoured the ends of the Earth for raw materials to fight the war. Iron-ore came from the mines of Kiruna and Gällivare in Swedish Lapland, from Algeria and Newfoundland and Sierra Leone. Bauxite for aluminum came from the mines of British Guyana, controlled by the Canadian corporation Alcan. Oil came overwhelmingly from the United States and Mexico—but also from Iraq, invaded by British forces in 1941; and from Iran, divided into spheres of influence by Britain and the Soviet Union.[11]

The quest for destruction reshaped even human bodies. In the

1970s Belarusian journalist Svetlana Alexievich interviewed Soviet women who had fought in the Second World War; one of them, V. Gromova, a medical assistant, told her: "I have enough metal in me . . . I carry a fragment from a wound I received near Vitebsk in my lung, within an inch of my heart. A second fragment in the right lung. Two in the region of the stomach. . . ."[12]

The war forced together two changes in the human relationship to the rest of nature that had played out over the nineteenth century: the first, within reach only of a privileged minority, was a revolution in the capacity to preserve, protect, and extend life; to thwart the newly visible pathogens that threatened human survival; to forestall decay and optimize every landscape for human flourishing. The second, both marker and maker of inequality, was a revolution in killing—a heightened capacity that the most powerful nations had to destroy human, animal, and vegetal life.

The sense that humans were an exception to the laws of nature had built slowly and partially over centuries and had grown more forceful in the nineteenth century age of industrialization and empire. Yet, amid the horrors of war, society seemed to revert, so many observers noted, to a "state of nature." As state after state collapsed from 1942 to 1945, any lingering sense of human mastery over nature dissolved into fear.

FIRST AND LAST THERE was the struggle for food. The Nazi leadership understood that the oldest and most basic form of human ecological control—control over the land and its produce—would decide the outcome of the war. Hitler described the struggle in May 1942: "It is a *battle for food*, a battle for the basis of life, for the *raw materials* the earth offers, *the natural resources* that lie under the soil and *the fruits* that it offers to the one who cultivates it." As soon as it became clear that the war would be prolonged, Germany's ability to fight rested on food from occupied lands. "Grain, grain and grain again," is how one Nazi regional leader summed up what Germany needed from the annexed areas of Poland. Anxiety about grain, alongside Hitler's fantasy of an inevitable showdown with Bolshevism, spurred the decision to invade the Soviet Union in 1941. Led by agricultural expert Herbert Backe, more grimly effective than Darré, the Nazis set out a scheme to plunder the east. The "Hunger Plan," formulated early in 1941, turned food into a weapon: to secure grain for the Reich, the Nazis decided that Slavic peoples should starve. German forces would cut food supplies from Ukraine to Russia's towns and cities and use it to feed the Wehrmacht. General Georg Thomas, shaper of the Hunger Plan, predicted in May 1941 that "umpteen millions of people will doubtless starve to death." Backe was more precise: that number would be thirty million people. It was the most naked plan for mass murder by starvation in human history. At every step, it was a struggle for environmental control.[13]

The strength of Soviet resistance wrecked the Nazis' systematic plan. What occurred instead were countless local famines, each driven by the same brutal calculations that had assembled the Hunger Plan as a whole. The ferocity of the German assault on the land killed everything on it: within 150 kilometers of the front, requisitioning was so comprehensive that it left behind an ecological "dead zone" without a single food plant growing, without an animal left alive. During the wartime occupation, German forces appropriated an estimated nine million tons of grain from the Soviet Union, an amount equivalent to the prewar consumption of twelve million Soviet citizens over a span of three years. What German forces could not seize, they strangled. The siege of Leningrad, which lasted for 872 days, killed a million people. Official propaganda upheld an image of Leningrad as "a Soviet Troy, defended by impeccably heroic inhabitants wholly dedicated to the manufacture of weapons and tanks for the war effort."[14]

Testimonies of suffering had little place in this story of resilience, and only decades later did the searing wartime work of Leningrad poets come to light. Soldier-poet Sergei Rudakov, who would die in battle a year after he wrote these lines, depicts city streets emptied of life:

> On the streets there's quite a chill.
> Wherever you look, they're dragging sleds
> Of sorrowful remains.
> Sewn into the white of linen.
> The row of frozen mummies slides along.

Rudakov conveys the hope that life will return; that this, too, would pass—coupled with stoic resignation that the cycle of death all around him is a pattern in the sweep of human history: "In this world, everything repeats."[15]

The Nazis' racial ideology infused every decision they made about the distribution of food. "If any one has to go hungry, it shall not be the Germans, but other peoples," Hermann Göering declared in August 1942. The war was being fought, chief propagandist Joseph Goebbels wrote, so that the German people could enjoy "a well laid breakfast, lunch and dinner table." With most German men of fighting age already conscripted, the Nazis' vision of who would eat and who would starve clashed with their need for workers. Millions of people were forced from the east to work in the German war economy, and their labor was so vital that the military-economic office of the Wehrmacht urged pragmatism: "the concepts of normal labour, heavy labour and extra heavy labour have to be regarded in objective terms, independent of racial consideration, as a through-put of calories and muscular effort." The science of human nutrition was reduced to a cruel essence: what was the minimal intake of calories compatible with toil? If essential workers had to receive scarce food to remain productive, it became even more important for the Nazis to identify those they called "useless eaters" (*unnütze Esser*)—who would receive none.[16]

The Nazis' use of starvation as a means of waging war set the stage for the singular horror that faced Europe's Jewish people.

Antisemitism was at the poisoned core of the Nazi ideology from the start, inciting pogroms, expulsions, discriminatory laws, and internment of Germany's Jewish population. In a speech to the German parliament on January 30, 1939, Hitler had predicted the "annihilation" of Europe's Jews in the event of global war. Local atrocities piled up as soon as war broke out. The systematic murder of Jewish people escalated after the German attack on the Soviet Union, carried out in village after village by *Einsatzgruppen* death squads. The genocidal impulse went beyond committed Nazi cadres. Walter von Reichenau, a Wehrmacht field commander, told the soldiers of his 6th Army in the fall of 1941 that they were "the carrier of an inexorable racial conception and the avenger of all bestialities which have been committed against the Germans." He sought their "complete understanding" in pursuing the "harsh, but just atonement of Jewish subhumanity."[17]

Starvation accompanied every step toward genocide. As the camps began their ghastly work of extermination, Jewish people throughout the occupied east were denied all rations. In the Nazis' murderous logic, the two kinds of killing presented as alternatives. In July 1941, Rolf-Heinz Höppner—who served the Security Police in Wartheland, part of the territory annexed from Poland—wrote to SS officer, key orchestrator of the Holocaust, Adolf Eichmann: "It should be seriously considered whether it would not be the most humane solution to finish off the Jews that are unfit for work through some fast acting means. In any case, this would be more agreeable than to let them starve to death."[18]

By the middle of 1942, one hundred thousand Jewish people in Wartheland had been murdered—and grain exports to Germany sped up. Historian Adam Tooze concludes that there was, in the end, no "grand contradiction between economics and ideology" within the regime. Rather, there was a "perverse functional connection" between the elimination of the Jewish population of the east, where most victims of the genocide lived and died, and the German scramble to feed an army of forced labor.[19]

Within the camps, the manipulation and withholding of food did the ideological work of rendering "life stripped bare of its humanness." In his indelible memoir of Auschwitz, Italian chemist and writer Primo Levi describes how the prison guards, and eventually the prisoners themselves, used the German word "fressen," not "essen," for eating: "this way of eating on our feet, furiously, burning our mouths and throats, without time to breathe, really is '*fressen*', the way of eating of animals, and certainly not '*essen*', the human way of eating, seated in front of a table, religiously." Nazi ideology projected a view of human beings as pure biology—as instinct-driven herds ("races") in a struggle to attain the conditions of life. At the same time the Nazi worldview also held that some human life, Aryan German life, was uniquely sacred. Here lies the significance of Reichenau's appeal to "bestiality" and "subhumanity," or of Heinrich Himmler's declaration, a year and a half later, that "Antisemitism is exactly the same as delousing." Their depraved worldview was so riven with inconsistency that many senior Nazi leaders were known for their acute sensitivity to, even love for, (non-human) animals, a trait they upheld as a mark of authentic Germanness.[20]

Himmler's chilling conclusion, on April 24, 1943: "We shall soon be deloused. We have only 20,000 lice left, and then the matter is finished within the whole of Germany." The substance that the Nazis used to murder so many millions of people in the gas chambers of Auschwitz, Zyklon-B, began life in the 1920s as a cyanide-based pesticide.[21]

FAMINES IN NAZI-OCCUPIED EASTERN Europe were the most orchestrated and the most brutal but far from the only episodes of large-scale starvation during the Second World War. They were famines of siege, they were famines of state failure, famines of bungling and selective neglect. Each famine marked the collapse of control that human institutions could exert over the environment they depended on. In occupied Europe, Greece suffered most.

When an Allied naval blockade stopped the arrival of food supplies in 1941, starvation followed. Food aid only began to arrive on neutral Swedish ships in late 1942: by that time whole villages had emptied. In the Netherlands, where perceived racial affinity had led to less harsh treatment by the occupiers, German authorities finally placed an embargo on food in late 1944 in revenge for a rail strike and sporadic resistance attacks. The miserable season of deprivation that followed is still known, in collective memory, as the *Hongerwinter*. In Asia, the scale of suffering was greater still: in Bengal, in Henan, in Tonkin, and in Java, the war eroded the buffer, already slim, that cushioned people from the ordinary vicissitudes of rain and drought.[22]

Extreme weather was the immediate trigger of the wartime Asian famines, but it was not their root cause. In the winter of 1942, a cyclone struck eastern Bengal that "in violence and devastation . . . surpassed any other natural calamity that befell this country." Cyclonic winds and a storm surge combined to cause havoc: they "swept the standing crops, blew off roofs, uprooted most of the trees, demolished the huts." Three-quarters of the region's livestock perished.[23]

Two years later, coastal Vietnam was battered by three successive typhoons, accompanied by a tidal wave that inundated 230,000 hectares of agricultural land. In the Chinese province of Henan and the Indonesian island of Java, the problem was not an excess of water but rather its dearth. Drought parched Henan's fields in 1941–42. The region had barely recovered from the catastrophic floods of 1938, unleashed by Chiang Kai-shek's retreating forces when they breached the Yellow River dikes at Huayuankou to stop the Japanese advance on Wuhan. Drought dried out riverbeds to make an ideal habitat for locust eggs. The locusts duly devoured a harvest already much diminished.

Rain fell short of expectations in Java two years later, in 1944, confounding the strategies of cultivators who had cut back their production for fear that any surplus would end up in the hands of occupying

Japanese forces. Each of these calamities wrecked farmland, flooded fields, drowned animals, and rotted stocks of grain. In normal times, the deficits would almost certainly have caused local hunger and deprivation, but not outright starvation; supplies would have arrived, for each region of deficit traded with places of plenty. But supplies did not arrive for hungry people in Bengal and Henan, Tonkin and Java. Even reserves that had been built up locally were shipped out to feed armies far away. Every layer of protection that rural societies had fought to build up over generations was stripped away.[24]

Expecting a Japanese invasion from Arakan, British authorities in riverine Bengal seized the boats that cultivators used to move rice to market. When local officials raised the alarm about shortages, the British political leadership ignored them. Churchill bore deep resentment toward Gandhi and his Indian National Congress, who had rebelled and launched the Quit India Movement in August 1942. He also expressed a common British racial hatred of India and Indians—let them starve, Churchill said, if never as explicitly as the Nazis. The effect was the same.

At the start of 1943, Churchill ordered a 60 percent reduction in shipping to the Indian Ocean: "There is no reason why all parts of the British Empire should not feel the pinch in the same way as the Mother Country has done," he insisted. Throughout Bengal's catastrophe, British authorities continued to export the surplus grain of Punjab to other theaters of war. As market prices soared and food supplies dwindled, the most vulnerable members of Bengali society succumbed to starvation and illness—worst off were people without land, people without incomes, and fishing communities, whose boats were taken. In greatest peril across all these groups—just as during the famines of the late-nineteenth century—were women and children, the elderly, and people with disabilities. Schoolmaster Bisweswar Chakrabarti described the condition of his home village simply in a letter to the Bengal Relief Committee: "The whole population seems to be moving silently towards death."[25]

In Vietnam and Java, too, the exigencies of war turned government officials stony in the face of people's distress. Japanese commanders prioritized the war effort as the prospect of victory receded week by week, while their earlier insistence that farmers plant oilseeds and fibers at the expense of food crops had already left rural Javanese vulnerable.[26]

Even if the political will had been mustered, relief efforts in Vietnam would still have confronted a devastated infrastructure. Coastal shipping was menaced by Allied submarines. The Transindochinois railway lay in tatters after repeated bombing by US forces, which destroyed bridges in Vinh, Yen Ly, Ninh Khoi, Yen Thai, Than Hoa, Hanrong, Dolen, Ninh Binh, Phu Ly, and Hanoi. "The French Indochina rail system, north from Vinh to the China border," the US military concluded, "was attacked in strength and rendered largely unserviceable." Meat vanished first. People subsisted on stale rice: on good days spiced with eggplant and salt, and most of the time eaten with shreds of water spinach and some sweet potato. And then the rice, too, disappeared from the market. Ngueyñ Thi Chúng, who was a girl of ten at the time of the famine, recalled people's cruel mirages and vanished hopes in a time of catastrophe:

> Eat hoping to ward off our hungry stomachs.
> Dry cakes pretending that they are rice dumplings filled
>   with green bean paste.
> People slit open sweet potatoes and smeared them with
>   ancient bran dregs
> To keep from wilting like swine.[27]

In China, with Henan haunted by starvation, a great exodus began. A planned resettlement of people, organized by the embattled Nationalist government, resembled earlier eras of settler colonization but was now compressed into just a few years. Around fifty thousand people from Henan settled in the Huanglongshan region of Shaanxi. There they cut down trees and eked out plots from hillsides to grow potatoes, corn, and buckwheat. "When the mountains

erode and the rivers grow murky," an official warned, "the harvests . . . are not abundant and erosion problems occur." So great
was the refugees' need, so desperate their quest for survival, that
some local observers predicted that in ten years the denuded land
would produce nothing.[28]

TO RENDER SUCH COLOSSAL human suffering in statistics risks
numbing the horror. Not to count the dead may be even worse: a
prelude to forgetting. Between two and three million people perished in the Bengal famine of 1942–43, and a further two million in
Henan; a million Vietnamese died in the famine of 1944–45, and at
least the same number of Javanese if not more. Nowhere did more
people die in wartime famines than in the Soviet Union, where the
death toll was between seven and nine million people, between six
and seven million of them in German-occupied territory. In Greece,
three hundred thousand people perished, around 5 percent of the
entire population; one hundred thousand died in Austria, and up to
twenty-five thousand in the Netherlands' *Hongerwinter.* Nowhere
are the numbers anything other than approximate. The struggle to
compile them, ever since the end of the war, has led scholars and
survivors to scour village records and local censuses, family memory and mass burial sites. To enumerate the dead has been a form of
witness. Hunger left intergenerational scars: nutritional research has
shown that prenatal exposure to wartime famine in the Netherlands
correlated in later life with lower body size, and an increased incidence of both diabetes and schizophrenia.[29]

In Europe and Asia, communities survived by salvaging niches
for growing plants in the midst of bombed-out cities and along their
suburban edges. Urban gardeners had provisioned their fellow citizens through the First World War's food shortages; in the 1940s, an
even larger number of people, and women most of all, turned to the
land. "The soil is a bowl," a Russian proverb said, "what you put
into it you can take from it" (*Zemlya e tarelka: chto polozhish, to i*

vozmesh). Half of all American households cultivated backyard and neighborhood plots during the war; even Boston Common and the White House gardens were turned to growing vegetables. The British Ministry of Agriculture announced the "Dig for Victory" campaign soon after the outbreak of war: by 1942, 1.6 million public allotments and more than 5 million domestic gardens supplied the British people.[30]

In the Soviet Union, more than anywhere else, kitchen gardens proved a lifeline. The pages of *Pravda* and the Communist Party's women's magazine, *Rabotnitsa*, were filled with columns of gardening advice—they instructed an eager reading public in using animal manure, ash, and turf to nourish the soil's fertility. Grow carrots, one columnist enjoined, for they were "a whole pharmacy in one plant." E. Sivakova, a factory worker with two young daughters, wrote a personal account of her quest in *Rabotnitsa*: "The soil was hard. We ploughed the virgin soil with horses, tractors and forks." Following a night shift at the factory, with only a couple of hours' sleep in her, Sivakova would head to the garden to work—"once in the fresh air all the tiredness disappears," she wrote. By 1945, Soviet official records registered 18.5 million kitchen gardens. Moscow's alone produced ten thousand boxcars worth of vegetables: potatoes in overwhelming quantities along with carrots, beetroots, cabbages, beans, and peas. The Soviet state suppressed stories about the less triumphant side of the kitchen garden movement: the scrounging for tools and supplies, and the proliferation of private markets that many gardeners turned to for a little money on the side.[31]

Where the conditions of life had been obliterated by fire and by bombs there remained defiant, snaking fringes of green. As rice rations shrunk in Japan in 1944 and 1945, as fish disappeared from people's bowls, desperate urban residents planted the edges of railway tracks with wheat, barley, potatoes, and yams. And in Japanese-occupied Southeast Asia, where food distribution had collapsed amid a rampant black market, no patch of soil was wasted. Yap Siong Eu, who lived through the war in Singapore, remembered that people planted tapioca everywhere, even along the edges of stormwater drains. The enterprising boss at the Ban Hin Lee Bank, where Yap worked, reared chickens for eggs in the firm's kitchen. When official routes of supply failed, informal ones stepped in: Yap's customers smuggled him red beans for protein to supplement the meager diet of kangkong and gruel served by the employees' kitchen. On lucky days, pieces of bean curd and leftover pork were purloined from Japanese military kitchens. A Japanese soldier, a "sympathetic" character as Yap remembered him, had a habit of "pok[ing] his sword" into the bags of rice that he deposited in the bank's vaults—he did this as if accidentally, allowing some precious grains to spill out to be swept up by employees.[32]

ONE COUNTRY STOOD ALONE. As Europe and Asia burned, the United States mainland was unscathed; as Asia and Europe battled hunger, American farms produced more than they ever had. Many social groups in America ate better during the war than they had in the lean years of the Depression. American agriculture was productive enough to supply vital grain, meat, and fats to Britain and the Soviet Union through the Lend-Lease scheme. The United States produced a tenth of all the food in the world by 1945.[33]

America's wartime abundance of food had a hidden side. Farmers struggled to meet the surge in demand for vegetables and fruits. A tenth of the agricultural output of California before the war had come from Japanese-American farms; they ceased production after February 1942, because 112,000 people of Japanese origin—79,000 of them American citizens—were forced to leave their homes and were imprisoned in camps in Arizona, Washington, Oregon, and California. To take their place, and to replace farmworkers serving in the military, the US government made a deal with the Mexican government: hundreds of thousands of short-term contract workers crossed the border to work on American farms and on the railroads beginning in 1942.[34]

The Bracero program took its name from a Mexican word for a manual worker, and it would outlast the war. Many *braceros* spoke of the privations and indignities of their lives through analogies with animals, akin to the experiences of so many others caught up in war. At the labor depot, Isidoro Ramírez recalled, "they put you up against the wall, and the contractors came like they were coming to buy livestock" (*como a ir a comprar ganado*). Cecilio Santillano described workers being packed into freight cars, "like sheep," up to El Paso. Chemical pesticides coated the bodies of migrant workers: "They sprayed us like rats, like insects" (*nos espragan como ratones así como insectos*), Isaías Sánchez remembered, "We left covered in powder."[35]

Along with human and animal bodies, swaths of America's farm-land were now "covered in powder"—coated with chemical insec-ticides. The war boom inaugurated the oil age in US agriculture. Petroleum drove motorized tractors; petroleum drove Massey-Harris self-propelled combine harvesters; petroleum drove aircraft that rained pesticides and fungicides upon the soil. A breakthrough in refrigeration revolutionized food preservation. Seabrook Farms of New Jersey, the largest agricultural firm in America, adopted Charles Birdseye's freezing technology at scale, to the benefit of America's allies as well as domestic consumers. Changes in the crop mix of American agriculture cast a long shadow. The area planted with soy in Illinois more than doubled. After the war, soy became dominant in animal feed on both sides of the Atlantic, and it became the crucial ingredient in processed foods.[36]

The productive power of the US economy was the deciding factor in the outcome of the war, and so in the future of the world. "We will emerge from this struggle as the dominant power," declared Ralph Watkins of the US National Resource Planning Board, in November 1942: "dominant in naval power, dominant in air power, dominant in industrial capacity, dominant in mineral production, dominant in agricultural production."[37]

Zoologist Henry Baldwin Ward was one of few people to voice

concern about the consequences of that dominance for what he called "the living and non-living materials that nature furnishes in the vast and little understood complex we call the environment." Ward trained at Williams and Harvard, and in the late 1880s he studied at Germany's premier universities—Leipzig, Göttingen, and Freiburg. He taught high school science back in the United States and then moved to university positions in Michigan, Nebraska, and finally at the University of Illinois. Before an audience at the Texas Academy of Science, in November 1942, Ward raised the threat of extinction amid mobilization for war: "Living things are easily destroyed," he said, "and once a particular type has been exterminated, it can not be restored."[38]

Ward narrated to his listeners a stylized history of the American frontier—the same story that Hitler and Himmler were so fond of telling—and although he embraced the notion that hardy white settlers had rightfully dispossessed Indigenous people, Ward drew a darker lesson. America's bounty was not infinite, Ward thought: "more than one half of the natural resources that the continent originally possessed had disappeared within the first two hundred and fifty years of our history." Ward's deepest fear was that "War is a carnival of waste." In America, the war might bring "enormous, disastrous" environmental consequences, he thought, but not "annihilating" ones, while in Europe, "destruction has already gone to an extreme." Whatever the postwar order looked like, Ward foresaw, it would demand the extensive restoration of nature's ruins.[39]

Students of the American war effort are mesmerized by it, even now. "One must risk hyperbole," economic historian Jonathan Levy writes, for the war brought the United States "global economic preeminence on a scale unmatched in history." Jill Lepore conveys the same sense of awe through numbers: during the war, American workers built three hundred thousand aircraft, eighty-six thousand tanks, three million machine guns, and seventy-one thousand ships. During the war the United States produced half the coal and two-thirds of the oil in the world. The Federal Government invested $70 billion in aerospace, arms, and electronics to propel another spurt of American industrialization, this time on the Pacific coast. The marriage of advanced scientific research and industrial capacity gave the United States its unassailable edge in destructive power, nowhere more than at the Los Alamos Laboratory where, in secret amid the high mesas— inspired by daily walks amid the pines, and a view of the Sangre de Cristo range—Berkeley physicist Robert Oppenheimer coordinated the Manhattan Project to produce the atomic bomb. When the Manhattan Project team witnessed the test explosion they conducted on July 16, 1945, they turned not to the language of military-industrial might but to expressions of awe at the unnatural power of what they had unleashed: "I thought that the explosion might set fire to the atmosphere and finish the earth," Emilio Segrè wrote. Oppenheimer, a student of Sanskrit, recalled that at the moment of the explosion, a line from the *Bhagavad Gita* came to him: "Now I am become Death, the destroyer of worlds."[40]

Twinned with the power of destruction, the strength and success of the American war effort lay in its construction of a new infrastructure of life support. The United States built runways to airlift supplies, pipelines to move oil, and factories to freeze vegetables. The clothing of American soldiers was coated with a new substance, Dichloro-diphenyl-trichloroethane (DDT), which insulated their bodies from insects. Aerial spraying of DDT moved from individual bodies to whole ecosystems to create zones of perceived human safety from malaria in the tropics. Satisfied US military medical officers found that DDT was "still killing—weeks after the first application."[41]

The technological struggle against hunger was manifest in every rectangular tin of SPAM—chopped-up pork mixed with salt, water, potato starch, sugar, and preserved in sodium nitrate to make a pink, oleaginous meat—shipped to every theater of war in a triumph of global logistics and imprinted on the culinary memories of people around the world. "Without SPAM we wouldn't have been able to feed our army," Soviet premier Nikita Khrushchev later recalled; "it tasted good," he added. Across the Pacific, wherever US troops went,

SPAM remained—"Hawai'i's soul food," a local food writer would call it, still, in the twenty-first century.[42]

In the mountainous, forested terrain between India, Burma, and China, the wartime quest to dominate natural environments reached a limit. The last three years of the war saw brutal struggles to stamp infrastructure onto unyielding landscapes. First the Japanese and then the Americans confronted the unfinished business of nineteenth-century colonization: they dusted off plans for roads and rail tracks that had been abandoned, now hastily revived to create supply corridors. The Japanese military forced the construction of a rail line from Thailand to Burma in 1942, using sixty thousand Allied prisoners of war and two hundred thousand Asian workers to hack through teak forest: they built six hundred bridges, viaducts, and embankments over the rivered ground to support a 250-mile stretch of rail. "The Japanese did not give me a proper shirt or blanket for seven months," testified a Tamil plantation worker in Malaya who had been bundled into a Japanese truck at gunpoint and forced to work on the railway. An estimated ninety thousand Asian workers and sixteen thousand Allied prisoners of war died in the effort. Richard Middleton-Smith, a private in the Straits Settlements volunteer force and a fluent Tamil speaker, noted in his diary—scrawled on the squared paper of school exercise books and on the backs of account ledgers—the large number of railway workers who staggered into relief camps at the war's end, having been forced to spend "agonising days clearing the jungle to build a camp of sorts."[43]

After the loss of the Burma Road to Japanese conquest in 1942, treacherous high-altitude flight over the Himalayas—The Hump, it was called—was the only way the Americans could keep Chinese allies supplied. To build a supplementary land route, fifteen thousand US soldiers, more than half of them African-American, worked alongside thirty-five thousand Asians, not all of them there willingly. Bengalis from the tea plantations of Assam, Garo porters, Indian and Chinese soldiers—all joined in the effort. To American

A photograph
of the Ledo
Road under
construction
in 1944.

planners, it all seemed a stretch too far, even with all the tools at their disposal. "The jungle is not an exotic green wilderness of gigantic trees, rare flowering plants, swarms of monkeys swinging from the vines, writhing snakes and vicious animals," a US Army report warned—it was worse than that: "The jungle, in reality, is tall and dark and silent as death." The troops and engineers soon found that the jungle was not quite silent: "just a decibel away from silence" there were "the buzzes and hums and whirrs" of the insects, "which died by the thousands every night." Assailed by winged tormentors, their clothes stinking of insecticide, insulation was for the troops a distant dream.[44]

General "Vinegar Joe" Stillwell's 1,000-mile road—to link northeastern India to the Burma Road connecting Burma and China—was built in two years. In aerial photographs the road looks like part of the landscape, embedded in the mountains and with no sense of what it had taken to create it. Lord Louis Mountbatten, commander of the Allied South East Asia Command, is said to have asked, the first time he flew over the Ledo Road, what river it was that he saw glinting in the sun. Convoys of trucks began to cross it in January

1945; over the next six months, they carried 129,000 tons of military and civilian supplies. Aircraft carried significantly more. The road was always secondary to the air corridor, which escaped the terrestrial threats of the jungle altogether.

It is hard to say which mattered more for what was to come: the speed with which the road was built, or the haste with which it was jettisoned. By January 1946, the British government of Burma would write to London that "we understand that U.S. forces have already abandoned it, or are on the point of doing so." Four decades later, American zoologist and big cat conservationist Alan Rabinowitz—who had obtained special permission from the junta to study the region in the 1980s, when Burma was closed to the world—described the ruins of the great Ledo Road: "skeletons of bridges, along with miles of old rusting pipe, battered oil drums, and numerous unrecognizable pieces of military hardware, now taken over by jungle."[45]

The Japanese Burma railway, which extinguished so many lives, suffered the same fate. In *The Narrow Road to the Deep North*, in which he imagines the experience of Australian prisoners of war on the railway, novelist Richard Flanagan describes the ruins of the railroad with taut ambivalence: a rampant, hopeful, recolonization by nature of the human wreckage; and an appalling erasure of human suffering through neglect. "The Line welcomed rain and sun. Seeds germinated in mass graves, between skulls and femurs and broken pick handles. . . ."[46]

Amid the war's powers of human and more-than-human destruction, the possibility of life, of survival and renewal, lay in cultivating the ruins of nature by the sides of ditches and in straggly blotches of green among shattered cityscapes. To claim human freedom was to reclaim kinship with the natural world. "Today, in this place, our only purpose is to reach the spring," Primo Levi recalled, as he brought vividly to life a day in the camp when "the sun rose bright and clear for the first time from the horizon of mud." It was a faint sun, "cold, white and distant," but it was enough that "a murmur ran through our colourless numbers." By contrast the camp of Buna, where the prisoners were forced to work, was a "huge entanglement of iron, concrete, mud and smoke"—in every way "the negation of beauty." On the camp's grounds, Levi wrote, "not a blade of grass grows and the soil is impregnated with the poisonous saps of coal and petroleum, and the only things alive are machines and slaves. . . ." To cling to one's humanity was to cling to a sense of communion, glimpsed or remembered, with the rest of nature.[47]

7:09 AM, AUGUST 6, 1945: *Fair weather, ready for air raid.*

Just over an hour later, "Little Boy" heated the air to several million degrees centigrade at the moment it exploded at 8:15 am, 1,800 feet above the ground. The thermal flash that accompanied the bomb's detonation killed seventy thousand people in an instant. Its impact touched almost every form of life. Birds dropped from the sky, hemorrhaging and denuded of feathers. At a stables near the hypocenter of the blast, 120 of 184 horses died; the equine survivors suffered burns, leukopenia, and suppurative conjunctivitis. Death mirrored art in trees that stood like Cubist paintings—the face turned toward the explosion was blistered and bare, the other was undisturbed: green and profuse with branches. Earthworms barely noticed the blast; all around them, the roots and stalks of plants survived underground.

At 9 o'clock on that morning of fair weather, rain started to fall. Black rain. Mutant raindrops gathered and disgorged the remnants of fire that whorled through city streets at a rate of 18 meters per second. Kimura Yasuko, who had been evacuated to a temple in the hills under the strict care of nuns, gazed down on what remained of her city. "The ruins from an ordinary fire are burned black, aren't they?" she mused many years later, "But the ruins of Hiroshima were brown, the color of unfired pottery." The uranium bomb unleashed by American forces on Hiroshima on August 6, 1945, and the even more powerful plutonium bomb on Nagasaki three days later, brought about the "total disintegration of human life."[48]

At the end of a war that had stripped the Earth of wood and ore and grain, at the end of a war that had forged new technologies of mass destruction—all that remained was the fragile creatureliness of the human body. So thin was the protective layer of skin that flapped or peeled in strips from people's bodies as they ran from the flames. So hallowed was the sensation common to all animals: the relief of water upon dry lips. But this water was radioactive.

The direct effects of the bomb—thermal injuries, blast injuries, radiation injuries—killed 140,000 people in Hiroshima, and 70,000 in Nagasaki. For those who lived, the trauma continued. Radiation stained the soil and water, causing a surge in leukemia, in thyroid and breast and throat cancers, in microcephaly in infants. Radiation destroyed "the reparative and regenerative processes of the living body" for years, for decades, afterward.[49]

President Harry S. Truman and US military leaders justified the atomic bombs as a necessary evil to end a war that had cost tens of millions of lives. The terrible swiftness of destruction, they argued, saved many lives that would have been lost in a ground invasion of Japan. Ever since the bombings of Hiroshima and Nagasaki, others have been skeptical. Japan was on its knees and close to surrender, critics say. The United States used the atomic bomb to demonstrate to the world, and in particular to the Soviet Union, that it commanded powers of earthly destruction without precedent.[50]

In the last two years of the war, even before the atomic bombs crossed a final threshold of ruin, Allied militaries wielded sufficient force to make an unnatural weather phenomenon: the firestorm. In the last week of July 1943, the Royal Air Force dropped so many bombs and incendiary devices on the city of Hamburg that hundreds of fires fused together in an 800-degree cyclone that devoured 256,000 dwellings, left forty thousand people dead, and injured more than one hundred thousand others. Aerial attacks on Dresden followed between February 13–15, 1945. The US bombing survey reported, "fire storms occurred, the violent fires generating a violent hurricane-like draft, which fed other fires and made all attempts at control hopeless." After two nights, all that remained of large parts of the city hung heavy in the air as clouds of smoke.[51]

Tokyo suffered the most devastating attack of all. As they contemplated the destruction of Japan's capital city, US military planners predicted "a degree of destruction never before equalled": they estimated that half a million people would die in a city where 90 percent of homes were made of wood. The night of March 9, 1945, American B-29 bombers unleashed 1,665 tons of bombs—a "great mushroom of boiling, oily smoke"—upon Tokyo. Many were cluster bombs, and each released a flurry of smaller devices a couple of thousand feet above the ground. The bomblets were filled with a substance discovered by Harvard chemists only three years earlier, a mixture of naphthenic and palmitic acids, their opening syllables squashed to make "napalm." Explosive compounds in the bombs ignited phosphorous, which burned hot enough in turn to ignite the napalm—a flammable, gelatinous liquid that adhered to the exposed surfaces of wooden houses and tarred roads, and human bodies. Napalm burns, blasts, asphyxiates its victims. When Tomie Akazawa spoke of the storm that had deranged everything, the detail that remained was the "tremendous updrafts that lifted from our shoulders the quilts with which we tried to protect ourselves." That night, in that man-made weather, more than 100,000 people died; a million lost their homes.[52]

In every fire of 1944 and 1945 there were echoes of earlier fires lit by German and Japanese dreams of world conquest—the fires across the frozen waste of Stalingrad, leaving "an enormous cloud of burning, blinding smoke"; the fires that obliterated the Arctic port city of Murmansk, bombed by German forces in June 1942; the fires that ate at the city of Chongqing, which Japanese forces bombed again and again from 1939 to 1944; the fires of Manila in 1945, where 100,000 Filipinos died amid the Japanese army's last acts of self-immolation; the fires that fed the crematoria of Auschwitz-Birkenau, where at least 1.1 million Jewish people were killed in gas chambers, among the 6 million murdered in the Holocaust.

"Mushroom cloud,"
Hiroshima, August 6,
1945.

Scientists have estimated that wartime fires emitted more than half a billion kilograms of soot into the atmosphere in 1944 and 1945—enough, in theory, to reduce the solar radiation reaching Earth's surface, though it has not been possible to demonstrate any clear impact of the Second World War on global climate. Even if the war's climatic signature cannot be proven, that such colossal impact is even plausible marks the dawn of a planetary power beyond comprehension. The iconic photograph of the Hiroshima explosion, taken with a handheld camera by the *Enola Gay*'s tail gunner, George Caron, shows an unnatural sky: a billowing "mushroom cloud" that engulfs the natural cloud forms around and beneath it.[53]

Years after the war, a group of Japanese scientists, doctors, and citizens constituted the Committee for the Compilation of Materials on Damage Caused by the Atomic Bombs in Hiroshima and Nagasaki: a prosaic name for an endeavor of lasting moral power and intellectual rigor. Only occasionally does the plain restraint of the committee's prose give way to something closer to anger. As the committee searched for words to describe the crimes of August 6 and 9, 1945, they chose: *genocide, ecocide, biocide, earthocide.* In this combination of horrors lies a new way to see not only the atomic bombings but the entirety of the Second World War—as the dark culmination of a century-long history that saw the twinned acceleration of both human and environmental destruction.[54]

PART III

THE
HUMAN
EXCEPTION

1945–2025

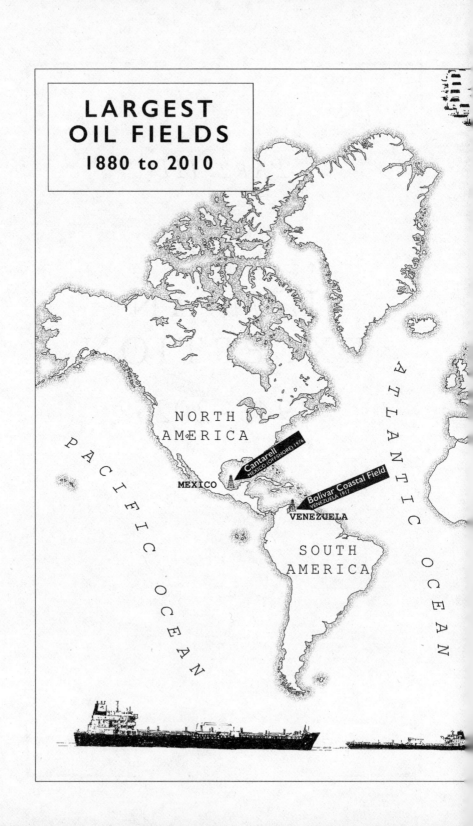

LARGEST OIL FIELDS
1880 to 2010

PACIFIC OCEAN

ATLANTIC OCEAN

NORTH AMERICA

MEXICO

Cantarell
MEXICO (OFFSHORE) 1976

Bolivar Coastal Field
VENEZUELA 1917

VENEZUELA

SOUTH AMERICA

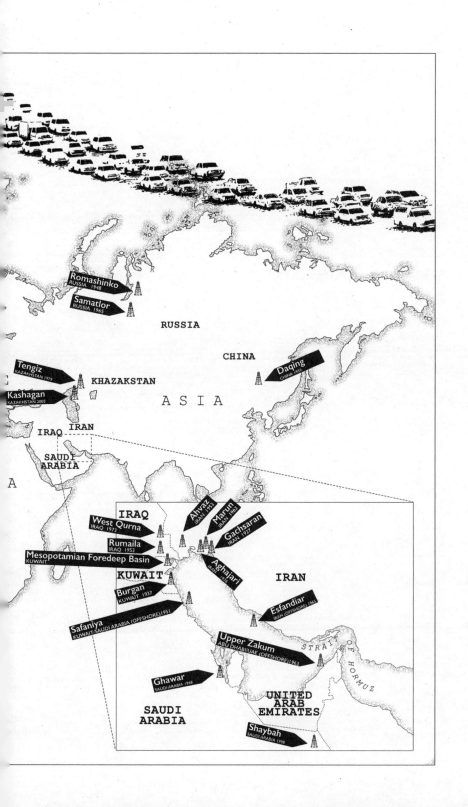

CHAPTER NINE

FREEDOM'S PROMISE

K ANJI WATANABE LEARNS THAT HE HAS STOMACH cancer and only months left to live. He is a cautious civil servant: a stickler for rules who makes nothing happen as director of public affairs in the municipal government. Shocked into questioning the values he has lived by, Watanabe devotes his remaining days to the pursuit of a simple human aspiration: for there to be space—green space, breathing space—where children can play.

This is the story of Akira Kurosawa's 1952 feature film, *Ikiru*, a pinnacle of achievement for the director and for a Japanese film industry that had pieced itself back together after the war. Inspired by Tolstoy's novella, "The Death of Ivan Ilyich," *Ikiru* touched an international audience with its animating question: what is a life well lived? Watanabe's quest poses a second, implicit, question—what are the environmental conditions for human flourishing, and how can they be achieved?[1]

Ikiru opens with the Kuroe Women's Association approaching the local government with a modest request: they submit a "Petition to Repair and Fill in Culvert." The final cut of the scene grew from the darkly comic sketch that Kurosawa added to the bare-bones scenario that Shinobu Hashimoto had written for him:

City Hall, the Public Affairs Section window.
Housewives have arrived to petition about the clogged drain.

"Thanks to the water I got this weird rash." "On top of that, it stinks and there are lots of mosquitoes." "Isn't there anything you can do about it?" . . .

The protagonist of the story, the section manager, states without feeling: "Civil Engineering Section . . ."

Civil Engineering Section: "This issue is the responsibility of the local Public Health Center."

Local Public Health Center: "Ah, that goes to the Sanitation Section."

The runaround continues until the women scream with frustration. Years after the war's end, the women of Kuroe still live amid its ecological wreckage.[2]

We do not see the site until halfway through the movie. By this point, Watanabe has died; the rest of the film unfolds in flashbacks and through the self-serving recollections of the colleagues at his wake. The camera cuts to a scene in the pouring rain. Watanabe and his reluctant staff stand arrayed under umbrellas; and then Watanabe steps out alone into the waterlogged, rubble-strewn square.

Akira Kurosawa, *Ikiru* (1952): the scene where Kanji Watanabe visits the site for the first time.

Soon earthmovers are shifting soil and leveling ground. The rattle of engines and the whine of drills reach a crescendo. A construction vehicle knocks over the frail Watanabe. Colleagues rush to help him, but he dusts himself off, a sense of wonder in his eyes at the momentous change taking place before him; he watches the machines work "as if he were watching his child or grandchild." What they are building is neither a dam nor a road, neither a steel plant nor a car factory. All this motorized activity comes together for a playground—a small, grassy patch of freedom with a view of the open sky.

NEVER HAD SO MANY people been promised so many freedoms as in the twenty years after the Second World War. At the San Francisco conference of 1945, which inaugurated the United Nations, four draped pillars on the ceremonial stage symbolized each of the "four freedoms" that FDR had first articulated in his State of the Union address of 1941, embraced as guiding principles for the postwar settlement: freedom of speech, freedom of worship, freedom from want, and freedom from fear. As Britain's cities lay cratered by German bombs, their shops' shelves grim with tinned meat and powdered egg, liberal politician William Beveridge had promised an "attack upon five great evils" in his 1942 *Report on Social Insurance and Allied Services*. The Beveridge report imagined an expanded set of human freedoms, inspired by a new egalitarian spirit still tinged with Victorian moralism: freedom from "physical Want," from "Disease which often causes Want," from "Ignorance which no democracy can afford among its citizens," from "Squalor which arises mainly through the haphazard distribution of industry and population," and from "Idleness which destroys wealth and corrupts men."[3]

Immediate political freedom took precedence for colonized people around the world who suffered hunger and terror through the bloody collapse of a European-dominated world order. War-shattered European nations had neither the funds nor the troops to hang on to their colonial empires. That did not stop them from trying.

After Indonesia's brief Proclamation of Independence on August 17, 1945, nationalist leader Sukarno made an effusive announcement: "So it is, Brothers and Sisters! We are now already free! There is not another single tie binding our country and our people!" But it would take Sukarno's forces four more years of war to defeat reoccupation, as the Dutch sought to cling to Indonesia's oil and timber—and to the status of an imperial power. Neighboring Malaya's rubber and tin were lucrative enough for the British to dig in to defeat popular radicalism with bombs and internment camps and promises of plenty. Vietnam's Communist leaders had an even longer and bloodier road ahead of them; so, too, did anticolonial movements in Algeria and Kenya. A Cold War between the two postwar superpowers, the United States and the Soviet Union, filled the international power vacuum left by retreating empires. With their promises of aid and expertise came new sorts of ties.[4]

Hard-won political freedom was only the start. Part of Ho Chi Minh's indictment of French rule, in Vietnam's September 1945 declaration of independence, was that the colonizers had "devastated our land . . . robbed us of our rice fields, our mines, our forests, and our raw materials." Freedom meant sovereign control over the products of nature.[5]

With that achieved, what would come next? Drafting India's democratic constitution, B. R. Ambedkar insisted that freedom required a degree of equality: "The fear of starvation, the fear of losing a house, the fear of losing savings . . . are factors too strong to permit a man to stand out for his fundamental rights." Ambedkar was a brilliant Columbia University–trained lawyer and political leader of India's Dalits; he devoted his political career to fighting the systematic discrimination, the violence, and the persistent indignity of untouchability that Dalits faced. In his last speech to India's Constituent Assembly, Ambedkar warned that the independent republic was about to "enter into a life of contradictions." He diagnosed the fundamental problem: "In politics we will have equality and in social and economic life we will have inequality." That tension would surely gnaw, Ambedkar thought, at the possibility of true freedom.[6]

Upholding the promise of freedom was a bedrock of confidence that the technological bonanza of the war years would bring a new level of human control over the conditions of life. In the postwar world, "man can be the master of his environment and not its slave," declared the United Nations' compendious *Preliminary Report on the World Social Situation.* Neither in the 1948 Universal Declaration of Human Rights ("Everyone has the right to life, liberty and security of person"), nor in any of the national constitutions drafted in those years, was there a reckoning with the ecological preconditions for freedom. It was enough to believe that the conquest of nature would be smooth—and that it would be sufficient. But environmental mastery, if not wholly illusory, was a capacity unequally distributed. The question was insistent: who could, and who couldn't, enjoy a measure of protection from the caprice of rain and drought, from flood and fire and infectious disease?[7]

IN 1950, THE MEXICAN artist Diego Rivera began work on what would be his last great public project. Rivera was a giant of a man: mercurial, demanding, and wildly creative. In his physical presence, and in his character, Rivera seemed to match the proportions of his murals. Rivera set out to paint the tunnels of the Cisterna Lerma, command center of a web of aqueducts built under Chapultepec Park to supply Mexico City with water from the hills. The site was rich with meaning. Tenochtitlan, city on a lake, was once a place of abundant water but had been dammed and drained by Spanish colonizers and then drained again during the Mexican Revolution. The Lerma project would honor the memory of Aztec hydraulic genius to forge a future where Mexicans would thirst no longer. Rivera called his mural *El Agua: Origen de la vida en la Tierra* (Water: Origin of Life on Earth). Rivera's epic celebrated the fusion of nature's power with the heroism of human labor, inspired by the evolutionary theories of Soviet biologist Alexander Oparin. Known for his celebration of industry, Rivera was always attentive to the vegetal and mineral origins of industrial power.

Witness this scene from the Lerma mural: a worker holds a pick-axe ready to strike rock; one step ahead of him, a man hands a bowl of water up to a young Indigenous girl. She sips from it as her parents look on in gratitude and astonishment, the mother cradling another baby. Nearby, a father and son irrigate their garden from a hose that gives them water on demand; the garden's profusion of green contrasts with the arid and dusty village in the background. Just above the archway to the tunnels, a pair of hands forms a cup; water spills through it, like a benediction on the nation. On the tunnel floor, Rivera painted a menagerie of extinct water creatures to evoke the origins of life. It is as if all that cumulative energy would now be harnessed to the project of building a just future. Overseeing it all, above the entrance to the tunnel, Rivera painted the wise engineers whose job it is to harness the power of nature. Here they are deep in discussion, bent over an unfurled chart; in the middle of the group stands Eduardo Molina, the brains behind the Lerma project.

Outside the building, standing guard, is Rivera's 100-foot-wide sculpture of Tlāloc, Mexican god of rain and harvest. The two-faced Tlāloc looks up at the sky and down to Earth. On Tlāloc's sandals, Rivera made a mosaic that shows the aqueduct slicing through mountains. Rivera designed the sculpture with a distinctive angle of vision in mind—he designed it to be seen from the air, from the window of descending aircraft. The Mexican citizen of the jet age would take in, at a glance, the whole hydraulic history of a civilization, and the direction of its progressive future.

Rivera's mural struck a universal chord. The same year the Lerma system opened, India's prime minister, Jawaharlal Nehru, dreamed a similar dream. In a speech to his Central Board of Irrigation and Power, Nehru described the Himalayas as "a suppressed source of vast energy" that "flows out in great rivers . . . watering the plains of India, running into the sea." India possessed "a mighty reservoir

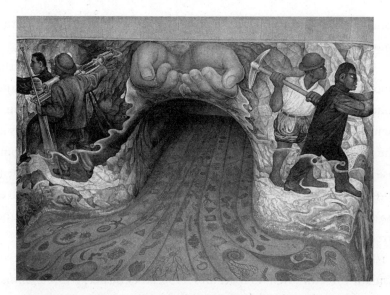

Diego Rivera's mural in the tunnels of the Cisterna Lerma, Mexico City.

A girl receives the gift of water: a scene in Rivera's mural.

of energy," Nehru thought, "which if only we could utilize it to full purpose, what could we not do . . . ?"[8]

Control over water, an ancient human desire, now symbolized the most modern ambitions for what the leaders of Asian, African, and Latin American countries called "development"—a word freighted with associations. It brought to mind tables of inputs and outputs in hundreds of pages of five-year plans; it brought to mind the promise and peril of World Bank loans and American or Soviet aid; it brought to mind an army of engineers, just like the figures in Rivera's mural. It also evoked plainer dreams of food and shelter and freedom for children to play.

Development fed the imagination. It was the beating heart of Indian director Mehboob Khan's 1956 blockbuster, *Mother India*. The opening scene of this epic film shows a frail old woman inaugurating a big dam in her village. It would be the key to her freedom and redemption. Told in flashbacks, Radha's lifelong struggle against a hostile nature becomes a metaphor for the Indian nation's struggle for freedom—hers is a life at the mercy of floods and haunted by famine, menaced by moneylenders and always under the shadow of death. Now she, her children, and her country would suffer no more. India's political freedom, *Mother India* imagines, will also bring India freedom from the vagaries of the monsoon. Mehboob's film was wildly popular in West Africa; it has been screened in Ethiopia continuously ever since the year of its release; it drew crowds across Southeast Asia, gained fans in the Soviet Union, won hearts in Greece where memories of wartime famine were still raw. *Mother India* captivated viewers around the world with a compelling story about turning the power of nature toward enhancing human life.[9]

Mother India proved especially popular with Egyptian audiences, who recognized the dam as a bulwark against imperialism. Egypt's charismatic leader, army officer Gamal Abdel Nasser, prevailed over an invasion by British, French, and Israeli forces in 1956; the attack was prompted by Egypt's decision to nationalize the Suez Canal in a dispute over the High Dam at Aswan, centerpiece of Nasser's plans.

US president Dwight D. Eisenhower feared that such flagrant colonial aggression by the British and French would undermine American strategic interests in the Middle East. While the United States would not directly import Middle Eastern oil in significant quantities until the 1970s, guaranteeing its easy flow to American allies in western Europe was a lever through which the United States exercised power in the world. Eisenhower put pressure on the Europeans to withdraw, even to the point of threatening to cut their petroleum supplies. Britain and France were forced into a humiliating climbdown.[10]

The dam rose as a symbol of both political and material freedom. Egyptians had built the High Dam not only "to reclaim two million feddans of desert land or secure ten million kilowatts of electricity," a government pamphlet declared, "but to prove also their independence which they wrested from tyranny and domination." The dam "is a symbol of moral struggle," Nasser told a fervent crowd: "a symbol of the abolition of imperialism, a symbol of determination"— Egypt would redirect the course of the Nile, "whether America wishes it nor not, and whether Britain wishes it or not."[11]

Infrastructure would be a salve for the wounds that accompanied the making and breaking of nations. Opening the 658-foot dam at Bhakra, built to irrigate the recently partitioned and still traumatized province of Punjab, Nehru was rhapsodic: what could be greater than this, he wondered aloud, "where thousands of men have worked or shed their blood and sweat and laid down their lives as well?" Speaking in Hindi and English, Nehru invoked the image of birth: "Mother India is in labour, producing and creating things," he said. The highest aim of the project and of his government, Nehru said, was "putting an end to the poverty of India"—poverty that two centuries of British exploitation had done much to deepen. The dam, and hundreds of projects like it, would awaken India and other postcolonial nations from their colonial torpor. Bhakra became an international symbol of India's rebirth. On the last day of 1956, Nehru took the visiting Chinese premier, Zhou Enlai, to visit the dam— the two men, and their countries, had started to build a rapport, though it turned out to be short-lived. "These are the new temples of India where I worship," Nehru told Zhou; "I am deeply impressed," Zhou replied.[12]

A REVOLUTION IN THE conditions of human life on Earth was wrought by millions of citizens of newly free nations. India's future was chiseled from rock by Velu Pillai, a stonecutter from Thanjavur who had honed his craft carving temple deities, and who now raised the Tungabhadra dam. It was engineered by Mr. Eswaraiah, supervisor of the country's first factory for the manufacture of sluice gates, his "sheer mechanical intelligence" having impressed the project's chief when he met Eswaraiah in "a Madras highway repair shop." India's future was built by the women, uncounted and unnamed in most archives, who hauled buckets of soil and water on their heads. It was jolted into motion by the clink of hammers and the thunk of spades and the clatter of conveyor belts.[13]

And Egypt's future was in the hands of workers like Dandarawi 'Abd al-Mun'im Hasan, who came from a water-scarce farm to "respond to the calls of the mountain to work in dynamite." His job was to drill into the granite cliffs and insert the sticks of explosive that would shatter them, making room for new canals to divert water. Hasan "trembles with life while he clings to the mountain," a profile in the pro-government *al-Ahram* newspaper described, "and he trembles with life while he collectes 45 piasters a day" for his work. With the dam's gift of water, "Everything in his life changes."[14]

An abundance of people, willing to move long distances to work—on their labor new nations would rise. Saint Lucia–born, London-trained economist W. Arthur Lewis published a paper in 1954 called "Economic Development with Unlimited Supplies of Labour." It captured how Lewis and, with him, many leaders of postcolonial nations perceived their task. This new movement of people would be no rehash of the nineteenth century's history of migration from Asia and Africa to other parts of the world, when the term "coolie" served as shorthand for a system of racial abuse from which there was never any question over who would gain. It would resemble only faintly, if sometimes uncomfortably, the settler migrations of the nineteenth century that pursued liberty for white people by taking it away from others. In a postcolonial age, development gave new meaning and purpose to human migration, now redirected within national borders from rural areas to the cities and factories that epitomized an industrial future.[15]

Collective labor on such a scale appeared to be a force of nature, to be channeled in much the same way as the energy of the Himalaya mountains. "Thirty years ago it was possible for one man to bring out that 'elemental force' from the Indian people," Nehru said, referring to Mahatma Gandhi's mass political campaigns; now, when freedom was won, "the question is how to regenerate that 'elemental force' and the urge to do things." Nehru and his contemporaries wanted workers on dam sites and steel plants to know what they were working so hard for. "Your work is to explain to the ordinary worker what he is doing in the scheme," Nehru admonished an engineer, who had neglected to do so. On another occasion, the religiously skeptical Nehru urged community workers to "search your hearts to find out whether you are going back to your States with the feeling of a crusader or missionary."[16]

Scratches appeared on the veneer of collective purpose. Workers were, after all, there to do a job. They took seriously the rights they had been promised. They formed unions. They demanded higher wages and better conditions. When workers at the Hirakud Dam site in eastern India went on strike in January 1954, the local magistrate authorized armed police to disperse them. The police deployed a tactic that had been a staple of colonial policing, used repeatedly against freedom fighters: they mounted a *lathi* charge on the protesting workers. Bamboo batons met flesh and bone. Fifty workers sustained injuries serious enough to put them in hospital; two of them died the next day.[17]

Neither human nature nor physical nature were as pliable as the orchestrators of development hoped. They turned, undeterred, to the power of fossil-fueled technology.

WHAT COULD WE NOT do? Nehru had asked, and many others asked the question with him. In the 1950s, the yellow construction vehicles of the Caterpillar corporation of Peoria, Illinois, trundled across the world to answer it. They bestowed upon engineers the power to move mountains and raise new ones. Caterpillar had started life making steam-powered tractors for Midwestern farms; in the 1950s, the corporation became the world's biggest manufacturer of earthmoving equipment—the description itself, "earthmoving," is a word recorded no earlier than the 1930s, and it signified a new kind of power. If today human activity moves more rock, sediment, and soil than all of Earth's natural processes, the 1950s marked the turning point in the human capacity to do so.[18]

Caterpillar brought out its self-propelled wheel tractor-scraper in 1951; its No. 6 shovel reached the market a year later—for "land clearing, digging, grading, truck loading, slope work," advertisements promised—and then, in 1954, came a machine of mighty capability: the 29-ton D9 tractor with a turbocharger in its diesel engine. Caterpillar was quick to see opportunity in the enthusiasm for development that swept Asia and Latin America that decade. In 1954, the company opened its second international subsidiary (the first was in England) in a warehouse in São Paulo. By the end of the 1950s, more than one hundred pieces of Caterpillar equipment were at work on the site of India's Bhakra Dam, supplied by a firm started in Bombay before the war by two Danish engineers, Henning Holck-Larsen and Søren Kristian Toubro. On the site of the Aswan High Dam, Caterpillar yellow was a presence long after Nasser had turned to the Soviet Union for aid. Earthmoving machines drove the race to build big: 60,000 tons of machinery shifted 13,000 cubic meters of rock a day; "this rate is expected to be accelerated in the future," the Egyptian Ministry of Information announced, the use of the passive tense ("is expected") suggested that this expectation was widely shared.[19]

Small as well as large countries deployed the alchemy of petroleum to remake themselves. On the island of Singapore, as independence from British rule beckoned, an ambitious government of educated men—lawyers, economists, engineers—turned from their youthful socialism toward pragmatic dreams of creating something from nothing. On 8,600 acres of marshland in the west, the finance minister, Goh Keng Swee, inaugurated a $122 million project to forge an industrial zone on an artificial island built from sand. An array of construction equipment dug and drained and hammered the land, overlaid it with earthworks and roads and bridges, secured it with sea walls. When Professor Jacques Rueff, head of the World Bank's economic mission, saw the site in October 1962, he said, simply: "it's a wonder." For years afterward, Goh would jokingly confess to his fear that the whole project would be a lost cause, forever to be known as "Goh's folly."

The son of a rubber plantation manager in Malacca, Goh went to Singapore's best schools, studied at the London School of Economics in the 1950s, and worked as an administrator in Singapore's Department of Social Welfare. With a "tremendous zest for work [and] a gift for concentration," Goh was imbued with the late-Victorian values of many of his generation. Accepting the Philippines' highest honor, the Ramon Magsaysay Award, in 1972, Goh said: "The virtues we need to cultivate in ourselves are the simple virtues propounded by nineteenth-century Scottish essayist, Samuel Smiles: 'thrift, industry, ambition, honesty and perseverance.'"

If Jurong Island began with an act of ecological destruction, it was also an act of repair. Once the Jurong River had been reengineered to make space for the industrial park and its bed had been dredged for sand, the government raised further artificial islands on the artificial lake it had created where the river once ran. On those islands, Singapore's planners built stylized Chinese and

Japanese gardens, which I used to visit as a child. A highly cultivated urban nature was created to take the place of what had
been destroyed.[20]

This was how oil insinuated itself into the hopes and dreams of the
postcolonial world: less as a means of individual mobility than as the
route to collective uplift; as fuel for dozers more than for cars. Wherever oil was discovered, in Latin America and in Asia and in Africa,
it promised to hasten the path to freedom. Brazil's discovery of oil
reserves in 1940 raised hopes that this new source of energy would
thrust the country up from the lowest rungs of the global economy. As
oil wells took the place of plantations, they redeemed landscapes dis-
figured by the baleful legacy of sugar and slavery. "This basic wealth
was not created by engineering nor by the hand of man," Congress-
man Alberto Pasqualini said in June 1953, "it has been bequeathed
by nature, and therefore it needs to be exploited only for the benefit
of the national collectivity." Brazil established a state oil monopoly
in 1953: Petrobras, the national oil corporation became a proud symbol of resource sovereignty. Brazilians celebrated the democratizing
bounty of oil in popular songs, in literature, and in photographs.
Seven decades after abolishing slavery (Brazil was last to do so, in
1888) Black Brazilians still confronted structural racism and limited
options—the "black gold" from the wells of Bahia promised a way
out. O petróleo é nosso, "the oil is ours," was the cry.[21]

The path to freedom through oil could, and often did, end abruptly.
It came to an end in Iran, which nationalized its oil fields in 1951
after pressure from a movement led by Mohammed Mossadegh, who
then became Prime Minister—many young Iranians believed, like
Brazilians, that "the oil is ours." But Iran's oil was more important
to Europe than was Brazil's. British intelligence and the CIA, who
believed the oil was really theirs, promoted Mossadegh's conservative enemies through a flurry of misinformation and manipulation,
trumped-up allegations, and manufactured protests, until a coup in
August 1953 brought down Mossadegh's elected government and

Mass protests in Iran in 1952 in support of Mohammed Mossadegh.

installed the pro-Western Shah, Mohammad Reza Pahlavi. A year later, the National Iranian Oil Company signed a profit-sharing agreement with a consortium of foreign oil corporations.[22]

The dream of using oil to promote justice and equality refused to die—and its risks began to flare. A decade after Mossadegh's nationalization of oil, director Ebrahim Golestan made a short film for the National Iranian Oil Company. *Yek Atash* ("A Fire") chronicled, in color, a seventy-day battle in 1958 to extinguish a fire at an oil well in the southern region of Khuzestan. Golestan's short documentary is a testament to the power of film to record, archive, and elicit an emotional response to the environmental restyling of the postcolonial world.

"Suddenly, a spark flew," the narrator begins, starting in midflow, and "soon after, the fire became a part of the landscape." Flames fill the screen. Jets of water pumped from the Karun River are feeble before the fire. Two sounds are constant, even when the narrator falls silent: the whoosh and roar of the blaze, and the

sputter of engines—the engines of tractors, trucks, and pumps that
fight the fire. At the climax, a tractor approaches the fire—likely a
Caterpillar—and it resembles a wounded but determined creature
crawling to its doom, its arm extended, clutching an insulated box
of dynamite. *Yek Atash* gave a twist to the familiar narrative of men
battling the hostile elements: this fire, created by human beings, was
no longer under human control; it could only be subdued by another,
even greater, human fire: an explosion that would bury the source
with cement.[23]

The haunting quality of Golestan's film comes from its visual
montage of the villagers who live in the shadow of the disaster. This
was the contribution of the film's editor: the modernist poet, New
Wave filmmaker, and cultural iconoclast, Forugh Farrokhzad, who
was Golestan's creative partner until her death in a traffic accident
in 1967. "Nights passed, days dawned—and harvest time came to
the neighboring fields," the narrator intones. Cutting through the
noise of the fire in the mix are the soulful notes of mothers singing
lullabies. Families share food and draw water from wells; they reap
what they can from a poisoned harvest. The flames are always there,
always part of the landscape. And then the villagers pile their bundled belongings onto trucks. They set out for a life unknown, which
we glimpse as an encampment of tents. They become refugees from
the fire—refugees from progress.[24]

In a scene that recalls photographs from Baku's conflagration in
1905, Golestan depicts the ruins of the dream in "the broken poles,
the twisted pipes and mangled hooks"—and in the haunted eyes
of exhausted firefighters. Carbon encrusts their faces, but this is
no longer the dark hope of plenty dramatized by Brazil's authoritarian populist leader, Getúlio Vargas, smearing his skin with
Bahia oil. *Yek Atash* reveals the price of fossil-fueled development,
but it also makes clear that it is a price humans would continue
to pay: "The fire was put out and the well was shut," the narrator
concludes—"and the efforts continued to drill another well, but that
is another story."[25]

"THERE IS A NEW war," Mao Zedong announced to Chinese Communist Party (CCP) officials in January 1958: "We should open fire on nature." Giving literal meaning to an old proverb, Mao told the Eighth Party Congress a few months later: "When we ask the high mountain to bow its head, it has to do so! When we ask the river to yield the way, it must yield!" Nowhere else in the postcolonial world was the conquest of nature imagined in such a violent way. Mao had just announced what he called the Great Leap Forward in 1958, with the goal of overtaking Britain's industrial capacity in less than two decades.[26]

Haste was a narcotic. However fast change came, it didn't come fast enough. However much production increased, it needed to increase more. Progress in increments might as well be no progress at all. To push the pace meant an ever-growing need for oil, machines, expertise, and loans from abroad. A decade after Mao Zedong's People's Liberation Army had prevailed over Chiang Kaishek's nationalists in 1949, China's gross domestic product per head remained, at best, 5 percent that of the United States. Mao sought to kick-start China's development using the sheer size of the country's workforce, imbued with the superhuman energy of revolutionary enthusiasm. What followed was a human and ecological disaster without precedent.

In August 1958, Mao decreed that China's production of steel would double in a year. Memories of the chaos are still vivid in oral testimonies that historian Xun Zhou collected fifty years later. Whole villages scrambled to build backyard blast furnaces, which they fed with every sliver of metal their households possessed: "knives, pots, hammers, door locks, and keys, even pegs for holding pictures on the wall," recalled Sun Po, who was in her forties at the time, living in Xushui. Xu Yongshing, then newly married and living near Chongqing, remembered the waste: "perfectly good weaving machines, as well as tables and chairs, were all smashed into pieces before being fed into the furnace." The furnaces devoured wood. "Our village was in the mountains," said Liang Xiansheng in Zhongshan, "It used to be covered with trees, but all of them were cut down in order to make iron and steel." It hardly mattered that the steel produced by the backyard furnaces was useless; local officials, always under threat of sanction from above, kept boosting targets and then issued wildly exaggerated accounts of achievement. The fear-saturated culture of official dishonesty made it impossible to register, let alone respond to, people's distress.[27]

Worst of all, the pressure to make steel dragged able-bodied farmers from their fields. Cultivation collapsed. Ill-judged advice from party officials to plant seeds more deeply in the soil made things worse: "there was no space for the growing crops to breathe," Mrs. Yue, a farmer in Anyue recalled, "how on earth could they grow?" Throughout rural China, famine tightened its grip. Outright starvation rather than infectious disease took the greatest toll, in contrast with earlier famines in China. It is a tragic irony that this owed something to the CCP government's notable progress in immunization and sanitation in the years before 1958, reducing the burden of cholera, smallpox, and plague.[28]

Political folly caused starvation—and still the rivers would not yield, the mountains would not bow. By the summer of 1960, drought in Shandong had diminished many rivers, and "it was possible to wade across the lower reaches of the Yellow River"; meanwhile in Sichuan, four excessively wet summers in a row, from 1958 to 1961, inundated crops. When the government acknowledged the people's suffering at all, they blamed "natural disasters"—as if the Maoist state hadn't left people vulnerable with its abrupt changes in policy, as if an avalanche of unrealistic goals hadn't buried rural China's preparedness for dearth. To survive, if they survived at all, families mined the collective memory of many previous famines during China's "century of humiliation," as the nineteenth century was known. They drew lessons from the very legacy of poverty that the Great Leap was determined to overcome. Starving villagers ate chaff, and

tree bark; they ate flower seed and sawdust and thistles; they ate
stone ground into flour. Around one and a half million people fled
Shandong province in 1960 alone, defying every official attempt to
limit migration.[29]

The Great Leap inflicted generational, perhaps irreversible, damage upon China's lands, waters, and forests. Breakneck irrigation
schemes flooded fields and turned fertile soils an alkaline, powdery
white. "Many paddy fields in the valley have turned into dry land;
some even became sandy beaches," a party official reported from
Fujian. Liu Jianxun wrote in distress to Zhou Enlai, in December
1961, that "in a few years the vast plain along the Yellow River will
turn into a total wasteland."[30]

The "war on nature" was also a war on animals, none more brutal than the collective assault on the common sparrow. Chinese officials thought sparrows consumed too much grain. Along with rats,
flies, and mosquitoes, sparrows were among the "Four Pests" to be
driven from the land. Children led the charge, some as young as
five years old. "The whole school went to kill sparrows," a Sichuan
man told political scientist Judith Shapiro in the 1990s, recalling his
childhood: "we made ladders to knock down their nests, and beat
gongs in the evenings when they were coming home to roost." The
cacophony was, for the birds, a kind of torture. Only later did regret
set in. "It was many years before we knew that sparrows are good
birds," the man said. "At the time, we only knew they ate grain." An
agricultural chemist in Chongqing told Shapiro about a local artist who had specialized in painting sparrows; during those terrible
years, the artist hid his work away in shame. The war on animals
hardened people's hearts, crushed their sympathy for other living
creatures. The destruction of the sparrows during the Great Leap
was motivated by a misguided sense of public purpose, always with
the end goal of increasing the production of food. In that sense, at
least, it never had the bloodlust and gratuitous cruelty of American and European colonial trophy hunting in the nineteenth century.
The birds' importance to the ecology of human flourishing, by their

feeding on insects, became evident only when it was too late. Hungry and broken villages complained of a plague of bedbugs.[31]

Because local governments ceased to keep records amid social collapse, and because they concealed anything that resembled truth, the number of people who died in the Great Leap famine will never be known with certainty—estimates vary between twenty million and thirty million people.[32]

China's suffering was extreme; but throughout the postcolonial world, the struggle for material freedom took its toll. Idealistic political leaders came to believe, even if they did not believe initially, that some people, some landscapes, and some species were disposable. The language of sacrifice seeped into every demand that states made of their citizens. An Indian government official told a public meeting of villagers threatened with displacement by a water project in Hyderabad that they "should not stand in the way of the construction of the project but should consider it a great sacrifice on their part." Nehru himself had said the same thing to the thousands evicted by the Hirakud Dam: "If you are to suffer, you should suffer in the interest of the country." In India, that "suffering" fell disproportionately on Adivasis, whose homes were in the forests drowned by reservoirs, whose compensation was inadequate when it was granted at all, whose places of resettlement felt like exile from the bonds of community and the affordances, however precarious, of a familiar ecology.[33]

In Egypt, the cost of the Aswan High Dam was no more equally shared. It fell to the people of Nubia, whose homes were drowned by Lake Nasser. Between 1963 and 1968, an international team of architects, archeologists, and artisans salvaged the temple of Abu Simbel—built by the Pharaoh Ramses II (1290–1224 BCE) in sandstone cliffs—from the rising waters. It was a $40-million project overseen by the United Nations Educational, Social and Cultural Organization (UNESCO). Piece by piece, the temple was dismantled by custom-made handsaws and reassembled on higher ground. Local people watched this happen. They heaved sand and rock as workers on the site—and they wondered, amid a rushed and inadequate program of resettlement, why their villages and homes could not be moved with the same loving care as the temple, "from the basement to the attic, the men and the animals, stone by stone."[34]

The uprooting of people by infrastructure rivaled the largest refugee movements of the twentieth century. From 1947 to the early twenty-first century, activists and scholars have found that at least forty million people in India alone were driven from their homes by large dams. In China, the numbers affected are harder to determine with accuracy, but they are likely to be even higher. Villages made way for dams, for pipelines, for oil wells, for steel plants, for roads. Across the postcolonial world, there emerged the "poignantly paradoxical figure" of the "development refugee." Scenes akin to the moment of the villagers moving away in Golestan and Farrokhzad's *Yek Atash* played out all over the world. The communities affected were not selected at random; for the most part they belonged to marginalized minorities.[35]

"Man can be the master of his environment and not its slave," the United Nations predicted. That search for mastery brought drinking water to millions of people, it filled dinner plates with grain, it made whole regions of the world safer for human habitation. The costs of progress were never quite concealed, but over time they became more visible. Engineered reservoirs submerged forests and uprooted communities; intensive irrigation salinated soils; land grabs deprived people of their homes; oil wells exploded, poisoning people and birds and animals.

ALL THE WHILE, ANOTHER part of the world pursued a different sort of freedom. By 1950, there were already 40.3 million cars on American roads, owned by 39.9 million families; just five years later, the number of cars had grown to 52 million. At home in America, the Caterpillar corporation sold a dream different from the one it sold to Brazil or India. In conjunction with the Federal-Aid Highway

Act of 1956, which set out to build 41,000 miles of interstate highways across America with 90-percent funding from the Federal government, Caterpillar hitched its roadbuilding armory to a vision of
unlimited personal freedom, embodied by the open highway. Pro-
ceeds from the federal tax on gasoline went directly to the Highway
Trust Fund, which built more and more superhighways.

In the 1950s, fractionated petroleum products seeped into American homes and into Americans' bodies: it was embedded in the
pills they ingested, the sanitary products they used. Oil changed the
American diet. The advance of fossil fuel use in American agriculture during the war now reached a position of absolute dependence.
The tractors that roamed industrial farms gulped diesel; petroleum
derivatives formed the base ingredient of fertilizers and pesticides;
their use, in turn, made possible a level of meat consumption "previously unseen in the history of human life."[36]

Petroleum advertising in the 1950s celebrated oil culture. A 1956
advertisement for Shell Oil reminded American consumers how
thoroughly their comfort and convenience depended on petroleum:
"Oil research helps with quick drying paints, no polish floors, durable plastic tabletops, and weather defying asphalt-shingle roofs."
Oil allowed Americans to get to the shopping center; and oil made
the things they bought there. The year of the 1956 Highway Act,
Vienna-born architect Victor Gruen completed his masterpiece, the
Southdale Shopping Center, in Edina, Minnesota, just off the I-294.
It was the world's first fully enclosed, fully air-conditioned shopping
mall, complete with a two-story parking lot: symbol of an automotive, consumer age. A 1962 advertisement for Humble Oil boasted,
under a picture of a snow-capped mountain: "Each day Humble supplies enough energy to melt 7 tons of glacier."[37]

"Your home is a home that oil built," Shell reminded Americans
through its advertising. In the 1950s, the New Deal–era Federal
Housing Administration pushed a surge in suburban housing development when its mortgage insurance underwrote the biggest construction boom in US history. The scheme favored large builders and

Four gasoline pumps in Yoder, Kansas, from the John Margolies
archive of Roadside America.

low-density developments of single-family homes in purely residential neighborhoods; it condemned as risky investments in the mixed-
use, racially diverse neighborhoods of the inner cities. Urban areas
were "redlined," a term that came from the red lines on Housing
Administration maps that marked out the areas that would not be
insured. The historic cores of many American cities were hollowed
out for a generation. Cars became indispensable to suburban sprawl,
while the combined pressure of oil companies, car manufacturers,
and developers undermined public transportation. At every highway junction stood clusters of motels, gas stations, fast-food restaurants, and truck stops. This landscape of the American highway
lodged in the world's consciousness through Hollywood movies and
popular music.[38]

NOWHERE IN THE WORLD did the automobile become as cen-
tral to living as it did in the United States; nowhere else did suburban
sprawl reach American dimensions. The western European allies of the
United States in the Cold War developed their own automotive cultures,

with a greater emphasis on compact vehicles proportioned to narrower city streets, and each with a distinctive stamp of national style.

In postwar Italy, cars spread with prosperity and became a symbol of a country reinvented. In the first of Elena Ferrante's "Nea-
politan Quartet" of novels—set in the postwar years and rich with
closely observed historical detail—the Fiat 1100 car, launched in
1953, appears as a signal of social change. The Solara brothers, Mar-
cello and Michele, sons of a successful bar owner, "bought a blue-
and-white Fiat 1100 and on Sundays paraded around the streets of
the neighborhood." Sitting in the public park, studying Latin, the
novel's protagonists, Lenù and Lila, perceive "a constant smell of
pitch" as steamrollers lay tarmac for new roads; land is cleared for
development, and they "heard the sound of annihilation for days" as
"the trees groaned" and "gave off the scent of fresh green wood."[39]

American economic assistance through the Marshall Plan spurred
Fiat's growth. The firm received $30 million to purchase plant and
equipment and put it to good use: through the 1950s, its factories
produced 2.9 million cars. The appearance of the nifty, rear-engined
Fiat 600 in 1955, affordable and made to seat four passengers, ush-
ered in the rise of mass car ownership. To celebrate the new model,
Fiat staged a parade of 600s through the streets of Turin. A year
later, designer Dante Giacosa released the 600 Multipla, a squat
people-carrier with rounded edges, flexible enough to furnish a fleet
of bottle-green-and-black taxis and also to transport goods.[40]

To fuel this new society, the Italian government established in 1953
the Ente Nazionale Idrocarburi (ENI), which acquired a monopoly
on hydrocarbon prospecting in the country. The Po Valley proved
rich in natural gas, but disappointing as a source of oil. So, ENI
ventured overseas. To gain new markets, ENI offered oil-producing
countries in North Africa and the Middle East deals more attractive
than the 50-percent profit share promised by the major oil corporations. Under ENI's offer, producing countries would become equal
partners in joint ventures if significant oil was found; and if not, ENI
would swallow the cost of failed exploration.

Advertisement for the Fiat Multipla 600, marketed as a flexible and democratic form of transportation in postwar Italy.

ENI's leader, Enrico "Enzo" Mattei, promised developing countries sovereignty over their own resources. ENI reached agreement with Nasser's Egypt in 1955, followed by Iran; and then, by the end of the decade, with Morocco, Libya, Sudan, Tunisia, and Nigeria too. At a speech in Tunis in 1960, Mattei declared outright, to assembled anticolonial leaders, "I am not afraid of decolonization." He said, "I believe in decolonization not only for moral reasons to do with human dignity, but for economic reasons to do with productivity." He gestured to Italy's own history as a mark of solidarity: "I, too, have to decolonize . . . indeed I would say that the south of the selfsame Italy was colonized by its north!" Mattei insisted that "the geography of famine is a myth"—the Third World remained poor not because of nature or climate, but because it had insufficient control over its natural wealth. What he offered, as effective a salesman as could be, was "parity, co-management, the formation of a technological elite," and above all the chance to be "the subject, not the object, of the economy."[41]

Mattei was charismatic and driven. The *New York Times* grudgingly dubbed him the "oil emperor of Italy." The US State

The allure of automotive modernity was strong even in the
poorest countries. Seydou Keïta, Malian portraitist and studio
photographer, captured the aspirations of ordinary Malians,
as in this photograph of women posing with a Citroën taken in
the 1950s.

Department mistrusted him. Mattei was born in 1906, one of five
sons of a noncommissioned officer of the Carabinieri, and during the
war he had commanded a partisan force fighting the Nazis after the
fall of Mussolini. After 1945, he dedicated himself to Italy's petrochemical future. ENI's advertisements beckoned to consumers with
the promise of a new era of prosperity, bright amid the drab constraints of postwar austerity. ENI's gleaming petrol stations sprang
up beside fast-expanding networks of highways all over Europe,
under the Agip brand that dated back to the Fascist era. In 1961, ENI
defied pressure from the US government and started importing large
quantities of cheap crude oil from the Soviet Union in exchange for
machinery and technical expertise. Mattei offered Italian consumers
autonomy from the "Seven (wicked) Sisters," as he dubbed the major
oil companies—the name stuck. His firm alone, he said, was "working in the interests of the country and not in search of profit."[42]

Mattei died in a plane crash in 1962. A bomb was the likely cause, though the details remain murky. Rumors alleged conspiracy: the suspects included the CIA and French settlers in Algeria, where Mattei had started talks with the nationalist insurgents of the FLN (National Liberation Front). By the time he died, ENI was a major player in the quest to stoke and satisfy the world's addiction to fossil fuels.

Global crude oil production in 1950 was approximately 9.5 million barrels per day, and ten years later it had nearly doubled. Neither figure counted the Soviet Union's considerable output. The United States and the Soviet Union remained the two largest producers of oil by 1960—the United States remained far ahead—but Middle Eastern states rose up the ranks, Kuwait, Iran, and Saudi Arabia foremost among them. Known reserves of crude trebled that decade following a rush of oil exploration, reaching 264 billion barrels by 1960. More than half of those known reserves were in the Middle East, thrusting the region into the crosshairs of strategic competition between the world's major powers. Global carbon dioxide emissions almost tripled between 1950 and 1973, but for now, only a small number of atmospheric scientists paid this any attention.[43]

THE AMERICAN PATH TO prosperity faced a challenge from the Soviet Union's equally energy-intensive model. Their competition began with power generation itself, and extended from there to alternative ways of organizing society. Superpower rivalry was strongest when it came to the most spectacular, the most promising, and by far the riskiest prospect on the horizon—harnessing the colossal energy released when neutrons split the atoms of the heaviest natural element: uranium. Nuclear power would generate electricity "too cheap to meter," promised Lewis Strauss, chair of the US Atomic Energy Commission. But its public perception was marked from the outset by the lag of almost a decade between its first use—to extinguish life in Hiroshima and Nagasaki—and its later civilian deployment. Neither in the 1950s nor at any time since could nuclear power be dissociated entirely from the power of nuclear weapons.[44]

"Atoms for Good and Evil" was the slogan of a public education exhibition that toured Britain's cities in the early 1950s at the initiative of Joseph Rotblat, the only atomic scientist to have resigned from the Manhattan Project on ethical grounds. In 1953, at the UN General Assembly, President Eisenhower made his "atoms for peace" speech, promising US technical support for the civilian development of nuclear power under the control of an international body (to be known as the International Atomic Energy Agency, which was started in 1957). The Soviets got there first. In June 1954, the world's first nuclear power station at Obinsk, 62 miles southwest of Moscow, was connected up to the capital's electricity grid. Within three years, France, Britain, and the United States possessed nuclear power stations of their own. West Germany and Japan would later join the small number of countries that substantially developed nuclear energy. Among them, France stood out. In France, the close relationship between the atomic energy commission and the nationalized electric utility underpinned large-scale investment in nuclear power—for decades to come France would rely on nuclear for a significantly larger proportion of its electricity than any other country. Nuclear power carried the banner of national pride in a country haunted by fears of post-imperial decline.[45]

Whether it came ultimately from petroleum or from nuclear power stations, American and Soviet visions of the good life both demanded substantial energy. By the time of Nikita Khrushchev's cautious repudiation of Stalin's terror at the Communist Party's twentieth congress in 1956, the Soviet leadership had come to realize that they could no longer dismiss as frivolous people's desire for small luxuries to ease their daily lives. The Soviet Union, too, now aimed toward "a complete abundance in our country of every type of consumers' goods," Khrushchev announced.[46]

Across the Soviet republics and eastern Europe, the Khrushchev era launched a sprawling program of residential construction, planned and implemented by the state rather than private developers. These first took the form of five-story apartment buildings, known with grudging affection as *khrushchevski*; in the 1960s, large tower blocks took their place. They were built at scale to identical designs, inside and out, prefabricated using modular concrete structures. With decent housing came a new level of control over the domestic environment. With decent housing came a new vision of collective life that inverted the values of the American single-family home: the apartments would come with public cleaning and public childcare—they would also come with the claustrophobia of constant surveillance.

Soviet-aligned East Germany went furthest in developing the petrochemical adornments of modern life. Nourished by the "friendship pipeline" that funneled petroleum from the oilfields of the Urals, East German factories manufactured polyethylene and polypropylene to furnish apartments with smooth, wipe-clean surfaces. "Chemicals Give Bread, Beauty and Prosperity!"—this was the hopeful slogan of the 1958 East German Chemical Conference. The pliability of plastic embodied a future where anything was possible. Using language that was not so different from Shell advertisements in America, Soviet propaganda praised the liberating qualities of oil. "From oil we take for the needs of our country a river of gasoline," announced a poster by graphic designer Viktor Karetsky, "oil and petroleum and in addition thousands of items for the home and for domestic comfort!"[47]

The showdown, when it came, took place over a kitchen. The American National Exhibition of consumer goods was held in Moscow in 1959, at a moment of easing in US–Soviet tension. Before a global television audience, US vice president Richard Nixon demonstrated to a skeptical Khrushchev the wonders of a Miracle Kitchen by Whirlpool, and a full General Electric kitchen in lemon yellow. The "kitchen debate" between the two men turned on whose system, and whose technology, could better "liberate" the housewife from domestic toil. (That this toil should always fall to the wife in a

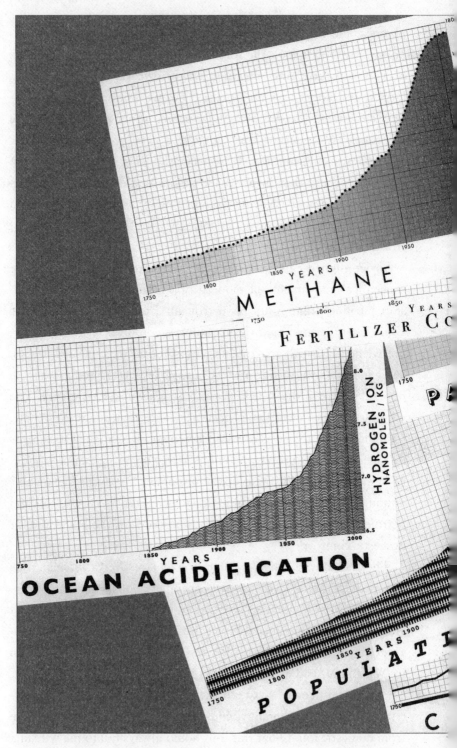

The great acceleration.

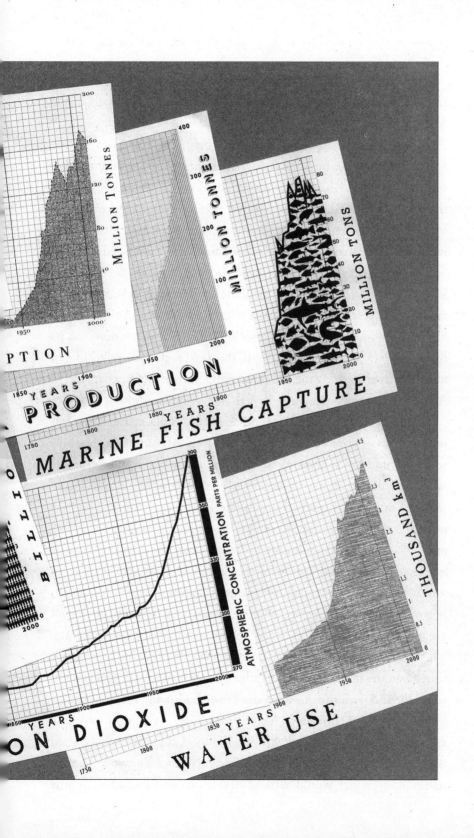

nuclear family—from that presumption only a few voices dissented, such as the Soviet construction engineer who quipped that "In the Miracle Kitchen a woman is just as free as a bird in a miracle cage.")[48]

For the most part, the debate took place on a basis of shared assumptions. "You think the Russian people will be dumbfounded to see these things," Khrushchev roared, but every Russian kitchen had them already—or they would, even if they didn't yet. By competing to satisfy the desires of modern consumers, Khrushchev entered a losing game. The Soviet economy proved unable to transcend its focus on heavy industry, born of the need to catch up with the West and forged by the trauma of war. Its planning machine lacked the local flexibility to respond to changing tastes. Both futures, American and Soviet, demanded a "river of gasoline." The Soviet version and its offshoots proved the most wasteful, the most recklessly polluting, of all paths to growth, while the more rapid and efficient expansion of American capitalism devoured oil at an even greater rate.[49]

So compelling was the kitchen battle between American capitalism and Soviet communism that it might almost have been possible to forget that the superpowers, boasting of their ever more refined ways to enhance domestic comfort, were at the same time devising ever more total ways to annihilate life on the planet. The fifty nuclear weapon tests carried out by the United States between 1948 and 1958 included Operation Castle on Bikini Atoll in 1954, which witnessed six nuclear explosions including a 15-megaton thermonuclear device, *Bravo*. The test brought lasting harm to the neighboring island of Rongelap. Women miscarried fetuses; people of all ages developed thyroid cancer; children suffered from leukemia. The blast's residue of radioactive strontium, cesium, and iodine poisoned aquatic life across 5,000 miles of ocean. With US government funding, and with the quest for data overshadowing the human suffering it revealed, brothers Howard and Eugene Odum traced how radioactive isotopes moved through the food chain in the Marshall Islands. The Odums pioneered the field of science known as ecosystem ecology, which would become vital to our understanding of how environmental harms reverberate across species. It has its dark origins in the harm caused by US nuclear testing in the Pacific.[50]

The Soviet Union conducted its own tests, dozens of them, in eastern Kazakhstan and in the Barents Sea. The "kitchen debate" took place during the three-year lull that followed the Limited Test Ban Treaty of 1958. It would not last, In October 1961, in the Arctic archipelago of Novaya Zemlya, the Soviet military tested the most powerful weapon in history—at 50 megatons, *Tsar Bomba* was more than three times more powerful than *Bravo*. A Russian military observer on the ground recorded that, following a "powerful, white flash," the sound of the explosion—"a remote, indistinct and heavy blow"—made him think, for a moment, that "the earth has been killed!"[51]

THE PERIOD OF GLOBAL history since 1945 has been called "the great acceleration" by climate scientists.[52] In the 1960s and 1970s, slowly at first and then with gathering force, evidence piled up to reveal a fundamental change in the human relationship with the rest of nature. Trends in how the Earth system was changing emerged like a bas relief from the solid rock of data generated by an apparatus built to monitor the effects of atomic tests and to support space exploration. The extent of observation increased simultaneously with the intensity of the changes being observed. Records of surface temperature, rainfall, and forest cover had been collected for centuries in different societies—Chinese records of all three reach back thousands of years. The global scale was new. The range of indicators amenable to scientific measurement was new. What the data revealed about the extent and scale of human intervention in the Earth's geophysical processes was not only new, but previously unimaginable.[53]

The surge in data collection came with the inauguration of the eighteen-month International Geophysical Year that ran from July 1, 1957, to December 31, 1958, first proposed by scientists Lloyd

Berkner and Sydney Chapman. It was the first comprehensive study of the planet: from pole to pole, from the upper atmosphere to the deep ocean. It involved sixty-seven nations and tens of thousands of scientists across the Cold War divide. The project gathered information on cosmic rays and glaciology, on seismic and solar activity. Its quest for transparent, universal knowledge stood in uneasy relationship with military secrecy. The Geophysical Year breached the protective layer of the atmosphere: it was the occasion for the surprise launch of the Soviet Sputnik satellite, in October 1957; and then, in response, America's Explorer 1 orbited the planet in January 1958, packed with temperature sensors and devices to detect micrometeoroids and cosmic rays. Fleets of ships mapped the ocean floor with sonar technology, discovering a landscape that mirrored terrestrial mountains and valleys.

The project of 1957–58 established permanent World Data Centers, which combined to create new series of indicators to measure planetary processes. American atmospheric scientist Charles Keeling established an observatory on the Mauna Loa volcano on Hawai'i in 1958 to measure atmospheric concentrations of carbon dioxide. The same year, the British Antarctic Survey began measuring total ozone over Halley Bay. Their continuing results would begin to tell a frightening story.

The International Geophysical Year sought a baseline of knowledge and observation; the notion that human activity was affecting geophysical processes was not yet a major concern. But neither was it an implausible suggestion. At the start of the international project, Scripps Institute oceanographer Roger Revelle had written, with his colleague the geochemist Hans Suess, that human beings were conducting, unwittingly, a "large scale geophysical experiment" with the world's climate. "Within a few centuries," Revelle and Suess wrote, "we are returning to the atmosphere and oceans the concentrated organic carbon stored in sedimentary rocks over hundreds of millions of years."[54]

The socioeconomic indicators that accompanied the Earth system trends depended on their own data-gathering machine. From the 1940s, the United Nations and its technical agencies churned out statistics, aggregating the information they received from national governments and conducting their own surveys, putting them all together in statistical yearbooks. A new infrastructure of knowledge arose from foundations laid by the League of Nations and the International Labour Organization before the war. Their data, too, began to tell a striking story.

Accounts of the human dimensions of the great acceleration tend to be descriptive rather than diagnostic: they mostly fail to grapple with how the Second World War and decolonization changed the world. One widely cited review of the evidence states simply that the great acceleration came about as a result of "the phenomenal growth of the global socio-economic system" after 1945—as if this "phenomenal growth" happened spontaneously rather than as a result of human struggles, human choices, and human conflicts. In the richest countries of the world, the great acceleration brought consumption and material security that was nothing less than shocking so soon after the war. The decades from 1950 to 1970 were a period of sustained expansion in industrialized countries: a "golden age" that saw a fourfold increase in world manufacturing output, a tenfold increase in world trade, together with a sharp rise in the consumption of petroleum and nitrogen—and in the emissions of both carbon and methane.[55]

The "golden age" left many people behind, even at its height and in the regions of greatest prosperity. The French term for that era, *"les trentes glorieuses,"* appeared only when those thirty "glorious" years had ended in the 1970s' bitter stew of inflation and unemployment. Success inspired fear. At the height of American economic and political power, US commentators were haunted by the specter of decline. For those with the fewest resources in wealthy countries, social mobility was hard-won, and always fragile. Growing industries in western Europe and North America depended on migrant workers from poorer regions: they were denied the benefits of welfare and the security of citizenship. Their sense of tenuous belonging is captured in the West German term *Gastarbeiter* ("guest workers"). In the Soviet bloc, the great acceleration was marked by a rapid rise in emissions and waste—but it fell short of delivering on the promises of greater choice for people to lead the lives they valued.

Most of all, the great acceleration meant something different in a postcolonial world poised between the tenuous promise of liberation and the intractable scale of the social and economic challenges ahead. For most of the Third World, the great acceleration was an aspiration several steps ahead of material reality—it was a dream of a better future, of faster progress and greater security. It was the dream of breaking out, finally, from the "waiting room of history," as historian and philosopher Dipesh Chakrabarty has called it. Confronted with the idea of a "great acceleration," most citizens and leaders of Asian, African, and Latin American countries would have said: yes, please, and it can't come soon enough. Mao Zedong had impressed this upon China's people, and he had tried to impress it upon China's rivers and its mountains too—we must go faster.[56]

Of all the hockey-stick charts, none touches the core of human experience so much as the graph of global population. Of all the changes that swept the postwar world, the most intimate was a transformation in the ecology of death. Between 1945–49, across a sample of eighteen "under-developed" countries—to use the UN's term of that time—the death rate fell by 15.2 percent; and from 1950–54, it fell by more than 20 percent. A UN investigation reported that "the extension of mass-disease control, which can eliminate scourges at relatively little cost, accounts in good part for these successes." Throughout the Third World—a term used assertively by countries of Asia, Africa, and Latin America as a mark of mutual solidarity—national health services aided by international agencies carried out vaccination against smallpox, sprayed DDT to reduce the transmission of malaria, and deployed antibiotics against infections like yaws; just as important were unheralded, halting improvements in municipal water supplies.[57]

Each step marked a more sweeping ecological intervention than even the clearing of land and the building of dams. Medical technologies were relatively inexpensive and so effective that they offered the prospect that Third World countries "do not need to become economically developed to reduce their death rates drastically." In India close to 133 out of every 1,000 babies born between 1945–49 died before they reached the age of one; by 1960, that number had fallen to 86.5; the figure for Thailand over the same period fell from 82.2 to 48.7; and in Nigeria it fell from 209, more than a fifth of all children born, to a still-devastating but significantly reduced 180. For most people, the fundamental conditions of human life on Earth— how long one could expect to live, whether one's children would die in infancy, whether a mother would survive childbirth—changed more rapidly in a decade than over the preceding several centuries.[58]

The big numbers of demography, even more than economic statistics, are distant from the lived experience of human beings. It took time for people to believe, in their own lives, that it was really true: that doctors could treat their fevers, that needles would deliver them protection from ancient scourges—that their children had a chance of life. Progress was fragile, and it was not equally accessible. In 1952, when victory was already being touted in the "war" against disease, Indonesian writer Pramoedya Ananta Toer penned a short story, "My Kampung" about those who had been forgotten. The word *"kampung,"* meaning village, had come to describe informal urban settlements—in this case, a shantytown but a stone's throw from the government headquarters at the palace, "where everyone's health, and every little detail is guaranteed." The story's acid-tongued narrator invites the reader on a tour of his neighborhood "where people die one after another," where "not even a small guerrilla squad" could survive. The kampung's residents died from the lead fumes that poisoned the air, from venereal diseases, from the tuberculosis infections that were so prevalent as to be "something routine." Mocking the promises of a new dawn, the narrator notes: "If killing with weapons is punished by the government, killing because of ignorance and poverty is not prohibited in my *kampung*...," which stands "in all its glory, defying the doctors and the technical professionals."[59]

The inhabitants of Pramoedya's fictional kampung were not alone in seeing every gain as tenuous. Addressing an international malaria conference in Delhi in 1959, Jawaharlal Nehru noted that, "In [malaria control], as in other matters which affect us underdeveloped countries the pace, the speed of advance, become all the more important." The risk, Nehru said, was that "if you don't go fast enough, the others will"—"others" such as evolving anopheles mosquitoes and human population growth. "In many of these regions of Asia, maybe elsewhere, malaria has been a more powerful determinant in the course of human history than people imagine," Nehru concluded, or perhaps warned: the implication was that it might still prove to be so.[60]

The great acceleration was a constant struggle. The conquest of death raised new fears about the control of life.

CHAPTER TEN

THE HUMAN
CONDITION

A PHILOSOPHER, A SCIENTIST, AND A POLITICAL leader. They were born just over a decade apart, between 1906 and 1917, on three different continents. To the best of my knowledge, they never met nor did they ever correspond. They came of age in the 1930s—one exiled from Nazi Germany; one forced by the Great Depression to abandon advanced study; one left to navigate a mother's illness with a father in and out of jail for anticolonial struggle. After the war each of them confronted, with uncommon insight, the cluster of changes that in retrospect we have called the "great acceleration."

By the end of the 1950s, a mass of data demonstrated how thoroughly human activity had affected forests and rivers, the oceans and the atmosphere. But how should societies respond? What did environmental change imply for the pursuit of justice? Three remarkable women reflected on how to navigate, morally and politically, a transformation in human life: German-born American Jewish philosopher Hannah Arendt (1906–75); American marine biologist and science writer Rachel Carson (1907–64); and Indian politician Indira Gandhi (1917–84), who served for almost sixteen years as prime minister.

AS HANNAH ARENDT WAS revising a set of lectures that would be published in 1958 as *The Human Condition*, the Soviet satellite Sputnik I orbited Earth. Arendt saw this as a pivot in human history more fundamental than the splitting of the atom. She perceived that the public response to space flight was "not pride or awe at the tremendousness of human power and mastery" in an era of postwar optimism. Rather, Arendt detected a sense of relief at the prospect of a "step toward escape from men's imprisonment to the earth," as an American news article had put it.[1]

Arendt elucidated the dilemma: "The earth is the very quintessence of the human condition," she wrote, "and earthly nature, for all we know, may be unique in the universe in providing human beings with a habitat in which they can move and breathe without effort and without artifice." First in science fiction (which Arendt disdained as "always disreputable"), and now in popular consciousness, that earthbound fate felt like "imprisonment." The quest to reach outer space shared something with the fight to extend the human lifespan: both expressed a sense of "rebellion against human existence as it has been given." The prospect that now beckoned was "cutting the last tie through which even man belongs among the children of nature."[2]

Arendt had fled Nazi Germany in 1933, moving first to London and then to New York. She remained steeped in a Western view of the world, and never thought to ask *who* sought this freedom from planetary boundaries. Did that dream extend to those, dispossessed and colonized, for whom life on Earth had not yet delivered its promise of the freedom to "move and breathe without effort"? Was the anticolonial struggle not itself a "rebellion against human existence as it has been given"?

In *The Origins of Totalitarianism*, the brilliant refugee philosopher located the roots of Nazi and Stalinist terror in the destabilizing churn of industrial capitalism. The monstrous violence of twentieth-century totalitarianism, she believed, had been presaged by the "new imperialism" of the 1880s and 1890s, most starkly in the genocidal thrust of German colonialism in Africa. Now, in *The Human Condition*, Arendt grappled with the prospect that technology would bring about an unmooring still more fundamental: an unshackling of people from their only habitable planet.

Arendt's paradox was this: by breaking the limits of "human existence as it has been given," technological change now threatened the "boundaries which protected the world, the human artifice, from nature." What might have appeared a decisive victory in this battle—the final human liberation from earthly nature—was anything but that, in Arendt's view. As technology broke one after another of the natural boundaries—creating life in the laboratory; deferring death; destroying disease; making land where there was none; breaking free of the Earth itself—the life sciences, unleashed, could now see human beings as an animal species like any other.[3]

Arendt feared self-destructive growth. She observed that a wasteful consumer culture had led Americans to "consume, devour, as it were, our houses and furniture and cars." Underlying this was a deeper fear: that runaway population growth menaced what was most precious in human culture. Arendt, who was mostly uninterested in the Third World, could not see that this "liberation of the life process" had, by reducing premature death, made possible simple and precious gains for millions of people.[4]

WHAT ARENDT DESCRIBED AS "cutting the last tie," Rachel Carson understood as hubris: a path of conquest. Carson, who as a farm girl in Pennsylvania had written, "Wild creatures are my friends," completed a master's degree in zoology at John's Hopkins in 1932, but family hardship during the Depression stopped her from pursuing a doctorate as she had hoped. Carson's literary talent found an outlet scripting public information radio broadcasts for the US Bureau of Fisheries, where she was then promoted to the role of aquatic biologist. With a lyrical prose style and an eye for close observation, Carson captivated a wide audience with her love of marine life. In 1937, the *Atlantic Monthly* published Carson's essay, "Undersea," which grew into her first book, *Under the Sea-Wind* in 1941. Carson evoked for her readers the whole evolutionary life of the ocean, in which "the life span of a particular plant or animal appears, not as a drama complete in itself, but only as a brief interlude in a panorama of endless change." Her 1951 follow-up, *The Sea Around Us*, was a commercial and critical success that inspired an Oscar-winning documentary; the breakthrough gave Carson the financial security to write full time.[5]

By now Carson, like Arendt, was aware that technological change rendered the world unrecognizable. Carson became concerned with the lasting effects of chemical pesticides, and she was indefatigable in pursuit of the story—her archive is full of letters she wrote to, and received from, scientists, naturalists, government officials, and citizens' groups across the United States. Carson solicited copies of scientific papers; she collated testimony and observation; she pursued elusive data. She described her achievement modestly to *New Yorker* editor William Shawn: "what I shall now be able to achieve is a synthesis of widely scattered facts, that have not heretofore been considered in relation to each other." She told him, in 1959, that she had enough material "to build up, step by step, a really damning case against the use of these chemicals as they are now inflicted upon us"; and what she had found was "terrifying." The following year, Carson was diagnosed with terminal breast cancer—she was determined to complete the work. Serialized in three issues of the *New Yorker* in June 1962, Rachel Carson's *Silent Spring* would become the most influential environmental writing of the twentieth century. Her message was clear, and clearly at odds with the governing values of the postwar decades: the "control of nature," she wrote, "is a phrase conceived in arrogance."[6]

Silent Spring begins with a parable of a settler idyll gone wrong: "There was once a town in the heart of America, where all life seemed to live in harmony with its surroundings . . . Then a strange blight crept over the area and everything began to change." The silence of the title echoes throughout the book—the "sudden silencing of the song of the birds" was the true sign, the true cost, of the mass spraying of chemical pesticides to boost agricultural production. Carson was unequivocal: what was happening was a "war against nature," an act of supreme violence. She believed that this war had already caused "irrevocable" and "irreparable" harm. In her research notes, Carson had typed up a quotation from an Alfred Etter of East Lansing, Michigan, who wrote in the *Audubon Magazine*: "I have little doubt that by raining death upon a country of defenseless and unsuspecting living things we have committed a crime." And by taking the lives of creatures who have "no rights," Etter believed, "I know that it decreases my small freedoms even further." Carson attached to the quotation a handwritten note on a page torn from a spiral notebook: "Chapter 4: Mass spraying becoming more and more prevalent— usually aerial application. . . ."[7]

All of life lay open to the assault, and in the end the harm reverberated back to human bodies. "For the first time in the history of the world," Carson wrote, "every human being is now subjected to contact with dangerous chemicals, from the moment of conception until death." Carson was prescient to see that the change was at once microscopic and planetary: "there is also an ecology of the world within our bodies," she wrote. Carson was attentive to new ways of conceiving of the relationship between bodies and their environments made possible by rapid advances in molecular biology, following James Watson and Francis Crick's discovery of the double helical structure of DNA in 1953. Carson feared that the "insidious effects" of chemical saturation would "include the most basic functions of every living cell."[8]

Silent Spring ends with an image, borrowed from Robert Frost, of forking paths: the path humanity was on resembled a "a smooth superhighway on which we progress with great speed, but at its end lies disaster." Just a few years after the Federal Highway Act, it was an apt metaphor. The road not taken, she insisted, writing less than twenty years after the end of the Second World War, "offers our last, our only chance to reach a destination that assures the preservation of our earth." Beneath Carson's language of rapture, her counsel was technocratic: it lay in harnessing expertise in the use of biological rather than chemical methods of insect control for the selective use of natural processes to push ecosystems more gently toward human convenience.[9]

Carson knew that by launching a double attack on chemical corporations and on US government agencies, she would be taking on formidable opponents. She did not flinch. In the margins of a *New York Times* cutting asking who benefited from the continued expansion of US agricultural production was Carson's penciled query: "Chem industry stake?" Throughout *Silent Spring*, Carson named the vested interests lined up behind "assaults upon the environment."[10]

Their response, which followed immediately upon *Silent Spring*'s publication, was vicious and misogynistic. "Why is a spinster with no children so concerned with genetics?" a former US Secretary of Agriculture demanded. Reviewers sought to discredit Carson's authority because she was a woman: they called her book "hysterically over-emphatic" and "more emotional than accurate." Others labeled Carson a communist, which proved a cheap way to cast suspicion on her amid an atmosphere of Cold War paranoia. Chemical industry spokesman, Robert White-Stevens, pulled out the argument that would recur in every subsequent effort to discredit environmentalists the world over—heed Carson's plea for environmental precaution, he warned, and "we would return to the Dark Ages."[11]

Carson did not back down from confronting powerful people, but her field of vision was almost entirely limited to the United States. *Silent Spring* insisted that the widespread dispersal of chemical pesticides was unnecessary at a time when the problem facing US agriculture was not dearth but excess. Carson's view of US agricultural surplus did not extend to an interest in how these surpluses were used as a tool to fight the Cold War through the "Food for Peace" scheme under Public Law 480, which distributed America's agricultural bounty to the postcolonial world with many strings attached. Only "in situations of extreme poverty and deprivation," Carson noted, would chemical "control of some sort" be justified. Her implication was that such situations were exceptional. For most of the world, they were not. Most of the world faced persistent hunger and "a permanent struggle against an omnipresent death," noted Martinican psychiatrist and anticolonial activist Frantz Fanon.[12]

The same blind spot led Carson toward a one-dimensional view of the use of DDT in public health. Carson was convinced that resistance to DDT was widespread among insects—in her view this, along with the lasting toxicity of the substance, was reason enough to discontinue its use. There was no shortage of evidence that Carson could turn to. Both in public and in private, the World Health Organization (WHO) worried that the fate of its global program to eradicate malaria—a project almost entirely dependent on spraying the walls of people's homes with DDT—faced the imminent threat of insecticide resistance. As early as 1952, following a few years of well-publicized success, public health officials in Greece reported that first houseflies, and then malarial mosquitoes, had evolved to dodge DDT. In Carson's view, this should have been a warning to slow down; the WHO drew the opposite lesson. To "heed the warning from Greece," said Emilio Pampana, Venezuelan malariologist, meant that eradication was now a race against time. In 1955, Pampana called for "huge areas" to be sprayed with DDT; he demanded "total coverage [and] great thoroughness of control." His insistence was driven by moral purpose as strongly as was Carson's opposition.[13]

In a 1961 exchange of letters with Carson, the Canadian Marshall Laird—head of environmental biology at the WHO's division of environmental sanitation—pointed out, without condescension, that she was not wrong to be concerned about DDT, but that she should also consider what its use had achieved. Laird shared Carson's enthusiasm for "naturalistic" methods, he said, but noted that "the whole question of scientifically manipulating biological equilibria to best advantage" was fraught and would require no less intensive an engineering of nature than chemical control. Laird emphasized the "tremendous savings of human life and foodstuffs for which the synthetic insecticides have already been responsible." Millions fewer people suffered from malaria, he noted. The fearsome wartime killer, typhus, had more or less disappeared because insecticides had eliminated the fleas that transmitted it. Both feats would "not have been possible" without chemical compounds.[14]

Carson's concern for the natural world was always part and parcel of her deeply felt concern for human well-being; but other, more misanthropic, American writers fretted that the very success of malaria eradication would prove self-defeating. By saving lives, they insisted, the scheme had sped up "overpopulation" in the Third World. On human numbers, the views of Carson and Arendt—otherwise so different in their diagnosis of the condition of the world—converged. Twice in her notes for *Silent Spring*, once copied by hand and the other time typed neatly, Carson highlighted a quotation from the Yale biologist and ecologist Paul Sears, who had written in *The Steady State* that "violence toward nature is no less an evil than violence toward man." Sears then noted: "I am far less interested in guessing how thickly mankind can be amassed on this planet than I am in the optimum quality of existence for those who [inhabit it]." What Sears did not see, what Carson and Arendt didn't see, was that the two processes could be the same: the "amassing" of people on the planet was the outcome of a modest, creeping, never sufficient improvement in the "quality of existence" for millions of people in the Third World, who were now more likely to survive to adulthood.[15]

NEITHER ARENDT NOT CARSON ever had to deal with the messy compromises of governing. When Indira Gandhi became prime minister of India in 1966, after the sudden death of the incumbent, Lal Bahadur Shastri, she was thrust straight into a crisis that affected the lives of hundreds of millions of Indians.

For two successive years, in 1965 and 1966, stretches of India waited for rain. "How helplessly we are at the mercy of the elements," a *Times of India* editorial lamented in 1965, arguing that all India had to show for the previous decade of development efforts were some "shallow and tentative improvements in irrigation." When the summer monsoon failed for a second successive year, in 1966,

India's food situation became critical. The Indian government dismissed early reports of starvation from Bihar as hyperbole—just as the British imperial government used to do. So much had the Indian government staked its legitimacy on the conquest of a dark colonial history of starvation that it fought to deny that famine could be also a post-independence fact. Bihar's suffering deepened, and it would not be silenced. Pictures of starving people appeared in newspapers across the country and around the world.[16]

On April 20, 1967, the government of India declared the existence of famine for the first time since independence, and did so in Palamau and Hazaribagh districts. Five more districts were added after that. The colonial famine codes of the nineteenth century, revised incrementally over the years, moved into action. PL-480 grain shipments from the United States arrived in bulk and were distributed to people by a network of twenty-thousand "fair price" shops. The government initiated public works to employ local people, augmenting incomes enough to encourage food imports from other regions of India. Under the leadership of the Gandhian socialist, Jayaprakash Narayan, the Bihar Central Relief Committee mobilized a legion of volunteers.

Despite severe shortages, the death toll was in the thousands rather than the hundreds of thousands. The Indian government had stepped in to prevent widespread starvation with the aid of the US farm surpluses that Rachel Carson had decried. The contrast with India's experience of famine under colonial rule was telling. Success came at a price: for a postcolonial state that had struggled in vain for self-sufficiency in food, India's stark reliance on US aid at a time of crisis was humiliating. "I don't ever want us to beg for food again," Indira Gandhi said—as it turned out, she would not need to.[17]

Even before Indira Gandhi came to power, India's agriculture minister, Chidambaram Subramaniam, was stunned by the results shown by Rockefeller Foundation–sponsored experiments in Mexico with high-yielding varieties of maize and wheat, and by concurrent trials with specially bred strains of rice in Taiwan and the Philippines. A team of scientists led by the Canadian plant pathologist

R. Glenn Anderson launched a series of experimental stations in India with pilot projects in Delhi, Ludhiana, Pusa, and Kanpur with seeds flown in from Mexico. Here lay the roots of what would come to be known as the "green revolution," which would recast Indian and global agriculture in the final third of the twentieth century.[18]

With the food crisis, the condition of India's soils, forests, and waters were catapulted to the forefront of Indira Gandhi's concerns. Her view of them was imbued with a love of nature that, like Carson's, had origins in childhood. As a girl Indira was constantly on the move: her father, Jawaharlal Nehru, rose to the first rank of India's anticolonial leaders while her mother, Kamala, ailed from tuberculosis and spent long periods of convalescence in sanatoria. Indira was educated in Geneva and Poona, and then at Santiniketan, Rabindranath Tagore's university devoted to the arts and to outdoor education. Works of natural history lined the household's bookshelves, among them, American botanist Donald Culross Peattie's *Flowering Earth* and *The Faber Book of Insects*.

Indira developed a love of birdwatching while she was imprisoned during the Quit India Movement of 1942–43, when Mahatma Gandhi spearheaded massive protests against India's forced incorporation into Britain's war effort. Her prison companion was *The Book of Indian Birds* by Salim Ali, a German-trained ornithologist and leading figure in the Bombay Natural History Society: the two forged a lifelong friendship. In 1950, Indira became one of the founding members of the Delhi Bird Watching Society, convened by the Quaker supporter of Indian freedom, Horace Alexander.[19]

Even as the Indian National Congress was consumed by factional strife after a poor showing in the 1967 elections, Indira Gandhi held on to her concern for nature. At a convocation speech at Bangalore University that year, she told students that "our building zeal is not accompanied by respect for the needs of conservation," and she warned that India would ultimately suffer from this neglect. Indira Gandhi implemented stepwise policies of environmental protection. She surrounded herself with sycophants but remained open to the advice of scientists. In 1969, on the advice of both Indian and foreign proponents of animal protection, Indira Gandhi's government banned the export of tiger skins despite the much-needed foreign exchange that came in from their sale. The ban came as her government took a populist turn, appealing directly to voters over the heads of regional party leaders. There was little public concern about tiger hunting, but the ban was justified as part of an all-out attack on special interests that would also lead Indira Gandhi's government to nationalize the banks and the coal industry: it would not have escaped notice that those who profited from the fur trade were often from former princely families who epitomized unearned privilege.[20]

A generation after independence, many Indians had grown impatient waiting for freedom's promises to be delivered. To most observers, the scale of unmet needs and frustrated expectations in India rendered environmental protection a distant concern. One of the first to challenge this view was physicist and industrialist Vikram Sarabhai, chair of India's Atomic Energy Commission and pioneer of its space research program. In a 1970 speech at the atomic research site at Trombay, Sarabhai noted that most of India's leaders still believed "that the problem of human environment was largely an affliction of the industrially developed, and that since India was still quite remote from this problem, we could tackle it in its own time." But Sarabhai insisted that "the ecology of the environment and the welfare of the human being are intimately connected," and that "this interdependence . . . puts on the whole problem of environmental protection a new dimension." He stressed, as Rachel Carson had done, the "cumulative" and "irreversible" character of environmental harm. Sarabhai formed part of Indira Gandhi's inner circle of scientific advisors.[21]

The same year, Indira Gandhi addressed another dimension of environmental harm at a meeting of the Non-Aligned Movement in Lusaka, Zambia—that it was a threat to peace and freedom. Established in 1961 by Nehru, Nasser, Sukarno, Ghanaian president Kwame Nkrumah, and the Yugoslav leader, Josip Broz Tito, the group of Non-Aligned countries fought to steer their own path through a Cold War world divided into US and Soviet alliances. They sought solidarity in a shared quest "to give to our people a better life and the opportunity to live in freedom, in dignity, and in peace," as Indira Gandhi put it in Lusaka. Addressing her peers, she highlighted what she saw as the biggest threats to the world in 1970: in addition to the ever-present "nuclear balance of terror," she added that "the war in Vietnam is said to be waged with 'conventional' weapons, yet these include chemical contamination of food and plant life." Martin Luther King Jr. had remarked on this a few years earlier, in his April 1967 speech at Riverside Church, New York City, condemning the American war in Vietnam. King enumerated acts of environmental destruction in pursuit of the war. The Vietnamese, he said, faced repeated horrors "as we poison their water, as we kill a million acres of their crops. They must weep as the bulldozers roar through their areas preparing to destroy the precious trees."[22]

By 1970, the US military had spent nine years raining chemical defoliants upon Vietnam's forests in an escalating and failing war, fought in a doomed attempt to deny Ho Chi Minh's forces the cover of the jungle they used as shelter and camouflage, and so to prevent a prominent "domino" from falling to Communism. In a far-fetched, if revealing, analogy with the everyday use of pesticides on American farms, military planners called it Operation Ranch Hand. Their arsenal was made up of the "rainbow" herbicides, each named for the color of the bands that secured the containers they were carried in: Agent Green, Agent Pink, Agent Purple, Agent Blue, as if they were characters in a children's comic book. Most of all, the US military used Agent Orange—more than 11 million gallons of it. Agent Orange contained dioxin, the most toxic substance ever produced in a laboratory. Vietnamese came to know it as *chat doc da cam*: orange-colored poison. It fell from the sky, dispensed from specially tailored C-123 cargo aircraft. Ngo Luc, who was serving in a guerrilla unit in Vietnam's Central Highlands, remembers his first encounter with the lethal spray. He saw a plane overhead one day, but it dropped no bombs; instead, "a fine yellow mist descended, covering absolutely everything." The soldiers thought little of it, for the spray even "smelled good." The next day, he said, "the leaves wilted and within a week the jungle was bald."[23]

Although the US government and chemical companies would for decades deny that they knew how toxic Agent Orange was, declassified secret files confirm the opposite. Harry Felt, commander in chief of US forces in the Pacific, left clear instructions: "Vietnamese personnel will be utilized to the maximum extent possible in the handling of chemicals for the defoliant operation." And if not by Vietnamese personnel, then the chemicals were handled by enlisted US soldiers that were disproportionately likely to be from poor and minority backgrounds. Vietnamese, American, Australian, and New Zealand soldiers who handled it the felt immediate effects. They suffered the agony of chloracne and peripheral neuropathy. The lasting harm suffered by Vietnamese people—cancers, diabetes, immunological disorders—carried across generations: through children stillborn; children born with spina bifida; children born with hidden disabilities. Dioxin pervaded the soil around US storage depots in Bien Hoa and Da Nang. It would bioaccumulate through the food chain—in the fat of animals, in the fish that formed the bulk of people's diets, and in up to 4.8 million human bodies.[24]

By the time of Indira Gandhi's speech to the Non-Aligned conference in Lusaka, the effects of Agent Orange were no secret. There was enough evidence of harm by February 1967 to prompt five thousand American scientists to write an open letter denouncing what they called the "chemical and biological weapons used in Vietnam." In February 1970, Yale University plant biologist Arthur Galston, speaking at a conference in Washington, described the use of Agent Orange as "ecocide": a conscious allusion to genocide. He asked the US government whether "any cause can legally or morally justify the deliberate destruction of the environment of one nation by another." The assault on Vietnam with defoliants was an aggressive amplification of the daily "rain of death" that Rachel Carson had seen and condemned on America's farms, now at fifty times the chemical concentration.[25]

Writer and translator of Vietnamese fiction Charles Waugh points out that the use of Agent Orange displayed a "casualness towards dangerous chemicals" only conceivable in the context of postwar America's petrochemical-saturated culture.[26] The war on Vietnam's forests joined Carson's worst fear with Indira Gandhi's—ecological destruction in Vietnam inflicted lasting chemical damage to the Earth and its inhabitants, and at the same time it threatened the hard-won freedom of postcolonial countries.

"MY MOTIVATION WAS THE message from Rachel Carson and her book *Silent Spring*," Jan-Gustav Strandenaes recalls. He was one among ten thousand people—mostly young, mostly white— who soaked up the carnival atmosphere at the People's Forum in Stockholm, Sweden, for two weeks in June 1972. The local hosts set aside camping space for those who could not afford hotel rooms and provided them with a supply of bicycles. The forum resounded with intense debates and theatrical, humorous protests; youth dressed as ancient Greek Olympians handed out "medals" to the world's most polluting companies. The activists and nongovernmental organizations were there to observe, protest, cheer, and advocate at the first United Nations Conference on the Human Environment. The conference slogan was "Only One Earth."[27]

The summit was first proposed in 1967 by the Swedish delegation to the United Nations. By the time it was held, five years later, the litany of ecological harm had only grown. The supertanker *Torrey Canyon* ran aground off the coast of Cornwall in 1967, spilling at least 25 million gallons of oil. Fish floated lifeless in the Rhine, so choked with effluent from Europe's industrial heartland that it was declared a "dead" river. In January 1969, an offshore rig, operated by Union Oil, exploded off the California coast. Gas and black oil rushed to the ocean's surface, escaping through cracks in the sea floor even after the rig was capped. "The bottom of the ocean exploded," remembers Bob Sollen, who was a *Santa Barbara News-Press* reporter at the time. Toxic waves hit the coast off Santa Barbara, one of America's wealthiest communities, and poisoned thousands of sea birds.[28]

If *Silent Spring* had sparked environmental consciousness in America, the Santa Barbara disaster galvanized action. Student groups, lawyers, ecologists, local residents, and legislators came together. As a direct response to the disaster, Wisconsin senator Gaylord Nelson proposed a nationwide teach-in on the environment—it was held in April 1970, and would come to be known as Earth Day. In America, Earth Day forged a coalition of support from college students, peace activists, suburban women, Sierra Club conservationists, and scientists. Its impact echoed around the world. An editorial in the *Times of India* called it "an exhilarating mass movement." The Indian journalist noted that "we in this part of the world tend to be smug about these matters, but we are no less culpable." From the fissure of India's gaping inequalities crept the question of blame; the *Times of India* chose to blame the "ignorance" of the poor as much as the inaction of government: "forests are denuded for firewood; soil is grossly overworked, there is thoughtless overuse of chemical . . . fertilizers and pesticides."[29]

It was in this atmosphere of expectation that Indira Gandhi took to the podium at the Stockholm conference. She was the only head of state to attend apart from the host, Swedish prime minister Olof Palme. The conference preparations had already fallen foul of Cold War tensions—since East Germany was not a member of the United Nations, only West Germany was invited to attend. The Soviet Union and its allied states boycotted the meeting, so its legitimacy was in question from the start. Third World countries, too, threatened not to attend: they feared, with cause, that environmental regulations would become just another tool for rich countries to keep them poor. It was left to the smooth-talking, well-connected Canadian oil executive and diplomat, Maurice Strong, to salvage the

Indian prime minister Indira Gandhi speaking at the United Nations Environment Conference, Stockholm, June 14, 1972.

summit as its chair. Film footage shows Strong waiting eagerly to welcome Prime Minister Gandhi at the entrance to the Folkets Hus, where the meeting was held. Her stature and moral authority would be vital to its success.[30]

Indira Gandhi did not disappoint. Her speech to the plenary session was visionary and hopeful—its theme was contradiction. Indira Gandhi set out the long list of ecological problems that were already of concern to her, and to India. "Some of our own wildlife has been wiped out, miles of forests with beautiful old trees, mute witnesses of history have been destroyed," she said. Indira Gandhi had a skilled team of speechwriters, led by H. Y. Sharada Prasad, and in her appeal to "mute witnesses of history" there is a lyrical echo of her father, Jawaharlal Nehru, who, in the 1930s, had written an epistolary primer of world history for Indira. She was motivated, above all, by "concern for the human being—a species which is also imperiled."

Indira Gandhi's diagnosis of the world's environmental crisis differed from that of many of the summit's promoters, whose vision borrowed the Malthusian fears epitomized by the views of Stanford biologist Paul Ehrlich, whose book *The Population Bomb* was published to acclaim in 1968. Ehrlich was at the Stockholm meeting, too: he spoke on many panels as the reasoned, scientific voice of alarm. But when he first saw Indira Gandhi's India, Ehrlich had been anything but dispassionate. The opening lines of Ehrlich's

book described a "stinking hot night" in Delhi, and the author's dis-
taste for all those poor, dark-skinned bodies was barely concealed;
his car was not insulation enough. "As we crawled through the city,
we entered a crowded slum area. . . . the streets seemed alive with
people," he wrote: "People eating, people washing, people sleep-
ing. People visiting, arguing, and screaming . . . People, people,
people, people."[31]

In response, Indira Gandhi argued environmental degradation was primarily a problem of distribution, not of numbers. She
reminded her audience that, notwithstanding the conference slogan,
"we inhabit a divided world." When it came to the origins of the
environmental crisis, India's prime minister was clear about where
the blame should lie. "Many of the advanced countries of today have
reached their present affluence by their domination over other races
and countries," she said—global economic inequality had its origins
in ecological violence and theft. And so, the rich world "got a head
start through sheer ruthlessness, undisturbed by feelings of compassion or by abstract theories of freedom, equality or justice."[32]

Now poor countries were being told that they could not do the
same—and they feared that the ladder would be kicked away from
them. "The riches and the labour of the colonized countries played
no small part in the industrialization and prosperity of the West,"
she reminded her audience. Yet the provision of dignified standards
of living to India's poorest citizens now took place amid an "eagle-
eyed watchfulness," and an awareness, which she felt acutely, of
finite resources and of time running out. "We do not wish to impov-
erish the environment any further," Indira Gandhi insisted, "and yet
we cannot for a moment forget the grim poverty of large numbers
of people." Her most resonant phrase, for which her speech is still
remembered, came in the form of an ambiguous question: "Are not
poverty and need the greatest polluters?"

Indira Gandhi raised the stakes when she asked: "How can we
speak to those who live in villages and in slums about keeping
the oceans, the rivers and the air clean when their own lives are

contaminated at the source?" India's prime minister held firm to the faith of her father's generation that "science and technology" would provide a solution. Here lay India's great hope, and the hope of all the Third World, that there might be a less ecologically ruinous path to prosperity. The green revolution, well underway, offered hope: it promised to boost food production without gobbling land, leaving space for protected areas. "For the last quarter of a century," Indira Gandhi concluded, "we have been engaged in an enterprise unparalleled in human history—the provision of basic needs to one-sixth of mankind within the span of one or two generations." In this evocation of speed and scale, Indira Gandhi offered her own perspective on the great acceleration that was sweeping the world.

Indira Gandhi's manifesto received support from many other representatives of Asian, African, and Latin American countries. Chua Sian Chin, Singapore's health minister and a former trade union lawyer, insisted that "if developed countries are genuinely interested in the improvement of the overall human environment" then they must be willing to contribute resources that poorer countries lacked— "after all, we all live in one world," he added, pointedly. Ghanaian diplomat K. B. Asante put it more starkly: the problems that Ghana and most African countries confronted, he said, were "simple, elementary ones of biological pollution"—providing people with safe drinking water was the greatest environmental challenge for human health and one so fundamental that it would be easy to forget amid all the talk of oil spills and industrial pollution.[33]

On the fringes of the conference, at the People's Forum attended by youth and activists, Indira Gandhi's vision received support from a voluble American cellular biologist who was drawn to socialism: Barry Commoner had graced the cover of *TIME* magazine's February 1970 issue as a prophet of a new ecological vision. At the Stockholm conference, he did not mince his words in setting out his radical vision of environmental justice. The environmental crisis, Commoner said, "cast a bright light" on "fundamental concerns that we've tended to push under the rug"—questions about "the validity of the private enterprise system," about "whether we can tolerate wars," and about enduring "racial discrimination." The Third World, he said, had been "victimized, ecologically . . . by colonialism." Commoner challenged the Malthusians when he noted that the "population explosion" was really a symptom of the "last remnants of the harmful influence of colonization"—for it was only now, at last, that most people on Earth were being given a chance at longer lives and broader choices. Commoner concluded his interview with the press at Stockholm with a call—years ahead of its time—for "ecological reparations," which he insisted was "a just idea."[34]

INDIRA GANDHI'S SPEECH AT Stockholm conveyed a humane, multifaceted perspective, insisting that the health of the planet was vital for human flourishing. It was a more generous vision of the future than either Rachel Carson's or Hannah Arendt's. In India, it would culminate in tragedy.

Two years before Stockholm, in Lusaka, Mrs. Gandhi had announced to her fellow leaders: "the 'revolution' of our times is unfinished." Most of her audience agreed. Postcolonial leaders felt that their political power was being eroded at every turn by economic dependence on the wealthy countries. The former colonial powers had stacked the rules of the global economy against the Third World. Ghana's leader, Kwame Nkrumah, had first used the term "neocolonialism" to describe a state of continued inequality after formal decolonization.[35]

Indira Gandhi embraced the idea. The brazen removal of elected governments by the CIA and former colonial intelligence agencies—in Iran, in Indonesia and, just the year after Stockholm, in Chile—gave Third World governments, especially those on the left, good reason to worry. Independent-minded governments allied to the Soviet Union viewed with the same alarm the brutal military crackdowns on democratic movements in Hungary and Czechoslovakia. Almost all postcolonial leaders faced restless and divided domestic constituencies, impatient for tangible improvements to their lives. Insecure leaders shored up their power by silencing opposition.

On June 25, 1975, Indira Gandhi invoked a constitutional provision intact from the colonial era to ask India's president to declare a state of emergency. The prime minister faced unrest, rolling industrial strikes, and a debilitating energy crisis after the price of oil spiked following the Organization of the Petroleum Exporting Countries (OPEC) imposing an embargo on exports to the United States in retaliation for US support of Israel in the Yom Kippur War. The night The Emergency was declared, police raided the homes of activists, opposition politicians, and journalists. Tens of thousands were detained. Mrs. Gandhi muzzled the press, shredded civil liberties.[36]

A sense of ecological emergency, of time running out, fed into a wider sense of all-pervasive crisis. Project Tiger had been launched in 1973 to protect the Bengal tiger by creating a series of nine tiger preserves. The Emergency's suspension of democratic niceties allowed an emboldened Forest Department to enforce the program with zeal, evicting Adivasi communities from their homes. The recovery in the number of India's endangered big cats was met with international celebration among conservationists.[37]

The Emergency's most brutal measures bore an ecological stamp. Despite the subtle way Indira Gandhi had articulated in Stockholm the relationship between population and ecology, she proved unable to resist the fear that population was an uncontrollable and destabilizing force: a threat to be met with violence. The prime minister's loutish son, Sanjay Gandhi, was unleashed in 1976 to oversee a nationwide push to sterilize poor families. The program targeted men, because of the greater ease of the surgical procedure. State governments set wild targets; local officials scrambled to meet them. "Some personal rights have to be kept in abeyance," Indira announced in 1976, "for the human rights of the nation, the right to life, the right to progress."[38]

In 1976–77 alone, eight million Indians underwent sterilization, many of them in mass camps. They came for the incentive of cash payments and transistor radios; they came because they had been threatened with the withdrawal of ration cards and state benefits. They came packed onto the backs of trucks by local thugs—beaten and threatened and lied to. The sterilizations struck hardest at the poorest families, from the least privileged castes and from religious minorities, Muslims above all. Countless people suffered injury because of botched operations. Tens or hundreds of thousands of bodies were violated without a shred of consent, and many people died or suffered lifelong disability. Human lives were reduced to statistical targets; their future choices reduced to the aggregate question of "population control." India's rush to population control—like China's, which was to follow with the declaration of the one-child policy in 1979 in the flurry of economic reforms after Mao's death in 1976—embodied a way of thinking that pitted individual against collective rights and saw the control of natural forces, including the size of a population, as a battle to be won. It embodied a way of thinking that measured success in large numbers and equated precaution with failure. Having posed the question—"are not poverty and need the greatest polluters?"—Mrs. Gandhi launched an assault on the poor.[39]

THE FATAL FLAW OF Indira Gandhi's approach was one that Arendt had foreseen as a danger. The answer to how we should live on a changed Earth, Arendt argued, could only be "subject to the agreement of many." No one person, no one idea, could decide on a path, "as though we dealt here with problems for which only one solution is possible." Arendt always emphasized the plurality of human beings and human interests even, or especially, when the human condition was on the threshold of such unforeseen alteration.[40]

Because of the brave advocacy of Rachel Carson, because of the work of delegates who attended the Stockholm conference, because of a much larger number of local activists who went unheralded— countries around the world moved to pass environmental legislation. The pressure-and-response that joined activists, scientists, and legislators within and across borders modeled the emphasis that Arendt placed on deliberation. The list is long. The United States passed the Air Quality Act in 1967, followed by the establishment of the Environmental Protection Agency (EPA) and the Clean Air Act in 1970. In 1969, Ethiopia opened the Simien National Park in the country's northern highlands. Mexico passed the first air pollution legislation in Latin America in 1971, with President Luis Echeverría Álvarez's Ley Federal para Prevenir y Controlar la Contaminación Ambiental. India soon followed. A year before her Emergency, Mrs. Gandhi's government sponsored the Water Act of 1974. It created pollution control boards at both the state and the national level: they had authority to determine permissible levels of pollution, setting limits on the composition and quantity of effluent that factories could discharge into water bodies. Countries around the world followed suit over the following decade. Indonesia passed its Act No. 4, which encompassed environmental protection, in 1982.

Because of the scale and pace of technological change, the cumulative effects of human activity grew uncontrollable. Arendt had used the phrase "action into nature" to describe the unstable ways that human activity could have irreversible consequences. The emergence of an international infrastructure for environmental policy and monitoring coincided with growing concern among scientists that human activity might already have placed the Earth on a dangerous trajectory. The World Meteorological Organization's first World Climate Conference, held in Geneva in 1979, predicted that growing concentrations of atmospheric carbon would lead surface temperatures to rise between 1 and 3 degrees Celsius by 2050, and that the problem was worrying enough to make it imperative to "reduce scientific uncertainty as rapidly as possible."[41]

This is the distinctive, and tragic, feature of environmental politics—how quickly we went from the stirring of awareness to despair that we might be too late.

Between 1972 and 1977, the newly formed Environmental
Protection Agency commissioned a photographic archive
of environmental harm in America, which assembled more
than twenty thousand images of polluted skies and rivers,
wastelands and decaying infrastructure. This blurred
photograph shows a dense smog over Los Angeles in
September 1973.

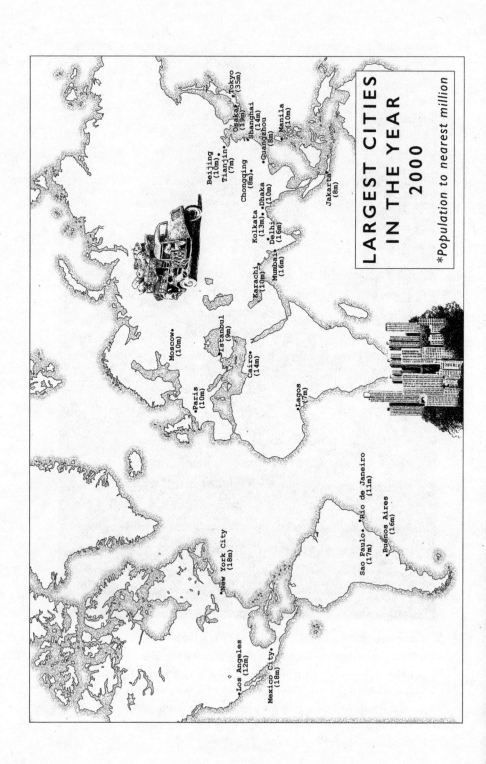

LARGEST CITIES IN THE YEAR 2000

*Population to nearest million

Tokyo (35m)
Osaka (19m)
Shanghai (14m)
Manila (10m)
Beijing (10m)
Tianjin (7m)
Guangzhou (8m)
Chongqing (8m)
Dhaka (10m)
Kolkata (13m)
Delhi (16m)
Jakarta (8m)
Karachi (10m)
Mumbai (16m)
Moscow (10m)
Istanbul (9m)
Cairo (14m)
Paris (10m)
Lagos (7m)
Rio de Janeiro (11m)
Sao Paulo (17m)
Buenos Aires (16m)
New York City (18m)
Los Angeles (12m)
Mexico City (18m)

CHAPTER ELEVEN

BURNING FORESTS

CONJURE IN YOUR MIND A THOUSAND-YEAR TIME-lapse of the Amazon rainforest, the camera high above Earth's surface. Nothing much seems to happen until the last few frames. Change is barely perceptible from this height—but at ground level, change is constant. For centuries people have sculpted the forest. They cut and burn it to make space for the fruit and nut trees that they need. When they move on, the forest closes in and covers their tracks. In places the detritus of human life is compacted into black soils a kilometer deep, made of burned seeds, pods, husks, leaves, bark and root, shards of pottery, ruined fragments of houses, and the ceremonial mounds that connected living people to their ancestors. Everything is movement: epiphytes grow with their roots in the air, trapping soil on the wind. Vines climb and strangle as they provide passage for forms of life unnamed and innumerable. Rivers muscle their way to new paths. The death of each aged tree brings a disruptive explosion, creating life from decay. Beneath the profound green of the canopy, there lives a kaleidoscope of color. Pinpricks of blue radiate from the flapping wings of Morpho butterflies, each little wing made of a million, tiny, overlapping scales that produce a lustrous structural color. The red and white of copaibas and the violet of jacarandas intensify the palette. The forest bursts into mass flowering every few years. From above, everything is still. And then you get to the 1960s. Bare patches start to puncture the green. By the 1980s, it is like a contagion. Roads appear like veins carrying flatbed

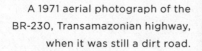

A 1971 aerial photograph of the
BR-230, Transamazonian highway,
when it was still a dirt road.

trucks. If the photographs could sing, a single, keening note would
rise above the symphony of the forest—the sound of the chainsaw.
Smoke obscures your vision. The forest ends in flames.[1]

For the world's tropical rainforests, concentrated in Amazonia,
central Africa, and Southeast Asia, the 1980s were uniquely catastrophic. Of all the great accelerations of the second half of the
twentieth century, none was as abrupt, and few were as consequential. In the 1980s, the planet lost 150 million hectares of tropical
rainforest—an area half the size of India. The greatest losses were
in the Brazilian Amazon, followed by the forests of the Indonesian
archipelago. Never in recorded human history—neither in temperate
nor in tropical lands, neither in modern nor in premodern times—
were so many trees killed so quickly. More than fifteen billion trees
fell each year. The term "biodiversity" only entered English in the
late 1980s, in conjunction with the loss of the forest, and it remains
an abstract, distant way to convey what has been lost through this
extraordinary assault. What was lost, what is still being lost, is a community of living beings, 15 percent of all the species on Earth. Working together, they capture more sunlight than any other ecosystem.
They recycle a significant portion of all the rainfall on the planet and

store billions of tons of carbon that would otherwise be released into the atmosphere. The Amazon and the Indonesian rainforest are also home to many Indigenous communities whose wellbeing is tied to the life of the forest and who are denied the political voice to protect it.[2]

THE ATTACK ON THE Amazon began with roads—roads laid with Caterpillar earthmovers crashing through the forest. It began with the populist, democratic government of the 1950s, which had promised Brazilians freedom through oil. In 1960, the government inaugurated the BR-153 highway: traversing 1,900 kilometers, it connected the port city of Belém, coastal gateway to the vast Amazonian region of Pará, with the country's purpose-built new modernist capital of Brasilia. With the expansion of the highway system into southeastern Pará, parts of the rainforest that were inaccessible came within range of a great migration. Land-grabbers and speculators, small family farmers and impoverished people without land—they all followed the road into the forest, and when the road was paved even more people made the journey. They went in search of freedom from the precarity of life in Brazil's arid northeast. Those who already had power and resources went in search of quick profits. The highway tore through the forest like a river of fire, leaving a broad swath of denuded land stretching for miles on either side of its path. The greatest portion of newly deforested land went to ranchers, who turned the rainforest into pasture for cattle that they raised for beef. They remade the ecology of Amazonia so fast and so fully that it would have consequences for all the world. The death of the forest served many needs—but above all it served the needs of cattle.[3]

Brazil's military coup of April 1964 hastened the conquest of the Amazon. The takeover was backed by the CIA and celebrated by the US establishment as a victory against Communist forces. The junta's most fervent supporters included big ranchers, alongside the most conservative sections of the Catholic Church: for landowners, the coup was a bonanza. The state dangled wildly attractive financial incentives before speculators. These giveaways were a death warrant for the forest. "Amazonian occupation will proceed as though we are waging a strategically conducted war," said General Castelo Branco in 1964. Even as it funneled land and power toward the wealthy, the military spoke the language of social justice: the government's aim, General Emílio Médici said, was to open up "a land without men, for men without land." The motto, ever masculine, tapped into old ideas of pioneer settlement.[4]

The junta's showcase scheme was the Transamazonian highway, which opened in 1972: it ran 5,400 kilometers from east to west and cut right through the rainforest. The government's stated goal, ambitious and alluring, was to grant land to one hundred thousand families within five years. In the end, only eight thousand came; their dreams of a better life died in Amazonian soils too poor in nutrients to sustain small farming. Instead, the ranchers moved in to amass even more pasture. A new frontier of gain lay in soybean plantations, as Brazil rose to become the world's largest producer of a crop that industrial American agriculture had elevated to a position of supremacy as animal feed ever since the Second World War.[5]

The state of Rondônia, further still from Brazil's centers of population, experienced the swiftest change of all. With another motorized acronym came another pathway to material freedom—and another engine of loss. The BR-364, from Cuiabá to Porto Velho, carried 160,000 migrants into Rondônia each year between 1984 and 1988. Settlers came from impoverished parts of the Nordeste, many of them Afro-Brazilians in search of viable subsistence; others took the four-day journey north by coach from Paraná, a region that had prospered from the export of coffee until hit by crop disease. The rapid intrusion of large soy plantations left local farming families, mostly of European descent, unable to compete. So they packed up and took their chances up the highway. All of Brazil's monstrous inequalities—inequalities of race, wealth, and political power—collided to propel the destruction of the forest. Humble migrants' hopes of sufficiency and safety faded while the coffers and

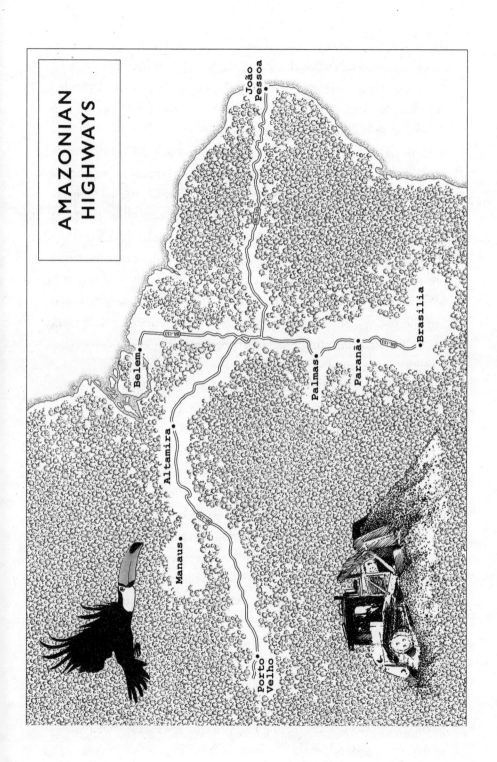

AMAZONIAN HIGHWAYS

João Pessoa

Brasília

BR-153

Palmas

Paranã

BR-153

Belém

Altamira

Manaus

Porto Velho

the paramilitary forces of landowners swelled. The Indigenous peoples of Amazonia suffered the violent destruction of their homes.[6] They faced the irreparable loss of the ecosystems they depended on: chainsaws and fire obliterated a whole web of kinship, human and more-than-human.

In Brazil, the producers of beef and soy orchestrated the destruction, while in Indonesia, rainforests fell to plantations of timber and palm oil. Just a year after the coup in Brazil, the CIA threw its weight of covert operations behind a military coup in Indonesia in 1965, led by the canny and dogged General Suharto against the charismatic, erratic, and left-leaning Sukarno, Indonesia's founding president. Suharto's supporters slaughtered hundreds of thousands of Indonesians, targeting Indonesia's Chinese communities and opponents they branded as communists. In Indonesia, as in Brazil, the military regime plundered nature for handouts to patch together a creaky coalition of supporters.

Beginning in the 1970s, loggers and plantation companies incinerated swaths of rainforest in Borneo, Sumatra, and Sulawesi. Settlers followed from Indonesia's heartland of population and political power, Java, sponsored by a government scheme of frontier colonization. The project of *transmigrasi*, or transmigration, with origins in the Dutch colonial era, treated people, like timber, as a resource to be managed. Just as in Brazil, the self-propelled movement of small farmers and families without land took place alongside, and probably outstripped, the schemes of official resettlement.[7]

Fire was the fastest way to clear the ground to turn rainforest into lucrative timber and palm oil plantations. The newcomers intensified the local practice of *ladang*, which had long made use of fire in the practice of shifting cultivation. Used on a small scale, fire had nourished and replenished the soil over centuries. Used on an industrial scale, fire became uncontrollable. Drought eased its spread. For the first time, in 1982, an El Niño year, the forests of Kalimantan burned out of control. Logging had mottled the forest with patches of dry, open ground, making a floor of kindling.

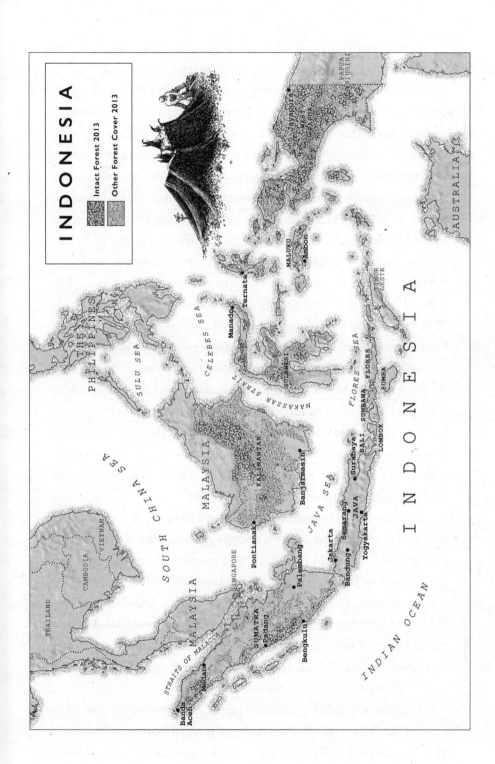

The crisis of Indonesia's forests galvanized widespread concern from students, academics, and clubs of nature-lovers across the country. The influential news magazine, *TEMPO*—founded and edited by dissident poet and playwright Goenawan Mohamad—featured regular columns under the heading *Lingkungan*, or "environment," starting from around 1976. The term *lingkungan* brought together diverse concerns—the loss of forests, the threats faced by birds and animals, urban air and water pollution, flooding, and land rights. In keeping with the new international norms that emerged following the first UN Environment Conference in 1972, Suharto's government created a ministry of the environment in 1978, and Berkeley-trained economist Emil Salim was put in charge. In 1980, a broad coalition of civil society groups came together to constitute WALHI (Wahana Lingkungan Hidup Indonesia), or the Indonesian Environment Forum. Just a few years after its founding, WALHI counted more than 350 member organizations across the country. As environment minister, Emil Salim proved receptive to working with WALHI and allied groups, so long as they did not stray beyond strictly "environmental" questions, which were deemed less threatening to state power than, for instance, land rights. But what the New Order conceded, it just as quickly took away. The profits to be made from destruction were simply too great.[8]

The booming global market for the products of Indonesia's forests enriched land speculators who belonged to the country's tight-knit political and financial elite. Suharto plundered Indonesia's vast natural wealth to finance his promise of progress and development to his constituents. By many measures he succeeded. Indonesia became the World Bank's poster child for the benefits of market-led development. But each year the fires burned longer. Indonesian journalists described the fires of 1987 as a "sea of fire," and the country's forests as the "charred lungs of the Earth."[9]

Along the way Suharto made his family and his associates wealthy beyond measure. One of the president's favored lieutenants was Bob Hasan, who held millions of hectares in timber concessions. Hasan

was dubbed "The Plywood King." His companies and front companies lay behind many of the fires that burned. The son of a modest
Chinese tobacco trader in the city of Semarang, Hasan gripped the
ladder to power and wealth through a century when the Indonesian
Chinese faced repeated atrocities. His corruption grew obscene, his
powers of destruction immense.[10]

IN THE STORY OF the rainforest's death in Brazil and Indonesia, avatars of greed are not hard to find. The Alves family of Acre,
Brazil, appear as something close to archetypical villains. From the
1960s to the 1980s they murdered and terrorized their way north-
ward, accumulating land, raising militias, and annihilating forest. They formed part of a cabal of ranchers who used violence to
impress their will along the highways into Amazonia, and in 1988
they would conspire to take the life of one of Brazil's most prominent
environmental activists.[11]

Only in the mid-1980s, when he was forty years old, did the word
ecologia enter Chico Mendes's political lexicon. Until then, he had
seen his fight as a very old one: a fight against the brutal unfreedom
of bonded labor, which still prevailed among the Amazonian rubber
tappers from whose ranks Mendes had emerged as a leader. Chico
Mendes's parents formed part of a large migration of labor to the
region of Acre during the Second World War when Allied demand
for Brazilian rubber surged because of the Japanese conquest of
Southeast Asia. Workers endured abusive conditions, bonded by
debt to the rubber barons who used loans and lethal force to keep
workers on the hook for life. Indigenous workers faced conditions
even harsher than migrant workers from the south. The same form
of debt bondage trapped workers who harvested piassava, the coarse
palm fibers used to make brooms. The most mundane of domestic
objects, produced at scale, came at huge cost to human life and to
the ecology of the forest.[12]

As a young person, Chico Mendes was schooled on weekends by

a lifelong rebel and labor organizer, Euclides Fernandes Tavora. In 1977, Mendes formed the Xapuri Rural Workers' Union in Acre, which grew to be thirty thousand people strong. Mendes was a modest, hearty person with a magnetic personality, always with a ready smile beneath his imposing mustache. He was an autodidact who learned of the world from the Portuguese-language programs of Radio Moscow, Voice of America, and the BBC: "These three programmes had a lot of power in the Amazon," he recalled in a 1988 interview. Mendes's rise to international prominence came by way of his friendship with Brazilian anthropologist Mary Allegretti, American conservationist Stephan Schwartzman, and British filmmaker Adrian Cowell, all of whom did sustained work in Acre. When Mendes left Brazil for the first time, it was to visit the World Bank and senior members of the US Congress; he was there to testify against the Bank's support for the environmentally and socially catastrophic Polonoroeste project in the Amazon.[13]

Mendes moved easily between the offices of Friends of the Earth in Washington and the campaign trail in Acre, spending weeks and months away from his wife and his two young children. Even as he began to advocate for the rights of the Amazon's peoples and its ecosystems on a global stage, Mendes stayed focused on local concerns. "The rubber tappers aren't saying that nobody should lay a finger on the Amazon," he insisted, "No. We've got our own proposals. . . ." At the heart of those alternatives was the idea of "extractive reserves"—designated areas for the industrial development of commercial forest products. The strand of conservation that rejected development altogether was, for the most part, an elite concern.[14]

Hard though it was for some conservationists to accept, the language of "extraction" was deeply embedded in the ecological consciousness of environmentalists in the Global South. *Empates*—occupations—staged by the rural unions Mendes supported turned back chainsaw gangs. Then they achieved a stunning and unexpected legal victory, winning a 61,000-acre tract of land to be set aside as the pioneer extractive reserve.

Chico Mendes, from Adrian Cowell's documentary *Decade of Destruction*.

For the powerful ranchers' association, the União Democrática Ruralista, Mendes's victory was a step too far. Locally, the quest for extractive reserves threatened the power of Darli and Alvarina Alves da Silva, landowners who commanded a phalanx of gunmen, and were determined to silence Mendes. Acre's landowners ruled by terror and assassination: by the start of December 1988, at least ninety murders had been recorded in Xapuri that year, few of them ever investigated by a local police force in the pocket of the ranchers. There had been more than one attempt on Mendes's life. He knew he was a marked man. He told a friend, "I am no longer afraid of dying and I know they can't destroy us."[15]

On the evening of December 22, 1988, the Alves family's gunmen lay in wait outside Chico Mendes's home; when Chico came out to bathe in the shed outside, they shot him dead.[16]

Some of the blame for hastening the destruction belongs with the cynicism and recklessness of US policy, expressed in American support for the coups in Brazil and Indonesia, driven by the belief that the combination of free markets and authoritarian rule would save the world from communism. There is no reason to think that popular democratic governments would have taken a radically different approach to the forest, at least not until the rise of a popular ecological consciousness later in the twentieth century. The conquest of nature for land, for livelihoods and for food, was integral to the promise of liberatory and democratic movements across Asia and Latin America. But the impunity and violence of the military regimes, emboldened by US intervention, surely accelerated the harm. Regimes that thought nothing of silencing, imprisoning, torturing, and murdering their opponents were unlikely to take heed of the concerns of Indigenous minorities—and still less to care for the suffering of other species. Blinded by righteousness, unaffected by criticism, they saw no reason for precaution.

A class of citizens became rich, but a terrible price was paid by the poorest people who suffered the degradation of precious ecologies. Just as China had experienced under Mao—as Indigenous Americans had experienced, centuries earlier, at the hands of European colonizers—the most rapid destruction of the rainforest and all the life in it accompanied the most brutal abuse of human beings. As we move beyond the obvious culprits, moral certainties blur, and responsibility for harm grows more dispersed.

TWO PLANETARY TRANSFORMATIONS SPED up in the 1980s, and both pushed the rainforest closer toward irrecoverable loss. The first was the agglomeration of ever more people in cities. For the first time in human history a large proportion of humanity, rapidly approaching half of all people, no longer lived from the land, no longer lived from growing food. Nowhere was the move to cities faster than in 1980s' China, as the Mao government's ideological restraint on urbanization caved to the force of the economic reforms that followed Deng Xiaoping's new maxim: "to get rich is glorious." Shenzhen, in the Pearl River Delta, was a small town of 60,000 people in 1980: by end of the decade, it was home—a temporary home, at least—to more than 800,000 people, and by 2000, to 6.5 million: the city's population had grown one hundred times larger in just twenty years, in what is probably the fastest growth of a city in human history. China's experience was unique in scale but not in kind. The population of Dhaka, the capital of Bangladesh, doubled between 1980 and 1990 from 3 million to more than 6 million people, and the population of Nigeria's largest city, Lagos, grew almost as fast.[17]

Leading the new ranks of "megacities," urban centers of over 10 million people, Mexico City added 2 million new residents in the 1980s to arrive at 15 million. They breathed diesel fumes, heavy metals, solvents, and the noxious compound that urban dwellers knew as *hupo*—*humo* (smoke) and *polvo* (dust). The city's topography, a long legacy of Spanish colonization, contributed to the problem: the drained bed of Lake Texcoco formed the impermeable base of a city in the shape of a bowl, surrounded by high mountains and prone to trapping pollutants. The air bore the emissions of the factories at the heart of the Mexican Miracle, which had promised Mexicans prosperity and self-sufficiency; by the 1980s, it also carried the exhaust of hundreds of thousands of automobiles. In 1986, pigeons dropped dead from the skies, their lungs scarred with lead, cadmium, and mercury.[18]

The Grupo de los Cien (the Group of 100), led by poet Homero Aridjis, mobilized for action. In the 1980s, Aridjis later recalled, Mexico City suffered "such a pollution that, sometimes as you were walking down the street, you have the feeling that you are probably going to die in the next corner." Aridjis enlisted the support of fellow writers—Octavio Paz, Carlos Fuentes, and Gabriel García Márquez—and allied with citizens' groups and young people. The Grupo de los Cien won many small victories: daily, public measurements of atmospheric pollutants, restrictions on vehicle use once a week, and stricter emissions standards. Chilangos, residents of Mexico City, struggled to breathe as Londoners and Angelenos had struggled in the 1950s—and their experience would be repeated across the Global South in the decades to follow.[19]

The green revolution made this migration to cities possible.

Hybrid seeds, petrochemical fertilizers, and abundant irrigation gave such a boost to harvests of wheat and rice that it seemed, by then, that the threat of population exceeding the world's food supply was gone. The 1970s' prophecies of doom, like Paul Ehrlich's prediction of a "Great Die-Off" that would kill billions of people, were shown to be fearful fantasies.

Between 1961 and 2014, the global production of cereals increased by 280 percent: far ahead of population growth and achieved with only a 16-percent increase in the total area of land devoted to raising staple crops. India, China, Mexico, and Brazil led the charge. Between 1970 and 2014, India's production of cereals outstripped the number of new mouths to feed with only a marginal increase in land area. In China the growth was even more dramatic: a 420 percent increase in cereal output with no appreciable rise at all in the expanse of cultivation. Mexico, home to pioneering research on high yielding varieties, did convert more land to wheat and maize—an increase of around a third—but this still sustained an increase in output of 224 percent.[20]

The green revolution was far from universal. Its secret weapon was inequality: it reinforced the gains of farmers who already had access to transportation, plentiful water, and enough money to invest in seeds and chemical pest control. Where those conditions were absent, as they were for small farmers in many regions of sub-Saharan Africa, or in rain-fed regions of South Asia, the green revolution recorded only modest and patchy results. Where it thrived, the green revolution changed everything—it changed how and where, and in what concentrations, human beings could live.

Without this leap in the collective ability of human societies to produce food, such a scale of increase in the world's urban population would have been unimaginable. High-yielding crops fed the voracious appetite of cities for grain as people moved off the land into cities, though often not into formal employment. The green revolution owed everything to fossil fuels: petrochemicals furnished the pesticides and fertilizers that high-yielding seeds depended on. Diesel

powered the groundwater pumps that decoupled harvests from rainfall in every region of agrarian prosperity, above all in South Asia.
The ecological costs of the green revolution accrued as silently as the
cancers that afflicted those who inhabited its heartlands. As farmers drilled deeper underground, groundwater tables dropped. As
pesticides permeated the earth, toxins dispersed. As monoculture
reigned, other forms of life receded. As irrigation water poured over
fields, soils grew saline and sterile.[21]

The green revolution improved and secured the futures of millions of people, many of them migrants to cities. And the green revolution wrecked the livelihoods of those who fell outside its creeping
embrace: those with land too measly, too stony, too unyielding to
accept new seeds. Most of all, it left out rural families who did not
own any land at all.[22]

High-intensity farming brought its own burdens. Since the late
twentieth century, India's farmers have committed suicide on a scale
without parallel in the world. Starting in the late 1990s, an estimated
seventeen thousand farmers every year have taken their lives in India,
at least two hundred thousand between 1997 and 2010. Debt is the
most common source of the intolerable pressure under which India's
farmers live and die—debt to pay for proprietary seeds, petrochemical fertilizers, ever-more-lethal pesticides, and diesel for pumps.
This shadow-side of the green revolution has contributed as much to
the urban transition as its gains. Rural families who felt robbed of a
future, caught in a pincer movement between indebtedness and the
creeping effects of a changing climate, put all their hopes in sending
their sons and daughters to the city.[23]

MANY NEW URBANITES WOULD find themselves precariously
employed through crushing economic vagaries, unsheltered and vulnerable to fire and flood and debilitating accidents, exposed to the
threats of unclean water and to fumes from dumping grounds. Success was never so elusive as to dissuade newcomers from taking their

chances. The transition to an urban planet could be born of desperation, but it was always clothed in dreams.

The big numbers of urbanization spellbind us. Beneath the statistics, however large, lie millions of individual decisions—decisions to leave, imposed by compounding debts or by sudden family illness; decisions taken in defiance of the brutality of caste, or made from dauntless hope. Writing in the 1970s, the critic, artist, and novelist, John Berger, working with photographer Jean Mohr, distilled the imaginative draw of cities:

> Every day he hears about the metropolis. The name of the city changes. It is all cities, overlaying one another and becoming a city that exists nowhere but continually transmits promises. These promises are not transmitted by any single means. They are implicit in the accounts of those who have already been to a city. They are transmitted by machinery, by cars, tractors, tin-openers, electric drills, saws. By ready-made clothes. By the planes which fly across the sky. By the nearest main road. By tourist coaches. By a wrist watch. They are there on the radio. In the news. In the music. In the manufacture of the radio itself. Only by going to this city can the meaning of all the promises be realized.[24]

Berger's astute observation—that the promise of the city lived in mundane objects ("tin-openers, electric drills, saws")—opens a window to understanding the tentacular reach of the world's cities into the rainforest and under the ground. In the everyday life of cities, petrochemicals and timber and paper were woven into the fabric of existence: at once alluring and unremarkable.

The more closely observed the account of urban life at this moment of global change, the more ubiquitous the plastic. Vivek Shanbhag's Kannada-language novel, *Ghachar Ghochar*, narrates the story of a south Indian family shaken by their sudden liberation from the grinding struggle for a respectable middle-class existence. It is in no overt sense an ecological novel, but in its fine detail provides more insight into a changing planet than almost any novel I have read. Once, the family had lived in a house "with four small rooms, one behind the other, like train compartments." Once, they had lived through times "when the whole family stuck together, walking like a single body across the tightrope of our circumstances." And then—at some unspecified moment in the 1980s or 1990s—Chikappa, the narrator's uncle, persuades the family patriarch to invest in a speculative venture that blooms with the liberalization of India's economy. Shanbhag traces the deeper meanings of the family's changing relationship to *things*.

Early in the novel, the trauma of the father's loss of his salaried job as a salesman comes through in the family's humiliating reversion from a gas to a kerosene stove. The ensuing turnaround in their fortunes depends on the most ubiquitous of all materials—plastic packaging. "It's a simple enough business: order spices in bulk from Kerala," the protagonist tells us, "parcel them into small plastic packets in our warehouse, and sell these to grocers in the city." As wealth flows, every relationship comes under strain. "It's true what they say—it's not we who control the money, it's the money that controls us," the narrator laments. It is as if that power were irresistible, no less than a force of nature: "Money had swept us up and flung us in the midst of a whirlwind." Even if that "whirlwind" only ever swept up a minority in the Global South, even if it left hundreds of millions of people out, it reached widely enough, and stimulated enough small desires, to leave a lasting imprint upon the Earth.[25]

The whirlwind uprooted the rainforests of Indonesia in the 1980s, and only indirectly through petroleum. The demand came first from the Japanese economic boom. Traders and construction companies from Japan negotiated favorable deals with Indonesia's political elite in the 1970s and 1980s. Cheap Indonesian plywood fueled the construction of skyscrapers and apartment complexes in neon-lit Tokyo, forming the taken-for-granted material fabric of the urban life evoked by that decade's shiny, alluring "city pop" churned out by the capital's music studios. Old-growth trees disappeared, replaced by monoculture plantations for pulp, paper, and cardboard to furnish retailers in Japan, Europe, and North America with attractive packaging—but also paper to furnish local schoolchildren, at long last, with textbooks and exercise books. Beginning in the 1980s, intensive pressure on the rainforest came from demand for another substance that began to infiltrate everyday life across the urban planet.[26]

Palm was, by the 1990s, the world's preferred vegetable oil, most of it extracted from palm fruit with a smaller proportion from crushing palm kernels. It makes shampoos lather and lends lipsticks their smoothness. It gives cookies their texture and raises the melting point of ice-cream. Palm oil, native to West Africa, had first been used as an alternative to animal fat in the late nineteenth century, forged by Liverpool's Lever Brothers into bars of "Sunlight"-brand soap. It was less pungent than tallow in candles, and in factories it lubricated engines. Palm was grown on plantations, most notoriously in the Belgian Congo, where coerced workers endured conditions not far removed from slavery.[27]

Only a whole century after its initial industrial deployment did palm acquire primacy among vegetable oils, and now with Southeast Asia rather than West Africa as the main region of production. For newly independent countries in Southeast Asia, palm offered a path out of poverty. General Suharto's bloody 1965 coup yanked Indonesia away from Sukarno's left-leaning economic policies. Declaring a New Order, the Suharto government "radically centralized" control over land. The state took over a significant proportion of Indonesia's forests, especially on the outer islands, which they operated directly as state-owned plantations or leased out to private interests. The Forest Department grew all-powerful in areas designated as "political forests," zoning different parts of the forest for development and preservation, but always at the expense of customary and Indigenous land claims. Finding a receptive ear

A palm oil plantation in Riau Province, Indonesia. Palm oil
became the most widely used vegetable oil in the 1980s, and
Indonesia and Malaysia became by far the largest producers.

in Suharto's government—now advised by a "Berkeley mafia" of
US-trained Indonesian economists—the World Bank promoted the
export of palm oil as a spur to growth. Neighboring Malaysia faced
a collapse in markets for its main export, natural rubber, thanks
to the rise of cheap synthetic alternatives. There, too, palm was a
promising replacement.[28]

The area planted with palm more than trebled in Indonesia
between 1970 and 1985, with state-owned and politically affiliated
plantations—the distinctions easily blurred—supported by loans
from the World and Asian Development Banks. In neither Indonesia
nor Malaysia was palm production exclusively in the hands of large
plantations. Around a third of global output has always come from
small farms—but because of how rapidly the fruit spoils, smallhold-
ers have often had no choice but to sell to the processing plants that
only larger firms could afford to build.[29]

In 1981, a humble breakthrough galvanized the advantage of
palm over competing oils, thrusting Malaysia to the top rank among
the world's producers. Leslie Davidson, a Scot who had worked for

Unilever from the age of twenty, commissioned a team of entomolo-
gists to investigate a phenomenon he had observed while working in
Cameroon. Yields there were better than in Malaysia, and Davidson
had noticed that the palm fruits were often surrounded by weevils.
Davidson's hunch proved right—the studies showed that palms were
pollinated by weevils, and not by wind dispersal. Unilever brought
weevils from Cameroon to Malaysia, and yields jumped—just in
time to meet rising demand. Concern about the health effects of
trans-fats in wealthy countries led to their substitution with palm oil
in processed foods. Palm was handy, too, as a cheap biofuel, ready
to be deployed when ecological concern about fossil fuels began to
escalate in Europe.[30]

In 1970, the total world production of palm oil was 2 million tons,
and palm was third behind groundnut and cottonseed among the
most commonly used vegetable oils. Palm oil production had leapt
to 7.5 million tons and the top rank by 1985, and by 1995 output
had doubled again. By 2005, the world produced more than 32 million tons of palm oil, almost six times more than groundnut. Since
the 1980s, Indonesia and Malaysia together have produced around
85 percent of the world's palm oil, and that figure has changed little to this day. Ten years after Davidson's weevil discovery, two
entrepreneurs—Singaporean Kuok Khoon Hong and Martua Sito-
rus, an Indonesian—cofounded Wilmar International. As demand
for palm surged in the 1990s, Wilmar quickly became its largest
trader and one of the biggest agribusiness firms in the world. Wilmar has faced accusations of both environmental irresponsibility
and exploitative labor practices.[31]

Palm oil has been used, first and foremost, in food production.
Most of the added production since the 1990s has been consumed
not in the Global North—demand from North America and the
European Union accounted for only 15 percent of global consumption of palm oil by the 2010s—but rather, and overwhelmingly,
within Asia. In India, in China, and in Indonesia itself, palm oil
was used primarily as a cheap and relatively nutritious cooking fat.

And as the growing middle classes of those countries sought convenience foods, palm oil insinuated itself ever more firmly into people's diets, not least as an essential ingredient in instant noodles. Palm met the nutritional needs of an urbanizing Asia with a colossal environmental impact—but an impact that was still smaller than would have been the case with any known alternative, given that palm uses only a fifth as much land, for the same yield, as soy and other vegetable oils.[32]

What palm demonstrates is more broadly true—the prime motor of environmental change in the 1980s and 1990s, still the factor above all others, was what and how people chose to eat.

During the 1980s, the proportion of the world's fisheries classed as overexploited—where rates of capture exceeded the ability of fish populations to reproduce—jumped from 13 percent to more than 26 percent. The ecological impact of meat was greater still. The main driver of forest loss in the Amazon was the search for pasture to raise cattle for beef. Until the end of the twentieth century, almost all of Brazil's beef was destined for domestic consumption, not for export—and the search for ever more meat was propelled by domestic politics. Ranchers trusted in the constant flow of handouts from the state to make their business viable, and they relied on the state's complicity in their landgrabs. But the story is incomplete without accounting for the politically assertive desire of Brazilian voters for beef on their dinner tables. Outside interests were ready and waiting to profit from Brazilians' taste for meat. The Brazilian state was so deeply in debt to Northern governments and Northern commercial banks that debt repayments, at one point in the early 1980s, added up to almost 30 percent of export revenues. To boost export earnings to keep up with loan payments, the state encouraged the further destruction of rainforest to be planted with commodity crops. Brazil's exports of both meat and soy surged as a result, with global markets now propelling a further spate of deforestation.[33]

The green revolution made hunger a distant memory for a substantial number of people though never for the poorest in each society,

and it did so permanently and securely enough that their very expectations of life changed. They desired to eat differently, and to eat
better. What the middle classes of Asia and Latin America desired
most of all was what had earlier been scarce—and that was the meat
and fish that European and American consumers had devoured with
abandon for a century or more, so much so that they considered it
almost a customary right. Now it was others' turn to eat.

CHAPTER TWELVE

TIPPING
POINTS

KIES DARKENED WITH PARTICULATE MATTER AS forests burned. Rivers as mighty as the revered Ganges ignited from time to time because they were so filled with petrochemical effluent. Days of extreme heat came more often than they did before. Rains grew more erratic. Deltas began to sink, pulled down by the withdrawal of oil and natural gas and groundwater from beneath them, and starved of silt by dams upstream. Industrial farms swallowed land, pumped out pesticides, sucked up petroleum. Governments sped up their quest to conquer nature: they built or licensed more dams, more roads, more mines, more wells—all to deliver development, to pay off loans, to enrich their supporters, or sometimes just to show that they could. Animals, trees, and birds died by the billions.

Through it all, in tandem with hastening harm, there emerged a formidable force of resistance. Environmentalism—not a single movement but a constellation of thousands—spread quickly and galvanized a broad base of support. Environmentalists brought a multiplicity of aims and tactics and a breadth of utopian visions. They raised urgent and challenging questions: Was conservation just another tool for the wealthy to appropriate more land and resources from the poor? What did living people owe future generations? What weight did the needs, or even the rights, of other species carry? Was the goal to make current systems of social and economic life less destructive to the living planet, step by incremental step—or was the goal a revolution how human beings lived on this Earth?

In western Europe, green political parties began to contest elections. None had more success than the West German Green Party (Die Grünen), formed in 1980 as a loose coalition of anti-nuclear protestors, peace activists, eco-socialists, and conservatives committed to landscape preservation. The Greens' arrival shook up the German political system: "we are neither left nor right, but ahead" (*Wir sind nicht rechts, nicht links, sondern vorn*) their 1980 manifesto announced. They had their electoral breakthrough in 1983, sending twenty-eight deputies to the Bundestag. The inevitable compromises of governing opened a rift between those dubbed Realists and their "deep green" Fundamentalist opponents, led by the charismatic countercultural hero, Petra Kelly. In the years to come, the German Greens would be elected to every level of government, from local to federal.[1]

In most of the world, green politics found a home not in formal parties but in social movements. Osmarino Amâncio Rodrigues, secretary of Brazil's National Council of Rubber Tappers, described in the late 1980s an urgent shift in perspective: "At first," he said, "people talking about ecology were only defending the fishes, the animals, the forest, and the river. They didn't realize that human beings were in the forest—and that these humans were the real ecologists. . . ." Rodrigues advocated for the view that human societies were not separate from, but part of, nature. Protecting the health of the forest, he insisted, was inseparable from defending the livelihoods of those who lived in the forest and whose wisdom had been crushed or exploited for others' gain. The target of Rodrigues's criticism was an older notion of conservation, still rooted in a nineteenth-century colonial worldview—embodied, in the United States, by President Theodore Roosevelt—that sought an absolute distinction between human settlement and wilderness, preserving the wilderness at least in part for the hunting pleasure of the men of the ruling elite.[2]

Distinctive articulations of an "environmentalism of the poor" proved to be the truly novel feature of the global environmentalism that emerged at the end of the twentieth century. It emerged from many streams of inspiration: the Chipko Movement of Himalayan women and men protesting deforestation in the early 1970s; the tree-planting Green Belt Movement in Kenya led by ecologist and activist Wangari Maathai; the broad and inclusive coalition of protest against the Sardar Sarovar Dam on the Narmada River in western India.

Diverse movements learned from and supported each other. La Vía Campesina was formed by a coalition of peasants' organizations in 1993: it brought together groups from the Global North and the Global South, aspiring to equality among them. The group was unusually attentive to gender equality within its ranks. La Vía Campesina never called itself an "environmental" movement, but always insisted that environmental crisis was an inevitable consequence of the erosion, by global agribusiness, of the land rights and livelihoods of small farmers. "Long-term food security depends on those who produce food and care for the natural environment," La Vía Campesina declared in its 1996 declaration on "food sovereignty," and small farmers could be "stewards of food producing resources."[3]

The environmentalism of the poor was fed by the legacy of anticolonial struggles for justice, now reframed to acknowledge what they had initially failed to see—that human freedom, political freedom, depended on the health and viability of the living planet. To identify specifically an environmentalism of the poor also comes with risks: it can romanticize the daily experience of scarcity that the world's poorest people face, making of them unwilling ecologists. And it elides the vital, binding role of activists from wealthy countries, or those from more privileged backgrounds within the Global South, as they take it upon themselves to advocate on behalf of the poor. These debates of the 1980s still shape, profoundly, how we now think about environmental justice.

"I KNOW THEY CAN'T destroy us," Chico Mendes had said when he knew his life was at risk. He was proved right. Mendes had known all along that "our biggest assets are the international environmental lobby and the press." The prominent coverage they gave his shocking murder embarrassed the Brazilian government out of its inaction. In the course of investigating Mendes's murder, the Brazilian government took the unprecedented step of removing the local police chief. Three months after the assassination, the Declaration of the Peoples of the Forest in Rio Branco, Acre, honored his memory with a commitment to bring together Indigenous and settler groups to defend "this immense, but fragile life-system that involves our forests, lakes, rivers and springs, the source of our wealth and the basis of our cultures and traditions." Because local struggles in Amazonia were already linked with a global environmental movement, the impact of Mendes's murder reverberated around the world. Only three years later, in June 1992, Rio de Janeiro would host the largest and most intensive meeting on the global environment ever convened: it came to be known as the Earth Summit. Over two weeks, 110 heads of state, 10,000 official delegates, and thousands of NGO representatives came together.[4]

Twenty years after Stockholm, the scope and purpose of international environmental politics had swelled, and so had the scale of the problem. The Rio meeting was the culmination of years of discussions and fraught negotiations. Its impresario, once again, was Canadian oilman Maurice Strong. In the lead-up to Rio, conventions, treaties, and declarations came so fast and so clustered together that they blurred into an encompassing sense of momentum.

The signal breakthrough, for diplomats and some environmentalists, was a 1987 agreement on ozone that would go on to become the first universally ratified treaty in history. By most measures, it has been a success. The 1987 Montreal Protocol, signed under the Vienna Convention for the Protection of the Ozone Layer, showed how quickly change could come when governments chose the path of cooperation. Atmospheric scientists recognized, in the 1970s, that highly stable chlorofluorocarbons (CFCs)—released into the atmosphere by refrigerators, aerosol sprays, and solvents—could deplete the unstable stratospheric ozone that protected life on Earth by absorbing harmful ultraviolet radiation. In 1985, scientists working for the British Antarctic Survey confirmed the worst fears when they found stratospheric ozone severely depleted: it soon came to be known in newspapers and school textbooks (including my own, I remember well) as a "hole in the ozone layer," which gave it a memorable image. The correlation of ozone depletion with skin cancers, especially in the southern hemisphere, lent urgency to the quest for a solution. The Montreal Protocol established a planned phase-out of different categories of ozone-depleting chemicals; it set enforceable targets for the elimination of CFCs; it established a fund to help lower-income countries meet their targets without compromising their current needs.[5]

For many Americans, another turning point in their awareness came in June 1988, when they watched on television the somber testimony to the Senate of NASA physicist and astronomer James Hansen, in the midst of the hottest summer anyone could remember. Hansen's conclusions were crisp, unambiguous—and shocking:

> I would like to draw three main conclusions. Number one, the earth is warmer in 1988 than at any time in the history of instrumental measurements. Number two, the global warming is now large enough that we can ascribe with a high degree of confidence a cause and effect relationship to the greenhouse effect. And number three, our computer climate simulations indicate that the greenhouse effect is already large enough to begin to affect the probability of extreme events such as summer heat waves.

Public recognition of the international community of climate scientists came the same year, with the establishment of the

Intergovernmental Panel on Climate Change (IPCC), established jointly by the United Nations Environment Programme and the World Meteorological Organization. The IPCC's periodic "assessment reports" have provided, since the first was published in 1990, a public record of the growing consensus on the existence, causes, and likely trajectory of anthropogenic climate change.[6]

To find a new political language for a new consciousness was the task of a commission led by the first female prime minister of Norway, Gro Harlem Brundtland, a politician of the center-left, and a qualified physician who would go on to lead the World Health Organization. The World Commission on Environment and Development came to be known by her name, as the Brundtland Commission, a mark of her impressive public presence and able leadership. She and her colleagues had absorbed Indira Gandhi's message at Stockholm, that environmental protection could not come at the cost of the poor. The Brundtland Commission promoted a new concept to take precedence over "conservation"—that of "sustainable development," which "meets the needs of the present without compromising the ability of future generations to meet their own needs." The hard question was: how to bring it about?

The nine hundred days over which the commission worked were filled with portents of ecological catastrophe. A text box within their final report condenses these episodes into a simple list: drought and starvation in the Horn of Africa; the disasters of failed engineering that caused a gas leak at a petrochemical plant in Bhopal, the meltdown of the Chernobyl nuclear facility in the Soviet Union, and a mercury spill into the Rhine from a factory fire in Switzerland.

Closing the list was a statistic orders of magnitude greater than any of the other harms they had outlined, and one that made clear that the basic struggle for material freedom was far from won: the commission estimated that *sixty million people*, most of them children, had died from diarrheal diseases over those nine hundred days between 1984 and 1987.[7]

The commission was doggedly optimistic but offered few

tangible solutions. Its success was in providing a new language, the language of sustainability, to discuss the hardest of political compromises.

Skepticism was soon to follow. In 1991, Indian environmental activists Anil Agarwal and Sunita Narain wrote a pamphlet on *Global Warming in an Unequal World*. "The idea that developing countries like India and China must share the blame for heating up the earth and destabilizing its climate," they declared, "is an excellent example of *environmental colonialism*." Historical responsibility for the accumulation of carbon in the atmosphere lay entirely with the advanced industrial countries of the world, they observed, and in per capita terms, India's or China's emissions were tiny. They denounced calls by Western political leaders and environmentalists to "manage the world as one entity," which, along with the language of "sustainability" itself, were simply a mask for continued exploitation.[8]

What Agarwal and Narain did not anticipate, in 1991, was that India itself was on the verge of change more rapid than they could foresee; that, within a generation, the country's overall contribution to planetary environmental change would no longer be minuscule— and the contribution of its richest citizens and corporations would grow enormous. China's own economic ascent was well underway, but its colossal scale and its implications for the world were only gradually becoming evident. The righteousness of the Indian environmentalists' language was well-earned, and had deep ethical foundations going back to Gandhi. But the austere, patriotic ethos to which they appealed was dwindling in popularity.

THE BRUNDTLAND COMMISSION LENT a sense of purpose and cohesion to the two years of hard negotiations, known as Agenda 21, leading up to the 1992 Rio Earth Summit. The summit was enlivened by a plurality of voices, including that of the Dalai Lama—spiritual and political leader of the Tibetan government in exile—who articulated the environmental crisis as fundamentally a moral problem. "Instead of caring for one another," he said, "we place most of our efforts for happiness in pursuing individual material consumption." The Dalai Lama observed: "We are not machine-made objects. If we were merely mechanical entities, then machines themselves could alleviate all of our sufferings and fulfill our needs." Drawing on Tibetan Buddhism, the Dalai Lama portrayed planetary harm as an outcome of a social order of atomized, desiring, acquiring individuals.[9]

Kenyan environmental activist Wangari Maathai, founder of the Green Belt Movement, echoed the Dalai Lama's emphasis on moral reformation. Speaking quietly, immensely dignified in the face of repeated harassment by the Kenyan police under the authoritarian government of Daniel arap Moi, Maathai told her audience at Rio that "we should speak more of hope"—"we should not discourage each other," she said.[10]

The discouragement came when US president George H. W. Bush took to the podium: amid platitudes ("growth is the engine of change") Bush made clear that the United States would not sign the treaty on biodiversity that had emerged from weeks of night-and-day negotiations. Most ominously for the future, Bush is reported to have said at Rio: "the American way of life is not up for negotiation."[11]

No amount of finesse around the idea of sustainability could cover the fissures. Recently declassified British documents show how deep divisions were among, and even within, the governments of wealthy countries. The British government supported a global environmental agreement, but opposed any substantial redistribution of resources to help poorer countries to adapt. A briefing memorandum to Prime Minister John Major identified the chief "difficulty" as the need to avoid "open-ended commitments to provide developing countries with new and additional money." "I do not think you need to make a new pledge [of funds]" a junior minister warned Major. This advice led to conflict within the government, as ministries concerned with the environment and foreign aid urged a somewhat more generous approach. A civil servant in the Overseas Development department complained of an "unseemly row" with the Treasury over spending commitments.[12]

For its part, the US government was dead set on blocking agreement altogether. When the delegations of Austria and the Netherlands pushed for a binding treaty limiting greenhouse gas emissions to 1990 levels by the year 2000, the United States bullied and threatened other countries not to support the effort. To divert discussions away from caps on energy use, the US delegation emphasized deforestation. Malaysia led the countries of the Global South that would not be cowed. Our role isn't to be the "lungs of the North," the Malaysian delegation declared. Malaysia's combative, self-aggrandizing prime minister, Mahathir Mohammad, was blunt: "You're asking us to cut back on our standard of living by asking us not to develop," he told a BBC interviewer: "Why can't we tell you to do the same?" Fiona Godlee, assistant editor of the *British Medical Journal*, dramatized the hypocrisy of northern countries through a small but telling detail: "all the delegations from developed countries had booths with roofs and air conditioning machines pumping out heat," she observed; those from poorer countries were "mostly roofless and sweltering."[13]

With the most powerful nation in the world conspiring against it, what the Rio summit still managed to achieve is astonishing. No fewer than 153 countries signed legally binding conventions on climate change (The United Nations Framework Convention on Climate Change) and biodiversity (The Convention on Biodiversity). Dozens of agreements followed in the years afterward: agreements on desertification, on the law of the sea, on persistent organic pollutants, on the trade in tropical timber. Utopian she may have been, but the moral and political transformation that Maathai envisaged was happening. An awakening of global environmental consciousness had begun.[14]

Its success was so menacing to vested interests that the petrochemical industry scrambled to stop the advance. The year after the Earth Summit, the Mobil oil corporation ran a paid "advertorial" in the *New York Times* entitled, "Apocalypse, No." Borrowing directly from the playbook of tobacco lobbyists in the 1970s and 1980s, the large US oil corporations sought to sow the seeds of doubt about climate change in American public consciousness. The "media hype proclaiming that the sky was falling did not properly portray the consensus of the scientific community," Mobil's publicists declared; appealing to readers' lived experience, they pointed out that after the Earth Summit, "colder than normal temperatures across the country cooled the warming hysteria." The more that oil corporations sensed a building consensus around climate action, the sharper their attack grew. As world leaders prepared to negotiate the Kyoto Protocol to set targets for reduced emissions, the oil companies did not let up. Climate action would bring "severe economic dislocation," Mobil warned in a 1996 statement. Oil publicists appealed to readers anxious about their jobs and their comforts: "World economic health will suffer as nations are forced to switch from fossil fuels, saddled with large carbon taxes and driven to prematurely scrap many factories and machinery."[15]

A forensic analysis of the climate-related communications of Exxon and Mobil identifies persistent themes, present since the 1980s: oil companies exaggerated the level of scientific uncertainty around anthropogenic climate change, emphasized the economic costs of climate action, and appealed to a distinctively American, late-twentieth-century ideology of freedom from regulation. The oil corporations' public disavowal of climate risks was at odds with the findings of their own internal research, to say nothing of a broader and overwhelming scientific consensus.[16]

In US politics, doubt carried the day. The 1997 Kyoto Protocol, the first to set binding targets under the UN Framework Convention on Climate Change, was signed by the Clinton administration; but even before it could be submitted for ratification, the Senate voted 95–0 to reject it.[17]

THE OIL CORPORATIONS' ATTACK on the global environmental movement did not stop at misinformation. In a very real sense, they waged war—and Nigeria stood at the front line. Kenule (Ken) Saro-Wiwa was an unlikely candidate to lead what would become Africa's largest movement for environmental justice. Born to an elite family from the Ogoni region of the Niger Delta in 1941, Saro-Wiwa came of age in the intellectual ferment that was the University of Ibadan in the early 1960s. He felt the pull of student politics. He loved the theater. And then his generation was swept up in Nigeria's civil war.

Prospectors had struck oil in Nigeria in 1956, just four years before the country's independence from colonial rule. Petroleum wealth sharpened conflicts over how power would be shared in a heterogeneous territory that had been thrown together cynically by the British in 1914. The eastern delta, where the oil lay, was dominated by the Igbo people; their leaders, motivated by personal ambition as well as public concern, resented how the northern Nigerian elite captured the benefits. Led by Colonel Odumegwu Ojukwu, the province of Biafra seceded in 1967, sparking a three-year civil war. The Nigerian federal government was dependent on oil revenues and could not afford to let Biafra go. More than one hundred thousand people died in the fighting; many more perished from famine that followed the disruption of food supplies. Federal troops benefited from the support of smaller ethnic groups in southeastern Nigeria who feared that living in an independent Biafra, dominated by the Igbo, would be even worse than having little voice in a larger federation.

Saro-Wiwa sided with the Nigerian federal government, along with many of his fellow Ogoni. An Ogoni patriot and a Nigerian nationalist, he believed that being part of an equitable, multiethnic federation would serve his people best. He hoped that Ogoniland would benefit from its wealth in oil. Over the following decades, the opposite happened.

The wounds of war had barely begun to heal when, in July 1970, there was a blowout at the oil well at Bomu in the Niger Delta. The oil flowed for three weeks; it soaked the soil and turned it to toxic sludge. "Everything just died like that," a local resident remembers. Shell made no effort to clean it up. Just months before the Bomu spill, Ogoni leaders Edward Kobani and W. Z. P. Ndizee had written to the military governor of the province of Rivers State with a plea for intervention. "A few years ago, our streams were blessed with pure and sparkling water," they wrote, and now the waters were fouled with crude oil. The oil had "killed off not only mangrove trees, but fishes and crabs, mudskippers, oysters, shell-fishes."[18]

Their petition received no response. Nigeria's National Oil Company stood between the multinationals and the residents of oil-rich lands. Oil revenues went to the treasury, and directly into the pockets of more than a few officials. In the two decades that followed the Bomu oil spill, the Ogoni saw less and less benefit from mineral resources, and they bore the heavy ecological cost of extraction. The oil flowed primarily to Britain and Europe, and then in increasing quantities to the United States. The suffering of the peoples of the Niger Delta lay hidden beneath the explosion of consumer culture in the industrialized world.

In the postwar years of the early 1970s, Saro-Wiwa served as a civilian administrator in the oil depot city of Bonny. He cycled through a succession of government positions. He did not shy away from criticizing the new regime. He described the Ogoni people as subject to "a Nigerian domestic colonialism, a colonialism which is cruel, unfeeling and monstrous." In 1973, Saro-Wiwa was dismissed from government. His advocacy for the Ogoni counted against him; but he lost his job also because he was not above using public office for personal gain. He had used government contacts to launch a succession of businesses. He dabbled in transportation and wholesaling, but the venture that stuck was his publishing company, Saros International. He had become wealthy enough by the late 1970s to send his family to England, where they would remain through the tumult of his political career.[19]

Ken Saro-Wiwa, 1995.

Saro-Wiwa's true calling was as a writer. His 1986 book *Sozaboy: A Novel in Rotten English* was linguistically inventive, playfully rendering Nigerian pidgin on the page. The following year, a story collection, *Forest of Flowers*, was shortlisted for the Commonwealth Writers' Prize, bringing Saro-Wiwa to international attention. His biggest success was on screen. Saro-Wiwa wrote and produced *Basi and Company*, a sitcom that ran from 1985 to 1990, the most successful ever to air on Nigerian national television. Its production was slick, complete with canned laughter. The program satirized corruption through the travails of Mr. B, a hustler who had gone to Lagos to get rich. Mr. B epitomized the dreams, and disappointments, of so many urban migrants in the Global South. The comedy's audience was Nigeria's newly confident, multiethnic middle class.

Saro-Wiwa was urbane and cosmopolitan with a ready smile and a quick wit, rarely seen without his trademark pipe. His commitment to democracy wavered. He tried to make his peace with the military dictatorship of General Ibrahim Babangida in the 1980s, returning briefly to an official role in 1989. Saro-Wiwa's admirers would describe him as a saint, but fellow writer Wale Okediran saw him, rather, as "one hell of a human maelstrom who leaves you breathless with his stamina and dexterity for discussion on every conceivable subject." Although Saro-Wiwa had long been concerned with the effects of the oil industry on his homeland, nothing in his life to that point suggested a deep interest in environmental questions.[20]

Saro-Wiwa's path swerved in 1990, when he fully confronted the ecological devastation of his native Ogoniland. Since the end of the civil war, the Ogoni region had generated billions of dollars in oil revenue; less than 2 percent of that money had remained in the region. The Ogoni, mostly fishers and cultivators, faced extreme poverty. The older generation of local leaders had become ineffective, their loyalty easily purchased by oil companies. Between 1976 and 1996, Ogoniland experienced seven thousand oil spills, and almost certainly many more that went unreported. There is a scene in Glen Ellis's 1994 documentary, *The Drilling Fields*, that shows Saro-Wiwa walking slowly across a desolate expanse of blackened crust, "what we are walking on now is crude oil, not soil," he says to the camera, "this land is lost forever. For the next thousand years, nothing is going to grow here." By this time, the most characteristic feature of the Niger Delta's landscape were flares from the natural gas trapped within oil reserves, burned off as waste. They are visible from satellites at night. Some have burned continuously for thirty years. Local people live surrounded by toxic flames. Day after day they breathe particulate matter, ozone, nitrogen oxides, volatile organic compounds, sulfur dioxide, and vaporized metals.[21]

In 1990, Saro-Wiwa founded the Movement for the Survival of Ogoni People (MOSOP). He was masterful in his ability to use his literary contacts to mobilize support from wealthy and influential people in Europe, including the Scottish writer William Boyd, and Anita Roddick, founder of the Body Shop. Saro-Wiwa's most effective strategy was to invoke the term "genocide" in relation to environmental harm, drawing directly on the language of the 1948 UN Convention on the Prevention and Prosecution of the Crime of Genocide—this is what brought MOSOP to global attention. Saro-Wiwa argued that ecological harm in Ogoniland amounted to "inflicting on the group conditions of life calculated to bring about its physical destruction. . . ." In a 1992 pamphlet, *Genocide in Nigeria*, he invoked the prospect of "extinction" for the Ogoni people and for every other form of life in the delta.[22]

Saro-Wiwa's grief for his homeland brought together a sense of human and non-human loss; "I hear in my heart the howls of death in the polluted air of my beloved homeland," he wrote. He mourned the animal life that had once "found sanctuary in mudbanks, under the protective roots of mangrove trees."

On January 4, 1993, at the start of the International Year of the World's Indigenous People, Saro-Wiwa and MOSOP drew three hundred thousand people to a public rally in Ogoniland.

Video footage shows that the atmosphere was joyful. The crowd sang and danced. Men and women chanted "Freedom! Freedom for Ogoni!" Saro-Wiwa stood before them, radiant, and professed his commitment to nonviolent struggle. He knew the risks he was taking; he wrote to a friend, "When I undertook to confront Shell & the Nigerian establishment, I signed my death warrant, so to speak."[23]

The Nigerian military government, with the alleged collusion of Shell, harassed Saro-Wiwa and watched his every move. They confiscated his passport, worried by his appeal to international public opinion. In May 1994, four loyalist Ogoni chiefs who opposed Saro-Wiwa were murdered along with many others. Impartial observers believed the security forces were responsible, but the government blamed MOSOP. Saro-Wiwa and eight other Ogoni leaders were imprisoned and hanged eighteen months later.

In the Niger Delta defeat turned to despair, and despair turned to nihilism. Saro-Wiwa's execution shocked the world. It led to Shell's withdrawal from Ogoniland, but they simply moved elsewhere in the delta. Saro-Wiwa's son and other relatives of the political prisoners sued Shell, claiming that the oil company was complicit in the harassment and executions of the Ogoni Nine. Shell eventually paid $15.5 million to settle the case, but denied all culpability. In the oilfields, Saro-Wiwa's death shattered his movement's commitment to peaceful protest. Interethnic conflict flared as rival gangs fought each other to control pipelines. They blew up oil fields, kidnapped oil workers, killed indiscriminately. By 2009, oil production was down by two thirds. The militants were "not communists . . . or revolutionaries," said their spokesman Jobo Ngomo, but "just extremely bitter men." But later, contradicting himself, he wrote to photographer Ed Kashi that they were fighting for "liberation of the niger delta peoples from 50 years of political and economic slavery."[24]

The misery of local communities deepened, caught between the rebels and the government's brutal counterinsurgency. A decade after Saro-Wiwa's murder, the United Nations Development Program reported that "vast revenues from an international industry have barely touched the Niger Delta's own pervasive poverty," and concluded, "for most people, progress and hope, much less prosperity, remain out of reach. . . ." The soil of the Niger Delta lay polluted to a depth of 40 meters; concentrations of benzene in the air were nine hundred times in excess of safe limits set by the World Health Organization.[25]

Saro-Wiwa's project of nonviolent resistance failed at home, but remained a "beacon of hope to marginalized peoples across the world," in the words of Nigerian environmentalist Godwin Ojo. In the twenty-five years since his death, Saro-Wiwa's example continues to inspire movements for environmental justice across the Global South, as well as in Europe and North America. Saro-Wiwa's activism inspired a slew of claims against Shell, alleging the corporation's culpability for environmental devastation. In March 2012, eleven thousand Nigerians from Bodo, Ogoniland, filed a suit against Shell in London, claiming compensation for an oil spill. Shell accepted liability, and paid out 55 million pounds.[26]

Ken Saro-Wiwa articulated a vision of individual and collective freedom in consonance with the health of the rest of the living planet. Saro-Wiwa's movement was distinctively modern, its language shaped by its place in a global network of activists concerned with human rights and environmental protection. But it also built on older traditions of thought and tapped into deep memories. It reverberated far beyond the Niger Delta like a familiar song.

Saro-Wiwa's movement was defeated by brute force. It was crushed because under the Ogoni soil lay a commodity for which the world's appetite was, and still is, insatiable. "Oil creates the illusion of a completely changed life," Polish writer Ryszard Kapuściński wrote. In the Niger Delta that illusion left a wreckage.[27]

THEY ARRIVED WITH HEADACHES and fevers, which turned into confusion and then delirium. Within days of feeling ill, many of them died. In September 1998, a cluster of patients sought treatment at a hospital near the city of Ipoh, in the western Malaysian state of Perak, all with the same alarming symptoms. At first glance their illness resembled Japanese encephalitis, an insect-borne infection that causes inflammation in the brain. It is a lethal but well-understood disease, and doctors have an effective vaccine. Two months later, similar cases appeared further south, in the state of Negeri Sembilan. The Malaysian health authorities launched a vaccination drive for farmers and fogged the affected areas with insecticide.

But there were some puzzling signs. The victims had all worked in close contact with pigs. The animals, too, had shown symptoms of the illness. Many pigs had died, which was unknown in previous outbreaks of Japanese encephalitis. The suspected virus affected mostly children and the elderly; but here, the sick people were adults of working age. Early in the new year, there was a third outbreak.

On March 1, 1999, Chua Kaw Bing, a microbiologist at the country's premier teaching hospital at the University of Malaya, received in his laboratory samples of bodily fluids and brain tissue from three victims of the disease: a truck driver from the hamlet of Sungai Nipah and two pig farmers from nearby Bukit Pelandok. Against the advice of their boss, and with minimal protective equipment, Chua and laboratory technologist P. S. Hooi placed droplets of infected body fluid onto cultures of kidney cells from pigs and monkeys, to see if they would cultivate the encephalitis virus. Every test they ran came back negative. The Malaysian government was committed to the idea that the cause of outbreak must be Japanese encephalitis. Now Chua was sure that it was not. Faced with disbelief and denial, Chua stood his ground. He was an unlikely hero. A modest and soft-spoken man, Chua had given up medical practice for laboratory research and was happiest behind the scenes. He credited the "faithful" support and courage of his assistant Hooi, though her name appeared nowhere in the press coverage that would follow. The head of his department, finally persuaded of the seriousness of the situation, turned philosophical. "Chua," he said, "why can't nature be more straightforward?"[28]

Chua lacked the specialized equipment he needed for further investigations, so he called a friend at the US Centers for Disease Control and Prevention (CDC). He planned to ship the samples to the CDC for testing, but no courier company would take them. So Chua packed them as carefully as he could and boarded a plane from Kuala Lumpur to Los Angeles, samples at his feet. At the CDC's offices in Fort Collins, Texas, and then at headquarters in Atlanta, Chua and his American colleagues identified the cause—a novel paramyxovirus. Paramyxoviruses are the cause of some severe human childhood infections, including measles and mumps. In animals they are responsible for the fearsome rinderpest. The novel paramyxovirus that Chua had discovered, soon to be named Nipah, joined a growing list of zoonotic infections that had spilled over to human hosts. "At that moment," Chua recalled, "a sense of great fear overwhelmed me."[29]

A mundane sign of the economic boom of the 1980s and 1990s was rising demand for pork in Malaysia's cities. In the years leading up to the Nipah outbreak, pig farming had become more intensive and more industrial. But pig farming was also a marker of cultural difference. Pork was taboo among the country's Malay Muslim majority at a time when public displays of religious piety were becoming politicized. So pig farming was the preserve of the ethnic Chinese minority in Malaysia. With a buoyant but limited domestic market, Malaysian farmers exported pork to Singapore and to other growing cities across Southeast Asia. The region's economic ascent faltered in 1997, with the shattering impact of the Asian Financial Crisis. But demand for pork held up.

Nipah virus devastated the pig farming communities of the area for which it was named. A local resident described what had befallen his friends and neighbors: "They took pigs and buried them. When they came back, they had headaches. By the third day, they were shivering. The fourth day, they were in a coma. The fifth day, they were dead." Hospitals reeled under the strain. Patrick Tan, head of the emergency room at the University of Malaya hospital, said, "At the peak, we were operating very close to our bare minimum standards for medical care." The case fatality rate was 40 percent. By the time the epidemic came under control, Malaysia had seen 265 cases, and 105 deaths. Workers in a slaughterhouse in neighboring Singapore came down with the illness when a shipment of infected pigs from Malaysia passed across the border undetected.[30]

As soon as it became known that pigs were spreading the Nipah virus, local authorities slaughtered them. Pigs were shot on sight; more than a million were killed. The government banned the transportation of pigs within the country as well as across Malaysia's borders. Residents of Bukit Pelandok remember the stench of death that accompanied the mass burial of the animals. It had the "look and feel of a ghost town," an American journalist reported.[31]

How had the pigs become infected in the first place? A few years earlier in Australia, a similar virus, Hendra, had jumped from racehorses to infect the people who worked with them. Researchers found that it had originated in bats. A year after the outbreak, Malaysian scientists confirmed that the Nipah virus, too, originated in a species of fruit bat, the *pteropus*, known as the flying fox. They found traces of the virus in the bats' urine, and in a piece of fruit that bats had chewed. It was likely that the infected pigs had scavenged fruit discarded by the bats, or that the bats' excretions had fallen directly into the pigs' enclosures. The virus was endemic to flying foxes—there was no evidence that they had ever infected other species before. Flying foxes navigate with keen eyesight. They display a capacity for the long-term storage and recall of information, tracing the same paths over years. Some change in their habits, or in their habitat, had forced them into closer contact with human settlements and domesticated animals.[32]

Flying fox, source of the Nipah
virus that crossed over to pigs and
then to human beings.

IN THE SUMMER OF 1997, forest fires raged out of control on flammable peat soil on the Indonesian island of Sumatra, and in Kalimantan, the Indonesian province that fills most of the island of Borneo. The fires burned so fiercely that smoke suffused the atmosphere for hundreds of miles around. The fires were a yearly event, but their effect was worse in 1997 because that summer they coincided with a prolonged drought, triggered by one of the twentieth century's strongest episodes of the El Niño Southern Oscillation. Forsaken by rain, the islands burned. Forests drowned in smoke. That year gibbons, confused by the dimmed sunlight, sang fewer, shorter, sadder songs. Orangutans came to know hunger. They moved less to conserve energy.[33]

"The haze," as it came to be known across the region in 1997, stretched up as far as Thailand—the mild, even romantic, term would suffice, since the visceral horror of smoky gulps for air was the daily lot of millions of people. The haze lingered over busy transportation corridors, with lethal consequences. On September 26, 1997, an Airbus flown by the Indonesian national airline, Garuda, crashed into a mountain as it descended toward the city of Medan in thick smoke, at the cost of 234 lives. Just hours later, 250 miles away, a supertanker collided with a cargo ship in the smog-choked Straits of Malacca, the narrow conduit for a quarter of the world's oil supplies.[34]

Far from such shocking headlines, a protracted crisis unfolded. Throughout the region, more than 200,000 people sought hospital treatment for respiratory illnesses. Air, food, and water contaminated by smoke caused an estimated 15,600 fetal, infant, and child deaths in the worst-affected parts of Sumatra. A long-term study showed that, many years later, the effects of smoke from the 1997 fires continued to impair the health, cognitive development, and educational attainments of local children.[35]

Confident in the triumph of technology over even the weather, Southeast Asian governments sent aircraft into the hazy skies to inject silver iodide into fugitive clouds. They tried to force rain by hastening the formation of ice crystals. They failed. Mosques and churches across the region held mass prayers for rain.

Walking around Singapore's MacRitchie Reservoir in the worst of the haze, conservationist Goh Si Guim related his melancholy experience:

> The smog-shrouded reservoir itself looked like a postcard from some foreign wintry land. The water levels were drastically down, with mudflats unusually exposed. Together the forest, the animals and myself, we all seemed to share in an over-whelming sense of unease, our biological clocks awry, with the sun nothing more than a dull orange glow. These are sad times.

In Goh's prescient intuition—a sense of "biological clocks awry"—lies the link between the fires of 1997 and the Nipah virus.[36]

Having established that the virus originated in flying foxes, a team of Malaysian scientists—among them Chua Kaw Bing, who had first identified Nipah—set out to discover how the bats had come into contact with the pigs they infected. It took them years to find the answer. Eventually they showed that the smoke haze had precipitated a decline in the flowering of forest fruit trees in peninsular Malaysia—the rambutan and mango, the *jambu air* ("wax apple"), and the spiky, pungent durian. In years of mass flowering the fruit trees explode in a fusillade of color spreading through the green canopy. The year of the fires the dimming of the light, which tinged the sky sepia, jolted the "biological clocks" of fruit trees and bats alike. The flowering was lackluster, and the fruit bats, confused and hungry, established colonies in the planted orchards adjoining the pig farms, where they had never been seen before.[37]

MORE THAN HALF THE cumulative total of carbon dioxide that human beings have emitted into the atmosphere since reliable records began has been emitted since 1990. That was the year the IPCC issued its first assessment report. The signs of trouble were clear long before 1990. They were particularly evident in countries that had contributed very little to global warming—countries that looked to the future in anticipation of their fair share of the riches of the world, but with a growing sense of foreboding. Indira Gandhi stated, as early as 1981, that "experts believe that the steady increase of carbon dioxide in the atmosphere because of large amounts of fossil fuels being burnt may lead to changes of temperature early in the next century." Two years later, the Indonesian news magazine *TEMPO* wrote about "Anticipating a Hotter Earth."[38]

The last two decades of the twentieth century saw the rise of powerful movements to repair the burning Earth. They found new ways to articulate why human wellbeing depends on the health of other species, and they showed how human inequality drives ecological harm. Their dedication and their imagination proved threatening enough to vested interests—those corporations, investors, and political leaders, North and South, who gain most from environmental harm—to provoke not only an intensified war on nature, but also a war on the environmentalists themselves. Over the past decade alone, close to two thousand environmental activists have been murdered around the world, the largest number of them in Brazil. A third of the environmental defenders killed come from Indigenous communities. Carmen Lusdary Rondón, Ana Marie Lemita-Evangelista, Raymundo Robles Riaño, Gurvinder Singh, Argentis Yatacué, Maria de Luz Benício de Sousa. We add their names, and hundreds more, to a dark list that reaches back to the 1980s—a list that includes Chico Mendes and Ken Saro-Wiwa. Their fights for justice live on.[39]

CHAPTER THIRTEEN

FOUR HUNDRED PARTS PER MILLION . . .

THE ATACAMA, SQUEEZED BETWEEN THE ANDES and the Pacific coast of Chile, is the oldest and driest desert on Earth. Parts of its hyperarid core might see rain only once in two decades. Since the early twenty-first century, international teams of scientists have studied the surprising richness of life in the Atacama's extreme conditions as an "analog model" for the possibility of life on Mars. The region's dark caves approximate the "last refuge used by life in an ever-drying planet."[1] In the Atacama's Coastal Range, where the sole source of life-sustaining water comes from low-hanging clouds—captured in nets by the region's Indigenous people—scientists have found microalgae harnessing the water they need for photosynthesis from condensation on spider webs. Scientists reason by analogy: in all that survives the dryness of the Atacama, they seek the possibility of life beyond the bounds of the only human planet.

Our best analogy to Mars has a surprisingly busy history of human exploitation. In the last quarter of the nineteenth century, *caliche*, the rock of the Atacama, became the world's leading source of nitrate fertilizer for agriculture. The lucrative substance had provoked the War of the Pacific from 1879–1883, in which Chile defeated its neighbors, Peru and Bolivia. After the war, and with extensive British investment, the caliche was blasted from the desert

The Atacama Desert, Chile, the driest place on Earth, studied as an analog for Mars.

surface: crushed, dissolved, and separated by indentured workers from Chile, Bolivia, and Peru, who then cleared the debris by hand. A railway line cleaved the desert, its rolling stock and coal imported from Britain, to take the desert rock to steamers bound for Europe and America. Only during the First World War, with sea lanes blocked and the synthetic Haber-Bosch process able to produce at greater scale, did Chile's boom come to an end. Left behind in the Atacama were the scars of extraction.[2]

The study of Earth's most extreme environments as analogs to other planets draws our attention back to the conditions that have made this one uniquely hospitable to life—and, in the Holocene era of relative climatic stability over twelve thousand years, uniquely hospitable to human life.[3] That, in turn, brings the shock of how many of those enabling conditions are now in peril. In the mid-2000s Johan Rockström, of the Stockholm Resilience Center, and colleagues around the world proposed a set of "planetary boundaries" that, if transgressed, would imperil the planet's life-support systems. Already exceeded are thresholds of danger for biodiversity loss and species extinctions. We have left far behind the safe limit of interference with natural cycles of phosphorous and nitrogen. Of rising concern are the levels of synthetic organic pollutants, heavy metal compounds, and radioactive materials in the oceans and in the atmosphere, for which safe limits have not even been defined.

The health of three vital ecosystems—the Amazon rainforest, Siberian permafrost, and the Greenland ice sheet—is so consequential for planetary processes that any further attack on their integrity risks provoking sudden, nonlinear changes in climate and sea level. All three are under strain, at least in part, because of another boundary that has been broken—the tolerable limit of human-induced climate change.[4]

A SILENT BOUNDARY CROSSED: in May of 2014, atmospheric concentrations of carbon dioxide crossed the threshold of 400 parts per million for the first time in several million years. The following year, that level was exceeded for the whole month of April. And in 2016, even the lowest reading for the year was above 400. When regular measurements first started in 1958, the level stood at 316. The average level in preindustrial times was around 280. The threshold of 400 parts per million is an arbitrary number, but we humans trade in symbols: this one was a signal that the impact of human activities on the Earth's climate was bigger and faster than was compatible with the concerted efforts, over those same years, to reach a binding international agreement to limit planetary warming.[5]

The measurement was taken at the Mauna Loa Observatory on Hawai'i, established there by Charles Keeling in 1958 as part of the International Geophysical Year. Its location was chosen to provide the closest thing to a representative sample of the planet's atmosphere, an amalgamated, placeless, global air, unmarked by traces of local pollutants. Mauna Loa sits above the marine boundary layer, far from a major center of industry and population but still in the Northern Hemisphere, where the majority of human beings live.

The threshold of 400 parts was crossed without being perceptible to any group of people, only visible to the technicians reading mass spectrometer analyses of flasks of air sent from Mauna Loa to Boulder, Colorado, by US mail. Similarly, none of us knew when exactly in 2007 another arbitrary boundary was crossed, and half of the world's population officially lived in cities. Other manifestations of that change in planetary state were only too visible. Every summer hotter than the last. Once-in-a-century storms every four or five years.

Animals experience these extremes as confusion: a scrambling of their sense of place and their expectations of the world around them. Fleeing unusual heat and unseasonal rain, many species are moving poleward and to higher elevations only to find their avenues of escape blocked by roads and settlements and mines. Land-based species confront a bewildering mismatch between sunlight and temperature, muddling the clues they rely on for survival. In the forests of the western United States, the balance of tree species is shifting toward those better adapted to warmer climates. But this process, known to ecologists as thermophilization, is advancing ten times more slowly than the climate is warming, so that "western US forests are becoming mismatched with their environments." The forests find themselves in a new and unfamiliar world.[6]

No corner of the planet has been untouched by species migrations. Crabs invade the continental shelf habitat of Antarctica to the detriment of seafloor echinoderms and mollusks. Kelp forests in Australia give way to seaweed turfs, reshaping the web of aquatic life. Across Europe and North America, heat waves have diminished site occupancy and species richness in colonies of bees that play an indispensable ecological role as pollinators.[7]

At the limit of adaptation lies the path to extinction. The checkerspot butterfly has vanished from the San Francisco Bay Area, driven out by the increased variability of rainfall. In Mexico, forty-eight species of lizard have disappeared as maximum air temperatures exceed the limits of their endurance. The Adrar mountain fishes in Mauritania have not survived the evaporation of local water bodies. The Yangtze river dolphin or baiji—poor in eye-sight, rich in hearing, and beloved as the "River goddess"—was last seen in the wild in 2006, driven to its doom by noise, water traffic, and pollution.[8]

In the oceans, which yearly absorb about a quarter of the carbon dioxide that human activity generates, the years between 2014 and 2017 witnessed the most severe and widespread episode of coral bleaching ever recorded. Intense heat stress sunders the symbiotic relationship between coral and microscopic algae called zooxanthellae. The coral expel the algae in an act of desperation that turns into self-harm: if conditions do not soon return to tolerable margins, the coral themselves die. Coral death reverberates across species—sea turtles, fish, crabs, shrimps, jellyfish, and seabirds. We live in the midst of a "universal redistribution of life on Earth."[9]

Human bodies, too, struggle to cope with new extremes. For at least twenty days each year a third of the world's population is already exposed to heat exceeding the deadly threshold at which the human body ceases to regulate its own temperature. Around 19 percent of the Earth's surface was affected by drought in 2020, a proportion that never exceeded 13 percent between 1950 and 1999. As temperature and humidity shifts, so too does the geography of threats to human health. Cases of mosquito-borne arboviruses—dengue, chikungunya, and zika—have doubled every decade since 1990. Cholera, the great scourge of the nineteenth century, has seen a resurgence.[10]

The very air we breathe bears harm, almost two centuries after the first "smoke nuisance" legislation. In February 2013, nine-year-old Ella Kissi-Debrah died of acute respiratory failure in London, after repeated bouts of asthma. She lived just off the South Circular Road in Lewisham, one of the city's poorest boroughs. On her walk to school every day, she breathed nitrogen dioxide from vehicular emissions far in excess of safe limits. After a long struggle for justice led by her mother, Rosamund, and supported by clean air activists, a coroner's court ruled that traffic fumes had contributed directly to Ella's death. It was the first time in Britain, and possibly in the world, that air pollution was listed as a "cause of death," though toxic air contributed to more than four million premature deaths worldwide in 2019 alone. The most poignant remark made by Rosamund Kissi-Debrah at the inquest was that, if she had only known how dangerous the air was that her daughter breathed every day, she would have moved without hesitation.[11]

The question, around the world, is where people can go for respite and refuge. The International Organization for Migration estimates that, between now and 2050, a billion people will be displaced from their homes by the effects of climate change. In South and Southeast Asia, in parts of Latin America and across much of sub-Saharan Africa, unprecedented peaks of heat, prolonged drought, more intensive storms, and sea-level rise are pushing many regions to the limit of ecological viability. Indigenous communities inhabit some of the most vulnerable edges, including the Yanomami of Amazonia, the Inuit in the Arctic, the Saami in Scandinavia, and the inhabitants of low-lying Pacific island-nations.[12]

In the Global North, media coverage of "climate migrants" often imagines them clustered at the gates of the wealthiest countries, demanding to be let in. But doors are closing in an era of racialized hostility to migration in the world's richest countries. The overwhelming majority of people who are forced to leave their homes by aridity or deluge will move within the borders of the countries where they live, almost all of them in the Global South. Most people who do cross an international frontier will cross the closest one to where they live, at risk of harassment by border guards and menaced by electrified barbed-wire fences.[13]

Throughout human history, migration has been a lifeline for communities facing sudden or prolonged changes in the ecologies that sustained them—often in the form of temporary movement over short distances. There is an odd historical echo to recent discussions of climate change and migration, for in the nineteenth century, too, many observers saw non-white migration as driven entirely by droughts and fearsome typhoons. And the use of liquid metaphors to describe migration still permeates even the most well-intentioned writing: a language of "floods" and "tides" and "waves."

But migration is not, or is no longer, an option for many people. The poorest people within the regions in the world most acutely vulnerable to the impact of climate change lack the experience, access to credit, and accumulated family connections that make long-distance migration possible. The slow effects of climate change are at least as likely to leave poor people stranded, unable to move, as they are to spark a rush of "climate refugees." Others steadfastly refuse to move. For many people around the world, the prospect of having to abandon lands of meaning, where ancestors are buried, is simply unimaginable—all the more so for communities that lost everything to the onslaught of colonial settlers.[14]

Anton Chekhov had seen in Siberia, 150 years ago, just what it takes to decide to leave home, "to sacrifice for this one's own locality, one's own beloved domestic nest. . . ." In the more recent words of the Somali British poet Warsan Shire: "no one leaves home unless / home is the mouth of a shark."[15]

AMID AN EXISTENTIAL INEQUALITY in the conditions of life, the most privileged part of humanity has fortified its place on Earth. An arsenal of nature-dominating technology upholds their freedom from nature's constraints: a "technosphere" of buildings and bridges, cables and tunnels, mines and plantations, laboratories and hospitals, factories and satellites, roads, railways, ports, airports. Since the mid-twentieth century, it has grown unfathomably large, with a combined mass of 30 trillion tons, including 11 trillion tons of urban settlements (the largest proportion), 3.76 trillion tons of cropland, and 2.25 trillion tons of ocean floor that has already been trawled for minerals. Buildings account for 40 percent of global energy-related carbon emissions, and homes alone account for nearly a fifth. Construction consumes almost all the world's cement, half of all steel produced, and around a quarter of aluminum and plastics.

No part of the planet lies untouched by the technosphere but, like fortifications of old, it is built to keep people out as well as to protect those within. Around the world, 1.6 billion people live in housing that the United Nations Human Settlements Programme describes as "inadequate," while an estimated 100 million people have no housing at all.[16]

China now plays a leading role in building the technosphere. The Belt and Road Initiative, launched by President Xi Jinping in 2013, is the largest infrastructure project the world has ever seen. It aims to connect Eurasia through highways, high-speed rail, and oil and gas pipelines in a sped-up repetition of the nineteenth-century's steam-powered globalization. In the ten years since its launch, the initiative has reached 147 countries, generated $596 billion in construction contracts, and now accounts for 45 percent of world trade in merchandise. It has also given China effective control over the materials required for the technosphere's further expansion, including 80 percent of the world's graphite and half of the world's capacity to process lithium, nickel, and cobalt—along with colossal amounts of fossil energy.[17]

The armed defense of the technosphere is itself a driver of environmental harm, and a behemoth in the way of effective action to curb it. The world's militaries contribute up to 5 percent of global carbon emissions, and the secrecy and opacity of their reporting means that figure could be even higher—the US military contributes the most by a substantial margin, and the US government has lobbied hardest to ensure that military emissions remain outside the ambit of international agreements. The military imperative to secure shipping lanes for the transport of hydrocarbons emboldens the corporate lobbyists who influence government policy, thwart regulation, and spread misinformation.[18]

The most grievous of environmental injustices is that the communities, countries, and whole regions that have done least to cause planetary warming are often most vulnerable to its effects. Their vulnerability is compounded by the unequal way the technosphere casts its shield. The more damaging its own impact on Earth systems, the more necessary the technosphere becomes to human wellbeing—and those outside its protective sphere grow more and more exposed.

IN PARIS, AT THE end of 2015, the governments of 196 countries signed a legally binding agreement to limit global warming to "well under" 2 degrees Celsius, and preferably not exceeding 1.5 degrees. The powerful advocacy of small island states impressed on the gathered delegates that climate change was no longer a distant risk. In his speech at Paris, Gaston Browne, prime minister of Antigua and Barbuda, insisted that island nations faced an existential threat. He quoted the St. Lucian poet, Derek Walcott: ". . . a morning could come in which governments might ask what happened not merely to the forests and the bays, but to a whole people."[19]

The Paris agreement fused moral urgency and messy compromise. Each party to the agreement agreed to an obligatory, yet unenforceable and self-determined, contribution toward reducing global emissions to net zero by 2050. Even if every national target were met, they would cumulatively fall short of the reductions necessary to meet the agreement's stated temperature goals. But the accords made substantial progress where previous climate summits had ended in acrimony. Though thin on specifics, the Paris preamble made reference to "environmental justice." Countries of the Global North pledged funds to help lower-income countries reduce emissions without placing even heavier burdens on the world's poorest people. And, in Paris, a door inched open to discussing what has come to be called the "loss and damage" suffered by countries that have made a negligible contribution to cumulative greenhouse gas emissions—but which now face a double burden from the effects of climate change and the rising cost of alleviating it.[20]

The goals of the Paris agreement, though many activists feel them to be too modest, will still require changes so rapid and far-reaching as to be unimaginable without new technologies. Many hopes, and billions of dollars in investment, are lodged in substitutes for hydrocarbons. The largest-scale response to climate change has been the dramatic rise in the availability and accessibility of renewable energy over the past ten years. Solar capacity increased by an average of 20 percent every year between 2010 and 2020, while its cost fell by 15 percent annually. The increase in onshore windfarm capacity was not far behind, with a 12 percent yearly increase. Without the continued and substantial expansion of renewable energy, there is no possibility that the decarbonization targets agreed to in Paris in 2015 will be met.[21]

Renewable energy presents a promising but not uncomplicated path to slowing the pace of planetary warming. Renewables will reduce greenhouse gas emissions but might do so by deepening human inequality and harming biodiversity. To generate as much electricity as a 1-gigawatt fossil-fueled power station, an array of photovoltaic solar panels needs about 80 square kilometers of land. In India, sprawling solar parks have seized land from small farmers and pastoralists in a manner that is uncomfortably reminiscent of the way large dams displaced millions in the twentieth century.

Advocates respond by promoting "symbiotic" solar: panels are raised above farmland, sheltering root vegetables and leafy greens that grow underneath, or they are built on stilts above grassland grazed by sheep. These technologies are unlikely to be within reach of farmers that barely own any land and struggle for access to water. And a further land-grab is underway, in ecologically imperiled lands, for the rare earth minerals that solar panels and batteries devour.[22]

Less proven, more expensive, and considerably riskier are efforts to capture carbon at the point of emission, and even to remove it from the air. Some carbon capture technologies are decades old, but their potential role in achieving climate goals has brought a surge in public and private investment. The most effective strategy has been to use amines to scrub the CO_2 from smokestack emissions, cutting the carbon impact of power plants and factories. By contrast, technologies of direct air capture are costly and have mostly failed to deliver on their promises. The most widespread use of the extracted CO_2 remains the oldest one: to repressurize depleted oil wells to force out more hydrocarbons. Carbon capture might yet increase the production of fossil fuels, delaying and obstructing more fundamental changes in consumption and energy use.

The carbon that is not reused is sequestered underground, drilled deep and sealed by layers of permeable rock. But that seal, many scientists warn, is "not necessarily permanent." It is prone to slow leakage—and also to spectacular failure, as with the Aliso Canyon gas leak in California, in 2015, where a burst pipeline released 97,000 metric tons of methane into the atmosphere.[23]

At the outer frontiers of technical possibility, a growing group of scientists argue that the only way to stall climate change fast enough to prevent catastrophe is to extend the technosphere as far as it will go—to engineer the climate itself. Solar geoengineering would inject aerosol particles into the stratosphere to reflect the sun's radiation back into space. When the Pinatubo volcano in the Philippines erupted in 1991, it spewed 20 million tons of sulfur dioxide into the upper atmosphere and cooled the planet by an average of 0.5 degrees Celsius over two years. The supporters of geoengineering, with a stronghold at Harvard University, propose to replicate this effect by design. With every target for reducing emissions missed, with the Earth on the brink of runaway warming—proponents of geoengineering argue that it is a radical solution worth considering.[24]

The unintended, often disastrous, effects of the twentieth century's attempts to engineer environments suggest the need for precaution. Critics insist that solar geoengineering is profoundly risky. Its use could alter patterns of rainfall, disrupt broader climatic systems, and trigger extreme events (though the geoengineers would point out that all of these things are happening already as a result of climate change). In the absence of agreed standards for regulation, the unilateral use of geoengineering is also likely to trigger international conflict. Even if the technology were perfectly calibrated, it bears the dangers of the quick fix. Solar geoengineering might alleviate climate change while leaving intact every other dimension of the environmental crisis—species loss, the depletion of fresh water, assaults on the forests and the oceans—and reducing the incentive for the wealthy and the powerful to change their behavior in any way. It epitomizes the furthest extension of the hubris that human beings can conquer nature.[25]

Well-intentioned critics present a misleading picture of solar geoengineering as a project forced by elite scientists in the Global North upon an unwilling Global South. That is, at best, a partial view. It underestimates, for a start, how fully China has embraced the prospect of weather modification. Most ambitious is a 2016 scheme to burn silver iodide to inject into clouds, creating a "Sky River" (Tian Shan) of forced precipitation that would turn the atmosphere itself into a sort of pipeline, mirroring in the air the mammoth terrestrial South-North Water Transfer Project to shift water from the Yangtze River to water-stressed North China. If the Sky River has subsequently vanished from public discussion, it nevertheless signals an openness to climate engineering on a grand scale. Chen Ying, at the Chinese Academy of Sciences, is China's leading advocate for solar geoengineering. She makes the case that radical measures may be necessary in response to the climate emergency. She also argues that China has no choice but to keep abreast of developments, or risk becoming a victim of the unilateral use of those technologies by the United States.[26]

Since the mid-twentieth century, postcolonial nations have been at least as attracted to top-down technological solutions as have wealthier countries—if not more so, given how much ground they felt they had to cover to catch up. There is some evidence that climate engineering enjoys broader public support in the Global South than in the Global North. The fear in poorer countries is not necessarily that they will be forced to accept tools to control the climate, but just as likely the opposite—that they will be excluded, with no say in the deployment and development of geoengineering technologies. They have well-founded fears that their voices will be nowhere on the expert panels that decide, for all of humanity, which risks are worth taking.[27]

MASKED BY THE ALLURE of planetary silver bullets are hundreds and thousands of smaller actions—and an even greater number of possible future actions—to reverse the damage to life on Earth.

Urban governments have made unglamorous but substantial improvements to how their cities function. Since the late 1990s Bogotá, Colombia, has cleaned its air and converted 17,000 square miles of roadway to pedestrian use with a fraction of the budget of European cities that have achieved similar feats. Under the leadership of mayor Enrique Peñalosa, the city rejected a plan for elevated highways and spurned an expensive subway system. Peñalosa's administration built instead the Bus Rapid Transit, a socially inclusive system of accessible public transportation. Its name, the Transmilenio (transmillennial), signaled the ambitious transition in urban life that it sought to bring to the twenty-first century. In two decades, Transmilenio has acquired one of the largest fleets of electrified buses in the world. Intersecting with the bus network are more than 500 kilometers of protected bicycle lanes, championed and claimed by a civil society group, La Ciudad Verde (The Green City), without waiting for government support.[28]

Beyond crowded cities, the quest to salvage coastal landscapes inches forward. The Indonesian government is in the midst of an ambitious project, launched in 2020, to restore 600,000 hectares of mangrove forest over the next few years, mostly in coastal Kalimantan and Sumatra. "Mangroves are among the far migrants of the plant kingdom, forever sending their young stages off to establish pioneer colonies," Rachel Carson wrote in 1955, pointing to their ecologically heroic role in "creating land where once there was sea."

The Transmilenio bus system in Bogotá, Colombia, is a model
of sustainable urban transportation in the Global South,
connected to a network of bicycle lanes.

With their rapid disappearance all over the world in the second half
of the twentieth century, the sea has clawed that land back.[29]

Planted seedlings will thrive only where the local soil and hydrology are receptive—and where structures of land ownership give
coastal people a stake in the forests' long-term preservation. A
vibrant WhatsApp group of Indonesian mangrove scientists buzzes
with ideas about the most promising sites for restoration, and so
far they have found a receptive ear in the government. Restored
mangroves would shelter fish, turtles, sharks, crocodiles, and—in
Indonesia alone—1,723 bird species, being a stopover on the major
bird migration route known as the East Asian–Australasian flyway.
Mangroves shore up sinking lands, protect coastal communities
from storm surges, and nourish the small-scale fisheries that could
enhance the livelihoods of artisanal fishers while augmenting the
food security of seventy-four million people.[30]

Repair is an urgent priority, too, when it comes to the most
harmful of human infrastructures. Every day, the leaky edges of
the technosphere emit a greenhouse gas thirty times more powerful

than carbon dioxide. Satellites of the European Space Agency and NASA have sensed previously invisible plumes of methane at more than two thousand locations around the world. The largest methane emissions surround oil and gas installations in the Permian Basin, New Mexico, and in Turkmenistan. Because methane remains in the atmosphere for only a decade, in contrast with carbon dioxide's lethal persistence, the number of "super-emitters" could be radically reduced simply by repairing leaks and making aging petrochemical infrastructure more secure. Repairing infrastructure could rapidly reduce harm—though without any of the positive reverberations across species of restoring ecosystems and at the cost of locking in destructive patterns of energy use.[31]

Will thousands of small acts of repair suffice to alleviate the cumulative impact of climate change, biodiversity loss, and new threats to human and animal health? Probably not. It is likely that large-scale technological intervention will play a part in sustaining human life within the limits that the Earth's systems will support. New technologies are emerging so rapidly, particularly in the area of artificial intelligence, that it would seem foolhardy to predict which of them will succeed.

ALMOST A THOUSAND YEARS after the transfer of Champa rice seeds spurred a rice revolution in southern China and opened new possibilities for the scale of human life on Earth, our most pronounced impact on the planet still comes from the most foundational of all human activities—growing food. Agriculture accounts for one quarter of all greenhouse gas emissions: 31 percent of this comes from livestock and fisheries, 27 percent from crop production, and 24 percent land use (of which only 8 percent is land devoted directly to human food, and the rest to livestock). Food production is by far the most important driver of biodiversity loss.[32] Meanwhile, an estimated one in ten people alive today do not have sufficient food to eat, including more than 20 percent of the population of Sub-Saharan Africa, and almost 16 percent of the population of South Asia. Human inequality determines how food shapes the world.[33]

Maldistribution is pervasive. No less than a quarter of greenhouse gas emissions from food—between 6 and 10 percent of the global total—come from food that is decayed, spilled, or simply thrown away before human consumption. Food *waste*, that is, accounts for a greater share of emissions than any single country on Earth other than China and the United States.

The first stage of loss is an ancient problem, eased but never solved by refrigeration and transportation—the farmer's struggle to preserve the harvest from rot. The intercontinental expanse of the trade in food, which emerged with the railroad and the steamship in the nineteenth century, made it possible for farmers to sell their surplus to distant markets but also introduced many intermediate steps where food could be ruined. And then came distinctive twentieth-century problems—food that rots on supermarket shelves before it is sold, food thrown out by restaurants after too much is cooked, food that households forget to eat. If it was once a plague of prosperity, it is no longer: with rapid urbanization, food waste is as characteristic of middle-income countries as it is of wealthy ones.

The need to reduce food waste is mostly uncontroversial. The steps toward it—better information; easier access to infrastructure for small producers; safer and better-labeled packaging; and public education, beginning in schools—are quiet, undramatic, and will grab no headlines. But they are eminently feasible.

An even more radical shift in food systems is urgent, and it is harder to imagine its success. No single change would have a more transformative impact on the health of the planet than human beings choosing to eat fewer animal products. A widely cited 2018 study, published in *Science*, estimates that if everyone alive were to move to an adequately nutritious, plant-based diet, we would see a 76 percent reduction in the land used to grow food, which is the most important threat to biodiversity. We would see a 49 percent drop in greenhouse gas emissions from agriculture, while acidification would fall by 50 percent.[34]

But food is where technical discussions of "climate change solutions"—the policymakers' abstract language of reductions and targets, adaptation and mitigation—collide with the essence of what it is to be human. The meaning of food is intrinsically bound to history, which alone can tell us why different cultures eat the way that they do: which foods they grant ceremonial value, which they offer to visitors, and which they reject as uncivilized or disgusting. Food has always been a marker and expression of cultural identity, a storehouse of collective memory. Above all, it is a source of joy and comfort. In most human cultures, the foods of greatest importance—the delicacies and cultural markers—are meats, and many European and Central Asian cultures also prize dairy products.[35]

Food preferences are deeply rooted but never static. Changes in culinary desire have driven sweeping changes in how human beings have exploited the Earth, and exploited each other—most pivotally, in modern history, the European taste for sugar and fine spices. In times of privation, as during both world wars, food habits have changed very suddenly. There are signs that they are changing again in response to ecological concerns. For now, plant-based diets and lab-grown meat substitutes appeal only to a small, wealthy group of urban consumers. Making them more affordable and more culturally appealing could have wider reverberations, for even halving the current consumption of animal products would achieve around 70 percent of the reduction in greenhouse gas emissions that would come from eliminating them entirely.[36]

Given how rampantly destructive it is to the viability of life on Earth, there is a strong moral and political case for advocating for a sharp reduction in the quantity of animal products eaten in the Global North—where meat and dairy have been abundant and cheap for two hundred years, where per capita consumption has long been above the global average, where industrial farming inflicts vicious cruelty on animals, and where alternative sources of nourishment could be made plentiful, even if currently out of reach for low-income and marginalized communities.

With an even stronger insistence on support for the poorest in society, some part of that case could plausibly be made for a country like Brazil, where levels of meat consumption are among the highest in the world despite massive social inequality. But to apply it to India would be both misguided and politically irresponsible. In India, a substantial proportion of the population does not receive even a bare sufficiency of protein despite rapid economic growth. In India, the forces of Hindu nationalism have wielded a militant vegetarianism as a marker of cultural purity, using it to persecute Muslims and Dalits to the point of public lynchings.

Neither justice nor environmental protection would be served by focusing on meat consumption in India. As the largest exploiter of groundwater in the world, India's contribution to addressing the planetary crisis might begin, instead, with the radical reform of the incentives that lead large farmers to deplete the water table at a rate that is hurtling toward disaster, with consequences not only for water security but also for the mighty South Asian monsoon. One of the lessons of the twentieth century's modernist failures is that global problems are not always best approached with standardized global solutions.[37]

To adopt too narrow a focus on carbon emissions, two leading geographers argue, runs the risk that we will "extract climate change from its social and environmental contexts," to see it as a "disembodied process acting on an undifferentiated world." An important dimension of this tendency to reductionism is the willful ignorance of history. The scale and rapidity of destabilizing changes to Earth systems have taken us into uncharted territory, outside the range of past human experience—but the institutions and the values with which human societies face the future are far from a blank slate.[38]

At the first global conference on the environment, in 1972, Indira Gandhi made two forceful observations that retain their bite, even if her own government proceeded to ignore them. Her first point was that "we live in a divided world"—she saw, and we see more clearly now, that the uneven forcing-together of peoples, plants, animals, and pathogens that began five hundred years ago leaves an imprint on the endowments and capacities with which different societies now confront the burning Earth. Her second enduring observation was that efforts at environmental protection will simply fail if they proceed in isolation from social justice.

No planetary scheme in the years ahead will be able to detach itself from these stubborn residues of history.

ROADS TO
REPAIR

I N 1997 THE JAPANESE DIRECTOR AND GENIUS OF ANI-
mation, Hayao Miyazaki, fashioned a parable about human
alienation from the rest of nature. *Princess Mononoke* is set during
Japan's iron age, in the late Muromachi era (1392–1573) and tells of
how the human assault on the forest gives rise to terrible vengeance
from the forest gods in the form of fearsome wolves and spectral
apes. In his search for a slice of pristine nature, Miyazaki had been
inspired by a real place: the thousand-year-old Shiratani Unsukiyo
forest on the island of Yakushima. The forest scenes in *Princess
Mononoke* are awash with a palette of greens, which tinge even the
shards of sunlight that slip through the canopy.[1]

On a quest for a cure after being bitten by a hate-filled boar god,
the protagonist, Ashitaka, stumbles into a war between humans and
nature. The settlement of Iron Town, under the rule of the capable and determined Lady Eboshi, has been built on the destruction
of the forest. The enraged forest gods, wounded but undefeated,
lie in wait.

Princess Mononoke is no simple story of human greed. Iron
Town is a place of conviviality and community, accepting of lepers
and prostitutes and others on the margins of society. It embodies the
material freedom that can come from razing forest and mining rock.
"When the forest has been cleared and the wolves wiped out," Lady
Eboshi tells Ashitaka, "this desolate place will be the richest land in
the world." The town's rice bowls are full, but there will be no peace.

Hayao Miyazaki, *Princess Mononoke* (1997).

Miyazaki's message is that there can be no victory in a war against nature. In the epic battle that follows, both Iron Town and the forest gods are destroyed. In the final scene, we glimpse a path to a more hopeful future. The forest regenerates from the ruins as wildflowers sprout over the burned-out hulks of buildings. The human survivors accept a humbler way of living. "This time, we'll build a better town," Lady Eboshi vows.

Many decades before Miyazaki, lonely but resonant voices warned of the estrangement of human beings from nature. Witnessing the cataclysm of the First World War, Rabindranath Tagore—poet, playwright, novelist, and the first Asian to receive the Nobel Prize in literature—described it not as a sudden convulsion but rather a slow culmination. "Turn a tree into a log and it will burn for you, but it will never bear living flowers and fruit," he said. The fundamental cause of the war was the alienation of industrialized societies from their "natural surroundings, from the fullness of . . . communal life, with all its living associations of beauty and love and social obligations." An exploitative approach to the natural world had in turn reduced human beings to "so many fragments of a machine for the production of wealth on a gigantic scale."[2]

The mechanized slaughter of the war, Tagore felt, was only possible because of the disregard that Europe's industrial civilization had shown toward the living planet—and toward the colonized peoples of Asia and Africa. A world built upon the domination of nature and of other societies was now collapsing on itself: "Suddenly, all the mechanism going mad, it has begun the dance of the furies, shattering its own limits, scattering them into the dust."[3] Tagore's description of the tight links between unrestrained capitalism, imperial domination, and militarism has lost none of its power.

To establish a wiser and less violent human relationship with the rest of nature would also be to restore and expand the breadth of our humanity—and in doing so it would continue a quest that has propelled the most sustained movements for justice of the past two hundred years. Feminists and anticolonial freedom-fighters, campaigners against racism and those for LGBTQ+ rights: what they have shared is an insistence on upholding the full range of human capabilities, a belief in the intrinsic value of different ways of inhabiting the world, and a rejection of the narrowing horizons that come inevitably from the denial of equality. It has taken longer to see that we may also have diminished, rather than enhanced, our sense of human possibilities by severing our bonds with other forms of life. In a world where human beings kill hundreds of billions of animals every year, we lose something of ourselves as well as inflict grave harm on other beings.[4]

When I first started out as a historian, I saw environmental concerns as secondary to political rights, economic empowerment, and social justice. I now believe that they are inseparable, and that the pursuit of environmental justice extends and builds on those earlier and still-unfinished struggles for human freedom. I have learned this not only from the years of research that have filled these pages, but also from my own children. They are under no illusions about the challenges ahead. And they feel a visceral need— for their own senses of self—to repair the human relationship with the rest of nature. "Why do people destroy the Earth when it's their only homeland?" my daughter asked me before she had even turned six. In a fourth-grade assignment about what he cares about most, my nine-year-old son wrote: "I worry about animals and climate change."

Rampant ecological destruction undermines the support systems that sustain the only habitable planet, as my daughter observed with the clarity that children have. But it is also a more intimate trauma, as my son expressed by using the language of worry. Social psychologists have observed the emergence of "ecological grief" in communities around the world. People mourn the loss, and anticipated future loss, of familiar landscapes and cherished animals. They mourn the erosion of hard-won local knowledge that can no longer account for weird weather and changing light and missing migratory birds. They mourn the breaking of bonds that forge human and more-than-human communities. If grief is "the price we pay for love, the cost of commitment," then ecological grief stems from the attachment that many human beings feel to the ecologies that sustain them. A member of the Inuit of Nunatsiavut, in Labrador, Canada, put it this way—"Inuit are people of the sea ice. And if there is no more sea ice, how can we be people of the sea ice?"[5]

In response, a refusal of the estrangement between human beings and the rest of nature has animated movements of resistance around the world. For several months in 2006, a group of 150 women surrounded the site of a marble mine on Mount Mutis, in the Indonesian province of East Nusa Tenggara that makes up the western half of Timor Island. The montane forests of eucalyptus, known as *ampupu*, were home to parrotfinch and red-capped plover, to civets and snakes. The whole living forest came under threat as the global market for marble fizzed with demand for photogenic kitchen counters and luxury apartment flooring.

The women came armed with handlooms. They wove brightly colored *tenun* cloth alive with ancestral symbols, they sang songs of praise to the spirits of the mountain. The women repeated a local proverb, which said:

Water is blood	*oel nam nes on na*
Forest is hair	*nasi nam nes on nak nafu*
Soil is flesh	*naijan nam nes on sisi*
Stone is bone	*fatu nam new on nuf*

By stripping the mountain, the miners threatened the spiritual fabric, as well as the livelihoods, of local people. Every day a new road inched closer to the outcrop of rock, guarded by the police and private security. Every day the women returned. The forest was precious to them. In the forest, women gathered natural dyes for their cloth, food and medicine for their families, honey and sandalwood for the market. The streams of Mount Mutis nourished the entire island. "If we are separated from any one of these natural elements, or if any one of the elements are destroyed," said the protesters' leader Aleta Baun, "we start to die and lose our identity." While the women protested, the men in their families cooked meals, cared for children and elders, and camped at the mining site overnight to make sure the guards did not seal it off. The Indonesian media took notice, and international news outlets followed. Within a few years of the protests, all mining activity in the region had ceased—though it was only a partial victory, for the mining companies moved on to exploit other regions.[6]

The 2008 Constitution of Ecuador went further. It shattered the anthropocentric presumption that had shaped every constitution in modern history by according Pachamama—a Kichwat and Aymara term often translated as Mother Earth—the "right to integral respect for its existence and for the maintenance and regeneration of its life cycles, structure, functions, and evolutionary processes." Granting legal personhood to rivers, bodies of water, or forests gives their interests representation in court by trustees. It is a bold, if imperfectly effective, way to give voice to nature in human decision-making. In an effort to heal the estrangement between human interests and the viability of ecosystems—but also to address the wounds of settler colonialism—New Zealand's Te Awa Tupua Act of 2017 protects the Whanganui River by appointing not one but two protectors: a Maori guardian, and a government guardian.[7]

Movements of repair and restoration have emerged not only from rural places, but also from the enormous cities where a majority of humanity now lives. Urban ecologists have grappled honestly with what human flourishing could look like in a world that embraces the density of cities, celebrating their human and more-than-human diversity rather than harking back to an irretrievable, antimodern vision of self-sufficient communities. They uphold plurality over purity.[8]

Novel visions of how to repair the rift between human desires and the health of the planet come from the creative hubs of cosmopolitan cities—from the very heart of global capitalism. In a recent estimate, one third of all people on Earth play video games in some form. Game designers have started to invite their avid followers to grapple with our ecological dilemmas with every choice they make as players. The Cape Town–based studio Free Lives responded directly to the city's dystopian experience of almost running out of water in 2018. *Terra Nil* reimagines the genre of the world-building game by prizing ecological repair and restoration. "Bring back life to a lifeless world by purifying soil, cleaning oceans, planting trees, and reintroducing wildlife, then leave without a trace," the game's tagline reads. Success, in this game, is to bring about human flourishing in consonance with lively streams and vibrant forests and clean air. In *Anno 1800*, by the game studio Ubisoft, the environment responds actively to the player's choices: punishing monoculture cultivation with soil erosion, and rewarding sustainable approaches to building community.[9]

Of the more than 389,000 people surveyed by the UN-supported project Playing for the Planet, 78.6 percent believed games could teach them about environmental problems. Most video games do not address the environmental crisis—many still celebrate the old story of frontier colonization and the conquest of nature—but the audience is so large that even the small number of games that raise ecological awareness will reach more people than other media.[10]

The irony is not lost on those who believe video games can help human beings reimagine their place in nature—because "every cutting-edge console, graphics card, and processor is the product of many carbon-intensive processes, including the mining of rare earth minerals." At the frontier of development, independent game-designers are responding to that dilemma. Canadian designer Kara Stone is experimenting with solar-powered servers, accepting the risk that the games would not always be available to players through the dark Canadian winter. And Stone is developing a new aesthetic of lower-resolution, reused, and recycled graphics.[11]

If not quite on the scale of video games, the cultural reach of hyper-urban Korean popular music is also enormous, with an esti-mated 150 million fans worldwide. In the world of K-pop, too, there are stirrings of a new ecological consciousness. Blackpink, the super-star girl group, put out a two-minute Instagram video in December 2020 on the fifth anniversary of the Paris Agreement, urging their legions of fans to take action in their own communities to slow the climate crisis.

The response was immediate. Nurul Sarifah, a twenty-two-year-old Indonesian college student studying international relations, teamed up with Dayeon Lee, a South Korean student of history, to form KPop4Planet, a group of K-pop fans around the world con-cerned with environmental justice, which soon counted tens of thou-sands of followers. Their slogan was instantly memorable—"After all, there's no K-pop on a dead planet."

They began with the environmental impact of the music indus-try itself: urging K-pop stars and record labels to cut back on lavish packaging, and to reduce the carbon impact of large concerts. They have not stopped there. They lobby governments and corporations to live up to promises of carbon neutrality. The daily experience of life in a megacity, together with her love of Korean music, inspired

Nurul Sarifah's activism: "I live in Jakarta," she said, "and there's so many coal plants around the area, it's affecting locals by creating air pollution." Along with lethal air, Jakartans live with the constant threat of floods: "it's becoming an annual thing that makes me realize the climate crisis is really happening," Sarifah said.[12]

There is a gap between passing a law on the rights of nature and enforcing it—and there is a gap between the advent of environmentally conscious video games and large-scale social change. In those gaps lie openings for positive action. Indonesia is not short on terrifying prospects of environmental collapse, but it tops a recent global survey of young people's attitudes when it comes to optimism. Almost 80 percent of those surveyed in Indonesia—Nurul Sarifah's generation, aged 15–24—are optimistic about the future. They answer positively the oldest of human questions—will tomorrow be better than today? Theirs is a brittle hope, emboldened by new educational opportunities, expanding employment, the newfound safety of universal health insurance, and most of all by a belief in their own agency as citizens, consumers, and voters—but it is tempered by daily exposure to extreme weather, collapsing infrastructure, smog-induced illness, and resurgent infectious diseases.[13]

Every tree planted, every school built, every sanctuary created is a bet on the future. Every act of care for other species is an assertion of a fuller vision of human life. In Shaunak Sen's 2023 documentary, *All That Breathes*, two brothers, Saud and Nadeem, run a makeshift basement clinic for the ailing black kites that drop from Delhi skies thick with vehicle emissions, construction dust, smoke from crop fires, and particles of burning waste. The brothers persevere when things seem hopeless—not only is the air poisonous, but their neighborhood lives in the shadow of murderous anti-Muslim violence fueled by India's Hindu nationalist government. To sustain a connection with the rest of nature is also to resist the politics of dehumanization.

"Life itself is kinship," the brothers insist, "we're all a community of air."[14]

IN A PIECE THAT he wrote after a 1959 visit to India to pay tribute to Mahatma Gandhi, Martin Luther King Jr. responded to cynicism that he could build a movement for justice on something as intangible as love, especially when the forces of hate showed no signs of relenting. "Non-violent resistance does call for love," King said, but he insisted that "it is not a sentimental love." Instead, his movement fostered "a very stern love that would organize itself into collective action to right a wrong by taking on itself suffering."[15]

As an educator I see every day that "stern love" for the world and its inhabitants, reaching across not only the boundaries of human cultures but also of species. I see it on university campuses and in school classrooms, in young people's climate strikes and in art studios. I see a new awareness that the absence of care and precaution has brought immense harm to human beings and to the rest of nature, even as it has generated unimaginable wealth for a few, and comfort and security for many more. In *The World Without Us*, journalist Alan Weisman painted an evocative picture of what the planet might look like if human beings were to vanish.[16] The most hopeful cultural shift of this century so far is the other side of that thought experiment: the growing realization that there is no "us" without the world.

More and more people are challenging the self-destructive folly that captured the imagination of the powerful and privileged for two hundred years, and which maintains a chokehold on our collective right to breathe—the idea that human ambition could simply disregard the health of rivers, the viability of forests, and the suffering of animals.

Once upon a time, all history was environmental history. It still is. The struggle ahead is to remember, and to integrate our creatureliness into new visions of human flourishing on Earth. Only then can we regain our freedom.

ACKNOWLEDGMENTS

FOR THEIR GENEROUS SUPPORT OF MY WORK, I AM grateful to the Infosys Science Foundation, the MacArthur Foundation, the Stichting Alfred Heineken Fondsen and the Royal Netherlands Academy of Arts and Sciences, the Harvard University Faculty of Arts and Sciences and the Harvard Center for History and Economics, and the Faculty of Arts and Sciences and the Whitney and Betty MacMillan Center for International and Area Studies at Yale University.

I have done the research that has fed into this book over the past twenty years, and my accumulated debt to librarians and archivists is immense—I thank the staff of the British Library in London, the National Library of Singapore, the Nehru Memorial Museum and Library in New Delhi, and the Widener Memorial Library at Harvard University. More than half the time I have spent writing the book was under Covid conditions, and I could not have continued work without the labor and dedication of librarians and archivists around the world who have digitized materials and made them accessible. I am grateful above all to the extraordinary librarians at Yale's Sterling Memorial and Beinecke libraries. While working on this book, I have benefited from excellent research assistance from Joseph Jones in London, and Po Eic Quah and Sai Rayala at Yale. Kelvin Ng found me a trove of environmentally focused articles from the 1970s and 1980s in the Indonesian news magazine, *TEMPO*.

My literary agent, Don Fehr, is always a dependable source of advice, encouragement, and good humor, and he has made it possible for me to work with a remarkable team of editors. Jon Durbin of W. W. Norton planted the seed for this book at a meeting back in 2018. When I told him I did not feel drawn to writing a general history of South Asia, he said, "then how about a global environmental history?" His positive energy and incisive feedback have continued throughout.

Alane Mason has been the greatest champion and the most astute critic of this book. It was exhilarating to work through her edits, attentive to each and every line, deeply aware of shape and structure, and alert to excavating the big ideas buried mid-paragraph. I have appreciated Mo Crist's efficient assistance and Rebecca Homiski's careful supervision of the book's production. This is the second book I have been fortunate to work on with Simon Winder at Penguin. I have benefited from Simon's unerring instinct for small changes that make a big difference. It has been a pleasure to work with David Atkinson, who has made such beautiful maps, and I am grateful for Rebecca Rider's meticulous and sensitive copyediting.

As this book draws on two decades of research, and it includes a debt to the first two institutions I worked at: Birkbeck College, University of London (2006–15), where the support of Hilary Sapire and Chandak Sengoopta was formative for me at the start of my career; and Harvard University (2015–20), where I appreciated the warm support of Dean Robin Kelsey, and the collegiality of Steve Biel, Sugata Bose, Vince Brown, Bruno Carvalho, Joyce Chaplin, Arunabh Ghosh, David Jones, Ian Miller, Ajantha Subramanian, Victor Seow, Michael Szonyi, Karen Thornber, and everyone associated with the Harvard Center for History and Economics. My collaborative work with David on air pollution in India, funded by the Harvard Global Institute, has been important to helping me think through the themes of this book, and I look forward to our joint work being published in years to come.

I began the writing just as I arrived at Yale University in 2020, and it owes most to the extraordinary sense of intellectual community I have found here. I am grateful to an exceptionally thoughtful leadership team—Tamar Gender, dean of the Faculty of Arts and Sciences, Kathryn Lofton, dean of Humanities, and Alan Mikhail, chair of History—for making my transition so smooth. My colleagues in History went out of their way to make me feel welcome, and for that I should thank in particular Dani Botsman, Mary Lui, Joe Manning, and Arne Westad. I feel fortunate to have found an intimidatingly brilliant but unfailingly kind group of colleagues at Yale with shared interests in South and Southeast Asia, and in environmental history. I am grateful to be able to work closely, in my various roles at Yale, with Anthony Acciavatti, Rohit De, David Engerman, Erik Harms, Rohini Pande, Paul Sabin, and Nurfadzilah Yahaya—as well as with K. Sivaramakrishnan, who has been a generous mentor to me since long before I arrived at Yale, and Steven Wilkinson, who has been warmly supportive in his role as director of the MacMillan Center. My work at the Council on South Asian Studies would not be possible without the leadership, energy, and vision of Kasturi Gupta, and more recently the support of Tara Giangrande.

I owe a great deal to the kindness and friendship of Tim Harper, Isabel Hofmeyr, Maya Jasanoff, Diana Kim, Sumit Mandal, Kazuya Nakamizo, Naoko Shimazu, Kavita Sivaramakrishnan, Eric Tagliacozzo, and A. R. Venkatachalapathy. Though time, distance, and a global pandemic have made our meetings less frequent over the years, my work always bears the stamp of their conversation and scholarly example. I owe an immeasurable debt to Emma Rothschild, who has supported me for more than two decades and continues to inspire me with her own work, most recently on the microhistories of methane.

For helpful exchanges of ideas, I am grateful to Jeremy Adelman, Aditya Balasubramanian, Debjani Bhattacharyya, Mark Bradley, Tim Bunnell, Cao Yin, Dipesh Chakrabarty, Shelly Chan, Elizabeth Chatterjee, Mel Chen, Patricia Clavin, Elizabeth DeLoughrey, Camelia Dewan, Prasenjit Duara, Ishita Banerjee Dube, Saurabh Dube, Amitav Ghosh, Ramachandra Guha, Sumit Guha, Cajetan Iheka, Derese

Kassa, Akiyuki Kawasaki, Prashant Kidambi, Kuntala Lahiri-Dutt, Charne Lavery, David Ludden, Tim Melley, Dilip Menon, Michele Navakas, Kerrill O'Neill, Ketaki Pant, Maya Prabhu, Gyan Prakash, Srinath Raghavan, Kalyani Ramnath, Mahesh Rangarajan, Stephanie Reents, Jonathan Rigg, Harriet Ritvo, Arupjyoti Saikia, Priya Satia, Jim Scott, Chandak Sengoopta, Karen Seto, Taylor Sherman, Tomoko Shiroyama, Matt Shutzer, Ben Siegel, Vineeta Sinha, Helen Siu, Sujit Sivasundaram, Glenda Sluga, Adam Sobel, Smriti Srinivas, Rory Stewart, Carolien Stolte, Tan Tai Yong, Francesca Trivellato, Paul Warde, Jeff Wasserstrom, Roland Wenzlhuemer, Jim Wescoat, Kathryn Yusoff, Christiana Zenner, and Ling Zhang.

The ideas in this book have benefited from feedback from seminars and lectures (both in person and remote) at the University of British Columbia, Colby College, the University of Colorado Boulder, Harvard University, Miami University Ohio, the Falling Walls Science Summit in Berlin, Nanyang Technological University, University College London, and the University of the Witwatersrand.

My understanding of the world of environmental policy has been enriched by many conversations with Jessica Seddon, who was generous enough to read parts of the manuscript and to give me invaluable feedback. Neel Mukherjee—one of the writers I admire most in the world—read every word at a busy time, buoyed my spirits when the task of finishing it felt forbidding, and provided deeply insightful comments.

I would never have contemplated writing a book on such a large subject without the experience of two decades of teaching. For more than half that time, I have taught classes on environmental history, and my ideas have been shaped by my students' curiosity and their desire to tackle the hardest questions. In the last phase of writing, I had the good fortune to convene a Yale undergraduate seminar— "Environmentalism from the Global South"—that serendipitously assembled the most cohesive and committed group of students I have ever taught. I learned a great deal from all fifteen of them. It gives me hope for the future that such talented and idealistic young people will form the next generation of policymakers and activists.

It has been my privilege to work with a remarkable group of graduate students at Yale, Harvard, and other institutions. They have inspired me, instructed me, and kept me on my toes. I am grateful to all the students I have taught in seminars over the years, and I name here only those I have worked with more closely as an advisor or committee member: Kamil Ahsan, Jibran Anand, Allegra Ayida, Sudarshana Chanda, Divya Chandramouli, Yi-Ning Chang, Aniket De, Hardeep Dhillon, Yuting Dong, Neeraja Durga, Swarnabh Ghosh, Junyi Han, Neelam Khoja, Adi Kumar, Kiran Kumbhar, Dante LaRiccia, Ayan Meer, Damanpreet Pelia, Chao Ren, Mindy Su, Darren Wan, Madeleine Ware, Alex Williams, Iris Yellum, and Nicole Yow. My work on *The Burning Earth* has benefited especially from all I have learned working with Meenakshi A., Shalini Iyengar, Sarah Kennedy Bates, Kalpana Mohanty, Kelvin Ng, Harsha Raghunandhan, Marcus Yee, and Xinyue Zhang.

IT WAS NOT EASY moving at the peak of the pandemic. That New Haven very quickly came to feel like home is thanks to the kindness of Lori Bruce, Sonali Chakravarti and Jac Mullen, Annette and Kerwin Charles, David Engerman and Stephanie Wratten, Hussein Fancy and Jane Lynch, and Erik Harms and Isabella Fiorentino—together with their wonderful children, who are good friends to mine. For steadfast trans-Atlantic friendship, I thank Morayo and Steve Fagborun-Bennett and their family.

My parents, Jairam and Shantha Amrith, have supported me in everything I have ever attempted. The older I get, the more I understand just how much they have given me. My brilliant sister, Megha Amrith, inspires me with her cutting-edge research on the anthropology of care and migration, keeps me supplied with recipes, and remains my favorite person to hang out with. Andreas Werner is the world's kindest and most gracious brother-in-law. I am always grateful to Barbara Phillips, and to Rachel Coffey and her family, for many years of support.

I have shared the whole of my adult life with the most ethical, creative, capable, and compassionate person I know. Many of the ideas in these pages began as conversations with Ruth Coffey, even as her contribution to the book accounts for only a sliver of why I appreciate her. Theodore and Lydia bring joy and wonder to my days, and seeing the world through their eyes has changed my perspective on just about everything. In a very tangible sense, this is their book. Their generation already has a deep environmental consciousness— and a fierce determination to make better choices than mine.

NOTES

Prologue: Dreams of Escape

1 Annie Proulx, *Fen, Bog and Swamp: A Short History of Peatland Destruction and Its Role in the Climate Crisis* (New York: Scribner, 2022), 3.

2 On reclamation, see Joshua Comaroff, "Built on Sand: Singapore and the New State of Risk," *Harvard Design Magazine* 39 (Fall/Winter 2014); Katy Lee, "Singapore's Founding Father Thought Air Conditioning Was the Secret to His Country's Success," *Vox*, March 23, 2015. A moving fictional perspective can be found in Rachel Heng, *The Great Reclamation* (New York: Riverhead Books, 2023).

3 Fernand Braudel, *L'identité de la France, Tome 1: Espace et Histoire* (Paris: Arthaud-Flammarion, 1992), 25.

4 Sunil Amrith, *Crossing the Bay of Bengal: The Furies of Nature and the Fortunes of Migrants* (Cambridge, MA: Harvard University Press, 2013); Sunil Amrith, *Unruly Waters: How Rains, Rivers, Coasts, and Seas Shaped Asia's History* (New York: Basic Books, 2018).

Introduction: Nature and Freedom

1 Nicholas A. Robinson, "The Charter of the Forest: Evolving Human Rights in Nature," in *Magna Carta and the Rule of Law*, eds. Daniel Barstow Magraw, Andrea Martinez, and Roy E. Brownell II (Chicago: American Bar Association, 2014), 311–77.

2 Jean Birrell, "Common Rights in the Medieval Forest: Disputes and Conflicts in the Thirteenth Century," *Past and Present* 117 (1987): 22–49, the Bilston case is on p. 44; Christopher Dyer, "Conflict in the Landscape: The Enclosure Movement in England, 1220–1349," *Landscape History* 28, no. 1 (2006): 21–33.

3 David Graeber and David Wengrow, *The Dawn of Everything: A New History of Humanity* (London: Allen Lane, 2021), 502–3.

4 Thomas Hobbes, *Leviathan*, ed. Richard Tuck, revised edition (Cambridge: Cambridge University Press, 1996), 170–71.

5 Dipesh Chakrabarty, "The Climate of History: Four Theses," *Critical Inquiry* 35, no. 2 (Winter 2009): 197–222, quotation on p. 208.

6 Angus Deaton, *The Great Escape: Health, Wealth, and the Origins of Inequality* (Princeton, NJ: Princeton University Press, 2013).

7 Leigh Shaw-Taylor, "An Introduction to the History of Infectious Diseases, Epidemics

and the Early Phases of the Long-Run Decline in Mortality," *Economic History Review* 73, no. 3 (2020): E1–E19; Max Rosen, Hannah Ritchie, and Esteban Ortiz-Espina, "World Population Growth" (revised 2019), published online at OurWorldinData.org.

8 International Human Genome Sequencing Consortium, "Initial Sequencing and Analysis of the Human Genome," *Nature* 409 (2001): 860–921, quotations from p. 914 and p. 860.

9 International Human Genome Sequencing Consortium, "Initial Sequencing and Analysis," quotations from p. 914.

10 *The Earth Charter* (Earth Charter Foundation, 2001), earthcharter.org.

11 Maggie Nelson, *On Freedom: Four Songs of Care and Constraint* (Minneapolis: Graywolf Press, 2021), 183; Bruce M. S. Campbell, "Nature as Historical Protagonist: Environment and Society in Pre-Industrial England," *Economic History Review* 63, no. 2 (2010): 281–314; J. G. Manning, *The Open Sea: The Economic Life of the Ancient Mediterranean World from the Iron Age to the Rise of Rome* (Princeton, NJ: Princeton University Press, 2018), 141.

12 Samantha Harvey, *Orbital: A Novel* (New York: Grove Press, 2023), 112.

Chapter One: Horizons of Desire

1 All quotations in this and the preceding paragraphs are from Yelü Chucai, "Record of a Journey to the West" [1228] in *Inscribed Landscapes: Travel Writing from Imperial China*, ed. and trans. Richard E. Strassberg (Berkeley: University of California Press, 1994), 229–34; Barry Cunliffe, *By Steppe, Desert, and Ocean: The Birth of Eurasia* (Oxford: Oxford University Press, 2017), 419–20.

2 Cunliffe, *Steppe, Desert, and Ocean*, 17.

3 Nicola di Cosmo, "The Scientist as Antiquarian: History, Climate, and the New Past," Institute for Advanced Study, *Ideas* (2018).

4 David Leeming, "Turko-Mongol Mythology," in *A Dictionary of Asian Mythology* (Oxford: Oxford University Press, 2001).

5 Population figures from Robert B. Marks, *China: Its Environment and History* (Lanham, MD: Rowman and Littlefield, 2012).

6 Francesca Bray, *The Rice Economies: Technology and Development in Asian Societies* (Berkeley: University of California Press, 1986); Ravi Palat, *The Making of an Indian Ocean World-Economy, 1250–1650: Princes, Paddy Fields, and Bazaars* (Basingstoke, UK: Palgrave, 2015).

7 Ping-Ti Ho, "Early Ripening Rice in Chinese History," *Economic History Review*, New Series 9, no. 2 (1956): 200–18; Dorian Q. Fuller, "Agricultural Origins and Frontiers in South Asia: A Working Synthesis," *Journal of World Prehistory* 20 (2006): 1–86.

8 Ho, "Early Ripening Rice"; Randolph Barker, "The Origin and Spread of Early-Ripening Champa Rice: Its Impact on Song Dynasty China," *Rice* 4, no. 3–4 (2011): 184–86.

9 Morris Rossabi, "The Reign of Khubilai Khan," in *The Cambridge History of China, Volume 6: Alien Regimes and Border States, 907–1368*, eds. Herbert Franke and Denis Twitchett (Cambridge: Cambridge University Press, 1994), 414–89, especially pp. 416–22. See also Morris Rossabi, *Khubilai Khan: His Life and Times*, 20th anniversary edition (Berkeley: University of California Press, 2009).

10 Roslyn Lee Hammers, *Pictures of Tilling and Weaving: Art, Labor, and Technology in Song China* (Hong Kong: Hong Kong University Press, 2011), quotations from pp. 9, 51, 88, 171.

11 Paul Ratchnevsky, *Un Code des Yuan*, vol. 1 (Paris: Presses Universitaires de France, 1937), 189–90; Rossabi, "Reign of Khubilai Khan," 447.

12 Jonathan Shepard, "Networks," *Past and Present* 238, no. 13 (November 2018): 116–57, quotation on p. 147.

13 Sheila S. Blair, "Rab'-e Raidi," *Encyclopaedia Iranica*, online edition (2016).

14 *The Travels of Ibn Battuta, AD 1325–1354*, vol. 4, ed. and trans. H. A. R. Gibb and C. F. Beckingham (Farnham, UK: Ashgate, 2010), 893.

15 Mark Bloch, *French Rural History: An Essay on Its Basic Characteristics*, trans. Janet Sondheimer (Berkeley: University of California Press, 1970), quotation on p. 16; Peter Biller, *The Measure of Multitude: Population in Medieval Thought* (Oxford: Oxford University Press, 2000), 218–27, quotations from Bartholomew on pp. 222–23, and p. 227.

16 Isidore of Seville, *Etymologiae*, in *Isidorus Hispalensis Etymologiae*, ed. J. Andre, book 17 (Paris: Les Belles Lettres, 1981): 147–49, cited in Paul Freedman, *Out of the East: Spices and the Medieval Imagination* (New Haven, CT: Yale University Press, 2009), 134.

17 "Mongol Exchange" from Marie Favereau, *The Horde: How the Mongols Changed the World* (Cambridge, MA: Harvard University Press, 2021); Marco Polo, *The Travels*, trans. Ronald Latham (Harmondsworth, UK: Penguin, 1958), 251; see also Freedman, *Out of the East*, 143.

18 Tana Li, "The Mongol Yuan Dynasty and the Climate, 1260–1360," in *The Crisis of the 14th Century: Teleconnections Between Environmental and Societal Change?* eds. Martin Bauch and Gerrit Jasper Schenk (Berlin: De Gruyter, 2019), 153–68, quotation on p. 157.

19 William Chester Jordan, *The Great Famine: Northern Europe in the Early Fourteenth Century* (Princeton, NJ: Princeton University Press, 1996), "*the* flood" quoted on p. 215, "unkynde" on p. 22.

20 Ian Kershaw, "The Great Famine and Agrarian Crisis in England, 1315–1322," *Past and Present* 59 (May 1973): 3–50, "A thusent winter" quoted on p. 14; Seung Hun Baek et al., "A Quantitative Hydroclimatic Context for the European Great Famine of 1315–1317," *Communications Earth and Environment* 1, no. 1 (September 2020): doi .org/10.1038/s43247-020-00016-3, Schmidtstedt memorial quoted on p. 2.

21 Quotations and translations from *Yuan Shi* are from Li, "Yuan Dynasty and the Climate," 153–68.

22 Li, "Yuan Dynasty and the Climate," 154.

23 Favereau, *The Horde*, 251–52.

24 Ole J. Benedictow, *The Black Death, 1346–1353: The Complete History* (Woodbridge, UK: Boydell Press, 2004); Giovanni Boccaccio, *Decameron*, trans. G. H. McWilliam (Harmondsworth, UK: Penguin, 1972), 50–58.

25 Abu Hafs Umar Ibn Al-Wardi, "Essay on the Report of the Pestilence" [ca. 1348], in John Aberth, *The Black Death: The Great Mortality of 1348–1350, A Brief History with Documents* (New York: Palgrave Macmillan, 2005), 16–18.

26 Georg Heinrich Pertz, ed., "Continuatio Movimontensis," in *Monumenta Germaniae Historica—scriptorium* (Hanover, 1851), IX:674–76, in *The Black Death,* ed. and trans. Rosemary Horrox (Manchester, UK: Manchester University Press, 1994), 59; Letter from Archbishop of York, July 28, 1348, in *Historical Letters and Papers from the Northern Registers*, Rolls Series, ed. James Raine (1873), 395–97, reproduced in Horrox, *Black Death*, 111.

27 Petrarch, *Epistolae de Rebus Familiaribus et variae*, ed. Joseph Fracassetti (Florence, 1859), I:13, 442–43, 443–45, in Horrox, *Black Death*, 248–49.

28 *Historia Roffensis*, British Library, Cottonian MS, Faustina B V folios 96v–101, in

Horrox, *Black Death*, 70; R. Butler, ed., *Annalium Hibernae Chronicon* (Irish Archaeological Society, 1849), 35–37, in Horrox, *Black Death*, 82–84.

29 John Aberth, *The Black Death: A New History of the Great Mortality in Europe, 1347–1500* (New York: Oxford University Press, 2020); Yaron Ayalon, *Natural Disasters in the Ottoman Empire: Plague, Famine, and Other Misfortunes* (Cambridge: Cambridge University Press, 2014), 21–60; Benedictow has the highest estimate of mortality, at 60 percent: *Black Death, 1346–1353*, 380–86; Emmanuel Le Roy Ladurie, "A Concept: The Unification of the Globe by Disease," in *The Mind and Method of the Historian*, trans. Siân Reynolds and Ben Reynolds (Brighton, UK: Harvester Press, 1981), 28–91.

30 Cantor quoted in Daniel Headrick, *Humans Versus Nature: A Global Environmental History* (New York: Oxford University Press, 2019), 128.

31 Richard Bulliet, *Cotton, Climate, and Camels in Early Islamic Iran* (New York: Columbia University Press, 2009).

32 Victor Lieberman, *Strange Parallels Southeast Asia in Global Context, c. 800–1830: Volume 2: Mainland Mirrors: Europe, Japan, China, South Asia, the Islands* (Cambridge: Cambridge University Press, 2011).

33 Letter from Madmun bin Hasan-Japheth to Abraham bin Yiju, in *India Traders of the Middle Ages: Documents from the Cairo Geniza "India Book,"* eds. Shelomo Dov Goitein and Mordechai Friedman (Leiden, Netherlands: Brill, 2007), 314.

Chapter Two: Winds of Death

1 On Zheng He's voyages, see Louise Levathes, *When China Ruled the Seas: The Treasure Fleet of the Dragon Throne, 1405–1433* (New York: Oxford University Press, 1994).

2 Sally K. Church, "The Giraffe of Bengal: A Medieval Encounter in Ming China," *The Medieval History Journal* 7, no. 1 (2004): 1–37; Xendu's poem quoted in Stewart Gordon, *When Asia Was the World* (New Haven, CT: Yale University Press, 2008): 141–42.

3 Dale Peterson, *Giraffe Reflections*, with photographs by Karl Ammann (Berkeley: University of California Press, 2013), 49; Quotation from *Shujing* in Church, "Giraffe of Bengal," 34.

4 Alvise Cà da Mosto, *The Voyages of Cadamosto and Other Documents on Western Africa in the Second Half of the Fifteenth Century*, ed. and trans. G. R. Crone (London: Hakluyt Society, 1937), 9; on the colonization of Madeira, see Jason W. Moore, "Madeira, Sugar, and the Conquest of Nature in the 'First' Sixteenth Century: Part I: From 'Island of Timber' to Sugar Revolution, 1420–1506," *Review (Fernand Braudel Center)* 32, no. 4 (2009): 345–90. Description of Elmina in Jean Barbot, *A Description of the Coasts of North and South-Guinea . . .* (London: A. and J. Churchill, 1732).

5 Cabot's patent quoted by Anthony Pagden, *Lords of All the World: Ideologies of Empire in Spain, Britain, and France, c. 1500–c.1800* (New Haven, CT: Yale University Press, 1995), 63.

6 "Letter of Dr. Chanca on the Second Voyage of Columbus," in *The Northmen, Columbus and Cabot, 985–1503: The Voyages of the Northmen; The Voyages of Columbus and of John Cabot*, eds. Julius E. Olson and Edward G. Bourne (New York: Charles Scribner's Sons, 1906), 281–313.

7 Michele de Cunco, quoted in Noble David Cook, *Born to Die: Disease and New World Conquest, 1492–1650* (Cambridge: Cambridge University Press, 1998), 28.

8 Cook, *Born to Die*, 28–30.

9   Massimo Livi Bacci, *Conquest: The Destruction of the American Indios*, trans. Carl
    Ipsen (Cambridge: Polity, 2008), 40; Clara Estow, "Reflections on Gold: On the Late
    Medieval Background of the Spanish 'Enterprise of the Indies,'" *Mediaevistik* 6
    (1993): 85–120.

10 Gregory Stone, *The Ethics of Nature in the Middle Ages: On Boccaccio's Poetaphysics*
    (New York: St. Martin's Press, 1998), 3.

11 María Elena Martínez, *Genealogical Fictions: Limpieza de Sangre, Religion, and
    Gender in Colonial Mexico* (Stanford, CA: Stanford University Press, 2008), 1.

12 Estimates of Hispaniola's population before the arrival of the Iberians range from one
    hundred thousand to several million people; after a careful review of the evidence,
    Livi Bacci proposes a range of between two hundred thousand and three hundred
    thousand. Livi Bacci, *Conquest*, 105; the Friars are cited in Cook, *Born to Die*, 60.

13 Gonzalo Oviedo y Valdés, *Historia general y natural de las Indias*, vol. 2 (Seville,
    Spain: Juan Cromberger, 1535), cited in Livi Bacci, *Conquest*, 117; Las Casas quoted in
    David Watts, *The West Indies: Patterns of Development, Culture, and Environmental
    Change since 1492* (Cambridge: Cambridge University Press, 1987), 78.

14 "Des Coches," *Essays of Michael Lord of Montaigne* [1603], trans. John Florio (Lon-
    don: Bent, 1928), 3:144.

15 W. F. Ruddiman, "The Anthropogenic Greenhouse Era Began Thousands of Years
    Ago," *Climatic Change* 61 (2003): 261–93.

16 Alexander Koch et al., "Earth System Impacts of European Arrival and Great Dying
    in the Americas after 1492," *Quaternary Science Reviews* 207 (March 2019): 13–36;
    Simon L. Lewis and Mark A. Maslin, *Human Planet: How We Created the Anthro-
    pocene* (New Haven, CT: Yale University Press, 2018), quotations on pp. 179, 184;
    Mauro Rubino et al., "Revised Records of Atmospheric Trace Gases, CO_2, CH_4, N_2O,
    and $\partial\ ^{13}C\text{-}CO_2$ over the Last 2000 Years from Law Dome, Antarctica," *Earth System
    Science Data* 11, no. 2 (2019): 473–92; Dagmar Degroot provides a clear overview of
    the uncertainties: "Did Colonialism Cause Global Cooling? Revisiting an Old Contro-
    versy," *Historical Climatology*, February 22, 2019.

17 Garcilaso de la Vega, *Royal Commentaries of the Incas and General History of Peru*
    [1609], trans. Harold V. Livermore (Austin: University of Texas Press, 1965), Part 2,
    chapter 1.

18 Felipe Guaman Poma de Ayala, *The First New Chronicle and Good Government: On
    the History of the World and the Incas up to 1615*, ed. Roland Hamilton (Austin: Uni-
    versity of Texas Press, 2009), 70–71; on Ayala's discussion of climate, see Sam White,
    A Cold Welcome: The Little Ice Age and Europe's Encounter with North America
    (Cambridge, MA: Harvard University Press, 2017), 24.

19 My description of mining is based on the excellent book by Kris Lane, *Potosí: The
    Silver City That Changed the World* (Berkeley: University of California Press, 2019),
    especially chapters 1 and 2; Luis Capoche, *Relación general de la Villa Imperial de
    Potosí*, Biblioteca de Autores Españoles, vol. 122, ed. Lewis Hanke (Madrid: Atlas,
    1959), 159, cited in Lane, *Potosí*, 74; Diego de Ocaña, *Viaje por el Nuevo Mundo de
    Guadalupe a Potosí, 1599–1605*, eds. Blanca López de Mariscal and Abraham Madro-
    ñal (Madrid: Iberoamericana/Vervuert, 2010), 257–58, cited in Lane, *Potosí*, 75–76.

20 Nicholas A. Robins, *Mercury, Mining, and Empire: The Human and Ecological Cost
    of Colonial Silver Mining in the Andes* (Bloomington: Indiana University Press, 2011),
    quotation from p. 48.

21 Martín de Murúa, *Historia General del Pirú* [1616] (Los Angeles: Getty, 2008), cited
    in Lane, *Potosí*, 86; the chronicle is cited in Lane, *Potosí*, 94.

22 On the circumnavigation, see Felipe Fernández-Armesto, *Pathfinders: A Global*

History of Exploration (New York: W. W. Norton, 2007), 197–200; on Chinese demand for silver, see Richard von Glahn, *Fountain of Fortune: Money and Monetary Policy in China, 1000–1700* (Berkeley: University of California Press, 2006); Timothy Brook, *The Confusions of Pleasure: Commerce and Culture in Ming China* (Berkeley: University of California Press, 1999); and Dennis O. Flynn and Arturo Giráldez, "Cycles of Silver: Global Economic Unity through the Mid-Eighteenth Century," *Journal of World History* 13, no. 2 (September 2002), 391–427. The figure for VOC exports of silver is from Timothy Brook, *Vermeer's Hat: The Seventeenth Century and the Dawn of the Global World* (London: Profile, 2008), 161.

23   The discussion of Manila draws on Brook, *Vermeer's Hat*, 162–84, quotation from Zhou Qiyuan on p. 168 and from a Spanish report on the cargo of Chinese ships from p. 170.

Chapter Three: Land and Freedom

1   David Moon, "Peasant Migration and the Settlement of Russia's Frontiers, 1550–1897," *The Historical Journal* 40, no. 4 (1997): 859–93.

2   Tale No. 159, "Historical Songs of the Russian People of the XVI–XVII Centuries," Collections of the Section of Russian Language and Literature of the Imperial Academy of Sciences [1915], cited in Clarence Augustus Manning, "Yermak Timofeyevich in Russian Folk Poetry," *Journal of the American Oriental Society* 43 (1923): 206–15, quotation from p. 207.

3   Jane Burbank and Frederick Cooper, *Empires in World History: Power and the Politics of Difference* (Princeton, NJ: Princeton University Press, 2010): 185–96.

4   John F. Richards, *The Unending Frontier: An Environmental History of the Early Modern World* (Berkeley: University of California Press, 2006), 242–55; John Darwin, *After Tamerlane: The Global History of Empire since 1405* (London: Penguin, 2009), 118–19.

5   Osip Mandelstam, "Black Earth," trans. Peter France, in *Black Earth: Selected Poems and Prose* (New York: New Directions, 2021).

6   Richards, *Unending Frontier*; Dominic Lieven, *Empire: The Russian Empire and Its Rivals* (New Haven, CT: Yale University Press, 2000).

7   On Remezov's life and work, see Leo Bagrow, "Semyon Remezov—a Siberian Cartographer," *Imago Mundi* 11, no. 1 (1954): 111–25; Valerie Kivelson, " 'Between All Parts of the Universe': Russian Cosmographies and Imperial Strategies in Early Modern Siberia and Ukraine," *Imago Mundi* 60, no. 2 (2008): 166–81; Emilie Hardman, "Early Maps of Siberia Digitized," *Houghton Library Blog*, October 4, 2010.

8   Jonathan Schlesinger, *A World Trimmed with Fur: Wild Things, Pristine Places, and the Natural Fringes of Qing Rule* (Stanford, CA: Stanford University Press, 2017), 132.

9   Alan Mikhail, *Under Osman's Tree: The Ottoman Empire, Egypt, and Environmental History* (Chicago: University of Chicago Press, 2017); Onur Inal and Yavuz Köse, eds., *Seeds of Power: Explorations in Ottoman Environmental History* (Cambridge: White Horse Press, 2019).

10   Chart and raw data, "Historical World Population: Comparison of Different Sources," in Max Roser et al., "World Population Growth," published online at OurWorldinData.org.

11   Helen Dunstan, "The Late Ming Epidemics: A Preliminary Survey," *Ch'ing-shih wen-t'i* 3, no. 3 (November 1975): 14–32.

12   Chen Zilong, "The Little Cart," from Arthur Waley, *Translations from the Chinese*

(New York: Alfred A. Knopf, 1941), 325; cited in Geoffrey Parker, *Global Crisis: War, Climate Change and Catastrophe in the Seventeenth Century* (New Haven, CT: Yale University Press, 2013), 103.

13 Extract from *Kuang Tung Hsin Yu* in Francesca Bray, *Science and Civilisation in China, Volume 6: Biology and Biological Technology; Part II, Agriculture*, ed. Joseph Needham (Cambridge: Cambridge University Press, 1984), 509; Peter Perdue, "Nature and Nurture on Imperial China's Frontiers," *Modern Asian Studies* 43, no. 1 (2009): 245–67.

14 Sucheta Mazumdar, "The Impact of New World Food Crops on the Diet and Economy of China and India, 1600–1900," in *Food in Global History*, ed. Raymond Grew (Boulder, CO: Westview Press, 1999), 58–78.

15 Mazumdar, "New World Food Crops," 66–67.

16 Robert B. Marks, *China: Its Environment and History* (Lanham, MD: Rowman and Littlefield, 2012), 205–7; Sow-Theng Leong, *Migration and Ethnicity in Chinese History: Hakkas, Pengmin, and Their Neighbors*, ed. Tim Wright (Stanford, CA: Stanford University Press, 1997).

17 Mark C. Elliott, *The Manchu Way: The Eight Banners and Ethnic Identity in Late Imperial China* (Stanford, CA: Stanford University Press, 2001); Robert B. Marks, "Asian Tigers: The Real, the Symbolic, the Commodity," *Nature and Culture* 1, no. 1 (Spring 2006): 63–87, quotation from Kangxi Emperor on pp. 67–8; Jonathan Spence, *Emperor of China: Self Portrait of K'ang Hsi* (New York: Alfred A. Knopf, 1974), 9.

18 On the fur trade, see Schlesinger, *World Trimmed with Fur*.

19 Peter C. Perdue, *China Marches West: The Qing Conquest of Central Eurasia* (Cambridge, MA: Harvard University Press, 2005), chapters 6 and 7.

20 Perdue, *China Marches West*, quotation on p. 283.

21 My account is based on Michael Khodarkovsky, *Where Two Worlds Meet: The Russian State and the Kalmyk Nomads, 1600–1771* (Ithaca, NY: Cornell University Press, 2018), quotation from Tsebek-Dorji on p. 230.

22 Khodarkovsky, *Two Worlds*.

23 Jos Gommans, "The Silent Frontier of South Asia, c. AD 1100–1800," *Journal of World History* 9, no. 1 (Spring 1998): 1–23; Christopher John Baker, *An Indian Rural Economy, 1880–1955: The Tamilnad Countryside* (Oxford: Clarendon Press, 1984).

24 Annette Susannah Beveridge, trans., *Babur Nama: Journal of Emperor Babur* (New Delhi: Penguin, 2006), quotations on pp. 93, 264–65; "Large cities" quoted in Sumit Guha and Kenneth Pomeranz, "Life and Energy," in *What China and India Once Were: The Pasts That May Shape the Global Future*, eds. Sheldon Pollock and Benjamin Elman (New Delhi: Viking, 2018), 27–62, quotation on p. 40.

25 John F. Richards, *The Mughal Empire* (Cambridge: Cambridge University Press, 1993).

26 Sumit Guha, *Ecologies of Empire in South Asia, 1400–1900* (Seattle: University of Washington Press, 2023), chapters 2 and 3.

27 Richard Eaton, *The Rise of Islam and the Bengal Frontier, 1204–1760* (Berkeley: University of California Press, 1993), quotations on p. 228.

28 Jos Gommans, *Mughal Warfare: Indian Frontiers and Highroads to Empire, 1500–1700* (London: Routledge, 2003); quotation from Henry Beveridge, trans., *Akbarnama of Abu-l-Fazl: A History of the Reign of Akbar Including an Account of His Predecessors*, vol. 3 (Calcutta: Asiatic Society, 1912), 135–36.

29 Eaton, *Bengal Frontier*: the story of Zindah Ghazi appears in the discussion of pioneer narratives on pp. 215–19.

30 François Pyrard, *The Voyage of François Pyrard of Laval to the East Indies, the Maldives, the Moluccas and Brazil*, ed. and trans. Albert Gray (London: Hakluyt Society,

1st ser., nos. 76, 77, 80, 1887–90; repr., New York: Burt Franklin, n.d.), 2:327, cited in Eaton, *Rise of Islam*, 201.

31   William Methwold, *Relations of the Kingdome of Golchonda, and Other Neighbour-ing Nations within the Gulfe of Bengala, Arreccan, Pegu, Tannassery, etc. and the English Trade in Those Parts* [1626], in *Relations of Golconda in the Early Seventeenth Century*, ed. W. H. Moreland (London: Hakluyt Society, 1931); Tomé Pires, *The Suma Oriental of Tomé Pires*, trans. Armando Cortesao (London: Hakluyt Society, 1944), 3:92–93; the estimate of 5 percent is from Guha and Pomeranz, "Life and Energy," 48.

32   Guha and Pomeranz, "Life and Energy," 48.

Chapter Four: Suburbs of Hell

1   Stephanie E. Smallwood, *Saltwater Slavery: A Middle Passage from Africa to American Diaspora* (Cambridge, MA: Harvard University Press, 2008), quotation from Jean Barbot on pp. 37–38.

2   W. E. B. Du Bois, *Black Reconstruction in America: An Essay toward a History of the Part Which Black Folk Played in the Attempt to Reconstruct Democracy in America, 1860–1880* (New York: Harcourt, Brace and Company, 1935), 727; the significance of Du Bois's observation is discussed in Marcus Rediker, *The Slave Ship: A Human History* (London: Viking, 2007), 4.

3   Frederick Cooper, *Africa in the World: Capitalism, Empire, Nation-State* (Cambridge, MA: Harvard University Press, 2014), 14; Jane I. Guyer, "Wealth in People, Wealth in Things—Introduction," *Journal of African History* 36, no. 1 (March 1995): 83–90.

4   "On Board the Unity, 1761–63," Zeeland Archives, zeeuwsarchief.nl; Prasannan Parthasarathi, *Why Europe Grew Rich and Asia Did Not: Global Economic Divergence, 1600–1850* (Cambridge: Cambridge University Press, 2011), 24; Kazuo Kobayashi, "Indian Cotton Textiles in the Eighteenth-Century Atlantic Economy," LSE Blog, June 27, 2013.

5   Smallwood, *Saltwater Slavery*, 43–44, quotation from Dalby Thomas on p. 44.

6   Rediker, *The Slave Ship*, quotation from Robinson on p. 38; Olaudah Equiano, *The Interesting Narrative of the Life of Olaudah Equiano, or Gustavus Vassa, the African. Written by Himself* [London, 1789] in *The Interesting Narrative and Other Writings* ed. Vincent Carretta (New York: Penguin, 1995), quotations on pp. 58–59.

7   The estimate is from the Slave Voyages database, slavevoyages.org.

8   Jason W. Moore, "Madeira, Sugar, and the Conquest of Nature in the 'First' Sixteenth Century: Part I: From 'Island of Timber' to Sugar Revolution, 1420–1506," *Review (Fernand Braudel Center)* 32, no. 4 (2009): 345–90; Jason W. Moore, "Madeira, Sugar, and the Conquest of Nature in the 'First' Sixteenth Century: Part II: From Regional Crisis to Commodity Frontier, 1506–1530," *Review (Fernand Braudel Center)* 33, no. 1 (2010): 1–24; On China, see Peter Perdue, *Exhausting the Earth: State and Peasant in Hunan, 1500–1800* (Cambridge, MA: Harvard University Press, 1987).

9   Laird Bergad, *The Comparative Histories of Slavery in Brazil, Cuba, and the United States* (Cambridge: Cambridge University Press, 2007), 96–131.

10   Gabriel Soares de Sousa, *Tratado Descriptivo do Brasil em 1587*, ed. F. A. de Varnhagen, trans. Loretta Porto Slover (Rio de Janeiro: Typographia de João Ignacio da Silva, 1879), 108–18, 121–42, reprinted in *New Iberian World: A Documentary History of the Discovery and Settlement of Latin America to the Early Seventeenth Century, Volume 5: Coastlines, Rivers, and Forests*, eds. John H. Parry and Robert G. Keith

(New York: Hector and Rose, 1984), 99–110; "Of those who came . . ." cited in Warren Dean, *With Broadax and Firebrand: The Destruction of the Brazilian Atlantic Forest* (Berkeley: University of California Press, 1997), 56–57.

11 This description of plantation labor draws on Stuart B. Schwartz, *Sugar Plantations in the Formation of Brazilian Society: Bahia, 1500–1835* (Cambridge: Cambridge University Press, 1985), quotation from Padre Vieira on p. 132; Mark Hauser, *Mapping Water in Dominica: Enslavement and Environment Under Colonialism* (Seattle: University of Washington Press, 2021).

12 C. L. R. James, *The Black Jacobins* (London: Secker and Warburg, 1938), 12–13; João Fernandes Vieira, "Instructions on How to Manage a Sugar Mill and Estate" [1663], in *Early Brazil: A Documentary Collection to 1700*, ed. Stuart B. Schwartz (Cambridge: Cambridge University Press, 2010), 224–29.

13 John Ovington, *A Voyage to Surat in the Year 1689* (London: Jacob Tonson, 1696), cited in Moore, "Madeira . . . Part II," 8; on the use of bagasse, see Ulbe Bosma, *The World of Sugar: How the Sweet Stuff Transformed Our Politics, Health, and Environment over 2,000 Years* (Cambridge, MA: Harvard University Press, 2023), 53–56.

14 Judith Carney and Richard Nicholas Rosomoff, *In the Shadow of Slavery: Africa's Botanical Legacy in the Atlantic World* (Berkeley: University of California Press, 2011), 123–38, quotation from Moreau on p. 127.

15 Alvin O. Thompson, *Flight to Freedom: African Runaways and Maroons in the Americas* (Kingston, Jamaica: University of the West Indies Press, 2006), quotation on p. 175.

16 John Gabriel Stedman, *Narrative of a Five Years' Expedition Against the Revolted Negroes of Surinam* [1796], ed. Richard and Sally Price (Baltimore: Johns Hopkins University Press, 1988), 157; quoted in Thompson, *Flight to Freedom*, 186.

17 Allan da Rosa, "The Sun Rises on Brazilian Bantu Culture," foreword to Marcelo D'Salete, *Run for It: Stories of Slaves Who Fought for Their Freedom*, trans. Andrea Rosenberg (Seattle: Fantagraphics Books, 2017).

18 Eurípedes A. Funes, "'I was Born in the Forest; I've Never Had an Owner': History and Memory of the Mocambo Communities in the Low Amazon Rainforest," in *Freedom by a Thread: The History of Quilombos in Brazil*, eds., Flávio Dos Santos Gomes and João José Reis (New York: Diasporic Africa Press, 2016).

19 Sidney W. Mintz, *Sweetness and Power: The Place of Sugar in Modern History* (New York: Penguin, 1985), 111.

20 Daniel Defoe, *A Tour Thro' the Whole Island of Great Britain. Divided into Circuits or Journeys. Giving a Particular and Entertaining Account of whatever is Curious, and worth Observation*, 3rd ed. (London: J. Osborn and c., 1742), Letter 5; William Cavert, *The Smoke of London: Energy and Environment in the Early Modern City* (Cambridge: Cambridge University Press, 2016).

21 Defoe, *A Tour*, Letter 5; Alexandra Logue, "'Saucy Stink': Smells, Sanitation, and Conflict in Early Modern London," *Renaissance and Reformation* 44, no. 2 (Spring 2021): 61–86; John Evelyn, *Fumifugium: or, The Inconvenience of the Aer and Smoak of London Dissipated* (London: W. Godbid, 1661); Cavert, *The Smoke of London*, 22.

22 E. A. Wrigley, "The Transition to an Advanced Organic Economy: Half a Millennium of English Agriculture," *Economic History Review* 59, no. 3 (2006): 435–80; Keith Thomas, *Man and the Natural World: A History of the Modern Sensibility* (New York: Pantheon Books, 1983), 37; Margaret Cavendish, *Poems and Phancies* (London: William Wilson, 1664), 137, cited in Thomas, *Natural World*, 170.

23 Jan de Vries and Ad van der Woude, *The First Modern Economy: Success, Failure, and Perseverance of the Dutch Economy, 1500–1815* (Cambridge: Cambridge University

Press, 1997), 27; Mike Cummings, "A Living Artifact from the Dutch Golden Age: Yale's 367-Year-Old Water Bond Still Pays Interest," *Yale News*, September 22, 2015.

24 de Vries and van der Woude, *First Modern Economy*, 27–30.

25 Eric H. Ash, *The Draining of the Fens: Projectors, Popular Politics, and State Building in Early Modern England* (Baltimore: Johns Hopkins University Press, 2017), Part II; H. C. Darby, *Draining of the Fens* (Cambridge: Cambridge University Press, 1956), 42.

26 C. Vermuyden, *A Discourse Touching the Drayning, the Great Fennes, lying within the severall counties of Lincolne, Northampton, Huntington, Norfolke, Suffolke, Cambridge, and the Isle of Ely as it was presented to his Majestie* (London: T. Fawler, 1642); William Dugdale, "To the Reader," in *The History of Imbanking and Draining the Fens and Marshes . . .* (London: W. Whittingham, 1792).

27 Richard Bridges quoted in Ash, *Draining of the Fens*, 158.

28 Quotations from H. C. Darby, *Draining of the Fens*, 2nd ed. (Cambridge: Cambridge University Press, 1968), 51-2.

29 Quoted in Darby, *Draining of the Fens*, 58.

30 Francis Bacon, "De Dignitate et Augmentis Scientarum" [1623], and "The Great Instauration" [1620], in *Works*, vol. 4, eds. James Spedding, Robert Leslie Ellis, and Douglas Devon Heath (London: Longmans Green, 1870), quotations on p. 296 and p. 20. The classic study is Carolyn Merchant, *The Death of Nature: Women, Ecology, and the Scientific Revolution* (New York: Harper and Row, 1980), Bacon discussed on pp. 168–69.

31 Poul Holm et al., "The North Atlantic Fish Revolution (ca. AD 1500)," *Quaternary Research* 108 (April 2019): 1–15; Pierre-François-Xavier de Charlevoix, *Journal of a Voyage to North America* [1720], Vol. 1 (London: R. and J. Dodsley, 1761), 69–70.

32 Richard Hakluyt, "Discourse of Western Planting" [1584], in *The Original Writings and Correspondence of the Two Richard Hakluyts*, ed. E. G. R. Taylor (London: Hakluyt Society, 1935), 234–35.

33 Sam White, *A Cold Welcome: The Little Ice Age and Europe's Encounter with North America* (Cambridge, MA: Harvard University Press, 2017), quotations from George Percy at p. 110, John Smith at p. 125; on the climatological evidence, see David W. Stahle et al., "The Lost Colony and Jamestown Droughts," *Science* 280 (1998): 564–67; *Bradford's History of Plymouth Plantation*, ed. William T. Davis (New York: Charles Scribner's Sons, 1908), 96; Alan Heimert, "Puritanism, the Wilderness and the Frontier," *New England Quarterly* 26 (1953).

34 William Cronon, *Changes in the Land: Indians, Colonists, and the Ecology of New England* (New York: Hill and Wang, 1983), 63–66; Francis Higginson, *New-Englands Plantation* [1630], in *Massachusetts Historical Society Proceedings* 62 (1929): 316; John Cotton, "John Cotton's Answer to Roger Williams," in *The Complete Writings of Roger Williams*, vol. II (New York: Russell and Russell, 1963), 46–47, both cited in Cronon, *Changes*, 55–57.

35 Cited in Daniel K. Richter, *Facing East from Indian Country: A Native History of Early America* (Cambridge, MA: Harvard University Press, 2003), 59.

36 Cronon, *Changes*, 71; Bernard Bailyn, *Voyagers to the West: A Passage in the Peopling of America on the Eve of the Revolution* (New York: Vintage, 1986).

37 John Locke, *Second Treatise of Government* [1690], §32, in *Locke: Two Treatises of Government*, ed. Peter Laslett (Cambridge: Cambridge University Press, 1988); Benjamin Franklin, *Observations Concerning the Increase of Mankind* [1751] (Tarrytown, NY: W. Abbatt, 1918), 224.

38 Toni Morrison, *A Mercy* (London: Chatto and Windus, 2008), 62.

39 Richard White, *The Middle Ground: Indians, Empires, and Republics in the Great Lakes Region, 1650–1815* (Cambridge: Cambridge University Press, 1991); on the

resilience of Native American communities, see Ned Blackhawk, *The Rediscovery of America: Native Peoples and the Unmaking of US History* (New Haven, CT: Yale University Press, 2023), and Pekka Hämäläinen, *Indigenous Continent: The Epic Contest for North America* (New York: Liveright, 2022).

40 Greg Grandin, *The End of the Myth: From the Frontier to the Border Wall in the Mind of America* (New York: Metropolitan Books, 2019), quotations on p. 16 and p. 20.

41 Thomas Jefferson to Charles Wilson Peale, April 17, 1813, in *The Garden and Farm Books of Thomas Jefferson*, ed. Robert C. Baron (Golden, CO: Fulcrum, 1987), 202; Alexis de Tocqueville, *Democracy in America*, ed. Phillips Bradley (New York: Alfred A. Knopf, 1946), II:74.

Chapter Five: Revolutions in Life and Death

1 Anton Chekhov, *Sakhalin Island* [1895], trans. Brian Reeve (Richmond, UK: Oneworld Classics, 2007), quotations on p. 3–4

2 Adam McKeown, "Global Migration, 1846–1940," *Journal of World History* 15, no. 2 (2004): 155–89; on South and Southeast Asia: Sunil Amrith, *Crossing the Bay of Bengal: The Furies of Nature and the Fortunes of Migrants* (Cambridge, MA: Harvard University Press, 2013), especially chapter 4.

3 Chekhov, *Sakhalin Island*, 75. An influential early text on the human transformation of the environment was George Perkins Marsh, *Man and Nature, or Physical Geography as Modified by Human Action* (New York: C. Scribner and Co., 1869).

4 Robert Brenner, "Agrarian Class Structure and Economic Development in Pre-Industrial Europe," *Past and Present* 70 (1976): 30–75; Terje Tvedt, *Water and Society: Changing Perceptions of Societal and Historical Development* (London: I. B. Tauris, 2016), 19–44; E. A. Wrigley, "The Transition to an Advanced Organic Economy: Half a Millennium of English Agriculture," *Economic History Review* 59, no. 3 (2006): 435–80.

5 Andreas Malm, *Fossil Capital: The Rise of Steam Power and the Roots of Global Warming* (London: Verso, 2016).

6 E. A. Wrigley, *Energy and the English Industrial Revolution* (Cambridge: Cambridge University Press, 2010), quotation on p. 206.

7 John Farey, *A Treatise on the Steam Engine: Historical, Practical, and Descriptive* (London: Longman, 1827), 4–5; Andrew Ure, *The Philosophy of Manufactures: Or, an Exposition on the Scientific, Moral, and Commercial Economy of the Factory System* (London: Charles Knight, 1835), 2; Lord Jeffrey, "Memoirs of Mister Watt," *The Scotsman*, September 4, 1819.

8 Farey, *A Treatise*, 7.

9 Correspondent to *Working Man's Friend* cited in Emma Griffin, *Liberty's Dawn: A People's History of the Industrial Revolution* (New Haven, CT: Yale University Press, 2013), 53; Bethune's piece appears in *Labour the Poor in England and Wales, 1849–1851: The Letters to the Morning Chronicle from the Correspondents in the Manufacturing and Mining Districts . . .*, ed. Jules Ginswick (London: Frank Cass, 1983), 3; R. Angus Smith, "On the Air of Towns," *Quarterly Journal of the Chemical Society of London* 11, no. 3 (1859): 196–235; Molesworth in *Manchester Guardian*, May 28, 1842: 20, Bethune, Smith, and Molesworth are discussed further in Stephen Mosley, *The Chimney of the World: A History of Smoke Pollution in Victorian and Edwardian Manchester* (London: Routledge, 2008), 20–22; Charles Dickens, *Hard Times* (London: Bradbury and Evans, 1854), 26.

10 Holland cited in C. Rolleston, "The Cloud Over English Life," *Westminster Review*,

162 (1904): 34; F. S. Mitchell, *The Birds of Lancashire*, 2nd ed. (London: Gurney and Jackson, 1892), ix, discussed in Mosley, *Chimney of the World*, 41–45.

11   Mrs. Haweis, *Rus in Urbe: or Flowers that Thrive in London Gardens and Smoky Towns* (London: Field and Tuer, 1885).

12   William Cooke Taylor, *Notes of a Tour in the Manufacturing Districts of Lancashire* (London: Duncan and Malcolm, 1842), 22; William Nicholson, *Smoke Abatement: A Manual for the Use of Manufacturers, Inspectors, Medical Officers of Health, Engineers and Others* [1905] (London: Charles Griffin, 1927), 63–64, in Mosley, *Chimney of the World*: 72–74.

13   W. Stanley Jevons, *The Coal Question: An Inquiry Concerning the Progress of the Nation, and the Probable Exhaustion of our Coal-Mines*, 2nd ed. (London: Macmillan, 1866), 2.

14   Jevons, *Coal Question*, 332; Francis Albert Rollo Russell, *The Atmosphere in Relation to Human Life and Health* (Washington, DC: Smithsonian Institution, 1896), 3.

15   Blanqui quoted in Abbott Payson Usher, *The Industrial History of England* (Boston: Houghton Mifflin, 1920), 247; on the trajectory of European industrialization: Jürgen Osterhammel, *The Transformation of the World: A Global History of the Nineteenth Century*, trans. Patrick Camiller (Princeton, NJ: Princeton University Press, 2015): 638–50, and Eric Hobsbawm, *Industry and Empire: From 1750 to the Present Day* (New York: The New Press, 1999), 34–56.

16   J. S. Ingram, *The Centennial Exposition* (Philadelphia: Hubbard Brothers, 1876).

17   William Dean Howells, "A Sennight of the Centennial," *Atlantic Monthly*, July 1876; "The Contributor's Club: Whitman," *Atlantic Monthly*, December 1877; for further discussion of the Exposition, see Richard White, *The Republic for Which It Stands: The United States During Reconstruction and the Gilded Age, 1865–1896* (New York: Oxford University Press, 2017), 308.

18   David B. Norman, "On the History of the Discovery of Fossils at Bernissart, Belgium," *Archives of Natural History* 14, no. 1 (1987): 59–75; Pascal Godefroit, ed. *Bernissart Dinosaurs and Early Cretaceous Terrestrial Ecosystems* (Bloomington: Indiana University Press, 2012).

19   Zoe Todd, "Fossil Fuels and Fossil Kin: An Environmental Study of Weaponized Fossil Kin and Alberta's So-Called 'Energy Resources Heritage,'" *Antipode*, November 8, 2022.

20   David Flath, *The Japanese Economy*, 4th ed. (Oxford: Oxford University Press, 2022), chapter 2; M. R. Anderson, "The Conquest of Smoke: Legislation and Pollution in Colonial Calcutta," in *Nature, Culture, Imperialism: Essays on the Environmental History of South Asia*, eds. David Arnold and Ramachandra Guha (New Delhi: Oxford University Press, 1995), 293–335, figure from the table on p. 320.

21   Svante Arrhenius, "On the Influence of Carbonic Acid in the Air upon the Temperature on the Ground," *Philosophical Magazine and Journal of Science* 41, no. 5 (April 1896): 237–76; "under a milder sky" from a lecture at Stockholm University, February 3, 1896, originally printed in *Nordisk Tidskrift* 14 (1896): 121–30, translated in Henning Rodhe, Robert Charlson, and Elisabeth Crawford, "Svante Arrhenius and the Greenhouse Effect," *Ambio* 26, no. 1 (1997): 2–5.

22   On railroad expansion, see Richard J. Evans, *The Pursuit of Power: Europe 1815–1914* (London: Penguin, 2016), 151–58; Richard White, *Railroaded: The Transcontinentals and the Making of Modern America* (New York: W. W. Norton, 2011); Reviel Netz, *Barbed Wire: An Ecology of Modernity* (Middletown, CT: Wesleyan University Press, 2004); Minute by Lord Dalhousie to the Court of Directors, April 20, 1853, in *Railway Construction in India: Select Documents*, vol. 2, ed. S. Settar (New Delhi: Indian Council of Historical Research, 1999), 23–57.

23 Julia Winterson, *Railways and Music* (Huddersfield, UK: University of Huddersfield Press, 2021), 11–12; Anonymous, "Paddy on the Railway" (c. 1860–1880), National Library of Scotland, L.C. Fol 178.A.2 (086).

24 Gordon H. Chang, *Ghosts of Gold Mountain: The Epic Story of the Chinese Who Built the Transcontinental Railroad* (Boston: Houghton Mifflin Harcourt, 2019); Jonathan Spence, *God's Chinese Son: The Taiping Heavenly Kingdom of Hong Xiuquan* (New York: W. W. Norton, 1996), quotation on p. 303.

25 Charles Nordhoff, *California for Health, Pleasure, and Residence: A Book for Travellers and Settlers* (New York: Harper and Brothers, 1873), 190; report in the journal *Independent*, August 9, 1882: 3, cited in Kelly J. Dixon et al., "Landscapes of Change: Culture, Nature, and the Archaeological Heritage of the Transcontinental Railroads in the North American West," in *The Chinese and the Iron Road: Building the Transcontinental Railroad*, eds. Gordon H. Chang and Shelley Fisher Fishkin (Stanford, CA: Stanford University Press, 2019), 126–38, quotation on p. 138; Description of the artifacts from Barbara L. Voss, "Living Between Misery and Triumph: The Material Practices of Chinese Railroad Workers in North America," in Chang and Fishkin, *Iron Road*, 110–25, at p. 122.

26 G. W. Macgeorge, *Ways and Works in India: Being an Account of Public Works in That Country from the Earliest Times Up to the Present Day* (London: Archibald Constable and Co., 1894), 220–21, 422–26; "Railway Accident in India," *Adelaide Observer*, October 2, 1897, 18.

27 Willa Sibert Cather, *My Ántonia* (Boston: Houghton Mifflin, 1918), 8.

28 Figure for value of fencing from Netz, *Barbed Wire*, 23; William Shakespeare, *Macbeth*, Act 4, Scene 1, 105–6 in *The Oxford Shakespeare: The Complete Works*, eds. Stanley Wells, Gary Taylor, John Jowett, and William Montgomery (Oxford: Oxford University Press, 2005); "The pioneer is insensible . . ." cited in William Cronon, *Nature's Metropolis: Chicago and the Great West* (New York: W. W. Norton, 1991), 205.

29 Ernst von Hesse-Wartegg cited in White, *Railroaded*, 460; Manu Karuka, *Empire's Tracks: Indigenous Nations, Chinese Workers, and the Transcontinental Railroad* (Berkeley: University of California Press, 2019).

30 M. A. Bartolomé, "Los pobladores del 'desierto': genocidio, etnocidio y etnogénesis en la Argentina," in *Etnografía de los confines*, eds. A. Medina and A. Ochoa (Mexico City: Universidad Nacional Autónoma de México, 2008): 247–64.

31 Richard Jefferies, *Field and Hedgerow: Being the Last Essays of Richard Jefferies* (London: Lutterworth Press, 1948), 182, as quoted in Chris Otter, *Diet for a Large Planet: Industrial Britain, Food Systems, and World Ecology* (Chicago: University of Chicago Press, 2020), 73.

32 Manisha Sinha, *The Slave's Cause: A History of Abolition* (New Haven, CT: Yale University Press, 2017).

33 Scott Reynolds Nelson, *Oceans of Grain: How American Wheat Remade the World* (New York: Basic Books, 2022).

34 Jonathan Levy, *Ages of American Capitalism: A History of the United States* (New York: Random House, 2021), 251; James Belich, *Replenishing the Earth: The Settler Revolution and the Rise of the Angloworld, 1783–1939* (Oxford: Oxford University Press, 2009).

35 E. H. Calvert, *The Wealth and Welfare of the Punjab* (Lahore: "Civil and Military Gazette" Press, 1922), 123.

36 Gibb Schreffler, "Western Punjabi Song Forms: *Māhīā* and *Ḍholā*," *Journal of Punjab Studies* 18, nos. 1–2 (2011): 75–96, quotation on p. 80.

37 James Douie, "The Punjab Canal Colonies," lecture delivered at the Royal Society

of Arts on May 7, 1914, *Journal of the Royal Society of Arts* 62, no. 3210 (May 29, 1914): 611–23.

38   Daniele Valisena and Antonio Canovi, "A Tale of Two Plains: Migrating Landscapes Between Italy and Argentina, 1870–1955," *Modern Italy* 26, no. 2 (2021): 125–40.

39   Cronon, *Nature's Metropolis*: 124–37.

40   Ulrike Schaede, "Forwards and Futures in Tokugawa-Period Japan: A New Perspective on the Dōjima Rice Market," *Journal of Banking and Finance* 13, no. 4–5 (September 1989): 494.

41   Otter, *Diet for a Large Planet*, 50, 67; quotation from 1903 report by the Counseller of the State Miller appears in I. M. Rubinow, "Russia's Wheat Trade," *Bulletin*, no. 65 (US Department of Agriculture, Bureau of Statistics, 1906): 10.

42   Michael Adas, *The Burma Delta: Economic Development and Social Change on an Asian Rice Frontier* (Madison: University of Wisconsin Press, 1974).

43   Adas, *Burma Delta*, 75, including a description of consumer goods valued in rural Burma.

44   On Chettiar banking activities and Indian migration: Burma Provincial Banking Enquiry (Grantham) Committee, *Volume 1: Report: Banking and Credit in Burma* (Rangoon: Government Press, 1930); see also Sean Turnell, *Fiery Dragons: Banks, Moneylenders and Microfinance in Burma* (Copenhagen: NIAS Press, 2009).

45   George Catlin, *Letters and Notes on the Customs and Manners of North American Indians*, 4th ed. (New York: Wiley and Putnam, 1842), I: 249, cited in Cronon, *Nature's Metropolis*, 215; Andrew C. Isenberg, *The Destruction of the Bison: An Environmental History, 1750–1920* (Cambridge: Cambridge University Press, 2012).

46   Cronon, *Nature's Metropolis*, both quotations on p. 216; Sheridan cited in Joshua Specht, *Red Meat Republic: A Hoof-to-Table History of How Beef Changed America* (Princeton, NJ: Princeton University Press, 2019), 43.

47   Ben Turner, *About Myself, 1863–1930* (London: H. Toumlin, 1930), 45–47, cited in Lizzie Collingham, *The Taste of War: World War II and the Battle for Food* (New York: Penguin Press, 2013), 18.

48   Netz, *Barbed Wire*, 46.

49   Cronon, *Nature's Metropolis*, quotations on p. 228 and p. 256.

50   Rudyard Kipling, *The City of Dreadful Night; American Notes* (New York: H. M. Caldwell, 1899); Rudyard Kipling, "Brown Bess," at www.kiplingsociety.co.uk.

51   Alfred Russel Wallace, *The Malay Archipelago* [1869], ed. Andrew Berry (London: Penguin Classics, 2014), 60–62; Peter Raby, *Alfred Russel Wallace: A Life* (Princeton, NJ: Princeton University Press, 2001). More broadly, see Priya Satia, *Time's Monster: How History Makes History* (Cambridge, MA: Harvard/Belknap, 2020).

52   Andrew Berry, Introduction to Wallace, *Malay Archipelago*, xxx–xxxi.

53   Andrea Wulf, *The Invention of Nature: Alexander Von Humboldt's New World* (New York: Alfred A. Knopf, 2015); Isabelle Charmantier, "Linnaeus and Race," Linnean Society of London, September 2020, linnean.org.

54   Wallace, *Malay Archipelago*, 631.

55   Rhodes's agent quoted in Saul Dubow and William Beinart, *The Scientific Imagination in South Africa* (Cambridge: Cambridge University Press, 2021), 119; on the genocidal wars in Aceh and in the process of German colonization in Africa, see Emmanuel Kreike, *Scorched Earth: Environmental Warfare as a Crime Against Humanity and Nature* (Princeton, NJ: Princeton University Press, 2021), chapters 9–10.

56   Rudyard Kipling, *From Sea to Sea, and Other Sketches: Letters of Travel*, vol. 2 (London: Macmillan, 1913), 166.

57   Mike Davis, *Late Victorian Holocausts: El Niño Famines and the Making of the Third*

World (London: Verso, 2001); Thaddeus Sunseri, "The African Rinderpest Panzootic, 1888–1897," *Oxford Research Encyclopedias: African History* (April 26, 2018); C. A. Spinage, *Cattle Plague: A History* (New York: Kluwer Academic, 2003).

58 Sunil Amrith, *Unruly Waters: How Rains, Rivers, Coasts, and Seas Shaped Asia's History* (New York: Basic Books, 2018), chapters 3–4.

59 Cormac Ó Gráda, *Famine: A Short History* (Princeton, NJ: Princeton University Press, 2009), 159–94; Ira Klein, "Plague, Policy, and Popular Unrest in British India," *Modern Asian Studies* 22, no. 4 (1988): 723–55.

60 Richard Powers, *Gain* (New York: Farrar, Straus and Giroux, 1998), 235; Edwin Merrall, *A Letter to Col. Arthur Cotton, upon the Introduction of Railways in India upon the English Plan* (London: E. Wilson, 1860).

61 Chekhov, *Sakhalin Island*, 31.

62 National Sample Survey cited in Joya Chatterji, "On Being Stuck in Bengal: Immobility in the 'Age of Migration,'" *Modern Asian Studies* 51, no. 2 (2017): 511–41; on China, see Kathryn Edgerton-Tarpley, *Tears from Iron: Cultural Responses to Famine in Nineteenth-Century China* (Berkeley: University of California Press, 2008).

63 C. H. Lushington quoted in Tarasankar Banerjee, *Internal Market of India, 1834–1900* (Calcutta: Academic Publishers, 1966), 90–91; Ó Gráda, *Famine*, 193.

64 Richard Strachey, "Physical Causes of Indian Famines," May 18, 1877, *Notices of the Proceedings of the Meetings of the Members of the Royal Institution of Great Britain* 8 (1879): 407–26.

65 "The Causes of Famine in India," *New York Times*, August 25, 1878, including the quotation from Nightingale on p. 6; Villiyappa Pillai, *Panchalakshana Thirumukavilasam* [1899], ed. M. P. Srinivasan (Chennai: Kavita Publications, 2014).

66 David Arnold, "Famine in Peasant Consciousness and Peasant Action: Madras, 1876–8," in *Subaltern Studies III: Writings on South Asian History and Society*, ed. R. Guha (New Delhi: Oxford University Press, 1984): 62–115; Amrith, *Crossing the Bay of Bengal*, chapter 4; Kathleen Pribyl et al., "The Role of Drought in Agrarian Crisis and Social Change: The Famine of the 1890s in South-Eastern Africa," *Regional Environmental Change* 19 (2019): 2683–95, discussion of migration on p. 2692.

67 "Chekhov, Sakhalin and the Russian Famine of 1891–92," British Library, European Studies Blog, February 20, 2018, bl.uk.

68 Alfred Russel Wallace, *The Wonderful Century: Its Successes and Its Failures* (New York: Dodd, Mead, 1898), 375–77.

69 Michel Foucault, "Governmentality," in *The Foucault Effect: Studies in Governmentality*, eds. Graham Burchill, Colin Gordon, and Peter Miller (London: Harvester Wheatsheaf, 1991); Didier Fassin, *Life: A Critical User's Manual* (Cambridge: Polity, 2018); figures on life expectancy are from Osterhammel, *Transformation of the World*, 170–71.

70 Simon Szreter, "The Importance of Social Intervention in Britain's Mortality Decline *c*. 1850–1914: A Re-Interpretation of the Role of Public Health," *Social History of Medicine* 1, no. 1 (April 1988): 1–38.

Chapter Six: Impossible Cities

1 The details of Kahn's life are drawn from the accounts in David Okuefuna, *The Dawn of the Color Photograph: Albert Kahn's Archives of the Planet* (Princeton, NJ: Princeton University Press, 2008); Paula Amad, *Counter-Archive: Film, The Everyday, and Albert Kahn's Archives de la Planète* (New York: Columbia University Press, 2010);

and Trond Erik Bjorli and Kjetil Ansgar Jakobsen, "Introduction," in *Cosmopolitics of the Camera: Albert Kahn's Archives of the Planet*, eds. Bjorli and Jakobsen (Chicago: Intellect Books, 2020), 1–24.

2 Sigolène Tivolle, "Le jardin de Boulogne, un conservatoire des arts horticoles à la Belle Époque," in *Albert Kahn: singulier et pluriel* (Paris: Albert-Kahn, Musée et Jardin Departmentaux, 2015), 125–40; *Bulletin municipal officiel de la Ville de Paris*, July 21, 1935: 3068.

3 On Kahn's pacifism, see Jay Winter, *Dreams of Peace and Freedom: Utopian Moments in the Twentieth Century* (New Haven, CT: Yale University Press, 2008): chapter 1.

4 Bjorli and Jakobsen, "Introduction," quotations from p. 5 and p. 11; Evans quoted in Amad, *Counter-Archive*, 261.

5 Richard D. Mandell, *Paris 1900: The Great World's Fair* (Toronto: University of Toronto Press, 1967), 73.

6 Mandell, *Paris 1900*, "outmoded . . ." quoted on p. 68.

7 Winter, *Dreams of Peace and Freedom*, 29.

8 Mandell, *Paris 1900*, 73.

9 On Nadar's images, see Matthew Gandy, *The Fabric of Space: Water, Modernity, and the Urban Imagination* (Cambridge, MA: MIT Press, 2014): 27–54; Jules Verne, *Voyage au centre de la Terre* (Paris: Pierre-Jules Hetzel, 1864).

10 Louis Rousselet, *L'Exposition Universelle de 1900* (Paris: Librairie Hachette, 1901).

11 The quotation from R. V. Selope Thema is displayed in the central gallery of the Apartheid Museum, Johannesburg, South Africa.

12 Peter Richardson and Jean Jacques Van-Helten, "The Development of the South African Gold Mining Industry, 1895–1918," *Economic History Review* 37 (1984): 319–40.

13 Henry Morton Stanley, *Through South Africa* (London: Sampson Low, Marston and Co., 1898), 78.

14 Cited in Peter Richardson and Jean Jacques Van-Helten, "Labour in the South African Gold Mining Industry, 1886–1914," in *Industrialisation and Social Change in South Africa: African Class Formation, Culture, and Consciousness, 1870–1930*, eds. Shula Marks and Richard Rathbone (London: Longman, 1982), 77–98, quotation on p. 82.

15 Charles van Onselen, *The Night Trains: Moving Mozambican Miners to and from the Witwatersrand Mines, 1902–1955* (London: Hurst, 2021), 9.

16 Mae Ngai, *The Chinese Question: The Gold Rushes and Global Politics* (New York: W. W. Norton, 2021), 189–220; Richardson and van Helten, "Development of the South African Gold Mining Industry."

17 "The Rand: What It Is, How It Is Worked, and at What Profit," *West Gippsland Gazette* (Warragul, Victoria), June 21, 1904, quoted in *Mining Landscapes of the Gauteng City Region*, Research Report #7, eds. Kerry Bobbins and Guy Trangos (Johannesburg: GCRO, 2018), 42.

18 Frederick H. Hatch and J. A. Chalmers, *Gold Mines of the Rand: Being a Description of the Mining Industry of Witwatersrand, South African Republic* [1895] (Cambridge: Cambridge University Press, 2013), quotations on p. 147 and p. 159.

19 J. MacArthur, "Gold Extraction by Cyanide: A Retrospective," *Journal of the Society of Chemical Industry* 24 (1905): 311–15.

20 Jonathan Cane, *Civilising Grass: The Art of the Lawn on the South African Highveld* (Johannesburg: Wits University Press, 2019), and Mark Gevisser, *Lost and Found in Johannesburg: A Memoir* (New York: Farrar, Straus and Giroux, 2015).

21 Randall Packard, *White Plague, Black Labor: Tuberculosis and the Political Economy of Health and Disease in South Africa* (Berkeley: University of California Press, 1989).

22 Quoted in Packard, *White Plague, Black Labor*, 85–87.

23 Packard, *White Plague, Black Labor,* 81.

24 Packard, *White Plague, Black Labor,* chapter 3; statistics from p. 76; Historian Gabrielle Hecht writes that "The term did not yet exist, but the Anthropocene was nevertheless etching itself into the lungs of generation after generation of young African men," in "The African Anthropocene," *Aeon,* February 6, 2018.

25 Patrick Harries, *Work, Culture, and Identity: Migrant Laborers in Mozambique and South Africa, c. 1860–1910* (London: Pearson, 1994).

26 Packard, *White Plague, Black Labor,* 77–78.

27 Jean Jacques Van-Helten, "Empire and High Finance: South Africa and the International Gold Standard, 1890–1914," *The Journal of African History* 23, no. 4 (October 1982): 529–48.

28 Hartley Withers, *The Meaning of Money* (London: John Murray, 1922), 283.

29 J. D. Henry, *Baku: An Eventful History* (London: Archibald Constable and Co., 1905), 12.

30 Henry, *Baku,* 12, including the quotation from Marvin.

31 Marco Polo, *The Travels,* trans. Ronald Latham (London: Penguin, 1958), 48; Scott Cameron Levi, *The Indian Diaspora in Central Asia and Its Trade, 1550–1900* (Leiden, Netherlands: Brill, 2002), Forster cited on p. 305.

32 Marvin, *Eternal Fire,* 202–3; the quotation about smoke is from an unreferenced newspaper article cited in Henry, *Baku,* 7–8; I have been unable to verify the original source.

33 This account of the Nobel family's history draws on Robert W. Tolf, *The Russian Rockefellers: The Saga of the Nobel Family and the Russian Oil Industry* (Stanford, CA: Hoover Institution Press, 1976), quotation on p. 34.

34 Tolf, *Russian Rockefellers.*

35 Tolf, *Russian Rockefellers,* cost of pipeline on p. 52.

36 Eve Blau with Ivan Rupnik, *Baku: Oil and Urbanism* (Chicago: Park Books, 2019), Villa Petrolea described on p. 43.

37 Henry Neuburger and Henri Noalhat, *Technology of Petroleum: The Oil Fields of the World,* trans. John Geddes McIntosh (London: Scott, Greenwood and Co., 1901), 82–83.

38 Henry, *Baku,* quotations on p. 14 and p. 7.

39 Audrey Altstadt-Mirhadi, "Baku: Transformation of a Muslim Town," in Michael F. Hamm, *The City in Late Imperial Russia* (Bloomington: Indiana University Press, 1986), 283–318.

40 Tolf, *Russian Rockefellers,* 153.

41 Luigi Villari, *Fire and Sword in the Caucasus* (London: T. Fisher Unwin, 1906), 205–6.

42 Villari, *Fire and Sword,* 205–6; Henry, *Baku,* caption facing p. 240.

43 Alfred Dutertre, Travel Diary (1908–9), typescript copy at the Kahn archives. Cited in Anne Sigaud, "Japan in The Archives of the Planet," in Bjorli and Jakobsen, *Cosmopolitics of the Camera,* 85–97, quotation on p. 86.

44 My account of the archive draws on Paula Amad's excellent *Counter-Archive*; quotation from Emmanuel Jaquin de Margerie on p. 49.

45 Amad, *Counter-Archive,* 49.

46 Jean Brunhes, *Human Geography* [abridged edition, 1910], ed. Mariel Jean-Brunhes Delamarre and Pierre Defontaines, trans. Ernest F. Row (London: George G. Harrap, 1952), 36.

47 "Moulting" quoted in Winter, *Dreams of Peace and Freedom,* 21.

48 A list of all of the photographers appears in Amad, *Counter-Archive,* 307–8.

49 Trond Erik Bjorli, "Photography, Gunpowder, and Fertilizer: Albert Kahn's Norwegian Journey," in Bjorli and Jakobsen, eds. *Cosmopolitics of the Camera,* 51–84.

50 Bjorli, "Photography, Gunpowder, and Fertilizer," 65.

51 Marguerite Mespoulet, travel diary, 1913, cited in Okuefuna, *The Dawn of the Color Photograph*, 21–22.

Chapter Seven: Nitrogen Nightmares

1   Timothy Mitchell, *Carbon Democracy: Political Power in the Age of Oil* (London: Verso, 2011), 67.

2   Avner Offer, *The First World War: An Agrarian Interpretation* (Oxford: Oxford University Press, 1989), quotation on p. 1; Christopher Clark, *The Sleepwalkers: How Europe Went to War in 1914* (New York: HarperCollins, 2013); Richard P. Tucker et al., eds., *Environmental Histories of the First World War* (Cambridge: Cambridge University Press, 2018).

3   *The Times*, December 27, 1915, 3; Lloyd George's speech provides the opening as well as the title for Adam Tooze's excellent book on the geopolitics of the war and its aftermath: *The Deluge: The Great War, America and the Remaking of the Global Order, 1916–1931* (New York: Viking, 2014), 3.

4   David Lloyd George, *War Memoirs*, vol. 1 (London: Odhams Press, 1942), 162.

5   Joseph E. Pogue, "Mineral Resources in War and Their Bearing on Preparedness," *Scientific Monthly* 5, no. 2 (Aug 1917): 120–34; "Chemistry and the War," *The Outlook* 117, no. 5 (October 3, 1917): 159.

6   "Chemistry and the War."

7   My account of Haber draws on the fine biography by Daniel Charles: *Master Mind: The Rise and Fall of Fritz Haber, the Nobel Laureate Who Launched the Age of Chemical Warfare* (New York: Ecco, 2005); see also Vaclav Smil, *Enriching the Earth: Fritz Haber, Carl Bosch, and the Transformation of World Food Production* (Cambridge, MA: MIT Press, 2000); the quotation is from Fritz Haber, *Aus Leben under Beruf* (Berlin: Verlag von Julius Springer, 1927), 30, cited in Charles, *Master Mind*, 10.

8   Charles, *Master Mind*; Smil, *Enriching the Earth*.

9   Letter from Clara Haber to Richard Abegg, April 23, 1909, Haber Collection, Archiv der Max-Planck-Gesellschaf; cited in Charles, *Master Mind*, 114–15.

10 On Bosch's technical innovation, Charles, *Master Mind*; Bernthsen quoted in Werner Abelshauser et al., *German Industry and Global Enterprise: The History of a Company* (Cambridge: Cambridge University Press, 2004), 151.

11 On BASF in World War I, see Abelshauser et al., *German Industry and Enterprise*, part II, chapter 3; Mittasch's letter to Eduard Farber dated April 22, 1953, quoted in Eduard Farber, "From Chemistry to Philosophy: The Way of Alwin Mittasch (1869–1953)," *Chymia* 11 (1966): 157–78, at p. 169.

12 Evelyn Blücher, *An English Wife in Berlin: A Private Memoir of Events, Politics, and Daily Life in Germany Throughout the War and Social Revolution of 1918* (New York: E.P. Dutton, 1920), 136; British nutritionist quoted in Alice Weinreb, "Beans Are Bullets, Potatoes Are Powder: Food as a Weapon During the First World War," in Tucker et al., *First World War*, 19–37, quotation on p. 28.

13 Ernst Langthaler, "Dissolution Before Dissolution: The Crisis of the Wartime Food Regime in Austria-Hungary," in Tucker et al., *First World War*, 38–61.

14 Zachary J. Foster, "Why Are Modern Famines So Deadly? The First World War in Syria and Palestine," in Tucker et al., *First World War*, 191–207; Zachary J. Foster, "The 1915 Locust Attack in Syria and Palestine and Its Role in the Famine During the First World War," *Middle Eastern Studies* 51, no. 3 (2015): 370–94, Yusuf al-Haddad quoted on p. 375.

15 Iaroslav Golubinov, "Food and Nutrition (Russian Empire)," in *1914–1918-online. International Encyclopedia of the First World War*, eds. Ute Daniel et al. (Berlin: Freie Universität Berlin, 2018).

16 Offer, *First World War*, quotation on p. 81; James Bryce, *South America: Observations and Impressions* [1912], rev. ed. (New York: Macmillan, 1917), 30.

17 Herbert Hoover, "The Weapon of Food," *National Geographic Magazine*, September 1917, 197.

18 Long and Clemenceau quoted in Daniel Yergin, *The Prize: The Epic Quest for Oil, Money, and Power* (New York: Touchstone, 1991), 177; Dan Tamir, "Something New Under the Fog of War: The First World War and the Debut of Oil on the Global Stage," in Tucker, et al., *First World War*, 117–35.

19 Yergin, *The Prize*, 170–72.

20 Statistics of wartime oil production in Oliver Gliech, "Petroleum," in *1914–1918-online* (2015); Myrna I. Santiago, *The Ecology of Oil: Environment, Labor, and the Mexican Revolution, 1900–1938* (Cambridge: Cambridge University Press, 2006), quotation from p. 122.

21 Letter from an unnamed South Indian Muslim soldier to a friend, February 9, 1915, in *Indian Voices of the Great War: Soldiers' Letters, 1914–18*, selected and introduced by David Omissi (New York: St. Martin's Press, 1999), 35; Letter from an unnamed Garhwali to his elder brother, February 12, 1915, in *Indian Voices*, 36; letter from a wounded Punjabi Rajput cited in Santanu Das, *India, Empire, and First World War Culture* (Cambridge: Cambridge University Press, 2018), 206.

22 Ross Mahoney and James Pugh, "Air Warfare," in *1914–1918-online* (2018); Stuart I. Granshaw, "Editorial: First World War Aerial Photography, 1916," *The Photogrammetric Record* 31, no. 156 (December 2016): 368–72.

23 John George Adami, *The War Story of the Canadian Army Medical Corps, Volume 1, 1914–1915* (London: The Rolls Publishing House, 1918), 101–4.

24 Peter Sloterdijk, *Terror From the Air*, trans. Amy Patton and Steve Corcoran (Los Angeles: Semiotext(e), 2009), quotations on pp. 13–14 and p. 16; Emmanuel Kreike, *Scorched Earth: Environmental Warfare as a Crime Against Humanity and Nature* (Princeton, NJ: Princeton University Press, 2021).

25 L. F. Haber, *The Poisonous Cloud: Chemical Warfare in the First World War* (Oxford: Oxford University Press, 1986), 27, cited in Charles, *Master Mind*, 154. On Clara Immerwahr's suicide, see Charles, *Master Mind*, 165–67; for a different perspective, see Bretislav Friedrich and Dieter Hoffmann, "Clara Haber, nee Immerwahr (1870–1915): Life, Work, and Legacy," *Journal of Inorganic and General Chemistry* (ZAAC) 642, no. 6 (March 2016): 437–48.

26 Gerard J. Fitzgerald, "The Chemist's War: Edgewood Arsenal, the First World War, and the Birth of a Militarized Environment," in Tucker et al., *First World War*, 62–96, quotation on p. 64; A. Y. Jackson's notes, cited in Susan Butlin, "Landscape as Memorial: A.Y. Jackson and the Landscape of the Western Front, 1917–1918," *Canadian Military History* 5, no. 2 (1996): 62–70, quotation on p. 66.

27 David Edgerton, *The Shock of the Old: Technology and Global History Since 1900* (Oxford: Oxford University Press, 2007), 143; Adami, *War Story*, vol. 1, 199.

28 Erich Maria Remarque, *All Quiet on the Western Front*, trans. A. W. Wheen (London: Heinemann, 1929), 209.

29 Letter from an unnamed South Indian Muslim soldier to a friend in India, February 9, 1915, in Omissi, *Indian Voices*, 35; letter from a wounded Garhwali soldier to his brother in India, February 12, 1915, in *Indian Voices*, 36; letter from Signaller Nattha Singh to Dafadar Wazie Sigh (7th Lancers, Force D, Mesopotamia), December 8, 1915, in *Indian Voices*, 125.

30 Letter from Sowar Sohan Singh (Dogra, 9th Hodson's Horse regiment) to Jodh Singh (Bitaspur, Punjab), July 10, 1915, in *Indian Voices*, 77; from Amar Singh Wawar (Garhwal rifles), to Dayaram Jhapiyal, Garhwal, April 1, 1915, quoted in Das, *India, Empire, and First World War Culture*, 212.

31 Joe Lunn, *Memoirs of the Maelstrom: A Senegalese Oral History of the First World War* (London: Heinemann, 1999), 135.

32 Ernest Harold Baynes, *Animal Heroes of the Great War* (New York: Macmillan, 1925), 21–22.

33 Ulrich Raulff, *Farewell to the Horse: A Cultural History*, trans. Ruth Ahmedzai Kemp (New York: Liveright, 2018), 106; A. W. Currie, "Foreword" in D. S. Tablyn, *The Horse in War and Famous Canadian War Horses* (1932), cited in Gene Tempest, "Horse and the History of War" (London: National Theatre, 2007).

34 Sisir Prasad Sarbadhikari, *Abhi Le Baghdad*, cited and translated in Das, *India, Empire, and First World War Culture*, 257–58; Donald Rayfield, "The Soldier's Lament: World War One Folk Poetry in the Russian Empire," *The Slavonic and East European Review* 66 (1988): 66–90, quotation on p. 71.

35 Baynes, *Animal Heroes*, 34.

36 Letter from Paul Nash to Margaret Nash, November 13, 1917: Nash Papers, Tate Archive, London: TGA 8313/1/1/162.

Chapter Eight: War on Earth

1 *Modern Times*, directed by Charles Chaplin (1936, Charlie Chaplin Productions, dist. United Artists).

2 Charles Chaplin, *My Autobiography* (London: Penguin, 1966), 335; M. K. Gandhi, "The Curse of Industrialization," *Young India*, December 20, 1928, 422.

3 Donald Worster, *The Dust Bowl: The Southern Plains in the 1930s*, 25th anniv. ed. (New York: Oxford University Press, 2004); Richard Hornbeck, "The Enduring Impact of the American Dust Bowl: Short- and Long-Run Adjustments to Environmental Catastrophe," *American Economic Review* 102, no. 4 (2012): 1477–1507; Great Plains Committee, *The Future of the Great Plains*, US House Doc 144, 75th Congress (Washington, DC, 1937), quotation from unpaginated insert; Lewis Mumford, "In Our Stars," *The Forum and Century* 88, no. 5 (December 1932): 338.

4 Stalin cited in Adam Tooze, *The Deluge: The Great War, America and the Remaking of the Global Order, 1916–1931* (New York: Penguin, 2015), 512.

5 Richard Overy, *Blood and Ruins: The Last Imperial War, 1931–1945* (New York: Penguin, 2022), Britain's first sea lord, Lord Chatfield, quoted on p. 71; Mumford, "In Our Stars," 338.

6 Adolf Hitler, *Mein Kampf*, trans. Ralph Manheim (Boston: Houghton Mifflin, 1971), 134. For further discussion, see Timothy Snyder, *Black Earth: The Holocaust as History and Warning* (New York: Tim Duggan, 2015); Richard Walther Darré cited in Adam Tooze, *The Wages of Destruction: The Making and Breaking of the Nazi Economy* (London: Penguin, 2006), 198.

7 "The critical problem . . ." quoted in Shin'ichi Yamamuro, *Manchuria Under Japanese Dominion*, trans. Joshua A. Fogel (Philadelphia: University of Pennsylvania Press, 2006), 17; Watsuji Tetsuro, *A Climate: A Philosophical Study*, trans. Geoffrey Bownas (Tokyo: Ministry of Education, 1961), 18–20.

8 For discussion of Nazi ideas of the frontier, see David Blackbourn, *The Conquest of Nature: Water, Landscape, and the Making of Modern Germany* (New York:

W. W. Norton, 2006), 291–97. See also Gert Gröning and Joachim Wolschke-Bulmahn, "The Concept of 'Defense Landscape' (*Wehrlandschaft*) in National Socialist Landscape Planning," in *Military Landscapes*, eds. Anatole Tchikine and John Dean Davis (Washington, DC: Dumbarton Oaks Research Library, 2021), 201–20, quotations on pp. 209–10.

9 Quoted in Sandra Wilson, *The Manchurian Crisis and Japanese Society, 1931–33* (London: Routledge, 2002), 58.

10 The most comprehensive general narrative of the war is Overy, *Blood and Ruins*.

11 Chris Pearson, "Environments, States, and Societies at War," in Michael Geyer and Adam Tooze, eds., *The Cambridge History of Second World War, Volume III, Total War: Economy Society and Culture* (Cambridge: Cambridge University Press, 2015), 220–44; David Edgerton, "Controlling Resources: Coal, Iron Ore and Oil in the Second World War," in Geyer and Tooze, *Second World War*: 122–48.

12 Svetlana Alexievich, *The Unwomanly Face of War: An Oral History of Women in World War II* [1985], trans. Richard Pevear and Larissa Volokhonsky (New York: Random House, 2017), 114.

13 My account draws on Lizzie Collingham's pathbreaking book, *The Taste of War: World War II and the Battle for Food* (New York: Penguin, 2012), quotation from Hitler on pp. 30–31; Christopher Browning, *The Origins of the Final Solution: The Evolution of Nazi Jewish Policy, September 1939 to March 1942* (Jerusalem: Yad Vashem, 2004), quotation from Georg Thomas on p. 235; Christian Gerlach, *The Extermination of the European Jews* (Cambridge: Cambridge University Press, 2016), 215–60, quotation from Backe on p. 218.

14 Kim Christian Priemel, "Scorched Earth, Plunder, and Massive Mobilization: The German Occupation of Ukraine and the Soviet War Economy," in *Paying for Hitler's War: The Consequences of Nazi Hegemony for Europe*, eds. Jonas Scherner and Eugene N. White (Cambridge: Cambridge University Press, 2016), 389–426; figures on grain from Gerlach, *Extermination*, 222; quotation about Leningrad in Polina Barskova, ed., *Written in the Dark: Five Poets in the Siege of Leningrad* (New York: Ugly Duckling Press, 2016).

15 Sergei Rudakov, trans. Anand Dibble and Matvei Yankelevich, in Piotr Florczyk, "Making Meaning Under Siege: On Five Leningrad Poets," *Los Angeles Review of Books*, October 27, 2016.

16 Goebbels quoted in Gerlach, *Extermination*, 219; Tooze, *Wages of Destruction*, 513–51, Goering and the Wehrmacht quoted on p. 540 and p. 546.

17 Quoted in Omer Bartov, *Hitler's Army: Soldiers, Nazis, and War in the Third Reich* (New York: Oxford University Press, 1992), 129–30.

18 Quoted in Gerlach, *Extermination*, 253.

19 Tooze, *Wages of Destruction*, 549.

20 "Life stripped bare" and the quotation from Himmler are in Hugh Raffles, *Insectopedia* (New York: Vintage, 2010), 155; Primo Levi, *If This Is a Man* [1958], trans. Stuart Woolf (London: Abacus, 1987), 84–85; Frank Uekoetter, *The Green and the Brown: A History of Conservation in Nazi Germany* (Cambridge: Cambridge University Press, 2006).

21 Heinrich Himmler, speech to SS Officers in Kharkov, Ukraine, April 24, 1943, reprinted in US Office of Chief Counsel for the Prosecution of Axis Criminality, *Nazi Conspiracy and Aggression* (Washington, DC: US Government Printing Office, 1946), 4: 574, also cited in Raffles, *Insectopedia*, 141.

22 For an overview, see Cormac Ó Gráda, "The Famines of WWII," *VoxEU Debate: The Economics of the Second World War: Eighty Years On*, September 2, 2019.

23 *The Ramakrishna Mission: Bengal and Orissa Cyclone Relief, 1942–44* (Howrah, India: Ramakrishna Mission, 1944), 1–2.

24 The accounts of the famines are based on: Gregg Huff, "The Great Second World War Vietnam and Java Famines," *Modern Asian Studies* 54, no. 2 (2020): 618–53; Gregg Huff, "Causes and Consequences of the Great Vietnam Famine, 1944–1945,"*Economic History Review* 72, no. 1 (2019): 286–316; Micah Muscolino, *The Ecology of War in China: Henan Province, the Yellow River, and Beyond, 1938–1950* (Cambridge: Cambridge University Press, 2015). I have written about the Bengal Famine in *Unruly Waters: How Rains, Rivers, Coasts, and Seas Have Shaped Asia's History* (New York: Basic Books, 2018); see also Christopher Bayly and Tim Harper, *Forgotten Armies: The Fall of British Asia, 1941–45* (London: Allen Lane, 2004), 282–91; and Collingham, *Taste of War*, 141–54.

25 Churchill quoted in Collingham, *Taste of War*, 145; Chakrabarti quoted in Paul R. Greenough, *Prosperity and Misery in Modern Bengal: The Famine of 1943–1944* (Oxford: Oxford University Press, 1982), 168.

26 Huff, "Vietnam and Java Famines."

27 United States Strategic Bombing Survey, *Air Campaigns of the Pacific War* (Washington, DC: Military Analysis Division United States Strategic Bombing Survey, 1946), 36; Huff, "Vietnam and Java Famines," 646–48; the poem by Nguễyn Thị Chúng is cited on p. 208 in Ken MacLean, "History Reformatted: Vietnam's Great Famine (1944–45) in Archival Form," *Southeast Asian Studies* 5, no. 2 (2016): 187–218.

28 Micah S. Muscolino, "Violence Against People and the Land: The Environment and Refugee Migration from China's Henan Province, 1938–1945," *Environment and History* 17, no. 2 (2011): 291–311, quotation on p. 305.

29 Overall estimates from Ó Gráda, "The Famines of WWII"; see also Cormac Ó Gráda, *Famine: A Short History* (Princeton, NJ: Princeton University Press, 2009) and the works on particular famines cited above, particularly Collingham, *Taste of War*, on Bengal, and Huff, "Vietnam and Java Famines"; L. H. Lumey and F. W. A. van Poppel, "The Dutch Famine of 1944–45 as a Human Laboratory: Changes in the Early Life Environment and Adult Health," in *Early Life Nutrition and Adult Health and Development: Lessons from Changing Dietary Patterns, Famines and Experimental Studies*, eds. L. H. Lumey and A. Vaiserman (New York: Nova Biomedical, 2013), 59–76.

30 Euridice Charon Cardona and Roger D. Markwick, "The Kitchen Garden Movement on the Soviet Home Front, 1941–1945," *Journal of Historical Geography* 64 (April 2019): 47–59, quotation on p. 59; Mark Bittman, *Animal, Vegetable, Junk: A History of Food, from Sustainable to Suicidal* (Boston: Houghton Mifflin Harcourt, 2021), 160–61; Collingham, *Taste of War*, 92–94.

31 Cardona and Markwick, "The Kitchen Garden Movement," Sivakova's story quoted on p. 57.

32 Sheldon Garon, "The Home Front and Food Insecurity in Wartime Japan: A Transnational Perspective," in *The Consumer on the Home Front: Second World War Civilian Consumption in Comparative Perspective*, eds. Hartmut Berghoff, Jan Logemann, and Felix Römer (London: German Historical Institute and Oxford University Press, 2017), 29–54. The bank story is from the National Archives of Singapore, Oral History Department. Interview with Yap Siong Eu, conducted August 16, 1983, by Liana Tan. Accession number 000316, quotations from reel 5. Audio and transcript at National Archives of Singapore, accessed May 3, 2023.

33 Bittman, *Animal, Vegetable, Junk*, 161.

34 Stephanie D. Hinnershitz, *Japanese American Incarceration: The Camps and Coerced*

Labor During World War II (Philadelphia: University of Pennsylvania Press, 2022); Ronald Mize and Alicia Swords, *Consuming Mexican Labor: From the Bracero Program to NAFTA* (Toronto: University of Toronto Press, 2010).

35   All quotations from oral history interviews with former bracero workers drawn from the National Museum of American History exhibition, *Bittersweet Harvest: The Bracero Program, 1942–1964*, transcripts available at National Museum of American History website; see also Jorge Durand, ed., *Braceros: las miradas mexicana y estadounidense: antología (1945–1964)* (Mexico City: Miguel Ángel Porrúa, 2007).

36   Charles H. Harrison, *Growing a Global Village: Making History at Seabrook Farms* (New York: Holmes and Meier, 2003); Collingham, *Taste of War*, 83–87; Bittman, *Animal, Vegetable, Junk*, 161.

37   Cited in Collingham, *Taste of War*, 75.

38   Henry Baldwin Ward, "Warfare and Natural Resources," *Science* 98, no. 2544 (October 1, 1943): 289–92. Biographical details from Smithsonian Institution Archives.

39   Ward, "Warfare and Natural Resources."

40   Jill Lepore, *These Truths: A History of the United States* (New York: W. W. Norton, 2018), 486; Jonathan Levy, *Ages of American Capitalism: A History of the United States* (New York: Random House, 2021), 439–51, quotation on p. 439; Mark Fiege, "The Atomic Scientists, the Sense of Wonder, and the Bomb," *Environmental History* 12, no. 3 (July 2007): 578–613, quotations on pp. 601–2.

41   "DDT-Weapon Against Disease," US Army film (1945), initially classified, available on YouTube; see also Edmund Russell, *War and Nature: Fighting Humans and Insects with Chemicals from World War I to Silent Spring* (Cambridge: Cambridge University Press, 2001), 160–64.

42   Robert Ji-Song Ku, *Dubious Gastronomy: The Cultural Politics of Eating Asian in the USA* (Honolulu: University of Hawai'i Press, 2014), 190, 211.

43   Survivor's testimony, in Paul H. Kratoska, ed., *The Thailand-Burma Railway, 1942–1946: Documents and Selected Writings* (London: Routledge, 2006), 4:308–9; Private Papers of Second Lieutenant R. Middleton-Smith: Archives of the Imperial War Museum, London, File number 02/50/1.

44   Leslie Anders, *The Ledo Road: General Joseph W. Stilwell's Highway to China* (Norman: University of Oklahoma Press, 1965), quotation on silence from pp. 28–29; Adie Suehsdorf, "Burma Was Jungle Noises," *American Scholar* 15, no. 3 (Summer 1946): 356–59, quotation on p. 357.

45   Letter from Burma Office to J. C. Sterndale-Bennett, Foreign Office, January 16, 1946: National Archives of the United Kingdom, file FO 371/53694; Rabinowitz quoted in Richard P. Tucker, "Environmental Scars in Northeastern India and Burma," in *The Long Shadows: A Global Environmental History of the Second World War*, eds. Timo Vuorisalo, Simo Laakkonen, and Richard P. Tucker (Corvallis: Oregon State University Press, 2017), 117–34, quotation on p. 130.

46   Richard Flanagan, *The Narrow Road to the Deep North* (New York: Alfred A. Knopf, 2013), 269.

47   Levi, *If This Is a Man*, 79–80.

48   Richard Ned Lebow and the Committee for the Compilation of Materials on Damage Caused by the Atomic Bombs in Hiroshima and Nagasaki, *Hiroshima and Nagasaki: The Physical, Medical, and Social Effects of the Atomic Bombings*, trans. Eisei Ishikawa and David L. Swain (New York: Basic Books, 1981), quotations from pp. 25, 55, 80, 337; the testimony cited is by Kimura Yasuko, "Forgetting Is a Blessing," in *Japan*

at War: An Oral History by Haruko Taya Cook and Theodore F. Cook (New York: The New Press, 1992), 395–400, quotation on p. 396.

49   Lebow and the Committee for the Compilation, *Hiroshima and Nagasaki*, casualty estimates on pp. 105–7; quotation from p. 115.

50   Henry L. Stimson, "The Decision to Use the Atomic Bomb," *Harper's Magazine* (February 1947): 97–107.

51   Richard J. Evans, *The Third Reich at War* (New York: Penguin Books, 2010), 444; The United States Strategic Bombing Survey, *Summary Report (European War)* (Washington, DC: US Bombing Survey, Over-All Economic Effects Division, 1945); Sinclair McKay, *The Fire and the Darkness: The Bombing of Dresden, 1945* (New York: St. Martin's Press, 2020).

52   Committee of Operations Analysts, "Economic Effects of Successful Area Attacks on Six Japanese Cities," September 4, 1944, available in the digital archive at japanairraids.org; ". . . great mushroom" from Martin Caidin, *A Torch to the Enemy* (New York: Ballantine Books, 1960), 154–55; Gregory T. Guldner and Curtis Knight, "Napalm Toxicity," StatPearls (May, 24, 2022); Tomie Akazawa's testimony in *Cries for Peace: Experiences of Japanese Victims of World War II* (Tokyo: Youth Division of the Sokka Gakkai International, 1978): 93–94; The United States Strategic Bombing Survey, *The Effects of Strategic Bombing on Japan's War Economy* (Washington, DC: US Bombing Survey, Over-All Economic Effects Division, 1946).

53   Alan Robock and Brian Zambri, "Did Smoke from City Fires in World War II Cause Global Cooling?," *Journal of Geophysical Research: Atmospheres* 123, no. 18 (2018): 10, 314–25; Dorothee Brantz, "Landscapes of Destruction: Capturing Images and Creating Memory Through Photography," in *The Cambridge History of the Second World War, Volume 3; Total War: Economy, Society and Culture*, eds. Michael Geyer and Adam Tooze (Cambridge: Cambridge University Press, 2015), 725–48.

54   Lebow and the Committee for the Compilation, *Hiroshima and Nagasaki*, 340.

Chapter Nine: Freedom's Promise

1   *Ikiru*, directed by Akira Kurosawa (Tokyo: Toho Co. Ltd., 1952), motion picture.

2   Shinobu Hashimoto, trans. Lori Hitchcock Morimoto, *Compound Cinematics: Akira Kurosawa and I* (New York: Vertical, 2015), 75.

3   *Report on Social Insurance and Allied Services*, Report by Sir William Beveridge (London: HMSO, 1942), 170.

4   George McT. Kahin, "Sukarno's Proclamation of Indonesian Independence," *Indonesia* 69 (April 2000): 3. On aid, see David C. Engerman, *The Price of Aid: The Economic Cold War in India* (Cambridge, MA: Harvard University Press, 2018).

5   Déclaration d'indépendance de la République démocratique du Việt Nam (Hanoï, September 2, 1945), text available through the Luxembourg Centre for Contemporary and Digital History.

6   B. R. Ambedkar, "Memorandum and Draft Articles on the Rights of States and Minorities," March 24, 1947, in *The Framing of India's Constitution: Select Documents*, ed. B. Shiva Rao et al. (New Delhi: Indian Institute of Public Administration, 1968), 2:100; B. R. Ambedkar, final speech to Constituent Assembly of India, November 25, 1949, in *Constituent Assembly Debates*, vol. 12 (New Delhi: Lok Sabha Secretariat, 1986): 979.

7   United Nations, Department of Social Affairs, *Preliminary Report on the World Social*

Situation, with Special Reference to Standards of Living (New York: United Nations, 1952), 35.

8   Speech to Central Board of Irrigation and Power, November 17, 1952, in *Jawaharlal Nehru on Science and Society: A Collection of His Writings and Speeches*, ed. Baldev Singh (New Delhi: Nehru Memorial Museum and Library, 1988), 94–95.

9   *Mother India*, directed by Mehboob Khan (1957, Mehboob Productions).

10 Odd Arne Westad, *The Global Cold War: Third World Interventions and the Making of Our Times* (Cambridge: Cambridge University Press, 2005), especially 73–109.

11 *The High Dam: Bulwark of Our Future* (Cairo: Information Department, United Arab Republic, 1963), 5; *Address by President Gamal Abdel Nasser at the Popular Rally Held by the Arab Socialist Union in Aswan, February 18, 1965, and Attended by President El Habib Bourguiba* (Cairo: Information Department, United Arab Republic, 1965), 5–6.

12 Jawaharlal Nehru, speech at the opening of the Nangal Canal, July 8, 1954, in *Jawaharlal Nehru: An Anthology*, ed. Sarvepalli Gopal (New Delhi: Oxford University Press, 1980), 213–15; for further discussion of Bhakra, see Sunil Amrith, *Unruly Waters: How Rains, Rivers, Coasts, and Seas Shaped Asia's History* (New York: Basic Books, 2018), chapter seven; "Nehru Shows Chou Indian Dam Project," *New York Times*, January 1, 1957, 4; Dipesh Chakrabarty, *The Climate of History in a Planetary Age* (Chicago: University of Chicago Press, 2021), 106. For the case of Ghana, where similar dynamics were at play, see Stephan F. Miescher, *A Dam for Africa: Akosombo Stories from Ghana* (Bloomington: Indiana University Press, 2022).

13 The stories of Vellu Pillai and Eswaraiah appear in Henry C. Hart, *New India's Rivers* (Bombay: Orient Longmans, 1956), 97, 115; India, Central Water-Power, Irrigation and Navigation Commission, *Quinquennial Report*, April 1945–March 1950, British Library, Asian and African Studies Collection, India Office Records, file IOR/V/24/4496; A. N. Khosla, "Our Plans," *Indian Journal of Power and River Valley Development* 1, no. 7 (1951): 1–4.

14 Ahmad Bahjat, "Wajhum fi'l-Ziham," *al-Ahram*, January 8, 1960, 4, cited and translated in Nancy Y. Reynolds, "Building the Past: Rockscapes and the Aswan High Dam in Egypt," in *Water and Sand: Environmental Histories of the Middle East and North Africa*, ed. Alan Mikhail (New York: Oxford University Press, 2012), 181–206, quotation on p. 189.

15 W. Arthur Lewis, "Economic Development with Unlimited Supplies of Labour," *The Manchester School* 22, no. 2 (1954): 131–91.

16 "Your work" cited in Chakrabarty, *Climate of History*, 109; "Thirty years ago," and "feeling of a crusader or missionary" in *Jawaharlal Nehru on Community Development* (New Delhi: Government of India, 1957): 17–18.

17 "Lathi Charge on Strikers," *Times of India*, January 31, 1954, 9.

18 Simon Lewis, "A Force of Nature: Our Influential Anthropocene Period," *The Guardian*, July 23, 2009.

19 "History of Larsen and Toubro, Limited," *Times of India*, July 10, 1954, AI; *Bulwark of Our Future*, 20–22.

20 All quotations from Goh in this and preceding paragraphs drawn from "Goh Keng Swee Biography," citation for Ramon Magsaysay Award, 1972 ; see also Tilak Doshi and Peter Coclanis, "The Economic Architect: Goh Keng Swee," in *Lee's Lieutenants: Singapore's Old Guard*, eds. Lam Peng Er and Kevin Tan (St. Leonard's, Australia: Allen and Unwin, 1999), 24–44.

21 Antoine Acker, "A Different Story in the Anthropocene: Brazil's Post-Colonial Quest

for Oil (1930–1975), *Past and Present* 249, no. 1 (November 2020): 167–212, quotation from Pasqualini on p. 202, discussion of race on pp. 186–87.

22   Odd Arne Westad, *The Cold War: A World History* (New York: Basic Books, 2017), 268.

23   *Yek Atash*, dir. Ebrahim Golestan (Studio Golestan, 1961).

24   *Yek Atash*; on Farrokhzad, see Saeed Kamali Dehghan, "Former Lover of the Poet Known as Iran's Sylvia Plath Breaks His Silence," *The Guardian*, February 12, 2017.

25   *Yek Atash*; on Vargas's action, see Acker, "A Different Story," 185.

26   "We should open fire on nature" cited in Frank Dikötter, *Mao's Great Famine: The History of China's Most Devastating Catastrophe* (London: Bloomsbury, 2010), 174; proverb from a speech on May 8, 1958, in Mao Zedong, "Speeches at the Second Session of the Eighth Party Congress," cited and translated in *Forgotten Voices of Mao's Great Famine, 1958–1962*, by Zhou Xun (New Haven, CT: Yale University Press, 2013), 104.

27   Zhou, *Forgotten Voices*, quotations from pp. 109, 111, 123.

28   Zhou, *Forgotten Voices*, p. 117; on the demography of the famine, see Cormac Ó Gráda, "Great Leap, Great Famine" (March 27, 2013): doi.org/10.2139/ssrn.2240590.

29   Roderick MacFarquhar, *The Origins of the Cultural Revolution, Vol 2: The Great Leap Forward, 1958–1960* (Oxford: Oxford University Press, 1983), quotations from p. 322.

30   "Report on the Damage to Forests in Fujian and Four Other Provinces and Eight Suggestions for the Region, June 1962," extracted and translated in *The Great Famine in China, 1958–1962: A Documentary History*, ed. Zhou Xun (New Haven, CT: Yale University Press, 2012), 87; "Comrade Liu Jianxun's Report on the Problem of Water-logged and Alkalized Farm Fields, as Well as a Proposal to Solve the Problem, December 24, 1961," extracted and translated in Xun, *Great Famine*, 89.

31   Judith Shapiro, *Mao's War Against Nature: Politics and the Environment in Revolutionary China* (Cambridge: Cambridge University Press, 2001), 67–94, quotations from interviews on p. 87.

32   Ó Gráda, *Famine: A Short History*, 96.

33   Proceedings of a meeting held on January 31, 1946, between representatives of Madras and Hyderabad: National Archives of India, Political Branch: Hyderabad Residency; File No. 92(2), 1946; Nehru's remark quoted in *The Bombay Chronicle*, April 12, 1948.

34   Reynolds, "Building the Past," the quotation from a Nubian villager is from Yusuf Chahine's 1968 film *al-Nass wa'l-Nil* [The people and the Nile], quoted on p. 195.

35   Rob Nixon, "Unimagined Communities: Developmental Refugees, Megadams and Monumental Modernity," *New Formations* 69 (Spring 2010): 62–81, quotations on pp. 63–64; on dam displacement in India, see Sanjoy Chakravorty, *The Price of Land: Acquisition, Conflict, Consequence* (New Delhi: Oxford University Press, 2013), 123–30.

36   Matthew T. Huber, *Lifeblood: Oil, Freedom, and the Forces of Capital* (Minneapolis: University of Minnesota Press, 2013), chapter 3, quotation on p. 88.

37   Huber, *Lifeblood*, Shell and Humble advertisements quoted on p. 83 and p. 76, respectively.

38   Christopher W. Wells, *Car Country: An Environmental History* (Seattle: University of Washington Press, 2013), 255–60.

39   Elena Ferrante, trans. Ann Goldstein, *My Brilliant Friend* (New York: Europa Editions, 2012), chapter 7.

40   Francesca Fauri, "The Role of Fiat in the Development of the Italian Car Industry in the 1950's," *Business History Review* 70, no. 2 (Summer 1996): 167–206.

41 Enrico Mattei, "On the Decolonization of States and of the Economy," speech in Tunis, June 10, 1960: Wilson Center Digital Archive, translated and annotated by Cyrus Schayegh, accessed July 15, 2023.

42 "Oil Emperor of Italy: Enrico Mattei," *New York Times*, January 6, 1958.

43 Statistics on oil from Walter J. Levy, "World Oil in Transition" (August 1961), collected in *Oil Strategy and Politics, 1941–1981*, Walter J. Levy, ed. Melvin A. Conant (Boulder, CO: Westview Press, 1982); *60 Years, BP Statistical Review of World Energy, 1951–2011* (London: BP, 2011). On carbon emissions, see Hannah Ritchie, Pablo Rosado, and Max Rosner, "CO_2 and Greenhouse Gas Emissions"(2023), published online at OurWorldinData.org.

44 Strauss cited in Helmuth Trischler and Robert Bud, "Public Technology: Nuclear Energy in Europe," *History and Technology* 34, no. 3–4 (2018): 187–212, quotation on p. 197.

45 Trischler and Bud, "Public Technology"; Andrew Brown, *Keeper of the Nuclear Conscience: The Life and Work of Joseph Rotblat* (New York: Oxford University Press, 2012); Dwight D. Eisenhower address to the 470th Plenary Meeting of the United Nations General Assembly, December 8, 1953; A. M. Petros'yants, "A Pioneer of Nuclear Power," *IAEA Bulletin* 26, no. 4 (1984): 42–46; on the French nuclear program, see Gabrielle Hecht, *The Radiance of France: Nuclear Power and National Identity after World War II* (Cambridge, MA: MIT Press, 1998).

46 David Crowley, "Thaw Modern: Design in Eastern Europe After 1956," in *Cold War Modern: Design, 1945–1970*, eds. David Crowley and Jane Pavitt (London: V and A Publishing, 2008), 133.

47 The slogan is quoted in Crowley, "Thaw Modern," 138; Susan E. Reid, " 'Our Kitchen Is Just as Good': Soviet Responses to the American National Exhibition in Moscow, 1959," in Crowley and Pavitt, *Cold War Modern*, 154–162, quotation from poster on p. 157.

48 Reid, "Our Kitchen," quotation on p. 159.

49 "You think the Russian people," quoted in Crowley, "Thaw Modern," 133.

50 Joel B. Hagen, *An Entangled Bank: The Origins of Ecosystem Ecology* (New Brunswick, NJ: Rutgers University Press, 1992).

51 On the US nuclear tests, see Elizabeth M. DeLoughrey, "The Myth of Isolates: Ecosystem Ecologies in the Nuclear Pacific," *Cultural Geographies* 20, no. 2 (April 2013): 167–84; Barbara Rose Johnston and Holly M. Barker, *Consequential Damages of Nuclear War: The Rongelap Report* (Walnut Creek, CA: Left Coast Press, 2008); on the Soviet test see Alex Wellerstein, "An Unearthly Spectacle: The Untold Story of the World's Biggest Nuclear Bomb," *Bulletin of the Atomic Scientists*, October 29, 2021.

52 Will Steffen et al., "The Trajectory of the Anthropocene: The Great Acceleration," *The Anthropocene Review* 2, no. 1 (2015): 81–98; J. R. McNeill and Peter Engelke, *The Great Acceleration: An Environmental History of the Anthropocene since 1945* (Cambridge, MA: Harvard University Press, 2016).

53 National Science Foundation, "Plans for Construction of Earth Satellite Vehicle Announced," press release, July 29, 1955, Dwight D. Eisenhower Records as President, Official File, Box 624, OF 146-E, International Geophysical Year, (1): NAID #16646897; Eisenhower Presidential Library, "International Geophysical Year," Documents online, eisenhowerlibrary.gov.

54 Roger Revelle and Hans E. Suess, "Carbon Dioxide Exchange Between Atmosphere and Ocean and the Question of an Increase of Atmospheric CO_2 During the Past Decades," *Tellus* 9, no. 1 (February 1957): 18–27, quotation pp. 19–20. On oceanography and the discovery of climate change, see Naomi Oreskes, "Changing the Mission:

From the Cold War to Climate Change," in *Science and Technology in the Global Cold War*, eds. Naomi Oreskes and John Krige (Cambridge, MA: MIT Press, 2014), 141–87.

55 Steffen et al., "The Trajectory of the Anthropocene"; Eric Hobsbawm, *Age of Extremes: The Short Twentieth Century, 1914–1991* (London: Michael Joseph, 1994), 261.

56 Dipesh Chakrabarty, *Provincializing Europe: Postcolonial Thought and Historical Difference* (Princeton, NJ: Princeton University Press, 2000), 6.

57 I discuss these health interventions at length in Sunil S. Amrith, *Decolonizing International Health: India and Southeast Asia, 1930–65* (Basingstoke, UK: Palgrave Macmillan, 2006).

58 Kingsley Davis, "The Amazing Decline of Mortality in Underdeveloped Areas," *American Economic Review* 46, no. 2 (1956), 305–18, quotation on p. 305; Samuel H. Preston, "Changing Relation Between Mortality and Level of Economic Development," *Population Studies* 29, no. 2 (July 1975): 231–48; figures compiled from United Nations, *World Population Prospects*, accessed May 14, 2023.

59 Pramoedya Ananta Toer, "My Kampung" [1952], in *Tales From Djakarta: Caricatures of Circumstances and Their Human Beings*, by Pramoedya Ananta Toer, ed. and trans. Sumit Mandal (Jakarta: Equinox Publishing, 2000), 75–86, quotations from pp. 82–84.

60 Opening Address by Jawaharlal Nehru at the Third Asian Malaria Conference, New Delhi, March 19, 1959, World Health Organization, Southeast Asia Regional Office, *Report on the Third Asian Malaria Conference, Delhi, 19–21 March 1959*, SEA/Mal/16, Annex 3, originally consulted at WHO Library, Geneva.

Chapter Ten: The Human Condition

1 Hannah Arendt, *The Human Condition* [1958], 2nd edition, with an introduction by Margaret Canovan (Chicago: University of Chicago Press, 1998), 1–3.

2 Arendt, *The Human Condition*, 1–3.

3 Arendt, *The Human Condition*, 126.

4 Arendt, *The Human Condition*, 126; "liberation of the life process" is Margaret Canovan's phrase in her introduction to *The Human Condition*, xiv.

5 Linda Lear, *Rachel Carson: Witness for Nature*, 2nd ed. (Boston: Houghton Mifflin Harcourt, 2009), 16; Rachel L. Carson, "Undersea," *Atlantic Monthly*, September 1937; *Under the Sea-Wind: A Naturalist's Picture of Ocean Life* [1941], rev. ed. (New York: Penguin Classics, 2007); Rachel Carson, *The Sea Around Us* [1951], 3rd ed. (New York: Oxford University Press, 2018).

6 Rachel Carson Papers, Beinecke Rare Book and Manuscript Library, Yale University, YCAL MSS 46, Series 1: Writings [hereafter, "Carson Papers"]: Rachel Carson to William Shawn, February 14, 1959: Box 35, folder 814; Rachel Carson, *Silent Spring* (Boston: Houghton Mifflin, 1962), 297.

7 Carson Papers, research notes for *Silent Spring*, subject heading: "Mass Spraying," typed quotation from Alfred G. Etter, *Audubon Magazine*, July–August 1959: Box 34, folder 621.

8 Carson Papers, "Insidious effects" from letter to William Shawn, February 14, 1959.

9 Carson, *Silent Spring*, 277.

10 Carson Papers, research notes for *Silent Spring*, subject heading: "Food Surplus," margin note on undated *New York Times* cutting: Box 34, Folder 603.

11 Quotations in this paragraph from Rob Nixon, *Slow Violence and the Environmentalism of the Poor* (Cambridge, MA: Harvard University Press, 2011), 145–46.

12   Frantz Fanon, "Medicine and Colonialism," in *Studies in a Dying Colonialism*, trans. H. Chevalier (New York: Monthly Review Press, 1965), 121–46, quotation on p. 128.

13   G. A. Livadas and G. Georgopoulos, "Development of Resistance to DDT by Anopheles Sacharovi in Greece," *Bulletin of the World Health Organization* 8, no. 4 (1953): 497–511; F. J. Dy, "Present Status of Malaria Control in Asia," *Bulletin of the World Health Organization* 11, no. 4–5 (1954): 725–63; E. J. Pampana, "Changing Strategy in Malaria Control," *Bulletin of the World Health Organization* 11, no. 4–5 (1954): 513–20, quotation on p. 518.

14   Carson Papers, Marshall Laird (WHO) to Rachel Carson, October 16, 1961: Box 43, Folder 802.

15   Carson Papers, research notes for *Silent Spring*, subject heading: "Philosophy," Box 46, Folder 883, quotation transcribed from Paul Bigelow Sears, *The Steady State: Physical Law and Moral Choice* (United chapters of Phi Beta Kappa, 1959).

16   "Years Before a Revolution," *Times of India*, August 22, 1965; *Economic Survey of Indian Agriculture for 1966–67* (New Delhi: Government of India, 1969).

17   Quoted in Mahesh Rangarajan, "Striving for a Balance: Nature, Power, Science and India's Indira Gandhi, 1917–1984," *Conservation and Society* 7, no. 4 (2009): 299–312.

18   Nick Cullather, *The Hungry World: America's Cold War Battle Against Poverty in Asia* (Cambridge, MA: Harvard University Press, 2010).

19   Rangarajan, "Striving for Balance"; Jairam Ramesh, *Indira Gandhi: A Life in Nature* (New Delhi: Simon and Schuster, 2017).

20   This follows the argument in Rangarajan, "Striving for Balance," quotation on p. 303.

21   Vikram Sarabhai, "Pollution and Human Environment," text of a speech delivered at a seminar on Pollution and Human Environment, Trombay, India, August 26, 1970: typescript is housed in the library of the Centre for Science and Environment, New Delhi.

22   Indira Gandhi, speech at the Non-Aligned Summit Conference, Lusaka, Zambia, September 9, 1970, reprinted in *India Quarterly* 41, no. 1 (1985): 140; Dr. Martin Luther King Jr. "Beyond Vietnam: A Time to Break Silence," address delivered April 4, 1967, Riverside Church, New York City, Internet Archive.

23   Ngo Luc quoted in Cathy Scott-Clark and Adrian Levy, "Specter Orange," *International Journal of Health Services* 34, no. 3 (2004): 557–66, quotation on p. 559.

24   Telegram from the Commander in Chief, Pacific (Felt), to the Chief of the Military Assistance Advisory Group in Viet-Nam (McGarr), December 28, 1961, *Foreign Relations of the United States, 1961–1963, Volume 1, Vietnam, 1961*, document 343; Diem T. Pham et al., "Predictors for Dioxin Accumulation in Residents Living in Da Nang and Bien Hoa, Vietnam, Many Years After Agent Orange Use," *Chemosphere* 118 (January 2015): 277–83; Ministry of Natural Resources and Environment, Office of National Steering Committee, *Comprehensive Report: Agent Orange/Dioxin Contamination at Three Hotspots: Bien Hoa, Da Nang and Phu Cat Airbases* (Hanoi, Vietnam, 2013); Charles Schmidt, "The Fog of Agent Orange," *Scientific American* 314, no. 6 (June 2016): 70–75.

25   Scott-Clark and Levy, "Specter Orange," 559; Robert E. Cook, William Haseltine, and Arthur W. Galston, "What Have We Done to Vietnam?," in *Ecocide in Indochina: The Ecology of War*, ed. Barry Weisberg (San Francisco: Canfield Press, 1970), 94; David Zierler, *The Invention of Ecocide: Agent Orange, Vietnam, and the Scientists Who Changed the Way We Think About the Environment* (Athens: University of Georgia Press, 2011), 18–21; Amy Hay, "The Origins of Ecocide," *Seeing the Woods: A Blog by the Rachel Carson Centre*, April 3, 2013.

26   Charles Waugh, "Introduction," in *Family of Fallen Leaves: Stories of Agent Orange*

by Vietnamese Writers, eds. Charles Waugh and Huy Lien (Athens: University of Georgia Press, 2010), 1–16, quotation on p. 2.

27 Interview with Strandenaes in "Stockholm: Birth of the Green Generation," *BBC News*, June 4, 2012.

28 Quotation from Bob Sollen in Kate Wheeling and Max Ufberg, "'The Ocean Is Boiling': The Complete Oral History of the 1969 Santa Barbara Oil Spill," *Pacific Standard*, November 7, 2018.

29 Lila Thulin, "How an Oil Spill Inspired the First Earth Day," *Smithsonian Magazine*, April 22, 2019; *Times of India*, April 23, 1970, 10.

30 United Nations Environment Programme, *1972 Conference on the Human Environment*, documentary film (United Nations Television and New York State Education Department, 1972).

31 Paul Ehrlich, *The Population Bomb* (New York: Ballantine Books, 1968), 15–16.

32 All quotations are from Indira Gandhi's "Man and Environment," speech given at the Plenary Session of United Nations Conference on the Human Environment, Stockholm, June 14, 1972, available in full at DownToEarth; Jairam Ramesh, "Poverty Is the Greatest Polluter: Remembering Indira Gandhi's Stirring Speech in Stockholm," *The Wire*, June 7, 2017.

33 Speeches by Chua and Asante from film footage in United Nations Environment Programme, *1972 Conference on the Human Environment*.

34 Interview with Barry Commoner in United Nations Environment Programme, *1972 Conference on the Human Environment*.

35 Indira Gandhi, speech at the Non-Aligned Summit Conference, September 9, 1970.

36 The best overall history of the Emergency is Gyan Prakash, *Emergency Chronicles: Indira Gandhi and Democracy's Turning Point* (Princeton, NJ: Princeton University Press, 2019); for a moving ethnographic account, see Emma Tarlo, *Unsettling Memories: Narratives of the Emergency in Delhi* (London: Hurst, 2003).

37 Rangarajan, "Striving for a Balance."

38 Robert Bendiner, "Mrs. Gandhi's Dilemma," *New York Times*, March 9, 1976, 31.

39 On forced sterilizations during the Emergency, see Tarlo, *Unsettling Memories*, and Prakash, *Emergency Chronicles*, chapter 7. For a global perspective, see Matthew Connelly, *Fatal Misconception: The Struggle to Control World Population* (Cambridge, MA: Harvard University Press, 2010), and on China's "one child" policy, Susan Greenhalgh, *Just One Child: Science and Policy in Deng's China* (Berkeley: University of California Press, 2008).

40 Arendt, *Human Condition*, 5.

41 World Meteorological Organization, *Thirty-First Session of the Executive Committee: Abridged Report with Resolutions* (Geneva: World Meteorological Organization, 1979), Annexe I: 88–89.

Chapter Eleven: Burning Forests

1 A. C. Roosevelt, "The Amazon and the Anthropocene: 13,000 Years of Human Influence in a Tropical Rainforest," *Anthropocene* 4, no. 1 (2013): 69–87.

2 John C. Kricher, *A Neotropical Companion: An Introduction to the Animals, Plants, and Ecosystems of the New World Tropics* (Princeton, NJ: Princeton University Press, 1989); Michael Williams, *Deforesting the Earth: From Prehistory to Global Crisis: An Abridgement* (Chicago: University of Chicago Press, 2006), chapters 13–14.

3 Williams, *Deforesting the Earth*, 441–42.

4   Branco and Médici quoted in Susanna Hecht and Alexander Cockburn, *The Fate of the Forest: Developers, Destroyers, and Defenders of the Amazon*, updated ed. (Chicago: University of Chicago Press, 2010), quotations on p. 104 and p. 122; on the military government of the 1960s, see Lilia M. Schwarcz and Heloisa M. Starling, *Brazil: A Biography* (New York: Macmillan, 2018).

5   Robert Walker et al., "The Transamazon Highway: Past, Present Future," in *Engineering Earth: The Impacts of Megaengineering Projects*, ed. Stanley D. Brunn (Dordrecht, Netherlands: Springer, 2011), 1:569–601.

6   Williams, *Deforesting the Earth*, 445–48.

7   Joan M. Hardjono, *Transmigration in Indonesia* (Kuala Lumpur: Oxford University Press, 1977); Peter Dauvergne, *Shadows in the Forest: Japan and the Politics of Timber in Southeast Asia* (Cambridge, MA: MIT Press, 1997).

8   "Kalau Bakau Tak Ada Lagi . . ." [When the mangroves are gone], *TEMPO*, March 11, 1978; "Mereka yang cinta alam" [Those who love nature], *TEMPO*, June 10, 1978; "Bahaya Asap Mobil (lagi)" [The dangers of car smoke (again)], *TEMPO*, July 1, 1978; "Duka Cita Bagi Walet" [Grief for the swallow], *TEMPO*, September 16, 1978; Anna Lowenhaupt Tsing, *Friction: An Ethnography of Global Connection* (Princeton, NJ: Princeton University Press, 2005); Nancy Lee Peluso, Suraya Afiff, and Noer Fauzi Rachman, "Claiming the Grounds for Reform: Agrarian and Environmental Movements in Indonesia," *Journal of Agrarian Change* 8, no. 2–3 (2008): 377–407; Colin MacAndrews, "Politics of the Environment in Indonesia," *Asian Survey* 34, no. 4 (1994): 369–80.

9   "Setelah hutan jadi lautan api" [After the forests become a sea of fire], *TEMPO*, October 10, 1987; "Terpanggangnya Paru-paru bumi" [The charred lungs of the earth], *TEMPO*, October 10, 1987.

10 Tokunori Mori, "Effects of Droughts and Forest Fires on Dipterocarp Forest in East Kalimantan," in *Rainforest Ecosystems of East Kalimantan: El Niño, Drought, Fire and Human Impacts*, eds. Edi Guhardja et al. (Tokyo: Springer, 2000), 29–45; Dauvergne, *Shadows in the Forest*; Peter Dauvergne, "The Political Economy of Indonesia's 1997 Forest Fires," *Australian Journal of International Affairs* 52, no. 1 (1998): 13–17.

11 For a detailed and well-documented account of the Alves family's activities, based on interviews, see Andrew Revkin, *The Burning Season: The Murder of Chico Mendes and the Fight for the Amazon Rain Forest* (Boston: Houghton Mifflin, 1990), 9–17. See also further references in the following notes.

12 Thais Lazzeri, "One Hundred Years of Servitude in Brazil," Inequality.org, April 5, 2018.

13 Tony Gross, ed. and trans., *Fight for the Forest: Chico Mendes in His Own Words* (London: Latin America Bureau, 1989), 5; Revkin, *Burning Season*.

14 *Fight for the Forest*, 35, 44.

15 *Fight for the Forest*, 77; the figures of ninety murders from Tony Gross's Introduction on p. 1.

16 The circumstances of his murder are related in Revkin, *Burning Season*, based on intensive investigative reporting. See also, Alex Shoumatoff, "Murder in the Rain Forest," *Vanity Fair*, April 1989.

17 All figures on urbanization from Hannah Ritchie and Max Rosen, "Urbanization" (2018, revised 2019), published online at OurWorldinData.org.

18 Ela Miljkovic, "Air Pollution in Mexico City," *Oxford Research Encyclopedias: Latin American History*, March 25, 2021; Enrique Tolivia Meléndez, "La contaminación atmosférica," in *El medio ambiente en México: Temas, problemas y alternativas*, ed. Manuel López Portillo Ramos (Mexico City: Fondo de Cultura Económica, 1982);

Vincent Schodolski, "On a Clear Day, You Can Nearly See Across the Street," *Chicago Tribune*, February 4, 1986.

19 Miljkovic, "Air Pollution."

20 All data from Hannah Ritchie, "Yields vs. Land Use: How the Green Revolution Enabled Us to Feed a Growing Population," August 22, 2017, published online at OurWorldinData.org.

21 Tim Bayliss-Smith and Sudhir Wanmali, eds., *Understanding Green Revolutions: Agrarian Change and Development Planning in South Asia* (Cambridge: Cambridge University Press, 1984); Vandana Shiva, *The Violence of the Green Revolution: Third World Agriculture, Ecology, and Politics* (Lexington: University Press of Kentucky, 2016); Thays Millena Alves Pedroso et al., "Cancer and Occupational Exposure to Pesticides: A Bibliometric Study of the Past 10 Years," *Environmental Science and Pollution Research International* 29, no. 12 (2022): 17464–475.

22 Investigations by the United Nations Research Institute for Social Development in the 1970s highlighted these contradictory effects: Cynthia Hewett de Alcántra, *Modernizing Mexican Agriculture: Socioeconomic Implications of Technological Change, 1940–1970*, UNRISD Studies on the Green Revolution, no. 12 (Geneva, Switzerland: United Nations Research Institute for Social Development, 1976); Ingrid Palmer, *The New Rice in Asia: Conclusions from Four Country Studies*, UNRISD Studies on the Green Revolution, no. 12 (Geneva, Switzerland, United Nations Research Institute for Social Development, 1976); Biplab Dasgupta, *Agrarian Change and the New Technology in India*, UNRISD Studies on the Green Revolution, no. 16 (Geneva, Switzerland, United Nations Research Institute for Social Development, 1977).

23 Aseem Shrivastava and Ashish Kothari, *Churning the Earth: The Making of Global India* (New Delhi: Viking, 2012), 176–83; P. Sainath, "Farm Suicides: A 12-Year Saga," *The Hindu*, January 25, 2010; P. Sainath, "The Largest Wave of Suicides in History," *The Hindu*, February 16, 2009; Akta Kaushal, "Confronting Farmer Suicides in India," *Alternatives: Global, Local, Political* 40, no. 1 (February 2016): 46–62; Barbara Harriss-White, "Introduction: India's Rainfed Agricultural Dystopia," *European Journal of Development Research* 20, no. 4 (December 2008): 549–61.

24 John Berger and Jean Mohr, *A Seventh Man: A Book of Images and Words About the Experiences of Migrant Workers in Europe* (Harmondsworth, UK: Penguin, 1975), 23.

25 Vivek Shanbhag, *Ghachar Ghochar*, trans. Srinath Perur (London: Faber, 2017), quotations from pp. 39, 21, 11, 53.

26 Peter Dauvergne, *Shadows in the Forest: Japan and the Politics of Timber in Southeast Asia* (Cambridge, MA: MIT Press, 1997).

27 Josie Phillips, "An Illustrated History of Industrial Palm Oil," *China Dialogue*, February 18, 2021; Jonathan E. Robins, *Oil Palm: A Global History* (Chapel Hill: University of North Carolina Press, 2021).

28 Peluso, Afiff, and Rachman, "Claiming the Grounds for Reform," 382; Nancy Lee Peluso and Peter Vandergeest, "Genealogies of the Political Forest and Customary Rights in Indonesia, Malaysia, and Thailand," *Journal of Asian Studies* 60, no. 3 (2001): 761–812; Bradley R. Simpson, *Economists with Guns: Authoritarian Development and U.S.-Indonesian Relations, 1960–1968* (Stanford, CA: Stanford University Press, 2008).

29 Vivek Voora et al., *Global Market Report: Palm Oil* (Winnipeg, Canada: International Institute for Sustainable Development, April 26, 2020).

30 The account of Davidson and the weevils is from Paul Tullis, "How the World Got Hooked on Palm Oil," *The Guardian*, February 19, 2019.

31 Voora et al., "Palm Oil"; Tullis, "How the World Got Hooked"; Duncan Brack,

Adelaide Glover, and Laura Wellesley, *Agricultural Commodity Supply Chains: Trade, Consumption and Deforestation*, research paper (London: Chatham House, 2016); "The Great Palm Oil Scandal," ASA 21/5184/2016, Amnesty International, November 30, 2016.

32 Brack, Glover, and Wellesley, "Agricultural Commodity Supply Chains"; Hannah Ritchie, "Palm Oil," February 4, 2021, published online at OurWorldinData.org.

33 Hannah Ritchie and Max Roser, "Fish and Overfishing," October 2021, published online at OurWorldinData.org; Brazil export and land use figures from supplementary chart 3 accompanying Karina Winkler et al., "Global Land Use Changes Are Four Times Greater Than Previously Estimated," *Nature Communications* 12, no. 2501 (2021), doi.org/10.1038/s41467-021-22702-2.

Chapter Twelve: Tipping Points

1 Silke Mende, "'Enemies at the Gate': The West German Greens and Their Arrival at the Bundestag—Between Old Ideals and New Challenges," *German Politics and Society* 33, no. 4 (2015): 66–79, manifesto quoted on p. 67.

2 Osmarino Amâncio Rodrigues, cited in Andrew Revkin, *The Burning Season: The Murder of Chico Mendes and the Fight for the Amazon Rain Forest* (Boston: Houghton Mifflin, 1990), epigraph.

3 For an early statement on the "environmentalism of the poor" by an Indian and a Catalan scholar, see Ramachandra Guha and Joan Martínez-Alier, *Varieties of Environmentalism: Essays North and South* (London: Earthscan, 1997); for further discussion, see Rob Nixon, *Slow Violence and the Environmentalism of the Poor* (Cambridge, MA: Harvard University Press, 2011); on La Vía Campesina, see María Elena Martínez-Torres and Peter M. Rosset, "La Vía Campesina: The Birth and Evolution of a Transnational Social Movement," *Journal of Peasant Studies* 37, no. 1 (2010): 149–75; La Vía Campesina, "Food Sovereignty: A Future Without Hunger," statement at UN Food Summit, Rome, November 11–17, 1996.

4 Tony Gross, ed. and trans., *Fight for the Forest: Chico Mendes in His Own Words* (London: Latin America Bureau, 1989), quotation from Mendes on p. 78 and from the Declaration of the Peoples of the Forest on p. 85.

5 Pamela S. Chasek and David L. Downie, *Global Environmental Politics*, 8th ed. (New York: Routledge, 2021), chapter 3.

6 Statement of James Hansen, June 22, 1988, in *Greenhouse Effect and Global Climate Change: Hearings Before the Committee on Energy and Natural Resources*, United States Senate, One Hundredth Congress, First Session, Part 2 (Washington, DC: Government Printing Office, 1988), 39; for a compelling narrative account, albeit one that focuses exclusively on the United States, see Nathaniel Rich, *Losing Earth: The Decade We Could Have Stopped Climate Change* (New York: Farrar, Straus and Giroux, 2019).

7 *Report of the World Commission on Environment and Development: Our Common Future* (New York: United Nations, 1987), 13.

8 Anil Agarwal and Sunita Narain, *Global Warming in an Unequal World: A Case of Environmental Colonialism* (New Delhi: Centre for Science and Environment, 1991).

9 "Universal Responsibility and the Global Environment—Address at the Rio Earth Summit," His Holiness the 14th Dalai Lama of Tibet, text at His Holiness the 14th Dalai Lama of Tibet official website: dalailama.com.

10 Fiona Godlee, "Rio Diary: A Fortnight at the Earth Summit," *British Medical Journal* 305, no. 6845 (July 11, 1992): 102–5, quotation on p. 105.

11 Godlee, "Rio Diary"; Bush's statement was made behind closed doors, but is often quoted, for example in John Vidal, "Rio+20: Earth Summit Dawns with Stormier Clouds than in 1992," *The Guardian*, June 19, 2012.

12 "Prime Minister's Briefing for Earth Summit," memorandum, June 9, 1992; confidential letter from Michael Portillo to John Major, June 9, 1992, headed "The Rio Earth Summit: Resources and Development"; letter from Tim Lankester, Overseas Development Administration, to Alex Allan, Prime Minister's Office, June 5, 1992: all documents contained in the file PREM19/3976 ("United Nations Conference on the Environment and Development"), National Archives of the United Kingdom.

13 Ranee K. L. Panjabi, "The South and the Earth Summit: The Development/Environment Dichotomy," *Penn State International Law Review* 11, no. 1 (1992): 77–138, quotation from Mahathir on p. 87; Godlee, "Rio Diary," 103.

14 A full list of the 1990s' environmental treaties and protocols appears in Chasek and Downie, *Global Environmental Politics*, 4–6.

15 Mobil, "Apocalypse, No," advertorial, *New York Times* (1993), cited in Geoffrey Supran and Naomi Oreskes, "Addendum to 'Assessing ExxonMobil's Climate Change Communications (1977–2014),'" *Environmental Research Letters* 15, no. 11 (2020); Mobil, "We're All in This Together" (paid advertorial), *New York Times* (1996), cited in Supran and Oreskes, "Addendum"; David Arkush and Donald Braman, "Climate Homicide: Prosecuting Big Oil for Climate Deaths," *Harvard Environmental Law Review* 48, no. 1 (2024), draft of January 23, 2023 available at: doi.org/10.2139/ssrn.4335779.

16 Supran and Oreskes, "Addendum."

17 Suraje Dessai, "The Climate Regime from the Hague to Marrakesh: Saving or Sinking the Kyoto Protocol?" Working Paper 12 (Norwich, UK: Tyndall Center for Climate Change Research, 2001).

18 "Everything died" quoted in Amnesty International, "Slick PR Can't Disguise Shell's Devastating Oil Pollution in Nigeria," press release, May 18, 2020; letter from Ogoni Divisional Committee to Military Governor, Rivers State, April 25, 1970, full text reproduced in Ken Saro-Wiwa, *Genocide in Nigeria: The Ogoni Tragedy* (Port Harcourt, Nigeria: Saros, 1992), chapter 5.

19 This account draws from the excellent biography by Roy Doron and Toyin Falola, *Ken Saro-Wiwa* (Ohio Short Histories of Africa) (Columbus: Ohio University Press, 2016), quotation from p. 58.

20 Wale Okediran, "Ken Saro-Wiwa at 50," *The Guardian,* October 19, 1991, 11.

21 Glenn Ellis, dir. *The Drilling Fields* (Catma Films, 1994).

22 Quotations in this and folowing paragraph from Saro-Wiwa, *Genocide in Nigeria*, "extinction" on p 24 and "I hear in my heart" on p. 83.

23 Letter from Ken Saro-Wiwa to Sister Majella McCarron, undated (c. 1994), in *Silence Would Be Treason: Last Writings of Ken Saro-Wiwa*, eds. Ide Corley, Helen Fallon, and Laurence Cox (Nairobi: Daraja Press, 2007), 77.

24 Michael Watts, "Sweet and Sour," and Ed Kashi, "Shadows and Light in the Niger Delta," both in *Curse of the Black Gold: 50 Years of Oil in the Niger Delta*, ed. Michael Watts (New York: powerHouse Books, 2008), quotations on p. 38 and p. 27. The Nigerian government reported oil losses, from theft and sabotage, of a billion dollars a year between 1998 and 2003. In 2005, rebel groups came together as the Movement for the Emancipation of the Niger Delta (MEND).

25 United Nations Development Program, *Niger Delta Human Development Report* (Abuja, Nigeria: UNDP, 2006), quoted in Watts, *Curse of the Black Gold*, frontispiece;

United Nations Environment Programme, *Environmental Assessment of Ogoniland* (Nairobi: UNEP, 2011).

26   Godwin Ojo, "Twenty Years On, Ken Saro-Wiwa's Legacy Echoes from the Grassroots to the United Nations," *Common Dreams*, November 9, 2015; "Shell Agrees $84m Deal over Niger Delta Oil Spill," *BBC News*, January 7, 2015.

27   Ryszard Kapuściński, *Shah of Shahs*, trans. William R. Brand and Katarzyna Mroczkowska-Brand (London: Quartet Books, 1982), 35.

28   Kaw Bing Chua, "The Discovery of Nipah Virus: A Personal Account," *Neurology Asia* 9 (2004): 59–63, quotation on p. 61.

29   My account is based on W. Wayt Gibbs, "Trailing a Virus," *Scientific American* 281, no. 2 (August 1999): 80–87; Chua, "The Discovery of Nipah Virus"; Kaw Bing Chua et al., "Fatal Encephalitis Due to Nipah Virus Among Pig-Farmers in Malaysia," *Lancet* 354, no. 9186 (October 9, 1999): 1257–59.

30   Local resident quoted in Keith B. Richburg, "Malaysia Slow to Act on Virus," *Washington Post*, April 29, 1999, A21; Patrick Tan quoted in Gibbs, "Trailing a Virus"; case statistics reported in Jeremy J. Farrar, "Nipah-Virus Encephalitis—Investigation of a New Infection," *Lancet*, 354, no. 9186 (October 1999): 1222–23.

31   On residents' memories, Michaeleen Doucleff, "A Taste for Pork Helped a Deadly Virus Jump to Humans," NPR, *Weekend Edition*, February 25, 2017; Richburg, "Malaysia Slow to Act."

32   Chua et al., "Fatal Encephalitis."

33   Susan M. Cheyne, "Effects of Meteorology, Astronomical Variables, Location and Human Disturbance on the Singing Apes: Hylobates albibarbis," *American Journal of Primatology* 70, no. 4 (2008): 386–92; Daniel J. Naumenko et al., "Evaluating Ketosis in Primate Field Studies: Validation of Urine Test Strips in Wild Bornean Orangutans (*Pongo pygmaeus wurmbii*)," *Folia Primatologica* 91, no. 2 (2020): 159–67.

34   Seth Mydans, "Indonesia Jet Crash Kills All 234 Aboard; Haze Was a Possible Cause," *New York Times*, September 27, 1997, A6; Hari S. Maniam, "Two Ships Collide Off Malaysia," *Washington Post*, September 28, 1997.

35   Maria C. Lo Bue, "Indonesia's Huge Fires and Toxic Haze Will Cause Health Problems for Years to Come," *The Conversation*, October 7, 2019; Maria C. Lo Bue, "Early Childhood During Indonesia's Wildfires: Health Outcomes and Long-Run Schooling Achievements," *Economic Development and Cultural Change* 67, no.4 (July 2019).

36   Goh Si Guim, *Nature News* (Nature Society Singapore), November–December 1997, 10.

37   Kaw Bing Chua, Beng Hui Chua, and Chew Wen Wang, "Anthropogenic Deforestation, El Niño and the Emergence of Nipah Virus in Malaysia," *Malaysian Journal of Pathology* 24, no. 1 (2002): 15–21.

38   Thorfinn Stainforth and Bartosz Brzezinski, "More than Half of All CO2 Emissions Since 1751 Emitted in the Last 30 Years," Institute for European Environmental Policy blog, April 29, 2020; Indira Gandhi, "Agriculture: Self-Reliance and Inter-Dependence," address to the UN Food and Agricultural Organization, November 9, 1981, in *Selected Speeches of Indira Gandhi, Volume 4: January 1980–December 1981* (New Delhi: Government of India, 1985), 253; "Menyambut bumi yang makin panas" [Anticipating a hotter Earth], *TEMPO*, November 5, 1983.

39   Jonathan Watts, "There Is a War on Nature. Dom Phillips Was Killed Trying to Warn You About It," *The Guardian*, June 16, 2022; Global Witness, *Decade of Defiance: Ten Years of Reporting Land and Environmental Activism Worldwide* (London: Global Witness, 2022); Global Witness conducts investigations and publishes a full list of environmental defenders killed every year at globalwitness.org.

Chapter Thirteen: Four Hundred Parts per Million . . .

1   Armando Azua-Bustos, Carlos González-Silva, and Alberto G. Fairén, "The Atacama Desert in Northern Chile as an Analog Model of Mars," *Frontiers in Astronomy and Space Science* 8 (2021); Armando Azua-Bustos, Luis Caro-Lara, and Rafael Vicuña, "Discovery and Microbial Content of the Driest Site of the Hyperarid Atacama Desert, Chile," *Environmental Microbiology Reports* 7, no. 3 (June 2015): 388–94.

2   Louise Purbrick, "Nitrate Ruins: The Photography of Mining in the Atacama Desert, Chile," *Journal of Latin American Cultural Studies* 26, no. 2 (2017): 253–78.

3   Christopher P. McKay, "Requirements and Limits for Life in the Context of Exoplanets," *PNAS* 111, no. 35 (2014): 12628–33.

4   Johan Rockström et al. "A Safe Operating Space for Humanity," *Nature* 461 (2009): 472–75; Will Steffen et al., "Planetary Boundaries: Guiding Human Development on a Changing Planet," *Science* 347, no. 6223 (2015): doi.org/10.1126/science.1259855.

5   Nicola Jones, "How the World Passed a Carbon Threshold and Why It Matters," *Yale Environment 360*, January 26, 2017.

6   Nick M. Haddad et al., "Habitat Fragmentation and Its Lasting Impact on Earth's Ecosystems," *Science Advances* 1, no. 2 (2015), doi.org/10.1126/sciadv.1500052; Kyle C. Rosenblad, Kathryn C. Baer, and David D. Ackerly, "Climate Change, Tree Demography, and Thermophilization in Western US Forests," *PNAS* 120, no. 18 (2023), doi.org/10.1073/pnas.2301754120; Camille Parmesan and Gary Yohe, "A Globally Coherent Fingerprint of Climate Change Impacts Across Natural Systems," *Nature* 421 (2003): 37–42.

7   Gretta T. Pecl et al. "Biodiversity Redistribution Under Climate Change: Impacts on Ecosystems and Human Well-Being," *Science* 355, no. 1389 (2017): doi.org/10.1126/science.aai9214; Cascade J. B. Sorte, Susan L. Williams, and James T. Carlton, "Marine Range Shifts and Species Introductions: Comparative Spread Rates and Community Impacts," *Global Ecological Biogeography* 19, no. 3 (2010): 303–16; Jeremy T. Kerr et al., "Climate Change Impacts on Bumblebees Converge Across Continents," *Science* 349, no. 6244 (2015): 177–80.

8   Francisca C. García et al., "Changes in Temperature Alter the Relationship Between Biodiversity and Ecosystem Functioning," *PNAS* 115, no. 43 (2018): 10989–94; Emily Osterloff, "The Baiji: Why This Extinct River Dolphin Still Matters," *Anthropocene* blog, Natural History Museum, London, September 15, 2022.

9   C. Mark Eakin, Hugh P. A. Sweatman, and Russel E. Brainard, "The 2014–17 Global-Scale Coral Bleaching Event: Insights and Impacts," *Coral Reefs* 38 (2019): 539–45; Eduardo Sampaio et al., "Impacts of Hypoxic Events Surpass Those of Future Ocean Warming and Acidification," *Nature Ecology and Evolution* 5, no. 3 (March 2021): 311–21, doi.org/10.1038/s41559-020-01370-3; "universal redistribution" quoted from Pecl et al., "Biodiversity Redistribution Under Climate Change," 1.

10 Marina Romanello et al., "The 2021 Report of the *Lancet* Countdown on Health and Climate Change: Code Red for a Healthy Future," *Lancet* 398, no. 10311 (2021): 1619–62; Camilo Mora et al., "Global Risk of Deadly Heat," *Nature Climate Change* 7, no. 7 (2017): 501–6; T. Vos et al., "Global Burden of 369 Diseases and Injuries in 204 Countries and Territories, 1990–2019: A Systematic Analysis for the Global Burden of Disease Study 2019," *Lancet* 396, no. 10258 (2020): 1204–22.

11 Clare Dyer, "Air Pollution from Road Traffic Contributed to Girl's Death from Asthma, Coroner Concludes," *British Medical Journal* 371 (2020): m4902; World Health Organization, "Outdoor (Ambient) Air Pollution," WHO Fact Sheets, December 19, 2022; Rosamund Kissi-Debra's comment is in Sandra Laville, "Ella Kissi-Debrah: How a

Mother's Fight for Justice May Help Prevent Other Air Pollution Deaths," *The Guardian*, December 16, 2020.

12 International Organization on Migration (IOM), Global Data Institute, "Climate Change and Future Human Mobility," *Thematic Brief* 1 (November 2022).

13 Intergovernmental Panel on Climate Change (IPCC), *Climate Change 2022: Impacts, Adaptation, and Vulnerability*, contribution of Working Group II to the IPCC Sixth Assessment Report (Cambridge: Cambridge University Press, 2022): migration discussed in chapter 7.

·14 Sunil Amrith, *Crossing the Bay of Bengal: The Furies of Nature and the Fortunes of Migrants* (Cambridge, MA: Harvard University Press, 2013), chapter 8; Joya Chatterji, "Dispositions and Destinations: Refugee Agency and 'Mobility Capital' in the Bengal Diaspora, 1947–2007," *Comparative Studies in Society and History* 55, no. 2 (April 2013): 273–304; International Federation of Red Cross and Red Crescent Societies (IFRC), *World Disasters Report 2012: Focus on Forced Migration and Displacement* (Geneva: IFRC, 2012), 38.

15 Warsan Shire, "Home," Facing History and Ourselves, January 5, 2017, facinghistory .org.

16 Jan Zalasiewicz et al. "Scale and Diversity of the Physical Technosphere: A Geological Perspective," *The Anthropocene Review* 4, no. 1 (2017): 9–22; Vaclav Smil, "Harvesting the Biosphere: The Human Impact," *Population and Development Review* 37, no. 4 (December 2011): 613–36; "The Construction Industry Remains Horribly Climate-Unfriendly," *Economist*, June 15, 2022; UN Environment Programme, "CO2 Emissions from Buildings and Construction Hit New High, Leaving Sector Off Track to Decarbonize by 2050," press release, November 9, 2022; Bhartendu Pandey, Christa Brelsford, and Karen C. Seto, "Infrastructure Inequality Is a Characteristic of Urbanization," *PNAS* 119, no. 15 (2022): doi.org/10.1073/pnas.2119890119; United Nations, Department of Economic and Social Affairs, "First-Ever United Nations Resolution on Homelessness," press release, March 9, 2020.

17 National Development and Reform Commission, People's Republic of China, "BRI: Decade of Achievements and Prospects of High-Quality Development Forum Held in Hong Kong," June 29, 2023; Christoper Nedopil Wang, *China Belt and Road Initiative (BRI) Investment Report 2022*, Green Finance and Development Center, February 3, 2023; Will Doig, *High Speed Empire: Chinese Expansion and the Future of Southeast Asia* (New York: Columbia University Press, 2018).

18 Mohammad Ali Rajaeifar et al., "Decarbonize the Military—Mandate Emissions Reporting," *Nature* 611 (2022): 29–32; on corporate resistance to climate action, see Naomi Klein, *This Changes Everything: Capitalism vs. The Climate* (New York: Simon and Schuster, 2014).

19 Statement by Gaston Browne, Prime Minister of Antigua and Barbuda, at the UN Conference on Climate Change, Paris, November 30, 2015.

20 Pamela S. Chasek and David L. Downie, *Global Environmental Politics*, 8th ed. (New York: Routledge, 2021).

21 Femke J. M. M. Nijsse et al., "The Momentum of the Solar Energy Transition," *Nature Communications* 14, no. 6542 (2023): doi.org/10.1038/s41467-023-41971-7; International Energy Agency (IEA), "Renewables," June 2023.

22 Stephen Battersby, "How to Expand Solar Power Without Using Precious Land," *PNAS* 120, no. 9 (2023): doi.org/10.1073/pnas.2301355120; Ryan Stock and Trevor Birkenholtz, "The Sun and the Scythe: Energy Dispossessions and the Agrarian Question of Labor in Solar Parks," *Journal of Peasant Studies* 48, no. 5 (2021): 984–1007; Sophia Kalantzakos, *China and the Geopolitics of Rare Earths* (Oxford: Oxford

University Press, 2017); Carolyn Gramling, "Rare Earth Mining May Be the Key to Our Renewable Energy Future. But at What Cost?" *Science News*, January 11, 2023.

23   Bruce Robertson, "Carbon Capture Has a Long History. Of Failure," *Bulletin of the Atomic Scientists*, online, September 1, 2022.

24   David Keith, *A Case for Climate Engineering* (Cambridge, MA: MIT Press, 2013); David W. Keith and Andy Parker, "The Fate of an Engineered Planet," *Scientific American*, 308 (January 2013): 34–36; Elizabeth Kolbert, *Under a White Sky: The Nature of the Future* (New York: Crown, 2021).

25   Marie-Valetine Florin et al., eds., *International Governance Issues on Climate Engineering: Information for Policymakers* (Lausanne, Switzerland: EPFL International Risk Governance Center, 2020); Center for International Environmental Law, *Fuel to the Fire: How Geoengineering Threatens to Entrench Fossil Fuels and Accelerate the Climate Crisis* (Washington, DC: CIEL, 2019); Heinrich Böll Foundation, *The Big Bad Fix: The Case Against Climate Engineering* (2017); J. P. Sapinski, Holly Jean Buck, and Andreas Malm, eds., *Has It Come to This? The Promises and Perils of Geoengineering on the Brink* (New Brunswick, NJ: Rutgers University Press, 2021).

26   Emily T. Yeh, "Sky River: Promethean Dreams of Optimising the Atmosphere," *Made in China Journal* (July–December, 2022); Scott Moore and Eyck Freymann, "China Doesn't Want a Geoengineering Disaster," *Foreign Policy*, February 21, 2023.

27   Jennie C. Stephens and Kevin Surprise, "The Hidden Injustices of Advancing Solar Geoengineering Research," *Global Sustainability* 3 (2020): E2, 1–6; for a response, see Olúfẹ́mi O. Táíwò and Shuchi Talati, "Who Are the Engineers? Solar Geoengineering Research and Justice," *Global Environmental Politics* 22, no. 1 (2022): 12–18; Masahiro Sugiyama, Shinichiro Asayama, and Takanobu Kosugi, "The North–South Divide on Public Perceptions of Stratospheric Aerosol Geoengineering: A Survey of Six Asia-Pacific Countries," *Environmental Communication* 14, no. 5 (2020): 641–56.

28   *From Transmilenio to Cycle Networks—Lessons Learned from Bogotá's Comprehensive Urban Mobility Planning* (New York: Institute for Transportation and Development Planning, 2022).

29   Rachel Carson, *The Edge of the Sea* [1955] (Boston: Mariner Books, 1998), 240.

30   Cassie Freund, "Indonesia's Mangrove Restoration Will Run Out of Land Well Short of Target, Study Warns," *Monagabay*, March 9, 2023; Sigit D. Sasmito et al., "Challenges and Opportunities for Achieving Sustainable Development Goals Through Restoration of Indonesia's Mangroves," *Nature Ecology and Evolution* 7 (2023): 62–70.

31   Berend J. Schuit et al., "Automated Detection and Monitoring of Methane Super-Emitters Using Satellite Data," *Atmospheric Chemistry and Physics* 23, no. 6 (2023): 9071–98, doi.org/10.5194/acp-23-9071-2023; Andrew Wang and Jane J. Lee, "Methane 'Super-Emitters' Mapped by NASA's New Earth Space Mission," NASA, Jet Propulsion Laboratory, October 25, 2022; Emma Rothschild, "Methane in 1,800 Histories," *Visualizing Climate and Loss*, Harvard Center for History and Economics, February 2022.

32   Hannah Ritchie, "Food Production Is Responsible for One-Quarter of the World's Greenhouse Gas Emissions," November 6, 2019, published online at OurWorldinData.org.

33   Hannah Ritchie, Pablo Rosado, and Max Roser, "Hunger and Undernourishment" (2023), published online at OurWorldinData.org; Hannah Ritchie, "Food Waste Is Responsible for 6% of Global Greenhouse Gas Emissions," March 18, 2020, published online at OurWorldinData.org.

34 J. Poore and T. Nemecek, "Reducing Food's Environmental Impacts Through Produc-
    ers and Consumers," *Science* 360, no. 6392 (2018): 987–92.
35 Paul Freedman, *Why Food Matters* (New Haven, CT: Yale University Press, 2021).
36 Poore and Nemecek, "Reducing Food's Environmental Impacts."
37 On groundwater in India, see Sunil Amrith, *Unruly Waters: How Rains, Rivers,
    Coasts, and Seas Shaped Asia's History* (New York: Basic Books, 2018); on modernist
    failures, the classic study is James C. Scott, *Seeing Like a State: How Certain Schemes
    to Improve the Human Condition Have Failed* (New Haven, CT: Yale University
    Press, 1998).
38 Jonathan Rigg and Lisa Reyes Mason, "Five Dimensions of Climate Science Reduc-
    tionism," *Nature Climate Change* 8, no. 12 (2018): 1030–32.

Epilogue: Roads to Repair

1 *Princess Mononoke*, dir. Hayao Miyazaki (DENTSU Music and Entertainment,
   1997).
2 Rabindranath Tagore, *Nationalism* (London: Macmillan, 1917), quotation on p. 37.
3 Tagore, *Nationalism*, quotation on p. 45.
4 Jeff Sebo, *Saving Animals, Saving Ourselves: Why Animals Matter for Pandemics,
   Climate Change, and Other Catastrophes* (New York: Oxford University Press, 2022);
   Martha C. Nussbaum, *Justice for Animals: Our Collective Responsibility* (New York:
   Simon and Schuster, 2023). Nussbaum argues that "an ethical attunement to the lives
   of animals and a sense of wonder at their complexity and dignity is part of our humanity, without which human life itself is impoverished" (p. 192).
5 Ashlee Cunsolo and Neville R. Ellis, "Ecological Grief as a Mental Health Response
   to Climate Change-Related Loss," *Nature Climate Change* 8 (2018): 275–81, quotation
   is from the documentary film *Attutauniujut Nunami* [Lament for the land], quoted
   on p. 277. Quotation on grief is from Colin Murray Parkes and Holly G. Prigerson,
   Bereavement: Studies of Grief in Adult Life, 4th ed. (New York: Routledge, 2010), 6,
   quoted in Consolo and Ellis, "Ecological Grief," 279.
6 My account of the protest is based on the video feature on its leader, Aleta Baun, on
   the Goldman Environmental Prize page, goldmanprize.org; Febriana Firdaus, "Inside
   the Weaving Protests of West Timor," *Mongabay*, November 20, 2020; Tessa Toum-
   bourou and Siti Maimunah, "Aleta Baun," *Mestras e Mestres do Mundo: Coragem e
   Sabedoria* (2020): alice.ces.uc.pt/mestrxs. Proverb quoted and translated in Firdaus,
   "Weaving Protests."
7 The text of the Ecuadorian constitution is at pdba.georgetown.edu/Constitu-
   tions/Ecuador/english08.html; for a broader discussion of the "rights of nature"
   movement, see Daniel P. Corrigan and Markku Oksanen, eds., *Rights of Nature:
   A Re-examination* (New York: Routledge, 2021); on the Indian case, where early
   legal successes were eventually overturned, see K. Sivaramakrishnan, "Environment, Law, and Democracy in India," *Journal of Asian Studies* 70, 4 (November
   2011): 905–28.
8 Matthew Gandy, *Natura Urbana: Ecological Constellations in Urban Space* (Cambridge, MA: MIT Press, 2022).
9 Lewis Gordon, "Can Video Games Change People's Minds About the Climate Crisis?" *Guardian*, January 26, 2023. The tag-line for *Terra Nil* from the *Terra Nil*
   page on Steam.
10 The figure on the industry's reach is from Playing for the Planet.

11   Quotation from Gordon, "Video Games"; Kara Stone's work is at karastone.itch.io.

12   Kpop4planet.com; quotation from an interview with Nurul Sarifah is in Ian Smith, "'No K-Pop on a Dead Planet': Meet the Stans Taking Up Climate Activism," *Euronews*, November 28, 2022.

13   UNICEF and Gallup, *The Changing Childhood Project: A Multigenerational, International Survey on 21st Century Childhood* (New York: UNICEF, 2021), 48–49.

14   *All That Breathes*, dir. Shaunak Sen (HBO Documentary Films, 2022); on Delhi's air, see Sarath K. Guttikunda et al., "What Is Polluting Delhi's Air? A Review from 1990 to 2022," *Sustainability* 15, no. 5 (2023).

15   Martin Luther King Jr., "My Trip to the Land of Gandhi," *Ebony*, July 1959: 84–92.

16   Alan Weisman, *The World Without Us* (New York: Picador, 2007).

CREDITS

179   Imperial War Museum. Art.IWM ART 1146

181   Universal History Archive / Shutterstock

202   Bernard Hoffman / The LIFE Picture Collection / Shutterstock

207   US National Archives, NAID: 542192

210   David Atkinson / Hand Made Maps

214   Toho / Kobal / Shutterstock

219   Photograph by Sunil Amrith

219   Photograph by Sunil Amrith

227   Everett / Shutterstock

235   John Margolies Roadside America Photograph Archive, Library
           of Congress, Digital image id: mrg 02113

237   Magic Car Pics / Shutterstock

238   Seydou Keïta, Untitled, 1954, Modern gelatin silver print, © Sey-
           dou Keïta / SKPEAC - Courtesy The Jean Pigozzi African Art
           Collection

242   David Atkinson / Hand Made Maps. Based on Will Steffen,
           Wendy Broadgate, Lisa Deutsch, Owen Gaffney and Cornelia
           Ludwig, "The Trajectory of the Anthropocene: The Great Accel-
           eration," *Anthropocene Review*, 2 (2015).

266   Everett / Shutterstock

273   DOCUMERICA: The Environmental Protection Agency's Pro-
           gram to Photographically Document Subjects of Environmental
           Concern, between 1972–1977. National Archives ID: 552394

274   David Atkinson / Hand Made Maps

276   John Dominis / The LIFE Picture Collection / Shutterstock

279   David Atkinson / Hand Made Maps

281   David Atkinson / Hand Made Maps

285   ITV / Shutterstock

293   Bagus Indahono / EPA / Shutterstock

309   Times Newspapers / Shutterstock

317   D Usher / imageBROKER / Shutterstock

322   Erich Fend / imageBROKER / Shutterstock

334   Sebastian Barros / NurPhoto / Shutterstock

341   Dentsu / Ntv / Studio Ghibli / Kobal / Shutterstock

INDEX

Page references in italic refer to illustrations.